The Gospel

The Gospel

Douglas W. Kennard

WIPF & STOCK · Eugene, Oregon

THE GOSPEL

Copyright © 2017 Douglas W. Kennard. All rights reserved. Except for brief quotations in critical publications or reviews, no part of this book may be reproduced in any manner without prior written permission from the publisher. Write: Permissions, Wipf and Stock Publishers, 199 W. 8th Ave., Suite 3, Eugene, OR 97401.

Wipf & Stock
An Imprint of Wipf and Stock Publishers
199 W. 8th Ave., Suite 3
Eugene, OR 97401

www.wipfandstock.com

PAPERBACK ISBN: 978-1-5326-3264-8
HARDCOVER ISBN: 978-1-5326-3698-1
EBOOK ISBN: 978-1-5326-3697-4

Manufactured in the U.S.A.   OCTOBER 24, 2017

This book is dedicated to
my students from diverse Christian traditions.

Contents

1. Introduction | 1
2. The Servant's Atonement in Isaiah | 21
3. Mark as Narrative Gospel | 30
4. Beatitudes to Kingdom | 32
5. Following Jesus' New Covenant Teaching of the Law in the Narrow Way | 44
6. Keep the Law of Love | 55
7. Kingdom Parables | 59
8. Forgiveness in the Synoptics | 68
9. Matthew 19:16—20:16: Standard and Poor | 77
10. Eschatological Reversal | 95
11. Sheep and Goats | 101
12. John 3: Believing Jesus Begets Everlasting Life | 104
13. Messiah unto Everlasting Life | 110
14. Believe in Jesus as Sent from God to Have Everlasting Life | 112
15. Jesus Is the Resurrection and the Life | 115
16. Jesus as Gospel | 117
17. Christ's Vicarious Atonement | 147
18. Gospel as Jesus' Death and Resurrection | 168
19. Christ's Imputation | 171

20　Mystical Justification by the Spirit | 177

21　Paul Identifies that Jesus Is Lord | 186

22　Redemption Victory Procession | 188

23　Paul's Narrow Way to Everlasting Life | 190

24　Christ's Atonement in Hebrews | 202

25　Petrine Redemption unto the Narrow Way to Kingdom | 215

26　Christ's Propitiation in 1 John | 224

27　The Overcomer in Revelation | 237

28　Putting It All Together | 244

Appendix: A Critique of Anselm's Cur Deus Homo (Why the God-Man?): Argument from Atonement | 247

Select Bibliography | 263

Author index | 283

Scripture index | 291

Subject index | 299

1

Introduction

THIS BOOK IS ABOUT the statement of the gospel, especially in the Bible. This first chapter surveys historical statements of the good news and their respective soteriologies. However, subsequent chapters will explore any biblical statement that either (1) identifies itself as gospel, (2) promises forgiveness, (3) promises everlasting life, (4) promises the kingdom, or (5) promises resurrection with Christ. These five statements indicate the outcomes that are normally associated with the gospel across Christendom. However, some traditions emphasize other aspects than these.

Often Christian salvation strategies argue for one gospel perspective to the exclusion of other options. One example of such an exclusive strategy is Simon Gathercole's recent *Defending Substitution*.[1] However, defending one element for inclusion within the gospel does not defend that all gospel statements must include that element, as though there is only one way to say the gospel. While Gathercole defends substitution as within Paul's salvation gospel strategy, he does not argue that if substitution is not mentioned other options cannot also be soteriologically Pauline. This present volume takes a different trajectory in drawing out all the ways that the Bible says the gospel message to bring the individual to the recognized outcomes of salvation. Of course, substitution is among them, but above I identified five ways to describe the goal of salvation. If these five statements indicate identifiers for biblical gospel statements, then the gospel can be said in varied ways and different traditions have focused on part of this statement.

This book is about soteriology but is more narrow than a discussion of everything that God accomplishes in the process or mechanism of salvation. That more expansive view of salvation has already been published

1. Gathercole, *Defending Substitution*.

2   THE GOSPEL

in my books *Biblical Covenantalism in Prophets, Psalms, Early Judaism, Gospels, and Acts. Volume Two Judaism, Covenant Nomism, and Kingdom Hope* and *Biblical Covenantalism: Engaging the New Perspective and New Covenant Atonement. Volume Three Biblical Covenantalism in New Testament Epistles*.[2] So this book focuses on the more restrictive task of identifying the legitimate gospel message that, if implemented, includes one in the benefits of this salvation.

The word εὐαγγελίου means "good news" or "joyous news" declared to others.[3] In classical Greek and Jewish contexts the word is used to describe the *good news* of announcing victory in battle (LXX: 1 Sam 31:9; 2 Sam 1:20; 4:10; 18:19–20, 27, 31; 1 Chr 10:9; Ps 67[68]:11).[4] By extension, the word announces the Lord's victory (LXX: Ps 95[96]:2). This victory might be that of spiritual cleansing and declared righteous by the priest through sacrifice (LXX: Ps 39[40]:9). The word announces entrance into the Lord's eschatological kingdom with peace (LXX: Isa 40:9; 52:7; 60:6; 61:1; Joel 2:32; Nah 1:15).[5] The word also announces the *good news* of who will be the next king, such as "David is lord" (LXX: 2 Sam 4:10; 1 Kgs 1:42).[6]

One expression of this gospel in the NT is the belief or confession that *Jesus is Lord*, who provides true knowledge in his teaching and everlasting life.[7] Those who confess Jesus is Lord and believe God raised him from the dead are saved because such a commitment can only be accomplished by

2. Kennard, *Biblical Covenantalism*, vols. 2 and 3.

3. GELS, 297; BDAG, 402–3; L & N, 412–13; *NIDNTT*, 2:107–15; *EDNT*, 2:69–74; *TDNT*, 2:707–37; *NIDIEC*, 3:10–15; Harnack, "Gospel: History of the Conception in the Earliest Church"; Schniewind, *Euangelion*; Betz, "Jesus' Gospel of the Kingdom"; Stuhlmacher, "Pauline Gospel," in Stuhlmacher, ed., *Gospel and the Gospels*, 53–74 and 149–72, respectively; Stanton, *Jesus and the Gospel*, 9–62; Horbury, "'Gospel' in Herodian Judea"; Dickson, "Gospel as News"; Mason, *Josephus, Judea, and Christian Origins*, 283–302; Pokorny, *From the Gospel to the Gospels*; Dunn, "Gospel and the Gospels"; Aune, "Meaning of Εὐαγγελίου in the *Inscriptiones* of the Canonical Gospels," in *Jesus, Gospel Tradition and Paul*, 3–24; Bird, *Gospel of the Lord*, 5–13.

4. Homer, *Od.* 14.152; Plutarch, *Demetrius* 17.5; *Pompeius* 41:3; 66.3; *P. Giss.* 27; Block, *Gospel According to Moses*, xii; also announces good news of a birth (Jer 20:15).

5. *Pss. Sol.* 10–11; Vanhoozer and Treier, *Theology and the Mirror of Scripture*, 53–57.

6. Also "good news" of Vespasian as lord, Josephus, *J.W.* 4.618, 656–57.

7. Clement of Rome, 1 *Cor.* 7–8; Ignatius, *Eph.* 15; *To Hero* 9; Papias, frag. 5; Justin Martyr, 1 *Apol.* 8; 45 (which contains Marcus Aurelius *Epistle to Senate*); *Dial.* 26; 35–38; Irenaeus, *Haer.* 1.10.1–2; 3.8.1; 3.9.13.10.2, 5; Clement Alexandria, *Paed.* 1.6; *Strom.* 6.15, 17; Origen, *de Prin.* 1.3.7; 1.6.2; 2.7.4; Cyprian, *Treatises* 3.20; 12.21; Gregory Thaumaturgus, *A Sectional Confession of Faith* 17; *The Clementine Homilies* 8.5–6; Chrysostom, *Hom. Act.* 18; Eusebius, *Hist. eccl.* 2.14; 3.4; Cassian, *Seven Books of John Cassian* 3.13–14; Wainwright, "Confession 'Jesus Is God' in the New Testament"; Bates, *Salvation by Allegiance Alone*.

the transformation the Holy Spirit brings (Rom 10:9–10; 1 Cor 12:3). The gospel statements in the book of Acts convey a statement that "Jesus is Lord" but it shows up elsewhere as well (see chapter 3 on Mark and chapters 16 and 20 on Paul's gospel). The rivals that drive Christians to identify that Jesus is the authority are polytheism, idolatry, and the claim that "Caesar is Lord." Christians repeatedly did not honor pagan deities or idols and suffered martyrdom for this refusal.[8] Irenaeus identifies that the unified faith preached is that *Jesus is Lord, raised to become the eschatological judge*.[9] As non-Christians, Marcus Aurelius, Pliny, and Lucian consider that the most defining feature of Christians at the start of the second century is that they pray to Jesus as God.[10] Especially before Rome recognized Christianity, the gospel is declared as "Jesus is Lord."

The Gospel of John presents that believing in Jesus is akin to a *loyalty commitment* to Jesus as Lord. This biblical theology approach recognizes that John's Gospel and epistles frame salvation in the present tense even though everlasting and resurrection life is not demythologized to an existentialized perspective as Bultmann advocated.[11] Instead, in this volume, chapters 12–15 and 26 develop John as advocating present believing in Jesus as the objectified person in the focus of Christians' faith. This faith provides believers with forgiveness and everlasting resurrection life now and beyond the grave.

The early church reflected this idea of a loyalty *belief articulated by their creeds*. Paul's preached gospel statement in 1 Cor 15:1–11 grounded on the historical death and resurrection of Christ serves as a model. The creedal statement for baptism and continuing church liturgy expand to differentiate true Christianity from surrounding heresies.[12] The most resilient

8. *Martyrdom of Polycarp* 9.2–12.2; Justin, *1 Apol.* 5–6; *The Acts of Justin and Companions* 5; *The Acts of the Scillitan Martyrs*; *The Acts of Cyprian* 3–4; Eusebius, *Hist. Eccl.* 5.1.53–54.7.11.7–10; *The Martyrdom of Perpetua and Felicitas* 6; *The Martyrdom of Crispina* 1–3; *The Martyrdom of Pionius* 9.9–11; Cyprian, *Laps.* 8–10; Trajan in Pliny, *Letters* 10.97.2; Minucius Felix, *Oct.* 6.1; 8.1–4; 9.1.

9. Irenaeus, *Haer.* 1.10.1–2.

10. Marcus Aurelius, *Epistle to Senate* as contained in Justin Martyr, *1 Apol.* 45; Claudius in *Praef.* 60, 163; Pliny Younger about A.D. 111–113, *Ep.* 10.96.7; Lucian, *Peregr.* 13; Celsus in Origen, *Cels.* 8.12–15; Porphyry in Augustine, *Civ.* 19.23; *Mart. Pol.* 17.2.

11. Bultmann, *Theology of the New Testament*, 2:75, 77–78.

12. Ign. *Trall.* 9.1–2; Justin, *1 Apol.* 61; *The Epistula Apostolorum*; Irenaeus, *Haer.* 1.10.1; *Epid.* 3; Tertullian, *Prax.* 2; *Virg.* 1; Hippolytus, *Trad. ap.* 21. Nicene Creed; Eusebius' *Creed of Caesarea*; Socrates, *H. E.* 1.8, in Bettenson and Maunder, eds., *Documents of the Christian Church*, 24–26. Apostles' Creed: Epiphanius, *Pan.* 72.3 "Old Roman Creed"; Rufinus, *Symb.* 21.335; Gallican creed from Caesarius, *pseudo-Augustinus* 244; *Dicta Abbatis Pirminii de singulis libris canonicis*, in Bettenson and Maunder, eds.,

4   The Gospel

expressions of these loyalty belief statements are the Apostles' Creed[13] and the Nicene Creed, with the later cited below.

> We believe in one God the Father All-sovereign, maker of heaven and earth, and of all things visible and invisible;
>
> And in one Lord Jesus Christ, the only-begotten Son of God, Begotten of the Father before all the ages, Light of Light, true God of true God, begotten not made, of one substance with the Father, through whom all things were made; who for us men and for our salvation came down from the heavens, and was made flesh of the Holy Spirit and the Virgin Mary, and became man, and was crucified for us under Pontius Pilate, and suffered and was buried, and rose again on the third day according to the Scriptures, and ascended into the heavens, and sitteth on the right hand of the Father, and cometh again with glory to judge living and dead, of whose kingdom there shall be no end;
>
> And in the Holy Spirit, the Lord and Life-Giver, that proceedeth from the Father, who with Father and Son is worshipped together and glorified together, who spake through the prophets;
>
> In one holy catholic and apostolic church;
>
> We acknowledge one baptism unto remission of sins. We look for a resurrection of the dead, and the life of the age to come.[14]

Documents of the Christian Church, 24. Campbell, *Gospel in Christian Traditions* identifies use of creeds as gospel among: proto-orthodox (20–29), ancient Christian community (32–40), Lutheran and Reformed (57), Methodist (71), and even evangelicals have begun to use them as gospel (97).

13. The Apostles' Creed has the following history: the Old Roman Creed was proposed in Rome around A.D. 340 by Marcellus to Julius, bishop of Rome. Epiphanius, *Patristics Greek*, 72.3 is the earliest copy we have. Around A.D. 385, Rufus, priest of Aquileia, added the start, "I believe in God Almighty," and left off "life everlasting" (*Expositio in Symbolum*, in *Patristics Latin*, 21.335). Caesarius, bishop of Arles, in a sermon between A.D. 503 and 543, cleaned up language of "conceived of" and added "he descended into hell" in the midst of a patristic debate on whether Jesus announced gospel to humans who died during Noah's flood (majority view remaining in literature of the time, so likely intended meaning) or announced judgment on fallen angels involved in the sin before the flood (minority view that eventually won out in historical exegesis, Kennard, *Messiah Jesus*, 344–47). The earliest copy of the Apostles' Creed as we have it now is in *Dicta Abbatis Pirminii de singulis libris canonicis scarapsus* around A.D. 750. Since the 1970s some restatements of the Apostles' Creed change the "descended to hell" to read "a full expression of death."

14. The Nicene Creed has the following history: Eusebius of Caesarea proposed his church's creed at the Council of Nicaea (*Epist. Euseb. Apud Socrates, Hist. eccl.* 1.8). The creed accepted at Nicaea (A.D. 325) added phrases to exclude Arianism (Bettenson and Maunder, eds., *Documents of the Christian Church*, 25–26). The final form of the Nicene

Such creedal statements serve in these traditions to be a belief loyalty affirmation, identifying gospel unto everlasting salvation.

Patristics and many contemporary gospel specialists view the gospel message as *the written narrative account about Jesus* that if believed provides salvation.[15] This gospel of Jesus story is the message that needs to be preached to all the nations before Christ comes again to establish his kingdom (Mark 13:10; [perhaps also 16:15–16]; Matt 4:23; 24:14). The *biblical gospel narratives* especially exemplify this gospel statement because Jesus is himself the gospel (especially evident in chapter 3 but also showcased in chapters 3–15).[16] Living by the wise counsel contained within these gospel narratives is salvation.[17] Origen considers that everything of the gospel narratives is contained within salvific gospel but that not everything found in the biblical epistles would be within this salvific message.[18]

Jesus' teaching is gospel. In Luke 16:16, Jesus said that since the beginning of his ministry that he had been about *preaching the gospel* (εὐαγγελίζεται) in all that he said (developed in chapters 4–15). Origen illustrates that Jesus' teaching about himself is gospel through Jesus' "I am" statements in the Gospel of John, such as, "I am the way, the truth, and the life," "I am the door," and "I am the resurrection" (John 10:9; 11:25; 14:6).[19] Summarizing Christianity, the Jewish Babylonian Talmud *Šabb.* 116a-b describes *Jesus' teaching as gospel*.[20]

The gospel for Jews, and especially Christian Jews, was to *obey the Law as a love relationship with God and one's fellow human unto everlasting life* (Matt 5; 19:16–22; 22:34–40; Mark 10:17–19; Luke 10:25, 28; 18:18–20; especially evident in chapters 5–6, 9–10).[21] N. T. Wright identifies, "The Torah

---

Creed smoothed this language to the version in Epiphanius, *Ancoratus* 118 (A.D. 375) and Cyril of Jerusalem, *Catechetical Lectures*. This final form was ratified at Councils of Constantinople (A.D. 381) and Chalcedon (A.D. 451).

15. *Did.* 8.2; Tertullian, *Ag. Marcion* 4.4–5; Irenaeus, *Haer.* 3.1.1; 3.10.5; 3.11.9; 4.20.10; Origen, *Comm. Jo.* 1.5, 7–9, 14, 27; Theodoret, *Dialogs* 1; Jerome, *Vir. Il.* 7–9; Eusebius, *Hist. Eccl.* 3.39=Papias, *Frag.* 3.15–17; Eusebius, *Hist. Eccl.* 3.24.1–15; 5.8.2–4; 6.14.5–7; 6.25; Augustine, *Cons.* 1.2.3–4; 4.10.11; Jerome, *Preface to the Four Gospels*; *Muratorian Frag.* 1–39; Marshall, "Luke and His 'Gospel,'" in Stuhlmacher, ed., *Gospel and the Gospels*, 283; Hooker, *Mark*, 33; Hengel, *Four Gospels and the One Gospel of Jesus Christ*, 91; Wright, "Foreword by N. T. Wright"; and McKnight, *King Jesus Gospel*, 12, 78–83.

16. Origen, *Comm. Jo.* 1.10, 39.

17. *The Clementine Homilies* 1.7; Origen, *Comm. Jo.* 1.11, 39.

18. Origen, *Comm. Jo.* 1.5.

19. Origen, *Comm. Jo.* 1.11.

20. *B. Šabb.* 116a-b; Betz, "Jesus' Gospel of the Kingdom," 55.

21. Kennard, *Messiah Jesus*, 107–52; Jer 31:31–34 and Ezek 36:24—37:28; Jdt

was the boundary marker of the covenant people: those who kept it would share the life of the coming age."[22] Jesus identified the greatest commandment in the Law as "You shall love the Lord your God with all your heart, and with all your soul, and with all your mind" (Matt 22:36–40). Such a love for God should captivate one's whole being. Such a focus on love resonates with the Jewish traditional understanding that the love of God is the greatest commandment (Deut 6:4–5; Luke 10:26–27).[23] The second command is like it in loving your neighbor as yourself (Matt 22:39; Luke 10:27).[24] This love emphasis is so essential that the whole Law and the Prophets depend upon (or are suspended from) this backbone of love (Matt 22:40). The affirmation of love as the core does not deny any of the specifics of the Law, for Jesus is recognized as teaching the Law correctly and thus not annulling any (Mark 12:32–34). In fact, it is the very same answer a scribal lawyer had earlier given to Jesus when Jesus asked him to summarize the Law (Luke 10:26–27). An affirmation that this love commitment to God and fellow humans identifies one as not far from the kingdom (Mark 12:34). Practicing this radical love commitment obtains the inheritance of everlasting life as sons of the divine Father (Matt 5:45; Luke 10:25, 28).

5:17–21; 8:18–23; 10:5; 12:2, 9–19; 13:8; *Pr. Azar.* 6–14; *Jub.*1:22–25; 2:17–33; 15:11–34; 1Q3 4, 5; 1QH 4, 5, 18; 4QShirShalb; Tob 1:10–12; 4:12–13; 1 Macc 1:48; 2:15–28; 2 Macc 6:18–31; 7; 3 Macc 3:4–7; 4 Macc 5:1—6:30; *T. Jud.* 26; *Jos. Asen.*; Josephus, *J.W.* 1.145–147, 157–60, 651–655; 2.169–74; *Ant.* 13.252; 14.237; 17.149–67; 18.55–59, 261–4, 267, and 271; *Gos. Nazarenes* 1 in Origen, *Comm. Matt.* 15.14; *mek.* Bachodesh 5.81–82; Wright, *Jesus and the Victory of God*, 301; Sanders, *Paul and Palestinian Judaism*; *Paul, the Law, and the Jewish People*; *Jewish Law from Jesus to the Mishnah*; and *Judaism*; and Dunn, *Jesus, Paul, and the Law*; *Jews and Christians*; and *Paul and the Mosaic Law* (especially interesting is Wright's chapter "The Law in Romans 2," 131–50). Furthermore, biblical texts like James, Matthew, and Acts indicate that Jews and Jewish Christians were zealous for the Law. However, especially at focus is Matt 5:17–48 and 19:16–22; Saldarini, *Matthew's Christian-Jewish Community* and Kennard, *Biblical Covenantalism*, 3:15–160; Klijn, "Study of Jewish Christianity"; Taylor, "Phenomenon of Early Jewish Christianity"; Velasco and Sabourin, "Jewish Christianity of the First Centuries"; Klijn and Reinink, *Patristic Evidence for Jewish-Christian Sects*; Strecker, "Appendix 1: On the Problem of Jewish Christianity," in Bauer, *Orthodoxy and Heresy in Earliest Christianity*, 257; Strecker, "Kerygmata Petrou," in Hennecke and Schneemelcher, eds., *New Testament Apocrypha*, 2:102–27, especially 210–22 and 270–71; Strecker, *Judenchristentum in den Pseudoklementinen*; Schoeps, *Theologie und Geschichte des Judenchristentums* and his abbreviated synthesis, *Jewish Christianity*; Van Voorst, *Ascents of James*.

22. Wright, *Jesus and the Victory of God*, 301.

23. B. Šabb. 31a; b. Ber. 63a; Josephus, *Contra Apionem* 2.206.

24. Rabbi Akiba considered love of neighbor in Lev 19:18 to be the great commandment (*Sifra Qed.* 4.200.3.7; *Gen. Rab.* 24.7).

As an expression of love for God, the Mosaic Law was replaced by early theologians with *universal natural law as a transcendental method for salvation*.²⁵ For example, Justin argues that eternal righteous acts are in keeping with nature. Furthermore, Tertullian sees all natural law virtues summed up in Christ and thus also in the eternal Logos, prior to the Law as the basis for identifying Noah as righteous. Additionally, Augustine claims that the Spirit graciously empowers the Christian to live the natural law. Eusebius dismisses the Mosaic Law as an unfortunate departure from the universal religion of the patriarchs, which grounds the antiquity of Christianity to which all ethnicities can belong.²⁶ Peter Abelard presents his "philosopher" affirming natural law as compelling faith sufficiently, providing a gracious salvation way of love toward God, who essentially loves and forgives those who are his.²⁷ Even today an occasional Christian philosopher grants such natural law as a means by which monumental non-Christian philosophers, such as Plato, might be saved.²⁸

Thomas Aquinas affirmed biblical law as binding, with natural law as an expression of God's general revelational light,²⁹ without reference to the written Mosaic Law.³⁰ On the basis of Romans 8:14, Aquinas makes the

---

25. Justin, *Dial.* 47.2; Irenaeus, *Haer.* 4.13.1, 4; 15.1; 16.1–5; Tertullian, *Virg.* 1.1; *Adv. Jud.* 2.7–10; Augustine, *De spir. Et litt.* 27.29; Pannenberg, *Systematic Theology*, 3:70–80; Troeltsch, *Social Teaching of the Christian Churches*, 115–17; Delhaye, *Décalogue*, 66–68.

26. Eusebius of Caesarea, *The Preparation of the Gospel*, books 1 and 2; Dulles, *History of Apologetics*, 53.

27. Abelard, *Dialogue of a Philosopher with a Jew and a Christian*, 24–27, 36–42 the way of Noah, Job, and patriarchs before Moses, 44 "sufficient for salvation of some people before the law or even now," 57–58 the Jew agrees perfect love saves Gentile as well as Jew, 90–94 Christian virtue is accessible to the moral pagan and thus also is Christian beatitude, 102–7, 119; Abelard, *Commentary on the Epistle to the Romans*, 2.9, p. 129; 2.14–15, pp. 133–34. Natural law provides the basis for *faith* (Abelard, *Theol. "Schol."* 2.2.1050d in emended form by Sikes, *Peter Abailard*, 53; Abelard, *Romans*, 4.13, p. 194; Weingart, *Logic of Divine Love*, 7). Abelard argues for *gracious synergism* following the Synod of Orange (Abelard, *Exp. In Epist. Ad Rom.* 2.3.835b; 3.4.1093bc; Weingart, *Logic of Divine Love*, 91, 180). God forgives because *God essentially loves* (Weingart, *Logic of Divine Love*, 88–89, 96).

28. Stuart Hackett made this claim in lectures during 1986 at Trinity Evangelical Divinity School.

29. Aquinas, *Summa Theologica*, p. 1, quest. 91, art. 2 and echoed in reply to obj. 1; Q 93, A 2, "On contrary," "I answer that" and "reply to objection 1." This is the same position as Abelard, *Romans*, 2.9, p. 129.

30. Aquinas, *Summa Theologica* I, 2nd part, quest. 91, art. 4; quest. 94, art. 2; art. 5, "I answer that" and "reply obj. 1." There would be slightly more basis for making a connection between natural law and biblical law through Augustine's *Confessions* bk. 11, pt. II.IV or 9, where Augustine claims theft is written on human hearts not effaced

case that the biblical law of grace is more efficacious than natural law, for only those "led by the Spirit" submit to biblical law, whereas many more submit to natural law.[31] Following natural law likely means that advocates choose their worldview preferences and intuitions from within their context as Immanuel Kant claims.[32] Additionally, to continue to utilize natural law would likely mean that the advocate assumes that what *is* should govern what *ought to be*, contrary to David Hume's claims that such a shift depends upon personal inference or preference rather than any observed data.[33]

In a priestly approach to justification, the believer does not earn her status by works but comes to the cult as a believer and *the priest declares her acceptable based on her allegiance of faith within covenant and perhaps whatever the appropriate sacrifice provides*. Eventually an elaborate system of sacrifices developed in the Mosaic covenant. By extension, Christ's sacrificial death provides a better everlasting forgiveness for believers in the new covenant. Christ's sacrifice is described as "propitiation" (ἱλαστήριον, Rom 3:25), identifying what is accomplished on behalf of the people at the "mercy seat" on the Day of Atonement (ἱλαστήριον, LXX: Exod 25:17–22; 31:7; 35:12; 38:5–8; Lev 16:2, 13–15; Num 7:89; Ezek 43:14–20).[34] Framing Christ's corporate atonement accomplishment through the lens of the Day of Atonement is a profoundly priestly image emphasizing the corporate atonement for the whole church (especially developed in Heb 9:1—10:18). Justification and atonement are not legal fiction but a priestly restoration of covenantal relationship. Isaiah, Hebrews, John, Paul and the early church

---

by iniquity and universally affirmed even by thieves. George, *Natural Law Theory*, 41. Notice that this only makes a case for one of the Ten Commandments, not the other nine. Schmidt (*Die Zehn Gebote im Rahmen altestamentlicher Ethik*, 20–21) claims that Luther defended that the Ten Commandments were understood by him as natural law.

31. Aquinas, *Summa Theologica* I, 2nd part, quest. 93, art. 6, obj. 1; quest. 94, art. 6, obj. 2 and reply to obj. 1 and 2.

32. Kant, *Critique of Judgment*, 459–613, and especially pt. 1, bk. 2, sec. 26, pp, 500–501, where the concept of the sublime "worldview" first appeared in 1790. Betz, "Zur Geschichte des Wortes 'Weltanschauung,'" in *Kursbuch der Weltanschauungen*, 18–28, but especially 18.

33. Hume, *Treatise of Human Nature*, bk. 3, pt. 1, sec. 1; this issue is known as "Hume's guillotine" by Max Black, "Gap between 'Is' and 'Should,'" *Philosophical Review*, 73.2 (April 1964) 165–81.

34. 1QIsa 52:14 replaces the MT "marring" (מִשְׁחַת) with a Qal singular "I have anointed" indicating that God established the sacrifice role for his Messiah, and 1QIsa 51:5 replaces the MT first-person "my righteousness" with a third-person "his arm" also indicating messianism; also 4Q541 9.1.1.2 "he will atone" (Hengel and Bailey, "Effective History of Isaiah 53 in the Pre-Christian Period," in Janowski and Stuhlmacher, eds., *Suffering Servant*, 101, 103, 108, 146; Fryer, "Meaning and Translation of *Hilastērion* in Romans 3:25"; Hofius, "Sühne und Versöhnung," 44, 48–49; Kruse, *Romans*, 187–89).

viewed Christ's death through this Jewish covenantal sacrificial model rather than a legal model, so such metaphors are not to be seen as inventions of the new perspective in Paul (Heb 9:7-28; John 1:29, 36; Rom 3:25; especially evident in book chapters 2, 17-19, 24, 26).[35] Remember that in a Levitical sacrifice the animal sacrificed is not declared to receive covenant curse. The earliest mention of the death of the scapegoat is around A.D. 200 in the Mishnah when the temple had been destroyed and there was no longer a liturgy occurring for the Day of Atonement; the rabbi's described that the

---

35. John 1:29; Heb 9:1—10:18; *Barn.* 7-8 Jesus' death parallels Day of Atonement and red heifer cleansing; Justin Martyr, *Dial.* 13.1-9, 40.1-4, 72.1, 111.2-3 develop Jesus' death as parallel to paschal lamb, Day of Atonement, and Isaiah 53 sacrificial lamb (Markschies, "Jesus Christ as a Man before God"; and Bailey, "'Our Suffering and Crucified Messiah' [*Dial.* 111.2]: Justin Martyr's Allusions to Isaiah 53 in His Dialogue with Trypho with Special Reference to the New Edition of M. Marcovich," in Janowski and Stuhlmacher, eds., *Suffering Servant*, 332-33 and 378-79; Cyprian, *Test.* 15 Jesus' death is parallel to Jewish sacrifice, Isaiah 53, and Passover lamb; *Letter* 63.14.4 in Filium, ed., *Corpus Scriptorum Ecclesiasticorum Latinorum*, 3c: 410-11; Origen, *Comm. Jo.* 1.40; 6.32-38 and Augustine, *Trin.* 4.14 or 19 and *On Forgiveness of Sins, and Baptism* 54-55 identify Jesus' death parallel to Jewish daily sacrifices; Theodoret of Cyrrhus, *Interpretation of the Letter to the Romans*, in Migne, ed., *Patrologia graeca*, 82; Chrysostom, *Hom. Rom.* 7, in Schaff, ed., *Nicene and Post-Nicene Fathers*, 11:378; both mentioned in Oden, *Justification Reader*, 62; Origen, *Comm. Romans* 2:110 cited in Oden, *Justification Reader*, 65; Cyril, *Catechetical Lectures* 13.3 develops Jesus' death parallel to Day of Atonement; Eusebius, *Hist. eccl.* 5.1.10; 5.13.5; 6.38; *Theoph.* 3.59, *Comm. Isa.* 2.42 on Isa 53:5-6 and 11-12, and *Dem. ev.* 3.2.61-2 develop Jesus' death as a Jewish sacrifice and sin offering (Markschies, "Jesus Christ as a Man before God: Two Interpretive Models for Isaiah 53 in the Patristic Literature and Their Development," in Janowski and Stuhlmacher, eds., *Suffering Servant*, 305, 308, 312-13); Gregory Nazianzen, *In Defense of His Flight to Pontus* 1.3-4 develops Jesus' atonement parallel to Passover; Ambrose, *Fid.* 3.11.67 parallel to Melchizedek sacrifice; Leo the Great, *Sermons* 55.3; 56.1; 57.3; 58.1; 59.5, 7; 62.5, 7; 68.3 parallel to daily Jewish sacrifice and Passover; Presbyterian Church of England, *Articles of the Faith*, 1890, art. 13, "Justification by Faith," in Schaff, ed., *Creeds of Christendom*, 3:918; also the abundance of early church iconography presenting Jesus as a sacrificial lamb show the profusion of Jesus' death conceived through the lens of Jewish sacrifice, for example: a third-century Roman catacomb lamb image for Christ, Jesus as lamb with cruciform halo in apex of dome in a 6th-century church of Ravenna, the 6th-century basilica of Saints Cosmos and Damian in Rome shows the Lamb of God on a rock surrounded by the twelve apostles as lambs indicating mimetic atonement, a 7th-century Roman altar portraying the Lamb of God on the altar with the cross, the 82nd canon of the A.D. 692 Council of Trullo affirmed Jesus was incarnate in human flesh by banning the very common practice of representing Jesus' death as a lamb, "we decree that henceforth Christ our God must be represented in his human form but not in the form of the ancient lamb"; Schaff, ed., *Nicene and Post-Nicene Fathers*, 2nd ser., 14:401; Sanday and Headlam, *Romans*, 122-24; Abelard, *Exp. In Epist. Ad Rom.* 2.5.874c; *Sermones* 2.5.874c, 388d-89c; 4.416a; 7.434d-35b; 9.445a; 11.454cd, 455a, 463d; 473c; 476d; Weingart, *Logic of Divine Love*, 134; Kennard, *Biblical Covenantalism*, 1:289-313; 3:46-61, 92-106, 164-72.

goat was to be led out into the wilderness and then pushed off a cliff.[36] Prior to this statement the scapegoat accomplished atonement by being let go in the wilderness, not as a penal sacrifice (the scapegoat would not receive covenant curse from God but would accomplish atonement; Lev 16:10). However, the scapegoat becomes part of the means to avert covenant curse in recovering believers within covenant blessing.

An alternative to the vicarious atonement sacrificial death of Jesus is that of a *victorious redemption that facilitates a new exodus for humanity from bondage* under: Satan, idolatry, impurity, lawlessness, class repression, and patriarchy.[37] This redemption approach presents Yahweh as a warrior to redeem Israel from an enemy, which threatens them so that Israel might enter the kingdom (Isa 49:23; 52:2).[38] Eschatological salvation banishes illness through kingdom healing (Isa 35:3–6; 53:5; 61:1–2; shown in this volume within chapters 2, 23, and 25).[39] Similarly, the military image describes a messianic figure that engages ungodly powers and redeems his people from them.[40] Jesus utilizes a bit of military imagery in casting out demons, especially with regard to "legions" of angels or demons (Matt 26:53; Mark 5:9, 15; Luke 8:30; shown in part of chapter 8 and 16),[41] and that the demons have a ruler that must be defeated (Matt 9:34; 12:24, 29; Mark 3:22, 27; Luke 11:15, 22). Irenaeus claims that the gospel is God's message of redemption unto victory defeating the devil and all his henchmen such as the beast.[42] This redemption includes being set free and forgiven by God.[43] Such redemption sets up a two-ways salvation model in the same manner as the exodus initiated the narrow way unto the promised land (Exod 12–19; Heb 3–4).[44] This redemption of "leading captive a host of captives" provides the

---

36. *M. Yoma* 6.4; *Bar.* 7.7, 9.

37. *Altereatio, Simonis et Theoophili* 6.24; Tertullian, *De Carne Christi* 17; Irenaeus, *Haer.* 3.18.6; 3.21.1; 3.23.1; 4.33.4; 5.17.2; 5.21.3; *Epiderxis* 37; Cyril of Jerusalem, *Cat.* 13.1; Gregory of Nazianzus, *Or.* 30.20; Hilary, *C. Ar.* 1.35; Augustine, *Trin.* 13.11–15, 18; Luther, *Luther's Works*, 22:24; 26:267; 52:156; Aulén, *Christus Victor*, 48; Gutiérrez, *Theology of Liberation*; Martyn, *Theological Issues in the Letters of Paul*, 298–99, 142–44; Ruether, *Introducing Redemption in Christian Feminism*.

38. Wis 5:16–23; Sir 35:22—36:17; 1QM 12.10–14; 19.2–8; *As. Mos.* 10.

39. *Jub.* 23.29–30; *T. Zeb.* 9.8; *2 Bar.* 73.2; *4 Ezra* 13.50.

40. *Pss. Sol.* 17.23–39; *2 Bar.* 39–42, 72–74; *1 En.* 37–71; *4 Ezra* 12.31–34; 13; Philo, *Prae.* 16(91–97); 1QSb 5.27; 1QSa 2.11–13; 4QpIsaa.

41. *T. Sol.* 11; Jesus' story repeated by *Epistula Apostolora* 5 in *NT Apocrypha* 1.253.

42. Irenaeus, *Haer.* 5.26.1; frag. 50.

43. Irenaeus, *Haer.* 3.23.1; 5.17.2.

44. Irenaeus, *Haer.* 3.18.6.

church with gifts from Christ's spoils of victory (Eph 4:8–13; 2 Cor 2:14–17; developed in chapter 22).

The narrow way within a two-ways orientation heads toward an eschatological justification that assesses every human at an eschatological forensic judgment according to her deeds (especially evident in chapters 4–8, 16, 20, 23, 25, and 27).[45] Such a narrow way framed virtues that imitate Christ and

45. This judgment according to deeds is continued in the two-ways teaching of the church: *Did.* 1.1.1–4; 4.14b; *1 Clem.* 34–35; *2 Clem.* 6.8; 8.4; Polycarp, *Phil.* 10; Ign., *Phil.* 5.1; *Eph.* 3.1; *Barn.* 16.7–8; 18.1–2; 19; Justin Martyr, *Dial.* 3.4; *1 Apol.* 16.8–9; *2 Apol.* 9; Irenaeus, *Haer.* 3.1.10 maintained this as the universal teaching all Christians held at the time; *Herm. Mand.* 2.7; *Herm. Sim.* 3.8.6–11; Clement of Alexandria, *Strom.* 4.6; Quis div., especially 1.6–7; 16.5; Commodianus, *Instructions* 28; Origen, *Comm. Matt.* 14.10–13; *Fr. Prin.* 2.9.7–8; 3.1.12; Cyprian, *Fort.* 12–13; Dionysius of Alexandria, *Exegetical Fragments 7 Reception of Lapsed*; Methodius of Olympus, *The Banquet of the Ten Virgins* 9.3; *Oration Concerning Simeon and Anna* 8; Lactantius, *Inst.* 3.12; 6.3–7; 7.10; *Epitome of Divine Inst.* 73; *Constitutions of the Holy Apostles* 7.1.1–2; *The Clementine Homilies* 18.17; Eusebius, *Hist. eccl.* 2.19; 3.20.6–7; 5.1.10, 48; 5.8.5; 5.13.5; *Council of Sardica Lengthy Creed*: Socrates Scholasticus, *Hist. eccl.* 2.19=Athanasius, *Syn.* 26; 351=Hilary of Poiters, *On the Councils* 34 and A.D. 359 *Sirmium Creed*: Socrates Scholasticus, *Hist. eccl.* 2.30=Athanasius, *Syn.* 27=Hilary of Poiters, *On the Councils* 38; *Synod at Ariminum Creed*: Socrates Scholasticus, *Hist. eccl.* 2.37; A.D. 359 *Seleucia Creed*: Socrates Scholasticus, *Hist. eccl.* 2.40=Athanasius, *Syn.* 8; A.D. 359 *Confession at Niké* and A.D. 360 *Constantinople Creed*: Athanasius, *Syn.* 30; A.D. 359 *Ariminum Creed* and modified for the A.D. 381 Council at Constantinople: Socrates Scholasticus, *Hist. eccl.* 2.41; Athanasius, *Inc.* 57; Cyril, *Catechetical Lectures* 15.1, 24–25, 33; Gregory Nyssa, *On Pilgramages*, para. 1; *The Great Catechism* 40; Gregory Nazianzen, *Letter 4 to Basil*; Ambrose, *Duties of the Clergy* 1.16.59; Augustine, *Conf.* 1.11.17; *Civ.* 13.8; 14.25; 19.11; 20.1–8, 12, 14, 22; 21.1; *Trin.* 8.7–8; *Enchir.* 15; 31–32; 55; 107; 113; *Doctr. Chr.* 1.12.10; *Perf.* 42–44; *Ennarat. Ps.* 31.25; 112.5; *Tract. Ev. Jo.* 124.5; Hilary of Poitiers, *On the Trinity* 12.45; Leo the Great, *Sermons* 46.3; 49.2, 5; 63.2, 7; 67.5–6; 72.1; 95.1–9; Vincent of Lérins, *The Commonitory* 23.57–59, which he claims is the teaching everyone held at that time, 23.4–6; John Cassian, *Cassian's Conferences* 1.1.5; 1.6.3, 8; 1.40.9; 2.13.13, 18; 2.14.3, 9; *Seven Books of John Cassian* 3.13–14; Leo the Great, *Sermons* 23.5; 24.1–5; 26.2; 66.7; 90.2; 95.1–9; John Climacus, *The Ladder of Divine Ascent*, 9.1; summary on step 30; Thomas a Kempis, *Of the Imitation of Christ*, esp. 1.23; 2.7; 3.44, 56; Bunyan, *Pilgrim's Progress*, esp. 18, 187; Reiche, "New Testament Concept of Reward"; Jeremias, *Neotestamentliche Theologie*, 209; Willard, *Divine Conspiracy*; Yinger, *Paul, Judaism, and Judgment According to Deeds*, 285 summary but argued through the book; Grindheim, "Ignorance Is Bliss"; Kim, *God Will Judge Each One According to Works*; Dunn, *New Perspective on Paul*, 72–73; "If Paul Could Believe Both in Justification by Faith and Judgment According to Works, Why Should That Be a Problem for us?" and "Response to Schreiner," in Stanley and Wilkin, eds., *Four Views on the Role of Works at the Final Judgment*, 135, 106–8. However, this view can be granted from outside the two-ways tradition, such as from the Reformed tradition: Calvin, *Institutes*, 3.15.8; 3.16.1 "we are justified not without works, and not by works, since in the participation in Christ, by which we are justified, is contained not less sanctification than justification," 16.3; 18.1; Schreiner, "Justification Apart from and by Works: At the Final Judgment Works will *Confirm* Justification," in Stanley and Wilkin, eds., *Four Views on the Role of Works at the Final Judgment*, 78–79.

identify a person in a love relationship with God and Christ (especially evident in chapters 6, 9, and 10). This narrow way is still a gracious salvation because the virtues identify one's loyalty unto either God and salvation or idolatry and damnation. For example in this framework, Augustine recognized that God's justification was graciously grounded upon Christ's death transformed into the inherent condition of the elect so that the believer might journey the narrow way (unhindered by previous legal debt) accruing virtue unto eschatological justification and the kingdom.[46] That is, for the New Testament, Augustine, and the patristics, a forensic justification retains an eschatological evidential aspect of "good works" to display the loyal commitment continuing in the narrow way (as evident in chapters 11, 23, 27) even though a past justification is already accomplished. Roman Catholic salvation portrays God's gracious placing those who encounter Christ into a mystical relationship in Christ so that his supernatural love would synergistically render Christians sufficiently mature so as to have meritorious works to vindicate us upon death (2 Cor 5:8; Phil 1:23; Heb 12:23) and before the eschatological judgment by Christ (Matt 25:31–46; John 5:28–29).[47] Protestant models tend to develop this narrow way as a pilgrimage or race in the wake of Christ's efficacious death for our sins.[48] A gracious patristic and charismatic Lutheranism results through the Holy Spirit fruiting lifestyle transformation fulfilling the virtues of the Law, which presently demonstrate a living justification in the life of the believer in Christ (evident in chapter 20).[49] These Spirit-fruiting virtues could also be

---

46. Augustine past justification: *Grat.* 17.33; 19; 21; Henninger, *Sanctus Augustinus et doctrina de duplici iustitia*, 79; McGrath, *Iustitia Dei*, 409; Augustine with narrow way to future justification: *Civ.* 13.8; 14.25; 19.11; 20.1–8, 12, 14, 22; 21.1; *Enchir.* 15; 31–32; 55; 107; 113; *Perf.* 42–44; *Ennarat. Ps.* 31.25; 112.5; *Tract. Ev. Jo.* 124.5.

47. *Catechism of the Catholic Church*, 487, no. 2011; *Council of Trent*, session 6, ch. 5; session 6, ch. 8, cited from Schroeder, trans., *Canons and Decrees of the Council of Trent*, 31, 35; Barber, "A Catholic Perspective: Our Works are Meritorious at the Final Judgment Because of our Union with Christ by Grace," in Stanley and Wilkin, ed., *Four Views on the Role of Works at the Final Judgment*, 161–84.

48. Bunyan, *Pilgrim's Progress*; Schreiner and Caneday, *Race Set before Us*.

49. Augustine, *Spir. et litt.* 26–29 and especially 46; Luther, *Lectures on Romans*, in *Luther's Works*, 25:243–44; *Lectures on Deuteronomy*, in *Luther's Works*, 9:179; Melanchthon, *Loci communes von 1521*, 123; Oecolampadius, *In Hieremiam prophetam commentariorum libri tres Ioannis Oecolampadii*, 2.162a; *The Thirty Nine Articles of the Church of England (1571)*, art. 7; Augustine, Ambroisiater, and Pelagius held this Christian life view (Bray, *Romans*, 205–6); Godet, *Romans*, 302; Murray, *Romans*, 283; Cranfield, *Romans*, 1:383–84; Keck, "The Law and 'the Law of Sin and Death' (Rom 8:1–4): Reflection on the Spirit and Ethics in Paul," in Crenshaw and Sandmel, eds., *Divine Helmsman*, 52–53; Sanders, *Paul, the Law, and the Jewish People*, 93–94; Räisänen, *Paul and the Law*, 65–67; Hübner, *Law in Paul's Thought*, 146–47; Schnabel, *Law and Wisdom from Ben Sira to Paul*, 288–90; Dunn, *Romans 1–8*, 423–24; Wright, *Climax*

understood as an Edwardsian Reformed demonstration of religious affections vindicating one's regeneration and thus indicating who the justified elect are.[50] This Edwardsian approach would subsume the two ways as a vindication of Christ's vicarious atonement for the elect. Thus, in a Reformed model, such Spirit-guaranteed vindication through virtues identifies those who are authentically the elect of God. The Synoptic Gospels also present a version of this narrow way within a relational human responsibility unto forgiveness (chapter 8). Within liberalism, this view softened the eschatological outcome of the narrow way to only the present virtuous ethical way in which Jesus is primarily a moral example.[51]

Especially the Eastern Church embraced an incarnation of Christ where *Jesus takes human nature upon himself so that he might mystically transform humans to become divinized as immortal* (2 Pet 1:4).[52] Part of this process is to provide humans with divine light so that believers would take on immortal knowledge.[53] Gregory of Nyssa claimed that when the divine nature of Christ fused with our fallible human nature, the divine nature as a consuming fire would eradicate the evil within our human nature.[54] Further divinization of the believer occurs through receiving a place within Christ's resurrection body through baptism and receiving Christ's resurrection body in Eucharist and then further in the believer's resurrection to be like Christ.[55]

---

of the Covenant, 212; Stuhlmacher, *Romans*, 120; Schreiner, *Law and Its Fulfillment*, 71–73; *Romans*, 404–8; Thielman, *Paul & the Law*, 242–43; Dabney, "'Justified by the Spirit,'" 50; Seifrid, *Christ, Our Righteousness*; Das, *Paul, the Law and the Covenant*, 226; McFadden, "Fulfillment of the Law's DIKAIŌMA."

50. Edwards, *Treatise Concerning Religious Affections*.

51. Harnack, *What Is Christianity?*; Scott, *Ethical Teaching of Jesus*; Marshall, *Challenge of New Testament Ethics*; Cox, *Secular City*; Rashdall, "Abelardian Doctrine of the Atonement." However, Abelard does not merely fund ethics for he envisions that eternal life salvation is the goal of the narrow way (*Dialogue of a Philosopher*, 27, 39, 57–58, 105, 108).

52. Irenaeus, *Haer.* 4.33.4; Athanasius, *De incarn.* 9; Gregory of Nyssa, *Great Catechism* 25, 37; *Ag. Eunomius* 5.5; Augustine, *Trin.* 3.4; *Doctr. chr.* 1.22.16–17; Leo the Great, *Sermons* 23.5; 24.1–5; 26.2; Ficino, *Platonic Theology*, bk. 14, chs. 1–2, 5, pp. 4:219–41, 251–63.

53. Clement, *Homily* 1.4; 1 *Clem.* 36.2.

54. Gregory of Nyssa, *Ag. Eunomius* 5.4; Lossky, *In the Image and Likeness of God*, 97–98.

55. Ignatius, *Ep. Smyrna* 6; *Ep. Eph.* 20.2 "breaking one bread, which is the medicine of immortality, the antidote against death which gives eternal life in Jesus Christ;" Irenaeus, *Haer.* 4.18.4–6; Gregory of Nyssa, *Great Catechism* 37; Cassiodorus, *Exp. S. Pauli epist. Ad Rom.*, in Migne., ed., *Patrologia latina*, 68:417B; Sedulius Scotus, *Col. In omnes B. Pauli epist.*, in Migne, ed., *Patrologia latina*, 103:42D; Hugh of St. Victor, *de sacramentis* 1.9.2 in *Patrologia Latina*. 176.317D; Bettenson and Maunder, eds., *Documents of the Christian Church*, 81–82.

When a person has the Holy Spirit, she has forgiveness (Acts 2:38).[56] Athanasius concluded that the Holy Spirit deifies the believer.[57] Athanasius also considered that this divinization process should be called "god adopting believers as sons."[58] Aquinas proposed that God infused justification beginning with an event of God's grace infused into a person, initiating a process to transform her toward faith and away from sin.[59] This divine action facilitates the believer growing in the narrow way toward being like Christ, and ultimately God will eschatologically forgive the believer's sin. McGrath summarized Aquinas' view as "man is translated from a state of corrupt nature to one of habitual grace; from a state of sin to a state of justice, with the remission of sin."[60] Morna Hooker defends this approach as "interchange in Christ" whereby "Christ became what we are, in order that we might become what he is."[61] Believers are transformed to reflect the exemplar Christ until in the kingdom we will all be like him.

Anselm proposed a *communal chivalry satisfaction* view in his book *Why the God-Man* within a context of late medieval feudal obligation in order to defend the Chalcedonian formula of Christ's hypostatic union (Jesus Christ is fully God and fully human within a unified person). Within this context, Anselm weaves an argument intended to be logically necessary and inescapable rather than any appeal to the biblical text.[62] However, most consider there are lapses of logic but that within Anselm's context the argument might be plausible. A literary opponent, Boso, is constructed to highlight aspects of the argument and to be a yes-man to compel the reader to grant the logic of the argument. Anselm's argument is as follows:

1. God must act for his greatest honor and such immutable honor cannot be diminished (1.14, 15).[63]

2. God made man for happiness and everlasting life (1.10, 21).

---

56. Clement of Alexandria, *Who Is the Rich Man that Shall Be Saved* 40.

57. Athanasius, *De decret.* 14.

58. Athanasius, *C. Ar.* 1.38; 3.25.

59. Aquinas, *Summa Theologica* 2.1, Q113, A5–A8; Matthew of Aquasparta, *Quaestiones disputatae de gratia* q. 2.

60. McGrath, *Iustitia Dei*, 46; Aquinas, *Summa Theologica* 2.1, Q113, A1–A2.

61. Hooker, *From Adam to Christ*, 13–26; summarizing Irenaeus, *Haer.* 5 preface.

62. Anselm, *Cur Deus Homo* 1.1; Leo the Great, *Sermon* 23.3, 5 anticipates Anselm's work; Leftlow, "Anselm on the Necessity of the Incarnation," *Rel. Stud.* 31(1995) 167–85; Aquinas is unconvinced of the necessity of Anselm's argument but also positions himself within Anselm's satisfaction model (*Summa Theologica* 3, Q48, A1–A4, especially in the "I answer that" sections).

63. References in parenthesis are from sections of Anselm's *Cur Deus Homo*.

3. Such human happiness and everlasting life cannot be obtained without freedom from sin (1.10).

4. All humans sin by not giving God his due honor (1.11).

5. Such sin obligates humans to the devil as their feudal lord (1.7, 22).

6. Therefore, to obtain human happiness, remission of sin is necessary by rehonoring God (1.10, 11, 24).

7. In a chivalry context, rehonoring God requires an infinite amount to be sufficient compensation or punishment (1.12, 13).

8. God's honor will not permit the same treatment provided for individuals who are guilty and forgiven individuals; either debt must be repaid or, in a chivalry context, guilt must be righteously punished to rehonor God (1.14).

9. In chivalry, God can be rehonored with regard to sin by judging the sinner to damnation (that is, a limited being dishonoring an infinite being requires an infinite payment of everlasting damnation to rehonor God (1.15).

10. Repayment cannot come from a human for his own dishonoring of God because he already owes everything to God (1.15).

11. Therefore, repayment must come from another with appropriate resources of at least equal value (1.14, 20).

12. To maintain God's honor for his creation design, the number and level of angels that fell must be made up by equal number and level of procreated beings associated with rehonoring God (1.16, 18; 2.22; LXX Deut 32:8).

13. Angel numbers cannot be made up by God creating more of that kind of angel because any increase of angelic creation would entail God's design had been flawed (1.17).

14. Therefore, the replacement beings for the angels that fell must be redeemed humans since they are the only procreated beings (thus able to expand beyond the original two, Adam and Eve) that can be elevated to sufficient angelic levels (1.17).

15. Therefore, divine atonement enables humans to replace fallen angels to complete kingdom happiness and despoil the devil (1.22, 23).

16. For redeemed humans to obtain happiness, they must be transformed to choose good in a restored condition as if they had never sinned (2.1, 3).

17. Therefore, in redemption sin must be removed from these human lives by God (2.4).

18. Atonement must be accomplished by a human, so rehonoring God is from humanity (2.6).

19. Atonement must be accomplished by someone of sufficient value for all the creation, therefore a divine one other than God the Father must rehonor God (2.6).

20. For 18 and 19 to be accomplished, divine and human natures must be fully instantiated in a hypostatic union with no alteration, comingling, or changing of these natures (2.7).

21. Christ's humanity cannot be directly created by God or he would not be of the human family as needed to satisfy rehonoring God from them (2.8).

22. Christ should come from a virgin woman alone as women originally came from man alone (2.8).[64]

23. Only one of the Trinity should be incarnated, so there is only one Son (2.9).

24. Christ's humanity must have the ability to sin so that Christ's impeccability and the devil's defeat is by a choice that rehonors God (2.10).

25. Humans are not essentially sinners, nor mortal, so that Christ willingly dies, and thereby he can resurrect as immortal (2.11, 17).

26. The Son set a pattern of generously giving to God beyond God's demand (2.18).

27. Christ lived the designed human life, preserving God's original honor and restoring the creation (2.19).

There are really three arguments in Anselm's: (1) God's original design must be maintained in the resolution to preserve God's honor; (2) within a narrow way eschatological judgment model, God's original design wisdom must show the narrow way is possible to be lived by Jesus living it, and redeeming humans so they can live the narrow way unto the kingdom; and

---

64. An undeveloped element in *Cur Deus Homo* is a likely Augustinian inclination for traducianism of the soul and seminalism in which each human participated in the sin of Adam and has that transferred to them through the sensual sex act. So to be free of the Adamic effect of sin is to be without a human father and the concupiscence of the sex act. So in this line of reasoning conception by a virgin is purer. In *Cur Deus Homo* the argument is that it is fitting that Jesus be born of a virgin, whereas in *De Conceptu* 13, 23, and 26 Anselm argues that Jesus must have been born of a virgin. Hopkins, *Companion to the Study of St. Anselm*, 202–12.

(3) to redeem the elect of humanity there must be an appropriate sacrifice (thus human) and an infinite sacrifice to rehonor the infinite God (thus the sacrifice must be divine). Within the original context of medieval interpretation, feudal obligation, and chivalry the argument could compel a generous reader such as Boso to the conclusion. However, several of the premises reflect worldview assumptions that are not dependent upon logical necessity or a biblical framework.[65] Anselm's approach will be discussed in an appendix, retaining the chapters of this book for biblical gospel statements.

The perspective of the Magisterial Reformation is that *Christ's death provides vicarious forensic penal substitution as individual justification* for each believer's sins.[66] Luther conceived of this justification through multiple realist personal encounter metaphors, including: covenantal marriage in which the believer weds Christ and our sin becomes his and his righteousness becomes ours,[67] and healing medicine that has begun to work the eradication of sin from the believer's life.[68] Calvin identifies a gracious justification by faith as an intimate act of the Spirit grafting the believer into Christ, thus blending covenantal, forensic, regeneration, and relational aspects of salvation.[69] Similarly, Martin Bucer appropriates forensic justification as beginning with a new covenant transformation of the mind and covenantal sanctification predisposing the believer with a devotion to godliness.[70] The new covenantal aspect of Reformation soteriology is especially evident in chapters 5, 19, 20, and 24. However, Melanchthon continues to tighten the justification metaphor of Christ's death to be an *extrinsic individual penal courtroom forensic declaration*.[71] This is a divine forensic

---

65. Because Anselm's model is not dependent upon the Bible, critique of this model is beyond the spectrum of the chapters of this book but it will be addressed in the appendix.

66. Forensic Justification works within a forensic context: Cicero, *Rhetoricum libro duo* 2.53; Justinian, *Institutio* 1; Luther, *Luther's Works*, 56:379.1–15; Melanchthon, *Loci communes*, in Bretschneider, ed., *Corpus Reformatorum*, 21.421; *Apologia* art. 4, par. 252 and 305; McGrath, *Iustitia Dei*, 211, 457; *Augsburg Confession*, art. 4.

67. Luther, *Luther's Works*, 5:608.16; Vidu, *Atonement, Law, and Justice*, xviii, 43, 132 clarified that penal substitution is not present until Luther.

68. Luther, *Luther's Works*, 2:503.34–36; 57:69.14–16.

69. Calvin, *Institutes*, 3.1.1, 3; 3.11.2, 6, 10.

70. Bucer, *Metaphrasis et enarratio in epist. d. Pauli apostolic ad Romanos* (Latin text retrieved online from *The Digital Library of Classic Protestant Texts*); Latin text translated and engaged by Parker, *Commentaries on Romans*, 1532–42, 146; Irons, *Righteousness of God*, 23–24.

71. Melanchthon, *Loci communes* in Bretschneider, ed., *Corpus Reformatorum* 21.421; *Apologia* art. 4 par. 252 and 305; *Commentary on Romans*, in Stupperich, ed., *Melanchthons Werke*, 5:65; McGrath, *Iustitia Dei*, 211, 457; *Augsburg Confession*, art. 4; Packer, "What Did the Cross Achieve?"

declaration concerning the passive believer, identifying that the believer has Christ's alien righteous condition actively imputed to her heavenly external legal leger, declaring full divine acceptance of the believer. Such a forensic gospel involves Christ taking the sinner's wrath in his death as a vicarious penal substitute to empower the benefits of salvation for the believer. This model attempts to replace the Jewish sacrifice model by a forensic legal justification. Immanuel Kant attacked this forensic model as a travesty of judgment, arguing that one person cannot stand in the legal place of another, especially in capital punishment.[72]

Within the Pietist movement, Melanchthon's external forensic declaration became a personal experience of new birth and relationship, refocusing on the Reformed *regeneration experience of revival*. John Wesley presents a good expression of this evangelical experience:

> In the evening I went very unwillingly to a society in Aldersgate Street, where one was reading Luther's Preface to the Epistle to the Romans. About a quarter before nine, while he was describing the change which God works in the heart through faith in Christ, *I felt my heart strangely warmed*. I felt I did trust in Christ, Christ alone for salvation, and an assurance was given me that he had taken away my sins, even mine, and saved me from the law of sin and death.[73]

In the wake of Melanchthon's external forensic declaration and Wesley's evangelical experience, D. L. Moody developed an individual gospel ticket approach from the time of the Chicago fire.[74] On Sunday night, October 8, 1871, while preaching at Farwell Hall, which was now being used because of the increased crowds, D. L. Moody asked his congregation to evaluate their relationships to Christ and return next week for the final sermon in the series to make their decisions for Christ. That crowd never regathered. While Sankey was singing a closing hymn, the din of fire trucks and church bells scattered them forever, for Chicago was on fire. The hall and all structures around were burned that night. Moody vowed never to send a crowd away again but to always press for a decisive salvation decision.[75]

72. Kant, *Religion within the Limits of Reason Alone*, 66.

73. Wesley, "I Felt My Heart Strangely Warmed," www.ccel.org/ccel/wesley/journal.vi.ii.xvi.html.

74. Some claim ticket Christianity begins earlier, but the use of the anxious bench and counseling of potential converts argues against this commitment being present in other options, such as Charles Finney.

75. Moody in his own words, from the twentieth-anniversary sermon in which he repreached his fire sermon contained within Hantzler, *Moody in Chicago*, Moody's reflection and vow on 194 with background from 184.

In Moody's day, a person could buy a ticket for a train to a destination. Salvation in this approach becomes viewed as having *a ticket grounded in past faith guaranteeing the destination of everlasting life*. In more recent times, ticket Christianity imagery has changed from that of a train to that of a theater where one tears the ticket in half, throwing the half of Jesus' teaching away to retain the half of Jesus' vicarious penal atonement death. With a past faith in Jesus' death, a person has his half ticket and he is good to go to the destination of everlasting life. If one has the ticket of faith then she is reassured of everlasting life even with no life change. Resisting Edward's religious affections as a vindication of regeneration, this model claims that a sufficient vindication is her past ticket faith in Christ's death and biblical promises that this faith provides unto everlasting life.

In the wake of Wesley's experience, much of popular American evangelicalism encourages people with another gospel ticket approach so that they might pray to *ask Jesus into their heart*.[76] The rationale is that Jesus presented by Revelation 3:20 is standing at the door and knocking to be let in to fellowship with the Laodicean church and subsequently into anyone's heart. John 1:12 reassures all who receive Christ through faith that they become children of God. Some may even encourage the new convert with Paul's prayer, "that Christ may dwell in your hearts through faith" (Eph 3:17). Some have challenged that these texts may not be a gospel presentation to unbelievers since they were written in contexts to those already Christian in Laodicean or Ephesus churches.

Likely, all of these statements of gospel are probably not right, but this survey has displayed a variety of gospel statements with hints as to where their ideas will be engaged in this volume. Any of the statements that legitimately have biblical grounding should be acknowledged as a legitimate gospel statement. Any statement that has biblical support for part of the tradition should probably be acknowledged to the extent that the tradition is undergirded by the biblical text. Which means that features within a tradition that do not have biblical support for them should be stripped away to the portion of the view that does have biblical support, even if it radically alters that tradition. Some of the gospel statements provide rival views from the same data. If the biblical data support a particular trajectory then alternative views built off the same data in a different direction should be diminished and discarded as not biblical enough.

---

76. Campus Crusade for Christ, *Four Spiritual Laws*, "Law Four," 8–10. Greear ("Should We Stop Asking Jesus into Our Hearts?" and *Stop Asking Jesus into Your Heart*; Greear's book is reviewed by Cary, "Anxious about Assurance") attacks this approach but gives testimony that he had followed it and that it is a very common prayer in evangelical gospel presentation, and that he would rather the gospel not be said this way.

Chances are that various traditions have latched onto one or more expression of the gospel through interpreting biblical texts through the lens of their traditions, making for a theological hermeneutic. Such an approach sets up an in-group cognitive bias that confirms the tradition through a consensus within that tradition.[77] In this setting, hermeneutics of tradition will not obtain a clear answer as to the essence and breadth of the gospel. That is, theological hermeneutics will cloud some of the distinctives of biblical texts in order to bring them into line with the reigning construct of that tradition. Such an approach has splintered Christianity into postmodern Christianities. Instead, biblical theology surfaces the meaning of biblical texts in their contexts transparently, obtaining gospel in its multiple facets.[78] Each chapter of this book attempts to explore one biblical context or one facet of approach to gospel from a biblical theology perspective. Several of these historical models will have biblical grounding provided for them in the chapters that follow, presenting a multifaceted gospel message but the same salvation. This book is a call to a new reformation driven by biblical theology to allow the different hues of the biblical text to shine through with the diversity of gospel thought forms. Which means that the gospel could legitimately be communicated in a variety of ways reflective of the biblical texts that: (1) identify themselves as "gospel," (2) promise forgiveness, (3) promise everlasting life, (4) promise the kingdom, or (5) promise resurrection with Christ. Each of the following chapters is a proposal for one manner in which gospel is communicated. If any of these chapters is considered by the reader to reflect the biblical texts developed, then one should recognize that these chapters are legitimate ways of communicating the gospel.

---

77. Chalmers, "Influence of Cognitive Biases on Biblical Interpretation."

78. A defense of this methodology is provided in Kennard, *Critical Realist's Theological Method*.

2

The Servant's Atonement in Isaiah

ESCHATOLOGICAL ATONEMENT WAS EXPECTED through the Messiah in his priestly ministry.¹ One possibility of this eschatological atonement was

1. 1QS text 7 1.19; 11QMelch 12.7–8; 4Q541; *1 En.* 39.4–6; 41.2 (much like Rom 8:28–30; Col 3:1–4); 48.1–4; 51.4–5; 61.4; 62.14; *T. Levi* 18; Kennard, *Messiah Jesus*, 302–5; Pate and Kennard (*Deliverance Now and Not Yet*, 173–76) discuss other possible allusions Paul may have made to Isaiah 52–53. Some of these claimed allusions (such as Romans 4:25 "justification" as reflecting Isaiah 53:11 "justify" only work on the level of Vulgate or English text, neither the MT nor the LXX have any similarity in phrase to that of Paul). For an explanation of and an apologetic for this see Wood, "Isaac Typology in the New Testament"; Daly, "Soteriological Significant of the Sacrifice of Isaac"; Gubler, *Frühesten Deutungen*, 336–75; Rosenberg, "Jesus, Isaac and the Suffering Servant"; Riesenfeld, *Jesus Transfiguré*, 86–96; Strack and Billerbeck, *Kommentar zum Neuen Testament*, 3:746; Vermès, *Scripture and Tradition in Judaism*, 193–97, 217–27; Schoeps, *Paul*, 141–49. An important issue that emerges is whether or not pre-Christian Judaism expected a suffering Messiah. Those who say yes include Cullmann, *Christology of the New Testament*, 55–56, 60; Lohse, *Märtyrer und Gottesknecht*, 104ff. Jeremias ("παῖς θεοῦ," *TDNT*, 5:677–717) summarizes the evidence for the messianic interpretation of the Isaianic Servant in Palestinian Judaism: (1) this interpretation was confined to Isaiah 42:1ff.; 43:10; 49:1–2 and 6–7; and 52:13ff.; (2) in relation to Isaiah 42:1ff. and 52:13ff., the messianic understanding is "constant from pre-Christian times;" (3) the messianic interpretation of the passion sayings of Isaiah 53 can be traced back at least with a high degree of probability to the pre-Christian period though not with the same certainty (παῖς θεοῦ). Those who do not think pre-Christian Judaism gives evidence of a suffering Messiah expectation include: Hooker, *Jesus and the Servant*, 56–67; Strack and Billerbeck, *Kommentar zum Neuen Testament*, 2:273–74; Menard, "*Pais Theou* as a messianic Title in the Book of Acts," especially 84–85; Longenecker, *Christology*, 105; Fitzmyer, *Luke*, 2:156–66. Strack and Billerbeck summarize the evidence for this view: The notion of a suffering Messiah is not found in the OT or in any texts of pre-Christian Judaism (2:273–99). It says the "Old Synagogue" knew of "a suffering Messiah, for of whom no death was determined, i.e. the Messiah ben David" and a "dying Messiah, of whom no suffering was mentioned," the Messiah ben Joseph (2:273–274). Yet when it cites the passages from Rabbinic literature (2:282–91) that speak of the suffering

through Isaiah's Servant. Such a vicarious atonement undergirds certain NT statements of gospel. The Servant's vicarious atonement could be considered to be gospel because it provides forgiveness and atonement for all participants entering into the kingdom.

Differing interpretations of the suffering of the Servant in Isaiah 53 are reflected in the translations, however David A. Sapp and Otto Betz present convincing cases for the following development: (1) in the MT the Servant's afflictions and death are portrayed as an individual vicariously atoning; (2) the LXX tones down the Servant's suffering (he does not die, but is divinely rescued), almost to the point of being representative atoning; (3) while *Targum Jonathan* to the Prophets transpose suffering from the Servant/Messiah to Israel's enemies.[2] This reinterpretation makes Israel's enemies become the sacrifice of atonement (Isa 43:3). There is perhaps an "Isaac typology" (based on Genesis 22:1–14) that lies behind Isaiah 53, and its influence is to be seen in early Judaism and the New Testament, where the motif of vicarious suffering and death in atonement emerges.[3] Sometimes adherents of a pre-Christian origin of the suffering Messiah appeal to three texts thought to be important exceptions to the rule: *4 Ezra* 7:28–30; *Targum of Isaiah* 53; and the "Pierced Messiah" text (4Q285). The first mentions the death of the Messiah as the climax of the temporal messianic kingdom. However, it is

---

Messiah ben David, they are all drawn from late texts, which scarcely show that the expectations of such a figure existed among Palestinian Jews in or prior to the time of Jesus. The same has to be said of the texts about the dying Messiah ben Joseph (2:292–299). Strack and Billerbeck rightly rejects the implication found at times in Christian commentators that Mark 8:31 and Matt 16:21 refer to a "suffering Messiah," and the latter is not a "messianic" title without further ado. Where in pre-Christian Judaism does one find a "Son of Man" as an agent of Yahweh anointed for the salvation, deliverance of his people? In *Targ. Jonathan* the "Servant" of Isaiah 52:13 is identified as "the Messiah": "See, my Servant, the Messiah, shall prosper; he will be exalted, great, very mighty," and 53:10c is made to read, "They will look upon the kingdom of their Messiah, many sons and daughters will be theirs." Yet no use of "Messiah" is made in the crucial verse, 53:12. It is not surprising that the "Servant" of Isaiah 52–53 was eventually identified with a Messiah in Jewish tradition; but it still remains to be shown that this identification existed in pre-Christian Judaism or in Judaism contemporary with the NT (Fitzmyer, *Luke*, 2:156–66). Wright, *Jesus and the Victory of God*, 591.

2. For numbers 1 and 2 see Sapp, "The LXX, 1QIsa, and MT Versions of Isaiah 53 and the Christian Doctrine of Atonement," in Bellinger, ed., *Jesus and the Suffering Servant*, 170–92; while Betz treats the *Targum* in "Jesus and Isaiah 53," in Bellinger, ed., *Jesus and the Suffering Servant*, 70–87, especially 73.

3. For an explanation of and an apologetic for this see Wood, "Isaac Typology in the New Testament"; Daly, "Soteriological Significant of the Sacrifice of Isaac"; Gubler, *Frühesten Deutungen*, 336–75. Rosenberg, "Jesus, Isaac and the Suffering Servant"; Riesenfeld, *Jesus Transfiguré*, 86–96; Strack and Billerbeck, 3:746; Vermès, *Scripture and Tradition in Judaism*, 193–97, 217–27; Schoeps, *Paul*, 141–49.

important to note that there the Messiah does not suffer; rather, after having lived long and well for four hundred years, he simply dies with the rest of humanity. His death, therefore, has no apparent theological significance. Likewise, the Aramaic translation (*Targum*) of Isaiah 53 is not evidence for the concept of a suffering Messiah when it transposed (probably in reaction to Christianity) the afflictions of the suffering Servant of Isaiah 53 *from* the Messiah *to* Israel or the surrounding Gentile nations. Moreover, both texts are dated after the birth of Christ and cannot be used as testimony for pre-Christian Jewish messianic understanding. The Pierced Messiah text cannot support the idea of a suffering Messiah because of grammatical reasons.[4] Thus that text should read, "The leader of the community [the Prince of the Congregation] will kill him [the leader of the Kittim]." N. T. Wright's comments represent a fair-minded solution to the issue:

> There was not such a thing as a straightforward pre-Christian Jewish belief in an Isaianic "Servant of YHWH" who, perhaps as Messiah, would suffer and die to make atonement for Israel or for the world. But there was something else, which literally dozens of texts attest: a large-scale and widespread belief, to which Isaiah 40–55 made a substantial contribution, that Israel's present state of suffering was somehow held within the ongoing divine purpose; that in due time this period of woe would come to an end, with divine wrath falling instead on the pagan nations that had oppressed Israel (and perhaps on renegades within Israel herself); that the explanation for the present state of affairs had to do with Israel's own sin, for which either she, or in some cases her righteous representatives, was or were being punished; and that this suffering and punishment would therefore, somehow, hasten the moment when Israel's tribulation would be complete, when she would finally have been purified from her sin so that her exile could be undone at last. There was, in other words, a belief, hammered out not in abstract debate but in and through poverty, exile, torture and martyrdom, that Israel's sufferings might be, not merely a state *from* which she would, in YHWH's good time, be redeemed, but paradoxically, under certain circumstances and in certain senses, part of the means *by* which that redemption would be affected.[5]

Let us then return to the MT and unpack what is meant by the "Servant of Yahweh" from the Servant Songs. The term "servant" is used several ways throughout Isaiah but in the four Servant songs it refers to a spiritually

---

4. Schiffman, *Reclaiming the Dead Sea Scrolls*, 346.
5. Wright, *Jesus and the Victory of God*, 591.

instructed individual in the midst of a sinful and blind nation Israel (Isa 40:2; 42:1, 19; 53:9). This Servant as an individual trusts Yahweh throughout discouragement and suffering for others sins, of which he is innocent (Isa 42:1; 49:4; 53:4–6, 9–11). In contrast, Israel is corporately spiritually deaf and dumb, doubting Yahweh in discouragement and suffering for its own sins (Isa 40:2, 27; 42:19). This Servant is a person who is chosen for a special ministry by God. Regal description "prohibits an understanding of "servant" as a slave or lackey, but determines its meaning as "trusted envoy" or "confidential representative."[6] Qumran noticed these features and even changed aspects in 1QIsa from the MT to be more messianic with regard to offering himself as atonement for humanity, and 4Q541 follows suit.[7]

In summary form, the Servant songs convey a good overview of the Servant's role. As a humble prophet, Yahweh's Servant will bring salvation and the proper order to the earth (Isa 42:1–4). Through the new covenant, Yahweh guarantees his Servant's mission for accomplishing salvation (Isa 42:5–9). Called by Yahweh, yet rejected by his own people, the Servant will bring salvation to the Gentiles and at the proper time restore Israel to the land and to Yahweh (Isa 49:1–13). The righteous Servant declares that by his being rejected while trusting Yahweh, he learned to comfort the weary (Isa 50:4–9). Yahweh applies the lessons from his Servant's experience to others by reminding believers to live by faith, while unbelievers are warned about judgment (Isa 50:10–11). Yahweh promises to exalt his Servant because he voluntarily provided a "substitutionary atonement," having *died as a vicarious sacrifice on behalf of guilty people* to cleanse and save them (Isa 52:13–15). Israel responds in a confession of their sin and belief in the Servant's atoning death (Isa 53:1–9; Zech 12:10–11). Israel's public confession probably takes place as the Servant is honored in the eschatological kingdom. The *Targum on Isaiah* 53:1 identifies this confession to be "our gospel."[8] This confession fits the pattern of the Servant offering himself as purification and guilt offering *on their behalf*, thus "vicarious atonement." The LXX translated the MT Isaiah 53:10 "guilt offering" (אָשָׁם) to be "sin offering" (ἁμαρτίας). Because of the effectiveness of the guilt (MT) or sin

---

6. Williams, "Poems about Incomparable Yahweh's Servant in Isaiah 40–55," 75.

7. 1QIsa 52:14 replaces the MT "marring" (מִשְׁחַת) with a Qal singular "I have anointed" indicating that God established the sacrifice role for his Messiah, and 1QIsa 51:5 replaces the MT first-person "my righteousness" with a third-person "his arm" also indicating messianism; also 4Q541 9.1.1.2 "he will atone" (Hengel and Bailey, "The Effective History of Isaiah 53 in the Pre-Christian Period," in Janowski and Stuhlmacher, eds., *Suffering Servant*, 101, 103, 108, 146).

8. *Targum of Isaiah* 53.1; Betz, "Jesus' Gospel of the Kingdom," 68, 73.

(LXX) offering by the Servant, the Servant will be blessed with a continuing inheritance (Isa 53:10–12).

Israel understands that the human abuse and death of the Servant was ultimately because Yahweh placed their iniquity and covenant curse upon the Servant as a vicarious substitutionary atonement as one would find in a guilt or purification offering (Isa 53:3–6, 10). Especially in Isaiah 53:4, the speaker testifies that they understood God to smite the Servant. The basic root נכה usually means "striking" or "violent killing" in OT and early Jewish contexts (Exod 21:12; Num 35:11, 15; Isa 14:6; 66:3),[9] unless the object of the beating does not kill, like Balaam's staff (Num 22:23–32). Thus, the emphasis is "violent killing" but the term does not essentially mean killing. The hophal passive participle מֻכֵּה (smitten) in Isaiah 53:4 when used as coming from God is identified by emphasis as *smiting with covenant curse* broadly in the OT, early Judaism, and in Isaiah (Lev 26:21; Num 11:33; Deut 28:59; Isa 1:6[10]; 10:26; 27:7; 30:26; 53:4).[11] However, in Ezekiel God claps (נכה) his hands together and no covenant curse is conveyed (Ezek 21:19 [Eng. 14], 22 [Eng. 17]; 22:13), showing that the term from God does not essentially mean death by covenant curse. However, in this Isaiah 53:4–5 instance based on emphasis of God doing the striking, the word implies that the Israelites confess an understanding that the Servant's death was "penal atonement." Thus, by emphasis the testimony was that the Servant *receives covenant curse from God* that would have come upon humans, resulting in the Servant's death. The place of decision is whether such a penal substitution is the factual truth or merely what those testifying consider to be so. If the atonement metaphors presented do not require a penal meaning then it could just be the testifiers' interpretation.

The theological meaning of the Servant's death is carried by the sacrificial terminology. The Servant atones for many nations and Israel in their sin through the pattern of covenantal atonement (purification or guilt offering). In his marred appearance the Servant is identified as "he will sprinkle many nations" (Isa 52:14–15; יַזֶּה/*yzh*). Such a concept of corporate sprinkling indicates the establishment of a covenant and the atonement forgiveness that accompanies this relationship (Exod 24:8; Heb 9:13; 1 Pet 1:2). Affecting this atonement forgiveness, the Servant was vicariously sacrificed by

---

9. *TDOT*, 9:415–8; this term (נכה) if accomplished by humans does not carry the semantic field of covenant curse, merely "killing," which term in Zech 13:7 conveys that the shepherd will be struck (נכה) by humans and his followers will scatter.

10. Perhaps Isa 1:6 מֻכֵּה is self-inflicted wounds rather than covenant curse due to Israel's sins.

11. Covenant curse when from God: Van Dam in Van Gemeren, ed., *NIDOTT*, 3:103–4; CD B 19.8; 4Q166 2.12; 4Q169 frag. 3–4 1.5; 11QTemple 55.6–8.

God (Isa 53:4–6). Is this vicarious sacrifice an instance of the cup of God's wrath (Isa 51:17, 22, then it is penal) or is this vicarious atonement as in the scapegoat "bearing" (נָשָׂא/nś') the sin away as on the Day of Atonement (Lev 16:20–22 vicarious but not developed as penal sacrifice; Isa 53:4)? The sins of the people are confessed upon the scapegoat to bear them away (נָשָׂא/nś') into the wilderness (Lev 16:22). This vicarious "bearing" (נָשָׂא/nś') of the people's sin is what the Servant accomplished (Isa 53:4, 10). *The Servant's death is to deal with our corporate iniquities, to bring atonement, and peace with God.* Such atonement and reconciliation are what one would expect as benefits from a *guilt offering* (Isa. 53:10 MT identifies אָשָׁם/'šm guilt offering, though the LXX identifies it as a sin offering: δῶτε περὶ ἁμαρτίας). There is no object taken, so no reparations are required, only Israel's conscious confession of their sin, which is in fact the voice of Isaiah 53:1, "Who has believed our message?" Isaiah presents this confession of corporate Israel as in the future kingdom era (Isa 52:7–10; 54:1–17). Presumably, individual Israelites could confess their sin earlier than that expression of the kingdom and have atonement benefits of the Servant applied to them. John Oswalt described this substitution sacrifice from Isaiah 53:4–6, 10–12.

> It is here and in vv. 10–12 that the issue of the substitutionary suffering of the Servant, and thus his capacity to deliver his people, comes to the fore. He does not suffer merely as a result of the people, but in the people. He suffers *for* them, and because of that, they do not need to experience the results of their sins.[12]

As has been shown, the Servant's substitutionary sacrifice is informed especially by the language of the cult, not a courtroom situation (especially Lev 5:1, 17; 10:17; 16:22; 17:16; 20:19; and Num 9:13; 14:34).

In Isaiah 53:5 the "piercing," "crushing," "chastening," and "scourging" are each metaphors of the death of the Servant, along with "slaughter" and "cut off" of Isaiah 53:7–8. We should not focus on the "pierce" and "scourge" as though they were specifically descriptive of Roman scourging and spear piercing on a cross, for neither was Rome present, nor was this means of death being used in Isaiah's eighth century B.C. For example, "scourging" (בַּחֲבֻרָתוֹ/bḥbrtw) in Isaiah 53:5 simply means "stripe" or "blow" or "strike" as in Genesis 4:23. So the word has no conscious allusion to Roman scourging. Likewise, we should not ignore the middle terms, especially "crushing," which is repeated again when this is identified as a guilt offering (Isa 53:5:

---

12. Oswalt, *Isaiah 40–66*, 385, and for contextual development 386–87, 401; for a discussion on a range of interpretations of Isa 53 see Pate and Kennard, *Deliverance Now and Not Yet*, 92–96.

מִדְכָּא/*mrk'*, 10: דִּכָּאוֹ/*dk'*). So I take these terms as metaphors of the Servant's death.

The NT refers to Isaiah 53 directly in several places but the amazing thing is that none of these references develop the vicarious atonement that Isaiah's Servant undertakes. For example, Matthew 8:17 describes that the miracles of healing accomplished by Christ are his carrying our infirmities (quoting Isa 53:4). 1 Peter 2:22 indicates the silence that Jesus maintained before his accusers as a mimetic[13] atonement pattern for the Christians to follow (quoting Isa 53:9). Luke 22:37 identifies (through Isa 53:12) that Jesus was to be classified with criminals. Acts 8:32-35 quotes some of the physical surroundings (identified with the wicked and rich in his death) to recognize the Servant's death as Jesus' death (quoting Isa 53:7-8). Paul makes two direct citations following the LXX and being rather dissimilar to the MT.[14] Isaiah 52:15b is quoted in Romans 15:21 and Isaiah 53:1a is quoted in Romans 10:16. Neither quote has christological or sacrificial value. Of these passages, only 1 Peter adds in the context that Jesus "bore our sins in his body on the cross," with imagery of Christians having strayed like sheep (1 Pet 2:24-25 probably alluding to Isa 53:4-6, 10). So at least Peter probably recognized that Isaiah 53 describes Christ's death as vicarious substitutionary atonement gospel, though his emphasis in the context is on instruction for servants suffering to follow Jesus in silent mimetic atonement (1 Pet 2:18-23). Additionally, with no actual clear statement for vicarious atonement, the Synoptic and Acts pattern identifies more with mimetic atonement.

In *1 Enoch* and some Qumran texts, the teaching about the Isaianiac Suffering Servant combine[15] with Merkabah[16] mysticism. *1 Enoch* joins

13. Mimetic atonement is where an example sets a pattern to emulate. Such a view was common in early Judaism and Greco-Roman literature (Pate and Kennard, *Deliverance Now and Not Yet*, 22-71; 2 Macc 6:18—7:42; 4 Macc 10:10; 11:12, 20, 27; 16:24-25; 17:2, 11-12, 18; Wis 3:5-6; 7:14; 11:19; 12:22; deaths of Socrates, Cato, Diogenes, Demonax, and Seneca: Seneca, *Epis.* 24.6-7; Epictetus, 4.1 168-72; Plutarch, *On the Tranquility of Mind* 475D-F 1.11; Tacitus, *Annals* 15.62; Seeley, *Noble Death*).

14. Pate and Kennard (*Deliverance Now and Not Yet*, 173-76) discuss other possible allusions Paul may have made to Isaiah 52-53. Some of these claimed allusions (such as Romans 4:25 "justification" as reflecting Isa 53:11 "justify") only work on the level of Vulgate or English text; neither the MT nor the LXX have any similarity in phrase or theology to that of Paul.

15. Pate and Kennard (*Deliverance Now and Not Yet*, 75-77) follow Nickelsburg (*Resurrection, Immortality, and Eternal Life in Intertestamental Judaism*, 71-72) in connecting these imageries in contrast to Sjöberg, *Menschensohn im ältiopischen Henochbuch*, 116-139.

16. Or Jewish divine chariot presentations of a real divine temple in heaven, simultaneous to that of God inhabiting the temple on earth. That is, both the heavenly and

mainstream Judaism in announcing that the afflictions of the righteous are to be seen as mimetic atonement, especially at the culmination of the messianic woes.[17] In this context, the Son of Man as Messiah[18] employs a representative role of suffering on behalf of the elect.[19] That is, the heavenly Son of Man appropriates to himself the afflictions of the elect so that the elect on earth may enjoy in heaven the glory of the Enochian Son of Man. This glory already exists in heaven[20] but the public resurrection of the elect will vindicate them before the wicked.[21]

However, meanwhile the Teacher of Righteousness viewed himself as Isaiah's Suffering Servant providing vicarious atonement for his community.[22] Thus, to be associated with him is to experience divine forgiveness.[23] The Qumran covenanter's identified the Teacher of Righteousness with Melchizedek, who was expected to atone for the Qumran covenanter's sins,[24] which equated with deliverance of the righteous from the age of the messianic woes into the kingdom.[25] After the Teacher of Righteousness died, his followers recalculated that deliverance would occur at the end of forty years, entailing their mimetic suffering to fill up what was lacking from the Teacher's sufferings.[26] However, after the forty years came and went with no rescue, the Qumran covenanters reinterpreted their deliverance mystically

---

earthly temples are real and different things may be occurring in these different realities. For example, the heavenly temple is normally thought to be where God's presence dwells (Isa 6:4), but the amazing thing is that with the cleansed tabernacle God dwells on earth, with the ark of the covenant serving as his throne (Exod 40:34–38). However, the uncleanness of the earthly temple dislodges the divine presence from the earthly temple, while it remains in the heavenly temple (Ezek 1:4–28; 11:22–25). The different conditions of the pure heavenly temple and the occasionally unclean earthly temple show that they are both real in this multidimensional Hebraic framework rather than the idealism of the earthly shadows that a Platonism would portray.

17. *1 En.* 43.4; 47.1–2; 48.6; 103.9–104.8.
18. *1 En.* 46.1–7; 48.2–10; 52.4.
19. *1 En.* 39.6; 48.1–4; 51.4–5; 61.4; 62.14.
20. *1 En.* 39.4–5; 41.2, much like Rom 8:28–30; Col 3:1–4.
21. *1 En.* 62.14–16.
22. 1QH 15.8–27 especially 15.18 and 16.4–17.36; 11QMelch. 6–25. The Teacher of Righteousness probably understood himself to be on the verge of exaltation in Jerusalem (1QH 14.28–36; 15.24–28). However, the Damascus Document suggests that the Teacher of Righteousness died before he could deliver on his promises (CD 19.34–35; 20.13–16).
23. Especially 1QH 15.18.
24. 11Q Melch. 6–8.
25. 11Q Melch. 9–25.
26. CD 19.34–35; 20.13–16. Deliverance was recalculated to be forty years later (CD 20.13–16; 11Q Melch.; 1QS 8.1–16).

to mean that they were caught up to heaven in the worship setting with and because of the Teacher of Righteousness's vicarious atonement.[27] This sentiment might inform NT textual development of Jesus' death as vicarious atonement.

Targum Jonathan of Isaiah 53:12 identified that the "Messiah" was the one who accomplished the guilt offering atonement of Isaiah 53:10 and 4–6. In such a non-penal vicarious atonement there is forgiveness and as such it could be considered to be gospel.

---

27. 1QH 11.19–38; 15.26–36.

3

Mark as Narrative Gospel

AT TIMES BIOGRAPHICAL WORKS were referred to as "good news" or "gospel." For example, the *Priene Inscription* 2.81–82 used the word "good news," (εὐαγγελίου) twice identifying a narrative describing Augustus's life up until the time when he began to rule as Caesar.[1] The Gospel of Mark utilized the term in the same biographical manner (Mark 1:1), which in the context identifies the good news of the narrative of Jesus Christ and his kingdom message (εὐαγγέλιον, Mark 1:14–15; 8:35; 13:10; 14:9; 16:15; Matt 4:23; 9:35), which is repeatedly proclaimed by the apostles (εὐαγγέλιον, Matt 24:14; 26:13; Mark 16:15). However, Mark's emphasis is that Jesus has authority to heal and meet the needs of people beyond other lords like Caesar. Jesus offers the kingdom of God (Mark 1:14–15) as an alternative to the Herodians' kingdom or Caesar's kingdom. So the gospel could be summarized as "Jesus is Lord."

The gospel can also be summarized as the narrative account of Jesus as he repeatedly heals and meets needs. The patristics concluded that there were four such authoritative gospels that contain these legitimate accounts about Jesus and that each of the four was authoritative salvific gospel.[2]

Such biographical accounts set up not only a belief in the authoritative Lord but a narrow way to follow exampled by the Lord's virtues. Hellenistic

---

1. *Priene Inscription* 105; similarly emperor Septimius Geta in *Inscriptiones Grecae* 3.1081; Dihle, "Gospels and Greek Biography."

2. Irenaeus, *Adv. Haer.* 3.1.1–2; 3.10.5; 3.11.9; Ignatius, *Smyrn* 1.1.1–2; John Chrysostom, *Hom. Matt.* 1.7; Justin, *1 Apol.* 66; *Dial.* 10.2; 103.19; 106; Eusebius, *Anti-Marcionite Prologue*; *Hist. eccl.* 2.15.1–2; 3.39.14–15; 5.20.6; 6.14.5–7; Tertullian, *Adv. Haer.* 4.2.2; 4.4–5; 4.5.3; Origen, *Frag. En Comm. in Matt.* 1.1–20; *Comm. Jo.* 1.5, 7–9; Gregory of Nazianzus, *Carmida dogmatica* 1.12.6–9; Theodoret, *Dialogs* 1; Jerome, *Vir. Il.* 7–9. Bauckham, *Jesus and the Eyewitnesses*, 300–305.

biography intentionally has virtues for the disciple and reader to imitate.[3] For example, Quintilian folds qualities of the person in narrative to be illustrated by the person's works.[4] Often the ancestry and origins indicate who the person will be like.[5] For example, Jesus is predicted to be the Messiah to bring in the Abrahamic and Davidic covenants, elevating the poor in eschatological reversal through his reign and destroying the opposition (Luke 1; 3:23–34), which means that a disciple imitates Jesus' virtues as they follow him (Mark 1:17; 2:14; 8:34).

Jesus called his disciples to follow him (Mark 1:17; 2:14), which is an invitation to follow the Father's will (Mark 3:35) in the same pattern as Jesus followed the Father's will (Mark 14:36). Such a life calls disciples to believe in the gospel (εὐαγγελίῳ, Mark 1:15). This believing life is alert to dangers but following Jesus in fervent prayer and forgiving others (Jesus: Mark 1:35; 2:5; 6:46; 14:32–36; disciples: 11:23–25; 14:38). Likewise, in the same manner as Jesus has come to serve, his disciples are to serve others (Mark 9:35–41; 10:42–45). Because of the contextual emphasis on service, Jesus gave his whole life (not merely his death) in service ransoming the many, such as Jesus rescuing the blind men so he might see after he calls his disciples to serve (Mark 10:45–52; Matt 20:28–34).[6] Furthermore, Jesus sent out his disciples to imitate his kingdom ministry to meet real needs and call others to repent to the narrow way unto the kingdom (Mark 4:11; 6:7–13; 11:10; 15:43). Amid the difficulties of persecution the disciples are to continue to follow and confess Christ even to their death (Mark 8:29, 34–38; 13:9–13). If a disciple does not continue but is ashamed of Christ and his words, then "the Son of Man will also be ashamed of him when he comes in the glory of his Father with the holy angels" (Mark 8:38). However, those who endure "to the end will be saved" (Mark 13:13).

---

3. Philo, *Moses* 1.158; Josephus, *J.W.* 1.4–8, 13–16; *Ant.* 1.1–2; Plutarch, *Aem.* 1.1, 5; Tacitus, *Agr.* 1; Dionysius, *Ant. Rom.* 8.56.1; Kurz, "Narrative Models for Imitation in Luke-Acts"; Fiore, *Function of Personal Example in the Socratic and Pastoral Epistles*, 26–44; De Boer, *Imitation of Paul*; Crouzel, "L'imitation et la 'suite' de Dieu et du Christ"; Cothenet et al., "Imitation du Christ"; Gutierrez, *Paternité spirituelle selon S. Paul*; Pate and Kennard, *Deliverance Now and Not Yet*, 369–72; Trompf, *Idea of Historical Recurrence in Western Thought*, 97–101; Talbert, "Biographies of Philosophers and Rulers as Instruments of Religious Propaganda in Mediterranean Antiquity," 1643; Fornara, *Nature of History in Ancient Greece and Rome*, 104–20.

4. Quintilian, *Inst.* 3.7.10–22; 5.10.24–31.

5. Quintilian, *Inst.* 3.7.12; Ps. Hermogenes, *Prog.* 15–17.

6. Kennard, *Messiah Jesus*, 275–77.

4

Beatitudes to the Kingdom

JESUS' GOSPEL (εὐαγγέλιον) is the core message taught (εὐαγγελίζω) by Jesus (Matt 4:23; 9:35; 11:5; Luke 4:18, 43; 7:22; 9:6; 16:16; 20:1).[1] Jesus preached this message repeatedly to those in need. Both Matthew and Luke provide exemplary sermons to capture the essence of Jesus' gospel. Jesus' characteristic sermons (the Sermon on the Mount and the Sermon on the Plain)[2] show Jewish-Jesus continuity within a narrow way unto the kingdom. Jesus has new things to say in these sermons but there is a great degree of continuity with early Judaism as well. Both the new and the continuity will be highlighted throughout this chapter and the next chapter.

Both the Sermon on the Mount and the Sermon on the Plain are addressed to Jesus' disciples (Matt 5:12; Luke 6:20). Of course, the multitude overheard his teaching (Matt 5:1; 7:28) but the thrust was for those already identified in relationship with Jesus as his disciples.

Jesus' sermons position themselves within a two-way approach unto the kingdom, much like early Judaism and John the Baptist had before him.[3]

---

1. Harnack, "Gospel: History of the Conception in the Earliest Church," 324–25; Stuhlmacher, "Pauline Gospel," in Stuhlmacher, ed., *Gospel and the Gospels*, 150. Some of the material in this chapter is reworked from Kennard, *Messiah Jesus*, 76–84 and used with permission from Peter Lang.

2. These two sermons are given historically at different times, since the miracle of healing the leper immediately follows the Sermon on the Mount as Jesus is coming down from the mountain (Matt 8:1–2), and precedes the Sermon on the Plain (Luke 5:12–15; 6:20–49), with Luke identifying that he writes his gospel in consecutive order (Luke 1:3). Additionally, the geography of mount and plain identify different locations (Matt 5:1; Luke 6:17). Any itinerant preacher will use his good material more than once. Loehr, "Jesus and the Ten Words."

3. Early Judaism develops a two-ways view unto the kingdom especially from a wisdom and prophetic perspective (Sir 11:26; 16:12, 14; 17:23; 35:11; 48:10; Bar 4.37; 5.5;

Both the Sermon on the Mount and the Sermon on the Plain follow this Jewish orientation as is apparent especially in the beginning and end of the sermons (Matt 5:3–16; 7:13–27; Luke 6:20–26). However, the clearest development of the two-ways approach is in the conclusion of the Sermon on the Mount in which five illustrations portray the two ways: 9 1) gates and ways, (2) sheep versus wolf in sheep's clothing, (3) trees, (4) claims demonstrated, and (5) builders (Matt 7:13–27). Each way has a goal to which it leads, either that of life and the kingdom (Matt 7:14, 21) or destruction (Matt 7:13, 19, 27; 16:18). Jesus begins his exhortation to enter by the narrow gate[4] and the way that leads to life. Only one of the two ways saves; the other damns. The narrowness of the strictured way (στενης and τεθλιμμένη) has implications that there are few who find it (Matt 7:13–14; Luke 13:23–25). The breadth of the way that leads to destruction indicates that many will follow this way (Matt 7:13, 22). The broad way includes those who take advantage of others, like wolves in sheep's clothing and false prophets. The basic way on which a person travels is evidenced by their consistency in obeying Jesus' and the Father's teaching (Matt 7:21, 24, 26). However, this is not earning one's place in the kingdom; the disciple shows in a natural fruiting manner that he has an intimate internalized discipleship relationship with the Son (Matt 7:15, 17–19, 23). The kingdom way is not shown in works like prophecy, exorcisms, or miracles (Matt 7:15, 22). Rather, *the kingdom way is shown in new covenant obedience rather than lawlessness* (Matt 7:21–24, 26). The good man or tree produces good fruit and generous speech from within his heart (Matt 7:16–20 with v. 12; Luke 6:43–45).[5] So works show what kind of person someone is. Such a good person builds on the firm rock foundation of obedience to Jesus and the Father (Matt 7:24–27; Luke 6:46–49).[6] Such strictured but wise living does not remove the troubles of life but enables one to survive them, because he has built upon the foundation of Jesus' teachings. Eschatological justification unto the kingdom assesses the disciple's aligning with Jesus from virtuous evidence consisting of righteousness,

---

2 *Bar.* 54.21; 2 Macc 1:27; 2:18; *Jub.* 1.15; 5.11, 15; *1 En.* 95.5; 100.7; *Pss. Sol.* 2.7, 16, 25, 348.34–35; 11.2; 14.9–10; 15.10; 17.8–9, 11–12, 28–31, 50; 18.6–9; *Jos. Asen.* 28.3; LAB 3.10; 44.10; 64.7; 1QM 2.2, 7; 3.13; 5.1; 11QT 8.14–16; 57.5; 1QS 3.18–4.26; 4Q228; 4Q473 frag. 2 2–4; *Charter of a Jewish Sectarian Association* 9.21; 11Q5 22.10; *Asher* 1.3–5; 6.4–6; Philo, *Rewards* 164; *4 Ezra* 7.6–8). Davies and Allison, *Matthew*, 1:439, 442–80 present these beatitudes as entrance requirements into the kingdom.

4. Luke 13:24 has narrow door instead of gate.

5. A similar good tree/bad tree comparison is made in the Jewish parables in *m. 'Abot* 3.18; *ARNa* 22.2; *ARNb* 34; *Tg. Ps.-J.* on Gen 4:8 and Deut 20:20.

6. *ARNa* 24.1–4, 22 makes similar building materials and on rock or sand comparisons in a two-ways Jewish salvation.

forgiveness, and doing good to indicate who is granted everlasting life (Matt 13:39–43, 49–50; 18:35; 25:12, 34–46; Luke 13:23–30).

Elsewhere in this two-ways soteriology, there is a way of light and a way of darkness (Matt 7:22–23; Luke 11:34–36).[7] In Judaism God is seen to dwell in light (Ps 104:2; Dan 3:3–4; Hab 3:3–4)[8] and thus he gives light to his people (Job 29:2–3; Pss 4:6; 18:28; 48:3).[9] The eschatological hope is light (Isa 60:20), but those who are God's are now illuminated by revelation light of life and wisdom (Pss 27:1; 56:13; Hos 10:12 LXX; John 1:4, 9).[10] This illumination impacts the righteous so that they are described as the people of the light (Isa 42:6; 49:6; Matt 5:14; 6:22; 1 John 1:5–10).[11] These "walk in the light of the Lord" (Isa 2:5). The way of the light shows the issues and allegiances clearly, demonstrating its sincere allegiance to God (Matt 6:22; Luke 11:34).[12] The way of the darkness can't see clearly. Darkness is duplicitous and is deceived, being unaware of its blindness and separation from God (Job 18:5–6; 38:15; Matt 6:23; Luke 11:34–35; 1 John 1:6, 8, 10).[13] For example, such a condition of Jewish "evil eye" is that of a selfish miser, signifying intent and remaining in darkness (Deut 15:9; Prov 23:6; 28:22).[14] In spite of fire, hell is described as a dark place with the outcome being darkened lives (Matt 8:12; 22:13; 25:30).[15]

BEATITUDES-SIMILITUDES

Both the Sermon on the Mount and the Sermon on the Plain begin with beatitudes characterizing the narrow way to the kingdom. In Luke the beatitudes render the two ways more explicit by a section of curses following the beatitudes (Matt 5:3–10; Luke 6:20–26). Each of the beatitudes begins with the word "blessed," serving as a repetitive[16] echo concerning the ben-

---

7. Davies and Allison, *Matthew*, 1:635–36.
8. *1 En.* 38.4; *Jos. Asen.* 6.3.
9. 1QS 11.3; *2 Bar.* 38.1.
10. Sir 8:1; Wis 7:10, 26.
11. *1 En.* 104.2; *T. Levi* 14.3; *LAB* 51.6; *T. Job* 31.5; 53.3.
12. Job 1:1 Aq.; *Barn.* 19.2; *T. Levi* 13.1; *Ps. Phoc.* 50; CR col. 3 and 4.
13. *T. Job* 43.5–6; *T. Sol.* 26.7.
14. Tob 4:7; Sir 14:8; 26.11; *m. 'Abot* 2.9, 11; 5.19; 1QS 4.9–11.
15. 1QS 2.8; *1 En.* 103.7.
16. While OT beatitudes do not group more than two together (Ps 84:4–5), the listing of nine beatitudes should not overwhelm the reader, since by early Judaism an occasional list of beatitudes is as long (Matt 5:3–11; five in 4Q525 including purity of heart and faithfulness to the Law; four in Luke 6:20–22). *2 En.* 52.1–14 has seven beatitudes and seven curses. Later, *Gos. Thom.* has ten beatitudes, some in series (7,

eficial condition that a disciple can possess provided he meets the criterion of each verse. This means that the beatitudes are first blessings and show God's grace, rather than requirements.[17] That is, the conditions evidence which disciples of Jesus will be so blessed. Or as Albert Schweitzer said it, the beatitudes "define the moral disposition which justifies admission into the kingdom."[18]

The blessed conditions are to be understood as realized within the kingdom. Matthew's beatitudes begin and end with identifying the blessing with "the kingdom" (Matt 5:3, 10).[19] The *inclusio*[20] (Matt 5:3, 10) of mentioning the kingdom serves to identify the other blessings as kingdom benefits as well. Additionally, some of the benefits are only believably received in the kingdom, such as when the meek and gentle inherit the earth (Matt 5:5). Luke's account begins with the kingdom but does not quite complete an *inclusio* in its close of promising great reward to come from heaven to earth (Luke 6:23).

These kingdom benefits have both present and future benefit in view. Matthew's *inclusio* and Luke's starting point of "theirs *is* the kingdom" evidences, by its present-tense verb, present kingdom benefits already for those who meet the criteria (Matt 5:3, 10; Luke 6:20). The other beatitudes evidence by their future-tense verb a future reward that is not yet received but will especially be realized in the future eschatological kingdom (especially clear in Matt 5:5, 12; Luke 6:23).

Thus the beatitudes must be taken together. No one benefit can be removed from the rest of the kingdom framework and a disciple relationship with Jesus the King; likewise no one quality can be lifted to promise kingdom benefits. For example, merely because a person grieves or is gentle does

---

18–19, 49, 54–58, 68–69, 103). Additionally, the Matthew beatitudes may have parallels with Isa 61, quoted in Luke 4:18–19; cf. Sir 14:1–2, 20–27; Davies and Allison, *Matthew*, 1:436–39.

17. Beatitudes are in Jewish wisdom (Sir 14:20–27) and prophetic texts (2 *En.* 52.1–14). As a genre, it is not really law or covenant, even though these genres possess statements of blessing and curse, but not in beatitude form (Deut 28–30).

18. Schweitzer, *Mystery of the Kingdom of God*, 53–54; *Kingdom of God and Primitive Christianity*, 93–101; Theodoret, *Dialogs* 1; Leo the Great, *Sermons* 95.1–9; Yoder, *Politics of Jesus*, 112–33. Thus the liberal ethical approach (Harnack, *What Is Christianity*; Scott, *Ethical Teaching of Jesus*; Marshall, *Challenge of New Testament Ethics*; Cox, *Secular City*) ignored the Jewish eschatological kingdom context and outcome for Jesus' teaching.

19. The kingdom focus of these beatitudes is like the beatitudes of *Pss. Sol.* 17.44 or 1 *En.* 58.2–3, "Blessed are you righteous and elect ones, for glorious is your portion. The righteous ones shall be in the light."

20. Latin for enclosing in a literary envelope.

not guarantee her involvement in the kingdom. However, when someone who has a discipleship relationship with Jesus grieves or is gentle, there is an appropriate reassurance that kingdom blessings are hers to meet that need.

"Blessed are the poor in spirit, for theirs is the kingdom" (Matt 5:3). Recognition of poverty in a disciple's spiritual condition identifies the disciple's trust and dependence upon her master (Jas 2:5).[21] So it is not a spiritual benefit for the able and wealthy, but for those who recognize their need. This reverses the popular secular sentiment: "blessed are the rich." Luke 6:20 simplifies the poverty to be material poverty, which is more emphasized in Luke than any other synoptic gospel (Luke 1:53; 4:18; 6:20; 7:22; 14:13, 21; 16:20, 22; 18:22; 19:8; 21:3).[22] This Lukan portrait is similar to Qumran's self-designation of the sect as the poor.[23] Whether material poverty or recognition of one's spiritual nature of inadequacy shows one to be in need of depending upon God, the results are the same. Both point to humility and dependence on God, as one admits to her own spiritual bankruptcy. Within Jewish tradition, such a reference to the poor refers to meek, humiliated, and oppressed people of God (Isa 10:2; 26:6).[24] This sentiment affirms one sense of Jewish tradition indicated in the *Sibylline Oracles* 8.208: "Blessed are the poor, for they shall be rich," especially in eschatological reversal. This is rather telling for American Christianity. For, in the twenty first-century, the world's richest 15 percent of people are those who own a house that keeps the weather out and also own a car. Whereas, if you own two cars and some recreational equipment as well, then you are among the top 5 percent of the world's wealthy.[25] Luke warns those who receive comfort now that their riches may indicate that they are not depending upon God and thus

---

21. Such fiscal poverty was a positive religious designation in Judaism (1QM 11.9, 13; 13.14; 14.7; 1QpHab 12.3, 6, 10; 4QpPs 37 fr. 1, 2.10).

22. This call to the poor is consistent with 4Q88 9.13–14 and the *Passover Haggadah* that calls all the poor (using similar phrases to that of Jesus in Luke) to the Passover feast. *Gos. Thom.* 54 follows Luke on *fiscal poverty* but Matthew on *third-person plural* (*their*) with, "Blessed are the poor, for theirs is the kingdom of heaven." That is, Luke personalizes it further by the second-person "*yours* is the kingdom." Additionally, *Gos. Thom.* 69.2 encourages that these hungry and thirsty will be satisfied.

23. 1QpHab 12.2–10; 1QM 11.9, 13; 13.14; 1QH 2.32; 3.25; 5.16, 18, 22; 4QpPs 37 1.9; 2.10; 4Q88 9.13–14; with only the *Damascus Document* using the term in the more common sense of poor people; cf. Dunn, *Christ and the Spirit*, 1:110.

24. *Pss. Sol.* 5.2, 11; 10.6; 15.1–3; 18:2; 5 *Apoc Syr. Ps.* 2:18; 1QpHab. 12.3; 1QM 14.7 where such poverty might mean fainthearted; 1QH 5.13–14; 4QpPs 2.9–10.

25. My attempt to conceptualize the *U.N. Human Development Report 2003* as summarized by http://www.trentu.ca/said/povertystats.html, which for example lists the average salary of the richest fifth of the world population to be $31,000 per capita per year in 1993 dollars, while the poorest fifth of the world population lives on less than $1 per capita per day.

there are no more benefits to come (Luke 6:24). Jewish tradition indicates that in the kingdom age to come there will be no poverty.[26] Luke later goes on to illustrate this point with Jesus' teaching on wealth, in the Parable of the Rich Man and Lazarus (Luke 16:19–31). Abraham in paradise summarized the point for the rich man as, "during your life you received your good things and likewise Lazarus bad things; but now he is being comforted here, and you are in agony" (Luke 16:25). However, for those whose dependence is on God, the present reality of the kingdom is their very real possession.

"Blessed are those who mourn, for they shall be comforted" (Matt 5:4; Luke 6:21). Perhaps picking up the Jewish traditional sentiment from Isaiah 61:1–2, quoted by Jesus as he began his ministry in the Nazareth synagogue, Jesus provided real comfort in the kingdom for the downtrodden and oppressed (Luke 4:18–21).[27] Jewish tradition continued to emphasize that the kingdom should be thought to be broadly comforting to us in our life of mourning (Isa 60:20; 66:10; Jer 31:13; Ps 126:2–6).[28] The mourning (Matthew's emphasis) and weeping (Luke's emphasis) that occur in this life are in contrast to the comfort and laughing that will come upon all who are beneficiaries of the kingdom in the future. The mourning refers to sorrow with the world as it is. Matthew uses "mourning" in one other place to indicate the inappropriateness of mourning when the disciples have Jesus with them, but Jesus reminds them that he will be taken away (Matt 9:15).[29] When Jesus is removed, mourning their loss is quite appropriate. However, this concept of mourning could be much broader, like sorrow for sin in one's life or context (Matt 25:75; Luke 7:38–48; 22:62).[30] This weeping could occur within areas of lack such as hunger or lack of love (Luke 6:21–22). Mourning can include loss of loved ones and the futility of wasted life (Matt 2:18; Luke 5:38). Jesus grieves over Jerusalem, which is rejecting him, and urges them to grieve as well (Luke 19:41; 22:28). For those who grieve in any of these ways, real comfort will be theirs in future kingdom benefits. Jesus' present kingdom healing even undoes the cause for grief for some now, in the promise of raising loved ones from the dead (Mark 5:34; Luke 7:13; 8:52). Luke warns those who laugh now and do not take to heart the

---

26. *Sib. Or.* 3.378; *T. Jud.* 25.4; *b. Pesaḥ.* 50 in contrast to *b. Šabb.* 151b and *Sipre* on Deut 15:11.

27. Sir 48:24.

28. *Thanksgiving Scroll* 13.14–15; Bar 4:23; 1QH 18.14–15; 11QMelch 2.20; perhaps also Ps 126:2–6.

29. While not in inspired Scripture as the earliest or the best manuscript, Mark 16:10 shows one example of how mourning and comfort surround the death and resurrection of Christ.

30. Tob 13:14; *Pesiq. R.* 28.3.

present context of grief that they shall mourn and weep in their destruction as they miss future kingdom benefits being poured out (Luke 6:25).

"Blessed are the gentle, for they shall inherit the earth" (Matt 5:5). The quality of πραεις is meekness, absence of pretension and gentleness. As such, this meek gentleness is a synonym to material poverty and poverty in spirit (Matt 5:3; Luke 6:20). In this statement, Jesus echoes the Jewish tradition evident in the Law[31] and articulated by *2 Enoch* 50:2: "In patience and meekness spend the number of your days so that you may inherit everlasting life." This meekness is a quality Jesus displayed in his humble offering of rest for the disciples (Matt 11:29). It is also a quality predicted of him by Zechariah 9:9, which indicates Jesus' peaceful intention in coming to Jerusalem on a colt of a donkey, to offer Israel the kingdom if they would have him as King (Matt 21:5). Those, like Jesus, who display this quality in relationship with him shall inherit the whole earth, and not merely a part of the land (γης in Matt 5:5, 13). This hope of land inheritance also reflects the Jewish hope for the kingdom (Isa 60:21–22; 61:7; Rom 4:13).[32] This eschatological reversal is a common Jewish hope (Luke 1:50–53).[33]

"Blessed are those who hunger and thirst for righteousness, for they shall be satisfied" (Matt 5:6).[34] Those with a desire for appropriate living to be developed in their lives and contexts will have their needs amply met. This quality of righteousness is developed in the next section, but here Jesus' sentiment also reflects Jewish traditional expectations (Pss 42:2; 63:1; 143:6; Amos 8:11).[35] This longing is the same sentiment as seeking above all else God's kingdom and his righteousness, where there is real encouragement that Jesus' disciples' needs will be met (Matt 6:33). Luke describes one who hungers for food, thus identifying the hungry with the poor, who may be oppressed (Luke 6:21 and connecting it by synonymy to Matt 5:3–5, 10–12). Especially the Lukan version resonates with the Jewish tradition of

---

31. The praise of meekness and gentleness is also evident in Jewish tradition through (Deut 4:1; Ps 37:11; Philo, *Vit. Mos.* 2.279; Josephus, *Ant.* 19.330; *m. Soṭa* 9.15; ARN 7; *b. Soṭa* 40a, 49b; *b. Šabb.* 30b; *b. Ned.* 38a; 4QPs 2.9–11) and in classical works as well (Plato, *Crit.* 120E; *Rep.* 375C; Lucian, *Somnium* 10; *Ep. Arist.* 257, 263).

32. *Jub.* 32.18–19; *2 En.* 5.7; 11QTemple 59.11–13; 4QpPs 2.9–12; 4QPs 37; *2 Bar.* 51.3; *m. Qidd.* 1.10.

33. Sir 35; Wis 5:1–20.

34. *Gos. Thom.* 69.2 takes this beatitude with reference to poverty, hungering and thirsting in need will be satisfied.

35. Wis 5:15; Philo, *Post.* 172; *Fug.* 139; *b. Sanh.* 100a; *m 'Abot* 2.2; *Sifra A.M.* par. 8.193.1.11; *Sifra Behuq.* 2.262.19; *b. Qidd* 396; *Pesiq. Rab. Kah. Sup.* 2.1; *Deut. Rab.* 7.9.

eschatological reversal (Pss 37:19; 107:5-9; 132:15; Isa 25:6-8; 32:1, 16-17; 49:10-13; 55:1-2; 65:13).[36]

"Blessed are the merciful for they shall receive mercy" (Matt 5:7). Jesus' teaching reflects the sentiment of rabbis elsewhere.[37] The merciful are benefactors who attempt to meet other's needs.[38] The dominant expression of mercy in the Synoptics is the healing done by the Son of David (Matt 9:27; 15:22; 17:15; 20:30-31; Mark 5:19; 10:47-48; Luke 1:58; 17:13; 18:38-39), whereas in Jewish tradition the primarily merciful one is God (1 Sam 23:21; Ps 72:13; Prov 14:21; Mic 6:8).[39] Mercy is one of the weightier matters of the Law and unfortunately was neglected by the scribes and Pharisees (Matt 23:23). One form of the Jewish neglect of mercy was their restrictiveness to their own Jewish group.[40] Jesus' disciples must have mercy in ministering to sinners and forgiving others without judging them (Matt 6:12-15; 7:1-5; 9:13; 12:7; 18:21-35; Mark 11:25). The good Samaritan exemplifies mercy in meeting his neighbor's and even enemy's needs (Matt 5:44-47; Luke 10:37). This sentiment of showing mercy universally was also a factor in some forms of Jewish tradition.[41] The merciful shall receive mercy (Matt 5:7). The future mercy to be received could be in this life or the kingdom beyond.[42] In response, praise is given to God for his mercy unfolding in his salvation plan (Luke 1:50, 54, 72, 78). Through Luke 16:24, Jesus warns us that those who do not give mercy (such as the rich man's abuse of Lazarus) will not receive mercy in the afterlife.

"Blessed are the pure in heart, for they shall see God" (Matt 5:8). The pure are the clean that recognize God alone as their hope (Ps 24:3-4; Matt

---

36. *1 En.* 58.4; *2 Bar.* 29.6; *Par. Jer.* 9.20; 1QSa; 4Q525; *T. Levi* 13.5. This theme is continued in 2 Pet 3:13 and *Gos. Thom.* 5.6; 69b.

37. This is parallel in *b. Šabb.* 151b, "He who has mercy on people obtains mercy from heaven;" also *t. B. Qam.* 9.30, "As long as you are merciful, the Merciful One is merciful to you;" *T. Sim.* 4.4; Josephus, *Ant.* 10.41. Additionally, the rabbis identified that God judged the world by two measures: justice and mercy (*Lev. R.* 29.3), so that following a verse about righteousness it is appropriate to develop the theme of mercy. This sentiment continues in early Christendom, *1 Clem.* 13.2; Polycarp, *Ep.* 2.3.

38. *T. Jud.* 18.3-4; Epict. *Disc.* 1.18.4.

39. *T. Zeb.* 5.1, 3; 7.1-8.6; Philo, *Spec.* 4.72, 76-77.

40. For example, Qumran, the Essenes, and other Jews maintained a mercy within the community and a hate to outsiders (1QS 1.4, 10-11; 2.4-9; 9:21-23; 1QM 4.1-2; 15.6; 1QH 5.4; *b. Ber.* 33a; *b. Sanh.* 92a; Josephus, *J.W.* 2.139).

41. A commitment to universal mercy is present in rabbinic Judaism (*Sipra* on Lev 19:18 and *Mek.* on Exod 21:35) and outside the Jewish tradition (Polybius 18.37.7; Hesiod, *Op.* 342-3, Solon, frag. 1.3-5; Plato, *Tim.* 17d-18a; *Rep.* 375c; *Meno* 71e; Tacitus, *Hist.* 5.5-6).

42. 2 Tim 1:18; Jude 21; *1 Clem.* 28.1.

23:26; 27:59).[43] The kind of purity described is one of whole moral purity. Such a person is sincere and not divided against himself. Examples of internal anger and adultery are developed as contrast to this purity in this context (Matt 5:22, 28). Such a commitment to purity of heart reflect Jewish tradition (Gen 20:5-6; Ps 24:3-4; Isa 61:1, "broken hearted" as in responsive from one's heart to God).[44] The privilege of the pure in heart in Jewish tradition is to see or know God in the kingdom (Job 19:26; Pss 11:7; 17:15; Isa 52:6; 60:16; Jer 24:7; 31:31-34).[45] Jewish tradition developed that such sight of God at the present tended to be beyond normal expectation,[46] so that it remained an eschatological hope (as in Matt 5:8).

"Blessed are the peacemakers, for they shall be called sons of God" (Matt 5:9). The peacemaker is one who reconciles humans into peaceful relationships as is evident in Matthew 5:23-26 and Mark 9:50. Such peacemaking is affirmed by Jewish tradition (Ps 34:14; Prov 10:10).[47] A peacemaker will not force God's kingdom but will humbly wait for it (Isa 25:6-9; 26:8; 30:15, 18; 40:30-31; 49:23; 50:10-11; 57:13; 64:4; Lam 3:22-26; Mic 7:7; Jas 5:7-9). A peacemaker is one who demonstrates that he is a son of the Father by generously loving and praying for his enemies that persecute him (Matt 5:39-45). Such peacemaking may be at significant cost or loss. Such peacemaking may require letting an abuse go in forgiving one's abuser. However, this peacemaking is not to be at the expense of denying Jesus as the Son, that is, the King. Associating oneself to Jesus' teachings may in fact separate one from others and work against peace (Matt 10:34). In maintaining a relationship with Jesus as the Messiah, we should work for peace and thereby identify ourselves as sons of God (Matt 5:9, 45; Luke 6:35; 20:36). Here, "sons of God" would imply that God has something of the same quality of loving and working toward peace that peacemakers as sons would have. A model for sons of God is Jesus, *the* Son of God, who by his mandate in the Davidic covenant works for peace (1 Chr 22:9-10; Matt 3:17; 4:3; 17:5; 27:9, 40, 43, 54). Being a son of God would identify one as a son of the kingdom (Matt 13:38) in contrast to the damned sons of hell (Matt 5:22; 23:15). This hope of becoming "sons of God" is one which Jewish tradition held out for the kingdom.[48]

---

43. *2 Bar.* 9.1; *2 En.* 45.3.1; *T. Jos.* 4.6; *Benj.* 8.2; 4QBeat.

44. *T. Naph.* 3.1; *T. Jos.* 4.6; 1 Tim 1:5; 2 Tim 2:22; Heb 10:22.

45. *4 Ezra* 7.98; *b. B. Bat.* 10a; SB 1; *b. Sanh.* 98b; Philo, *Contempl.* 11-12; *Abr.* 57-59; *Mut. nom.* 81-82; Matt 16:27; 24:30; 26:64; Mark 13:26; 14:62; 1 Cor 13.12; Heb 12:14; 1 John 3:2; Rev 1:7; 22:4.

46. Exod 3.6; 19:21; 33:20, 23; John 1:18; 1 Tim 6:15-16; *Sipre* on Num 12:8.

47. *2 En.* 52.11-15; *m. 'Abot* 1.12; *m. Pe'a* 1.1; *Mek.* on Exod 20:25.

48. *Pss. Sol.* 17.27; *Sib. Or.* 3.702. Everlasting reward is promised for peacemaking

"Blessed are those who have been persecuted for righteousness sake, for theirs is the kingdom" (Matt 5:10-12; Luke 6:22).[49] "Those who have been persecuted" is a perfect participle that emphasizes that we are dealing with qualities which in this case we have little control over. This kind of persecution includes: hatred, ostracism, insults, spurning through defamation, excommunicating,[50] and saying all kinds of evil against one falsely on account of Jesus (Matt 5:11; Luke 6:22). Such persecution is essentially for those who have identified with Jesus and maintain obedient, righteous character. This is consistent with the Jewish traditional expectation that the righteous will suffer persecution.[51] Such persecution has the potential of devastating a person so that he falls away (Matt 13:21; Mark 4:17). Such persecution identifies Jesus' disciples with the prophets who were persecuted by the religious leaders before them. This virtually guarantees the certainty of the religious leaders persecuting the disciples (Matt 10:23, 38-39; 16:21, 24-26; 23:34-35; Mark 8:31, 34-38; 10:30; Luke 9:21-24; 21:12). Early Jewish tradition identified that the fate of God's prophets was that of martyrdom.[52] In this context it is a bad sign if all speak well of you, for this is the way the religious leaders' fathers treated the false prophets (Luke 6:26). To be identified with God's prophets, and with the Son, in persecution is a cause for rejoicing because it indicates that you will be blessed with life and reward in the kingdom (Matt 5:11-12; 16:24-27; Mark 8:35-38; Luke 9:24-26). This joy in suffering resonates with a Jewish traditional approach,[53] but more clearly provides the kingdom rationale for such gladness. It is in this way of identifying with God's prophets that Jesus teaching resonates with the Jewish revelation heritage. Other than this, persecution in the OT is not developed as a condition of blessing. This encouragement to joy is rather unusual for Matthew's more somber character in his persecution environment, in contrast to Luke, who writes at great length about rejoicing since he normally identifies with kingdom realizations occurring and the lost be-

---

(*m. 'Abot* 2.8; *Pe'a* 1.1; *ARN* 40A).

49. 1 Pet 3:14 and *Gos. Thom.* 68 retain the same sentiment. Polycarp, *Ep.* 2.3; Clement of Alexandria, *Strom.* 4.6.

50. Perhaps implied by a wooden reading of the text in Matt 5:11 and Luke 6:22, namely, "cast out your name as evil on account of the Son of Man," which probably has beneath it a Semitic expression, "to cause an ill name to go out." Davies and Allison, *Matthew*, 1:462.

51. Wis 1:16—5:23.

52. *Jub.* 1.12; 4QpHos 2.3-6; Josephus, *Ant.* 10.38; *Ascen. Isa.* 2.16; 5.1-14; *Par. Jer.* 9.21-32; *Tg.* on Isa 28:1.

53. Jdt 8:25; 2 Macc 6:28-30; 2 *Bar.* 48.48-50; 52.5-7; *b. Sanh.* 101a; Acts 5:41; Rom 5:3-5; Phil 4:10-13; Jas 1:2, 12; 1 Pet 1:6; 4:13-14.

ing saved (Luke 1:14, 47; 2:10, 13, 20; 10:20; 15:5, 7, 10, 24, 32; 24:41, 52). Perhaps it is in this Lukan joy (when present kingdom benefits get realized) that Matthew identifies that blessing is also expressed by a *present* benefit of having the kingdom now (Matt 5:10). However, Matthew's joy goes further, in that it realizes that suffering now for Christ identifies one as a beneficiary of greater kingdom benefit from heaven in the future (Matt 5:12).

"You are the salt of the earth" (Matt 5:13). Salt was gathered from evaporation pools or from the edge of the Dead Sea (Ezek 47:9–11; Zeph 2:9).[54] Salt was a primary implement in keeping food from putrefying (Exod 30:35).[55] It was also used as a condiment to season food (Job 6:6; Isa 30:24) and was a mandatory accompaniment in some sacrifices (Lev 2:13; Ezra 6:9; Ezek 43:24).[56] As such, salt was considered one of the valuable staples of life along with oil and wine.[57] For example, Antiochus IV gave salt, oil, and wine to all the Jews who aided him against Ptolemy Philopater (ca. 170 B.C.). None of the synoptics describes an ethical meaning to this salt description, as though we had a salty task to perform. In fact, since the statement is a descriptive comment of being, "You are salt," there is no charge at all to do some salty purpose like preserving the world. Rather, as a descriptive comment, it recognizes these disciples to be valuable as they are identifying with these beatitude traits. The contextual emphasis of Jesus and all the synoptics is to take this condition of saltiness as something that instead unfortunately can be lost (Matt 5:13; Mark 9:50; Luke 14:34). That is, salt is more soluble than the impurities contained within it, so the salt could be leached out, leaving a non-productive soil worthy only to be trod upon by feet.[58] This loss of salt (μωρανθῇ) is elsewhere taken as an ethical condition of becoming fools (μωρανθῇ; Matt 5:13; Luke 14:34; Rom 1:22; 1 Cor 1:20).[59] Here is where the ethical charge lays. In the same way that salt can leach out and become unrecoverable in unproductive soil, so too could the disciples depart from their beatitude traits and be rejected from the kingdom program already begun with them. The exhortation is to stay true to the beatitudes as qualities of one's being, for being this way indicates the blessing of the kingdom.

---

54. Josephus, *Ant.* 13.128.
55. Ignatius, *Magn.* 10; Diogenes Laertius, *Vit.* 8.1.35.
56. *Jub.* 21.11; 11QTemple 20; *m. Mid.* 5.3.
57. Sir 39:26; Pliny, *Nat. hist.* 31.102; *m. Soṭa* 9.15.
58. Pliny, *Nat. hist.* 31.82.
59. This allusion also works in Aramaic and Hebrew, further underscoring that loss of salt and foolishness are related.

"You are the light of the world" (Matt 5:14). Again, this is a declaration of a quality of being. Jewish tradition developed that people could be light (Isa 42:6; 49:6; Dan 12:3).[60] The disciples in their beatitude traits are like light. Here the emphasis is not on losing the quality of being (such as salt) but on doing what light does. A lit-up city is visible at night on a hill, so also oil lamps that are lit are used to shine light to their whole environment, not to be under a basket (Matt 5:14–15; Mark 4:21; Luke 8:16; 11:33).[61] The disciple is to let this light quality of his life be visible to others *by doing good works reflective of the beatitude virtues* (Matt 5:16). The purpose (ὅπως) of being light is so that others may see our good works and praise the Father as a result.

This look at the beatitudes and similitudes has provided a brief overview of the way to obtain the kingdom. It is a virtue salvation in disciple relationship with Jesus, that is, possessing beatitude qualities of behavior or character while being aligned with Jesus. For example, evangelicals tend to emphasize salvation by faith. Jesus in the Gospel of John would recognize faith as the critical salvation virtue. However, this discussion currently is unpacking the Sermons on the Mount and Plain, which neither deny nor develop faith in that manner. Actually, synoptic gospels identify faith with obtaining healing.[62] So this virtue salvation is dependent upon a relationship with Jesus, which obtains, retains, and exhibits these beatitude qualities evidenced through good works. Loss of these qualities spells a rejection from the kingdom. Continuation in these qualities as a disciple of Jesus indicates great blessing in the kingdom.

---

60. *1 En.* 104.2; *2 Bar.* 77.13–16; *T. Levi* 14.3–4; *T. Job* 31.5; *Par. Jer.* 9.14; *Apoc. Adam* 83.3–4; *b. Sanh.* 14a; *b. B. Bat.* 4a; *ARN* 25; 1QS 3.3, 19–22; 1QM 13.5–6, 14–15; *T. Job* 43.6/4; *Sib. Or.* fr. 1.26–27.

61. A similar point is made in *Gos. Thom.* 33b about preaching instead of good deeds.

62. Kennard, *Messiah Jesus*, 33–36.

5

Following Jesus' New Covenant Teaching of the Law in the Narrow Way

THE GOSPEL CAN BE said as *following Jesus in the narrow way unto the kingdom* and thus departing from any participation within the broad way that leads to destruction. Within Pharisaic Judaism, this narrow way would include *loving God in following the Law*. Within sectarian Judaism, this narrow way of the Law would also be viewed as *a new covenant internal responsiveness to God*. Within these frameworks, one expectation for the Messiah was that he would teach the good news of the Law in a new covenant manner.

Israel interpreted God as establishing the nation in covenant nomism with the Mosaic covenant such that they must obey the Law or his people will lose God's blessing.[1] Some sectarian Jews saw this passion for the Law as a realization of the new covenant in which God was giving them a "new heart" and a "new spirit."[2] Judaism's hope for the kingdom was in part a divine work that would transform Israel into a new covenant people responsive to the Law (Deut 30:1–6; Jer 31:33–34).[3] As a result, Israel insisted on defining practices including: circumcision, kosher, and Sabbath keeping as expressions of this purity.[4]

---

1. Jdt 5:17–21; 8:18–23; *Pr. Azar.* 6–14; CD 10.14–11.18; Some of this material is reworked from Kennard, *Messiah Jesus*, 107–51 and *Biblical Covenantalism*, 2:155–81 and used with permission by Peter Lang and Wipf and Stock.

2. As in Jeremiah 31:31–34 and Ezek. 36:24—37:28 so too in: *Jub.* 1:22–25; 1Q3 4, 5; 1QH 4, 5, 18; 4Q Shir Shalb; CD 4Q266 frag. 2 1.6–8; B 19.12–13; 1QpHab 2.3; 11.13; 4Q434 frag. 1 1.4; 4Q437 frag. 1 1.14.

3. CD 6.19; 8.21; 20.12; 1QpHab 2.3; Kennard, "Jeremiah and Hebrews"; *Biblical Covenantalism*, 2:73–89 and 3:162–74.

4. *Jub.* 2:17–33; 15:11–34; 12:2; Tob 1:10–12; 4:12–13; Jdt 10:5; 12:2, 9–19; 13:8;

Covenant nomism informed national policy in Israel as well. For example, Hasmonean John Hyrcanus broke off an important siege because of the coming of the Sabbath year.⁵ The *Letter of Aristeas* 139-42 identifies this covenant nomist mindset.

> In his wisdom the legislator (Moses) ... surrounded us with unbroken palisades and iron walls to prevent our mixing with any of the peoples in any matter ... So, to prevent our being perverted by contact with others or by mixing with bad influences he hedged us in on all sides with strict observances connected with meat and drink and touch and hearing and sight, after the manner of the law.⁶

Jews risked their lives to be faithful to the Mosaic covenant. For example, in 5 B.C. Herod had erected a golden eagle over the temple as a votive offering, and two learned teachers (Judas and Matthaias) inspired the young men to pull down the image.⁷ Herod responded with having many of them arrested, tried, and burned alive. Furthermore, Josephus describes instances such as that in A.D. 26 when Pilate introduced Roman standards and a bust of Caesar into Jerusalem. Here Jews were ready to die rather than transgress the Law.⁸ A large group followed him to his residence in Caesarea and sat outside his house for five days. When they were summoned to tribunal and troops surrounded them with drawn swords, the Jews fell to the ground extending their necks and exclaiming that they were ready to die rather than to transgress the Law. Pilate was impressed and withdrew the standards. Likewise, in A.D. 41 Caligula ordered Petronius to set up his statue in the temple. Josephus claims that the protestors said, "slay us first before you carry out these resolutions ... we will sooner die than violate our laws."⁹ Their hope was that God would intervene and prevail with blessing from the Mosaic covenant.¹⁰ Presumably, God did since Caligula died before the

---

1 Macc 1:48 and 2:15-28; 2 Macc 6:18-31; 7; 3 Macc 3:4-7; 7:11; 4 Macc 5:1—6:30; also *Joseph and Aseneth*; Horace, *Sat.* 1.9.69-70; Philo, *Som.* 2.123-24; *Leg. Gai.* 158; *Migr. Abr.* 89-93; Josephus, *Ant.* 1.10.5; 13.252; 14.10.12; 14.237. 16.2.3; 16.6.2-4; *J.W.* 1.145-7.

5. Josephus, *J.W.* 1.157-60; Jews compliance with Sabbath law was well known in the ancient Near East (Josephus, *Ant.* 14.10.12; *Ag. Ap.* 2.2, 39; Philo, *Vit Mos.* 2.21) and even more so in sectarian Judaism (CD 10.14-11.18; *Songs of the Sabbath Sacrifice*; *Temple Scroll*=11Q19).

6. *Letter of Aristeas* 139-42, quoted in Dunn and Suggate, *Justice of God*.

7. Josephus, *J.W.* 1.651-5; *Ant.* 17.149-67.

8. Josephus, *J.W.* 2.169-74; *Ant.* 18.55-59.

9. Josephus, *Ant.*18.261-4 and 271.

10. Josephus, *Ant.*18.267.

statue was completed and it never was installed in the Jerusalem temple. These examples reflect merely a sample of Israel's commitment to Yahweh under the framework of corporate covenant nomism.[11]

The eschatological expectations among the Prophets and Qumran were for a messianic teacher, "the interpreter of the Law" (Isa 42:4).[12] *Messianic Apocalypse* (4Q521) presents the character of the hoped for messianic teacher as echoing Isaiah 61:1.

> For the heav]ens and the earth will listen to his anointed one, [and all] that is in them will not turn away from the precepts of the holy ones. Strengthen yourselves, you who are seeking the Lord, in his service! Will you not in this encounter the Lord, all those who hope in their heart? For the Lord will consider the pious, and call the righteous by name, and his spirit will hover upon the poor, and will renew the faithful with his strength. For he will honor the pious upon the throne of everlasting kingdom, freeing prisoners, giving sight to the blind, and in his mercy ... the Lord will perform marvelous acts such as have not existed, just as he sa[id for] he will heal the badly wounded and will make the dead live, he will proclaim good news to the poor.[13]

Such a messianic expectation hoped for a Jewish king who is a healer, a spiritual teacher of the Law, and a rescuer of the needy. Early Jewish literature expected the Teacher of Righteousness to teach righteous Jews God's Law and revelation in a new covenant form.[14] He would serve as a rival to the man of the lie, a wicked priest who tried to destroy the Teacher of Righteousness. However, the Teacher of Righteousness (as the Messiah of

---

11. Challenges to this view have been marshaled (Elliott, *Survivors of Israel*). However, the impact of this work on this question is in my opinion significantly diminished because of the highly selective sectarian documents it surveys and admits it surveys (pp. 13–26). At this point I believe Sanders and Dunn presented a broader reflection of Judaisms of this era (cf. 1QM; 1QS; CD; Josephus, *J.W.* 1.5.2; 2.8.14; 2.162–3; *Ant.* 13.10.6; 13.172; 13.288; 17.2.4; 18.12–15, b. *Yom.* 19b; b. *Nidd.* 33b; *Life* 12; *Yadayim* 3.7; 4.6; *Makkot* 1.6; *Niddah* 4.2; perhaps *Pss. Sol.* 1.8; 2.3; 7.2; 8.12–13; 17.5–8, 23). Additionally, biblical texts like James, Matthew, and Acts indicate that Jews and Jewish Christians were zealous for the Law.

12. 4Q174 (4QFlor) 1.11–12 (different from the "branch of David" but possibly identified with the priestly Messiah); CD 6.7; 7:18 (identified with the star but different than the Davidic Messiah); 20.1, 28, 32.

13. 4Q521, frag. 2, col. 2, vv. 1–12; overlap with Isa 35:5–6 and 61:1, and Luke 7:21–22.

14. 1QpHab 1.11–13; 2.1–3; 7.1–5, 10–11; 8.1–3; 9.9–10; 11.4–8, 13; 4Q165 frag. 1–2; 4Q171 3.14–17; 4.3–4, 26–27; 4Q173 frag. 1 4.

Aaron)[15] will prepare those faithful to the Law for eschatological blessing of everlasting life[16] instead of God's judgment on the unfaithful.[17]

When Jesus announced his ministry in his home town Nazareth, he identified that this hoped for expectation was realized in him by citing Isaiah 61:1–2.

> The Spirit of the Lord is upon me, because he anointed me to preach the gospel to the poor. He has sent me to proclaim release to the captives, and recovery of sight to the blind, to set free those who are downtrodden, to proclaim the favorable year of the Lord (Luke 4:18–19).

Jesus identified that this very reality was being realized in his own ministry.[18]

The Law is the framework for Jesus' context and the context of Matthew's Jewish-Christian readership.[19] Matthew is written for a Jewish audience following Jesus.[20] The other synoptic gospels merely treat the binding nature of the Law as a non-emphasized historical feature of Jesus' ministry,[21] while Matthew emphasizes Jesus binding the Law upon his disciples and his readership. A new covenant compliance with the Law provides the kingdom (Matt 5:3, 10, 20; perhaps 6:4; 6:10, 20; 7:12–13, 21) and forgiveness (Matt 6:12, 14–15) in contrast to damnation (Matt 5:22; 29–30; 7:23, perhaps 26–27). In all the gospels, but especially in Matthew, Jesus radically teaches and lives the Law in three ways. (1) Jesus maintained a more pervasive new covenant internalizing of the Law (Jer 31:33).[22] (2) Jesus emphasized the

15. 1QpHab 2.2–9; 4Q171 3.15.

16. CD 3.12–16, 20; *Tg. Onq. Lev.* 18.5; *Tg. Pseudo-Jonathan*; *Sipre Lev.* 193 on Lev 18:1–30.

17. 1QpHab 2.2–10; 5.3–8.

18. Josephus, *Ant.* 18.63–64; *J.W.* 6.312–313; 3.400–402; *b. Sanh.* 107b; 104b; 43a; 67b; *b. Soṭah* 47a; *Sib. Or.* 8.206–7.

19. Saldarini, *Matthew's Christian-Jewish Community*. However, I would date the composition of Matthew as before the destruction of the temple, since Matthew's comments concerning Jesus on this topic appear to reflect prophecy awaiting fulfillment rather than having been fulfilled, but likely after the Gentile ministry had begun (Kennard, *Messiah Jesus*, 69–155; Overman, *Matthew's Gospel and Formative Judaism*; Levine, *Social and Ethical Dimensions of Matthean Salvation History*; Park, "Covenant Nomism and the Gospel of Matthew."

20. Irenaeus, *Adv. Haer.* 3.1.1–2; Eusebius, *Hist. Eccl.* 3.24.6; 6.25.4; Epiphanius, *Pan.* 30.3.7; Jerome, *Ep.* 20.5; Augustine, *The Harmony of the Gospels* 1.2–3, 3–6; 1.6.78–79; Hebrew Matthew preserved in the 14th-century text *Even Bohan*; Howard Hebrew Matthew text based on Add no. 26964 (British Library) for Matt 1:1—23:22 and Ms. 2426 (Jewish Theological Seminary of America) for Matt 23:23—28:20.

21. Kennard, *Biblical Covenantalism*, 2:214–47; *Messiah Jesus*, 153–56.

22. Rabbinics saw that there was a continuity of law into the Messiah's new covenant

priority of the Law's design over against its permissions. (3) Jesus emphasized the priorities that the Law sets up within itself, such as generosity and compassionate love. Each of these radical extensions is consistent with the Law and a new covenantizing of the Law, so that, *for Jesus in Matthew, the gospel way of salvation is via the Messiah and a new covenant embracing of the Law.* Jewish contextual communities expected the same thing.[23] In fact, the charge that sectarian and some Pharisaic Jewish communities would have against Saducean and other forms of Pharisaic Judaism is that they were not faithful enough to the Mosaic Law.[24] In this way, Jesus could be seen as cultivating and raising up a new sect of peacemaking messianic Judaism, with the same charge that other forms of Judaism were not faithful enough to the Law (Matt 5:20; 23:23).

JESUS' TEACHING OF LAW IN A NEW COVENANT MANNER

Jesus lives the Mosaic Law zealously in a new covenantal manner and mandates a zealous teaching and living of the Law by his followers as their narrow way unto the kingdom.[25] In the Sermon on the Mount, Jesus set out a two-way approach unto the kingdom, much like early Judaism and John had before him[26] (Matt 5:3–16; 7:13–27). The sermon is in a very similar style to that of the rabbis of his day, in a *midrash* (interpretation) style, evident

---

ministry and the kingdom to come (*Gen. Rab.* 98.9; *Eccl. Rab.* 11.1; *Mid. Tanh., Ki Tavo,* par. 4; Midrash fragment, *BhM* 6.151–52; Hildesheimer, ed., *Halakbot G'dolot,* 223 top; Azulai, *Hesed l'Avraham* 13c–14a; Vital, *Sefer haHezyonot,* 160; *Mid. Talpiyot* 58a; Yemenite Midrash, 349–50; Yitzhaq of Berdichev, *Imre Tzaddiqim,* 10 [5b]).

23. Sanders, *Jesus and Judaism*; *Paul, the Law, and the Jewish People.*

24. Josephus, *J.W.* 1.5.2; 1.97; 2.8.14; 2.162–3; *Ant.* 13.10.6; 13.172; 13.288, 298, 380; 17.2.4; 18.12–15, 17; *b. Yom.* 19b; *b. Nidd.* 33b; *Life* 12; *Yadayim* 3.7; 4.6–7; *Makkot* 1.6; *Niddah* 4.2; *Pss. Sol.* 1.8; 2.3; 3.3–7; 4.1, 8; 7.2; 8.12–13; 9.3; 10.6; 13.6–12; 15.6–7; 17.5–8, 23; 1QpHab col. 8–12; 4QoNah 1.6–7; 2.2, 4; 4QMMT C 5–21a.

25. Matt 4:23; 5:2, 19; 7:29; 9:35; 11:1; 13:54; 15:9; 21:23; 22:16; 26:55; 28:15, 20; Mark 1:21–22; 2:13; 4:1–2; 6:2, 6, 30, 34; 7:7; 8:31; 9:31; 10:1; 11:17; 12:14, 35; 14:49; Luke 4:15, 31; 5:3, 17; 6:6; 11:1; 12:12; 13:10, 22, 26; 19:47; 20:1, 21; 21:37; 23:5; John 3:2; 6:59; 7:14, 28, 35; 8:2, 20, 28; 9:34; 14:26; 18:20; Acts 1:1; Josephus, *Ant.* 18.63.

26. Early Judaism developed a two-ways view unto the kingdom especially from a wisdom and prophetic perspective (Sir 35:11; 48:10; Bar 4:37; 5:7; 2 Macc 1:27; 2:18; *Jub.* 1.15; *Ps. Sol.* 8.34; 11.2; 14.9–10; 15.10; 17.11–12, 28–31, 50; 18.6–9; 1QM 2.2, 7; 3.13; 5.1; 11QT 8.14–16; 57.5; 1QS 3.18–4.26; 4Q228; 4Q473 frag. 2 2–4; *Com. Rule* 9.21; *Asher* 1.3–5; 6.4–6; Philo, *Rewards* 164; *4 Ezra* 7.6–8); Davies and Allison, *Matthew,* 1:439, 442–80 present these beatitudes as entrance requirements into the kingdom.

in the oral *Torah* and the later Talmud.²⁷ Jesus utilizes the *kĕlāl* teaching pattern of a general principle stated first, which is later developed through examples.²⁸ Similar to Jewish teachers of his day, Jesus' teaching goes beyond Law conformity to press application home in the lives of his listeners.²⁹ Jesus' kingdom teaching to Jews incorporates the Law as the ethic to be lived toward the kingdom. The other Synoptic Gospels merely treat the binding nature of the Law as a non-emphasized historical feature of Jesus' ministry, while Matthew emphasizes Jesus binding the Law upon his disciples and his readership. In all the gospels, but especially in Matthew, Jesus radically teaches and lives the Law in three ways. Jesus' kingdom way incorporates the Law as part of the ethic to be lived in order for his Jewish disciples to obtain kingdom everlasting life. Jesus radically extends the Law in three broad patterns. The first radical extension of the Law is through a more pervasive new covenant internalization of the Law as is evident in Jesus' treatment of anger, adultery, and seeking God's kingdom and righteousness (Jer 31:33).³⁰ The second radical extension of the Law emphasizes the priority of design over permission as evident in Jesus' treatment of commitment in marriage, honesty, and Sabbath strictness. The third radical extension of the Law emphasizes the priority of generosity as is evident in Jesus' treatment of legal rights, practical love, judging, and Sabbath healing. Matthew portrays that Jesus requires his Jewish disciples to keep the Law in order to obtain the kingdom and its everlasting life (Matt 5:20). Jesus' view is what the Pharisaic and sectarian Jewish communities would have thought,³¹ though each version of Judaism would differ on the extent of what this means. In fact, the charge that sectarian Jewish communities had against more conservative Judaisms was that they were not faithful enough to the Mosaic Law.³²

27. Bokzer, *Judaism and the Christian Predicament*, 194.

28. Davies and Allison, *Matthew*, 1:481–503; Kennard, *Messiah Jesus*, 107–52.

29. Baba Mezia 88a; Mekitta on Exod 18:20; Loader, *Jesus' Attitude towards the Law*.

30. Rabbinics saw that there was a continuity of law into the Messiah's new covenant ministry and the kingdom to come (*Gen. Rab.* 98.9; *Eccl. Rab.* 11.1; *Mid. Tanh., Ki Tavo*, par. 4; Midrash fragment, *BhM* 6.151–52; Hildesheimer, ed., *Halakbot G'dolot*, 223 top; Azulai, *Hesed l'Avraham* 13c–14a; Vital, *Sefer haHezyonot*, 160; *Mid. Talpiyot* 58a; *Yemenite Midrash*, pp. 349–50; Yitzhaq of Berdichev, *Imre Tzaddiqim*, 10 [5b]).

31. Sanders. *Jesus and Judaism*; *Paul, the Law, and the Jewish People*; 1QM; 1QS; CD; Josephus, *J.W.* 1.5.2; 2.8.14; 2.162–3; *Ant.* 13.10.6; 13.172; 13.288; 17.2.4; 18.12–15, *b. Yom.* 19b; *b. Nidd.* 33b; *Life* 12; *Yadayim* 3.7; 4.6; *Makkot* 1.6; *Niddah* 4.2; perhaps *Pss. Sol.* 1.8; 2.3; 7.2; 8.12–13; 17.5–8, 23.

32. 1QpHab col. 8–12 on the wicked priest; 4QoNah 1.6–7; 2.2, 4; 1QM; 1QS; CD; *b. Yom.* 19b; *b. Nidd.* 33b; *Life* 12; *Yadayim* 3.7; 4.6; *Makkot* 1.6; *Niddah* 4.2; perhaps *Pss. Sol.* 1.8; 2.3; 7.2; 8.12–13; 17.5–8, 23. Josephus, *J.W.* 1.5.2; 1.97; 2.8.14; 2.162–3; *Ant.* 13.10.6; 13.172; 13.288; 13.380; 17.2.4; 18.12–15; contrary to Elliott, *Survivors of Israel*.

In Matthew 5:17, "Do not think that" is a rabbinic rhetorical device designed to set aside potential misunderstandings. So when Jesus points out that his purpose for coming is not to abolish but to fulfill, his insistence on his disciples doing the Law and Prophets indicates teaching consistent with the Law and Prophets but with qualifications not immediately apparent in his brief statement.

The "Law or the Prophets" mean the OT or the Pharisaic scriptures of Jesus' day (Matt 7:12; 11:13; 12:5; 22:40; Luke 16:29, 31).[33] The disjunctive "or" makes it clear that neither is abolished. The Prophets answer the Law, so that the referent does not change when only the Law is mentioned in verse 18.

Jesus calls his disciples to see that their lifestyles need to be about fulfilling the Law and the Prophets. "Abolish" means a destruction or removal from experience (Matt 24:2; 26:61; 27:40). Jesus denies that he will destroy or remove the Law from the experience of his disciples. "Fulfill" (πληρωσαι) means to fill or complete. There is no evidence that πληρωσαι translates the Aramaic קום (*qum*), meaning "establish, validate, or confirm" the Law. The LXX never uses πληρωσαι to render קום (*qum*) or cognates. Instead, the verb πληρωσαι renders the Hebrew מָלֵא (*ml'*), which means "fulfill." Matthew's use of the verb πληρωσαι is to "fill up a pattern," not "a one-to-one correspondence."[34] In Matthew 5:17 the issue is not Jesus' keeping the Law and the Prophets so that he might be a perfect human able to die in our place; the issue is that the ethical lifestyle of Jesus' disciples (reflective of his teaching) is to fit within the Law and the Prophets, and contribute toward identifying them with the kingdom.[35]

In Matthew 5:18, "For truly I say to you" emphasizes that the connection with the preceding is very important. This "amen faithfully" emphasizes the connection with the preceding, showing why Jesus' disciples need to fit within the Law pattern in identifying themselves with the kingdom.[36]

The Law is still in effect such that even the smallest letters and stroke remain binding (Matt 5:18; Luke 16:17). The smallest Hebrew letter is *yod* or י.[37] The *yod* is the center of much rabbinic discussion as the smallest letter. For example, Rabbi Honnah said that Rabbi Acha described a tradition from Rabbi Hoshaia.

---

33. 4 Macc 1:34; 2:5–6, 9; 9:2; Josephus *Ant.* 17.151.
34. Matt 1–3 use of "fulfill;" Kennard, *Messiah Jesus*, 17–18.
35. Davies and Allison, *Matthew*, 1:485–87.
36. Ibid., 1:487–91.
37. I realize that the typeset *yod* is smaller than most instances of manuscript written *yod*, but the argument still holds up as is evident by the following manuscript quotes and Second Temple discussion about *yod*.

> The letter yod which God took out of the name of Sarai our mother was given half to Sara and half to Abraham. A tradition of rabbi Hoshaia: The letter yod came and prostrated itself before God, and said, 'O eternal Lord, thou has rooted me out of the name of the holy woman.' The blessed God answered, 'Hitherto thou hast been in the name of a woman, and that in the end [viz. in Sarai]; but henceforth thou shalt be in the name of a man, and that in the beginning.' Hence is that which is written, 'And Moses called the name of Hoshea, Yehoshua.'[38]

This Jewish teaching is concluded "So you see not even the smallest letter can pass from the Bible."[39] The name *Yehoshua* is that of Joshua or Jesus, so *yod* matters if you say "Jesus." When sages declared that Solomon threatened to uproot a *yod* from the Law, God responded that he would instead uproot a thousand Solomons.[40]

Likewise, every stroke (a very small extension on several Hebrew letters that distinguishes these from similar ones [ה and ח, or ו and נ or ז, or ר and ד, or כ and ב]) is retained in the Law. Even Luke joins Matthew in identifying that "it is easier for heaven and earth to pass away than for one stroke of a letter of the Law to fail" (Luke 16:17; Matt 5:18). The rabbis also speak directly to the absolute importance of every stroke in the text.

> It is written (Lev. 22:32) לֹא תְחַלְּלוּ אֶת־שֵׁם קָדְשִׁי *Ye shall not profane my holy name:* whosoever shall change ח into ה, destroys the world (for then לֹא תְחַלְּלוּ written with ה, makes this sense, *Ye shall not 'praise' my holy name.*) It is written (Ps.150:6) כֹּל הַנְּשָׁמָה תְּהַלֲלֵיהּ *Let every spirit praise the Lord:* whosoever changeth ה into ח destroys the world. (It would read *"Let every spirit profane the Lord."*) It is written (Jer. 5:12), כִּחֲשׁוּ בַּיהוָה *They lied against the Lord:* whosoever changeth ב into כ destroys the world. (It would read *"Like the Lord they lied."*) It is written (Deut. 6:4) יְהוָה אֱלֹהֵינוּ יְהוָה ׀ אֶחָד *The Lord our God is one Lord:* he that changeth ד into ר destroys the world. (It would then read *"The Lord our God is another [god]."*).[41]

Much like the rabbis claiming that the world would be destroyed if strokes were changed, so Jesus claims that the strokes of the Law will

---

38. B. Sanh. 20.3.

39. B. Sanh. 107ab; p. Sanh. 2.6.2; Gen. Rab. 47.1; Ex. Rab. 6.1; Lev. Rab. 19.2; Num. Rab. 18.21; Song Rab. 5.11.3–4.

40. P. Sanh. 2.6.2; Ex. Rab. 6.1.

41. *Tanchum* 1.1; Lightfoot, *Commentary on the New Testament from the Talmud and Hebraica*, 2:102.

be preserved until heaven and earth pass away (Matt 5:18). In a parallel construction, the descriptive event that heaven and earth *will pass away* (παρέλθῃ) is mentioned as a contrast to not even the slightest letter or portion of a letter from the Law *will pass away* (παρέλθῃ). Jesus affirms that what the Law says about all its minutia being preserved is still applicable for his disciples. Using the same verb *pass away* (παρέλθῃ), Jesus makes the same kind of parallel statement in Matthew 25:35: "Heaven and earth *will pass away*, but my words *will not pass away*." In both these statements, the ethical binding condition is in view and not merely a remembrance or preservation of words. The two "until" (ἕως) clauses in Matthew 5:18 designate the duration of the binding authority of the Law. The first "until heaven and earth pass away" means "until the end of the age" or "never, as long as the present world order persists." The second "until" (ἕως) clause, "until all is accomplished," is parallel to the first. The word πάντα ("all" or "everything") probably refers to the prophecies in the Law or the whole OT that carry on through the whole eschatological kingdom program. An example of the Law's prophecies that have not happened yet would be that Israel will be regathered into the land in a responsive believing condition (Deut 30:3–10). Therefore, until the present order of the world realizes the complete description of this OT program, the Law and the rest of the OT are still binding upon Israel.

This doctrine of the immutability of the *Torah* is consistent with Jewish teaching that understood the *Torah* would in the future be understood better than it had to that point (Jer 31:33).[42] Therefore, Jesus' revisions and intensifications are consistent with the practice of the Jewish rabbis affirming the *Torah*.[43]

In Matthew 5:19, "these commandments" refer to the ethically binding material in the OT, especially the Law.[44] In Matthew, ὅς ("this" or "these") never points forward, so Jesus does not include his commands of Matthew 5:20—7:27 within "these commands." However, it is possible that "these commands" could include 5:3–16. Matthew elsewhere uses the verb cognate to "commandments" (ἐντολῶν) of Jesus' teaching in 28:20 (ἐνετειλάμην), but the noun as used in 5:19 is never used of Jesus' teaching. Much more likely than referring to the preceding discussion of 5:3–16 is the immediate context concerning the continued ethical relevance of the Law. Here it cannot be restricted to the Ten Commandments since all the OT program

---

42. 1 Macc 4:46; *b. Šabb.* 151b; *Lev. Rab.* on 7:11–12 and 11:2; *Yal.* on Prov 9:2; and *Midr. Ps.* 146.7; Davies and Allison, *Matthew*, 1:492.

43. 11QTemple or Hillel introduction of the prozbul (*m. Seb.* 10.3–4).

44. Davies and Allison, *Matthew*, 1:496.

is still in effect within this age, even those funded by the minutia of the Law. Furthermore, the kind of commands that Jesus has in mind with regard to the Law come from all over the Law, even several minor laws beyond the focus of the Ten Commands.

All these commandments are still binding so that they inform the disciple's life and teaching. The one who by lifestyle or teaching *annuls* or *loosens* (λύσῃ) one of the *least* (ἐλαχίστων) commandments has the consequences in his life of being *least* (ἐλάχιστος) in the kingdom. Likewise, the one who keeps and teaches the commandments has the consequences of greatness in the kingdom. Least and greatness refer to gradation with the kingdom ranks as is evident elsewhere in Matthew (11:11; 18:1–4). Least and greatness probably does not refer to exclusion and inclusion, for Jesus is not placing the disciples under a standard of absolute perfection to be included; there is still a place for poverty of spirit and forgiveness. John Fisher concludes:

> No one can break or set aside even the least of the commands, without jeopardizing his future status (v. 19). As if this were not enough, he concluded this section (v. 20) by emphasizing that his followers needed to be even more observant and devout than the Pharisees, going beyond even their exemplary practice of the traditions![45]

Jules Isaac summarizes this in saying, not only did Jesus "not overthrow the Law . . . or empty it of its content, but on the contrary I increase that content, so as to fill the Law to the brim."[46] So part of Jesus correct teaching of the Law includes the full implications and complete meaning of the spirit of the commandments. In effect, this new covenant spirit of the commandments is building a "fence around the Law," which would be indicative of the Aramaic for "fulfill" (קום/*qum*) and consistent with what earlier sages had done.[47]

Jesus points out that entrance into the kingdom requires a practice of righteousness warranting their place as surpassing the scribes and Pharisees (Matt 5:20). Jesus' criticism here is not that the scribes and Pharisees were not ethically good, but rather that they were not good enough. As the scribes and the Pharisees taught the Law from "Moses' seat," they could encourage their society to be good, but their pattern of life did not match their teaching (Matt 23:2–3). They placed a burden upon the people that was too heavy

---

45. Davies and Allison, *Matthew*, 1:496.

46. Isaac, *Jesus and Israel*, 66.

47. *Pirke Avot* 1.2; cf. Lachs et al., *Jewish Sources of the Sermon on the Mount*; Lapide, *Sermon on the Mount*.

to comply, focusing on peripheral matters as tithing, clothes, baths, and monuments for the dead (Matt 23:4–36). Later Jesus confronts the negative qualities in the scribes and Pharisees that needed to be transcended. Their fundamental failure was a disregard for the weightier matters of the Law, such as the kingdom, the Messiah, justice, mercy, and faithfulness. In the Jewish leaders' radical externalizing of the Law they show themselves to be hypocrites, full of robbery, self-indulgence, and lawlessness. Some Jewish teaching permitted calling others fools and sexually lusting after others, but Jesus identified that these actions damn (Matt 5:22, 29). Instead, Jesus called for a proper valuing of the Law from the weightier matters down to the minutiae.

The righteousness required in the passage is not a past positional righteousness; for the passage is on *doing and teaching the Law*, and *looking ahead* to that which will in the future provide entrance into the kingdom. So to these Jewish disciples, Jesus identified that those who will enter the kingdom identify themselves by a radical practice of righteousness that surpasses the scribes' and Pharisees' practice and teaching of the Law. Jesus has already shown himself to be a practitioner of such righteousness (Deut 6:13–14; 8:3; Matt 4:4, 7, 10). Of course, such a radical practice of righteousness is evident in the preceding beatitudes (Matt 5:6, 10), but also in Jesus' subsequent teaching. Probably also the "woe" side of the Sermon on the Plain indicates what needs to be transcended: the rich, well fed, laughing life, of which all speak well (Luke 6:24–26).

6

Keep the Law of Love

A LAWYER (OR SCRIBE)[1] came to test Jesus and asked, "Teacher, What shall I do to inherit everlasting life?" (Luke 10:25). Obtaining everlasting life is analogous to entering the kingdom and being saved (Matt 19:16, 23, 24, 25; Mark 10:17; Luke 18:18, 24–25).[2] Jesus' answer for the lawyer is the covenant nomist option, keep the commandments of the Law (Luke 10:26). Jesus does not say to try to do the Law until you find out you can't and then throw yourself on the mercy of God; Jesus says keep the Law. N. T. Wright identifies this perspective: "The Torah was the boundary marker of the covenant people: those who kept it would share the life of the coming age."[3] This should not surprise us because it is what Jews repeatedly expected and Christian Jews for several centuries tried to do in keeping the Law as the way to everlasting life (Mark 10:17–19; Luke 10:25, 28; 18:18–20).[4] Since the lawyer was informed, Jesus put the question back to

---

1. Νομικός is Luke's term for scribe (Luke 7:30; 11:45–52; 14:3).

2. Early Jewish sources support this point as well (1QS4.6–8; CD3.20; 4Q1811.3–4; *1 En.* 37.4; 40.9; 58.3; 4 Macc 15:3; *Ps. Sol.* 3.12). Also, Augustine, *Serm.* 35.1.

3. Wright, *Jesus and the Victory of God*, 301.

4. Kennard, *Messiah Jesus*, 107–52; Jer 31:31–34 and Ezek 36:24—37:28; Jdt 5:17–21; 8:18–23; 10:5; 12:2, 9–19; 13:8; *Pr. Azar.* 6–14; *Jub.*1:22–25; 2:17–33; 15:11–34; 1Q3 4, 5; 1QH 4, 5, 18; 4QShirShalb; Tob 1:10–12; 4:12–13; 1 Macc 1:48; 2:15–28; 2 Macc 6:18–31; 7; 3 Macc 3:4–7; 4 Macc 5:1—6:30; *T. Jud.* 26; *Jos. Asen.*; Josephus, *J.W.* 1.145–147, 157–60, 651–655; 2.169–74; *Ant.* 13.252; 14.237; 17.149–67; 18.55–59, 261–4, 267, and 271; *mek. Bachodesh* 5.81–82; Wright, *Jesus and the Victory of God*, 301; Sanders, *Paul and Palestinian Judaism*; *Paul, the Law, and the Jewish People*; *Jewish Law from Jesus to the Mishnah*; and *Judaism*; and Dunn, *Jesus, Paul and the Law*; *Jews and Christians*; and *Paul and the Mosaic Law* (especially interesting is Wright's chapter "The Law in Romans 2," 131–50). Furthermore, biblical texts like James, Matthew, and Acts indicate that Jews and Jewish Christians were zealous for the Law. However, especially

him as to what the Law says (Luke 10:26). The lawyer responded with two love commands that summarized the Law in the same manner that Jesus and Jews elsewhere affirmed: "You shall love the Lord your God with all your heart, and with all your soul, and with all your mind" (Deut 6:5; Luke 10:27-28; Matt 22:36-40)[5] and "love your neighbor as yourself" (Lev 19:18; Luke 10:27-28; Matt 22:39).[6] This love emphasis is so central that the whole Law and the Prophets depend upon (or are suspended from) this backbone of love (Matt 22:40). Such an affirmation identifies one as not far from the kingdom (Mark 12:34). Practicing this radical love commitment obtains the inheritance of everlasting life as sons of the divine Father (Matt 5:45; Luke 10:25, 28). The Law applies this command of love to all vulnerable, such as sojourners (Lev 19:19, 33-34).[7] Jesus concurs, even extending such love to one's enemies (Matt 5:44; 22:39; Luke 6:27-28; 10:29-39; 23:34).[8] Jesus

---

at focus is Matt 5:17-48 and 19:16-22; Saldarini, *Matthew's Christian-Jewish Community* and Kennard, *Biblical Covenantalism*, 3:15-160; Klijn, "Study of Jewish Christianity"; Taylor, "Phenomenon of Early Jewish Christianity"; Velasco and Sabourin, "Jewish Christianity of the First Centuries"; Klijn and Reinink, *Patristic Evidence for Jewish-Christian Sects*; Strecker, "Appendix 1: On the Problem of Jewish Christianity," in Bauer, ed., *Orthodoxy and Heresy in Earliest Christianity*, 257; Strecker, "The Kerygmata Petrou," in Hennecke and Schneemelcher, eds., *New Testament Apocrypha*, 2:102-27, especially 210-22 and 270-71; Strecker, *Judenchristentum in den Pseudoklementinen*; Schoeps, *Paul* and his later abbreviated synthesis, *Jewish Christianity*; Van Voorst, *Ascents of James*; Park, "Covenant Nomism and the Gospel of Matthew."

5. Luke or the lawyer add additional all-embracing terms to describe the extent of one's love for God beyond what the LXX contains (καρδίας, ψυχῇ, δυνάμεως [in LXX but not in Luke]), including mind (διανοίᾳ) and strength (ἰσχύϊ). The LXX expressed that this love is "out of" (ἐξ) these descriptions of the human while Luke expresses that such love is "out of" one's heart but "in" (ἐν) soul, mind, and strength. Jewish affirmation of the summary of the Law as love for God: *b. Šabb.* 31a; *b. Ber.* 63a; Josephus, *Contra Apionem* 2.206. The Law was summarized by the combination of both love commands: *T. Iss.* 5.1-2; *T. Dan.* 5.3; Aisteas, *Ep.* 229; Philo, *De virt.* 51; 95; *Spec.* 2.63; *Abr.* 208; *T. Naph.* 8.9-10; *Jub.* 7.20; 20.2; Josephus, *J.W.* 2.139. Other Jewish texts summarize the Law as "fear God and love neighbor": *T. Ben.* 3.3; *Jub.* 36.4-8; Philo, *Spec.* 2.15 sec. 63. The church followed this same double love perspective (1 John 4:21; *Did.* 1.2; Polycarp, *Ep.* 3.3; Justin, *Dial.* 93; Sextus, *Sent.* 106a-b; Tertullian, *Adv. Marc.* 5.8; Augustine, *Trin.* 8.28).

6. Rabbi Akiba considered love of neighbor in Lev 19:18 to be the great commandment (*Sipre* on Lev 19:18; *Sifra Qed.* 4.200.3.7; *Gen. Rab.* 24.7).

7. Other OT and early Jewish texts that concur: Exod 23:4-5; 1 Sam 24:17-19; 2 Sam 19:6 LXX; 1 Kgs 3:11; Job 31:29 (cf. Eusebius, *Dem. ev.* 1.6); Ps 7:3-5; Prov 24:17-18 (cf. *m. 'Abot* 4.19); 24:29; 25:21-22; Jer 29:7; Jonah 4:10-11; *T. Iss.* 7.6; *Jub.* 7.20; 20.2; 36.4; Philo, *Decal.* 108-10.

8. Jewish parallels include: *Ep. Arist.* 207, 227, 232; Philo, *De. virt.* 116-18; *T. Gad.* 6.1-7; *T. Zeb.* 7.2-4; *T. Iss.* 7.6; *T. Benj.* 4.2-3; *2 Bar.* 52.6; *2 En.*50.4; *b. Ketub.* 68a; *m. 'Abot* 1.12; 2.11; 4.3; 5.16. Early Christian literature echoes this love of enemies: Acts 7:60; Rom 12:14, 17-20; 1 Cor. 4:12-13; 1 Thess 5:15; 1 Pet 3:9; Polycarp, *Ep.* 12.3;

recognized that the Law has its primary focus on the loyalty relationship to the Lord (Matt 22:37–38), however, when the lawyer tried to justify himself to escape from being under conviction, Jesus focused on the human side of the Law by emphasizing the love relationship to others as demonstrating practically whether one truly loves the Lord (Luke 10:27–36; Matt 22:39). Practicing this radical love commitment identifies and obtains the goal of the kingdom; to really love one's neighbor as oneself means sharing one's possessions with those in need.[9] For example, Rabbi Chiyah identified that the righteous come into the kingdom by loving others with practical good deeds.[10] Tobit 12:9 identified that, "It is better to give alms to the poor than to lay up gold, for almsgiving saves from death and purges away every sin."

The lawyer protested, "Who is my neighbor?" Jesus told the Parable of the Good Samaritan to answer that your neighbor is anyone who is there in your context, especially anyone with needs (Luke 10:30–37). The road from Jerusalem to Jericho was well known and traveled by Jesus (Matt 20:34—21:1; Mark 10:46; 11:1; Luke 19:1, 11) and others. A man traveling down the road was beat up, robbed, and left half dead (Luke 10:30). However, a number of Jewish leaders traveling down the road away from Jerusalem avoided the mugged man. According to rabbinic texts, a priest might have a reason to maintain purity if he was hastening toward his priestly responsibility in Jerusalem.[11] Richard Bauckham excused the priest, because the priest "cannot get close enough to tell without risking defilement from corpse if that is what it turns out to be. This is because, in first-century Jewish thought about such matters, corpse-impurity travels vertically through the air. If any part of the priest's body were to be above any part of a corpse, he would contract impurity."[12] However, the priest was heading down from Jerusalem away from any priestly service so the impression the parable gives is that he just didn't care enough to help, so he avoided the mugged man (Luke 10:31). There is no evidence that the priest becomes an emblem for the Law, nor that the Levite is identified with the Prophets, nor that the Samaritan is identified with the second coming of Christ, nor that the inn symbolizes the church as some traditions have developed; these are simply a variety of people traveling down this familiar twenty-mile stretch of road.[13] Then there

---

Irenaeus, *Adv. haer.* 3.18.5; *Ps.-Clem. Hom.*3.19; *Ep. Apost.*18; 2 *Clem.*13.4; Justin, 1 *Apol.*14.3; Athenagoras, *Supp.* 12.3.

9. A similar spirit is shared and complied with by *Jos. Asen.* 13.2.

10. *Semachot de Rabbi Chiyah* 3.2.

11. Lev 21:1; Sir 12:4–6; *m. Naz.* 7.1; *Midr. Sam.* 5, sec. 9(31a); *y. Naz.* 56a; *b. Naz.* 43b; *b. Soṭah* 44a–b threatens unclean priests with flogging.

12. Bauckham, "Scrupulous Priest and the Good Samaritan."

13. Contra Egelkraut, *Jesus' Mission to Jerusalem*, 89–90; additional views are

was a Levite (who would have lesser responsibility in the temple), and Jesus does not tell which way he is traveling but he also avoided the robbed man (Luke 10:32). However, the drama heightens to prompt the question, "who will love this dying man?" The person who stops to help is a Samaritan (a kind of Jew considered unclean by other Jews[14] because of their mixed-race nature from the Assyrian repopulation of Samaria and their allegiance to the Samaritan Pentateuch and temple). However, Jesus did not maintain such animosity concerning Samaritans, having traveled through Samaria several times (Luke 9:52; Matt 10:5; John 4:4–42). The Samaritan of Jesus' parable saw the man and felt compassion and practically helped the injured man by bandaging him and removing him to the inn for continued care paid for perhaps about a week (two denarii), with the addition that he offered to pay for more at the inn on his return trip if more would be required (Luke 10:35). The issue was not whether either of these travelers lived near the mugged man, rather, Jesus asked which of them *became* (γεγονέναι) a neighbor by his deeds (Luke 10:36). The lawyer identified that the Samaritan in his sharing mercy (ἔλεος) became the neighbor who loved. Jesus commanded the lawyer to do the same in meeting real needs of others (Luke 10:37).[15]

By the choice of the characters in the parable, Jesus clearly highlights that obedience to the Law is especially expressed through practical love to meet real needs, rather than the much lesser concern for ritual uncleanness. The fact that the mugged man was not dead indicates that none of the travelers would have been defiled if they stopped to help him, so maintaining ritual uncleanness was not the issue. This is especially the case because the priest was going away from Jerusalem. Maintaining the Law by loving God means that a person should become a neighbor to all vulnerable that they come across through helping those they can. Mercy is more significant than ritual purity. The issue of gospel through Law is: *do you care about others in practical ways to meet their needs as Jesus did?*

---

contained in Fitzmyer, *Luke*, 2:885.

14. 2 Kgs 17:21–28; *m. Šeb.* 8.10; *Sanh.* 57a; *m. Nid.* 4.1–2; Josephus, *Ant.* 11.306–12; certain Jewish texts excluded love for Samaritans (*Mekilta de Rabbi Ishmael*, tractate *Nezikin* 11 on Exod 21:35).

15. The present tense looks like a continuous response (Plummer, *Luke*, 289).

7

Kingdom Parables

WHEN JESUS BEGAN TO proclaim the kingdom of God, he did so by teaching parables. Generally these parables are to be understood as providing good news about gaining the kingdom amid warnings about the alternative of damnation. For example, Jesus addressed the multitude through parables from a boat and then interpreted the parables later to his disciples, who asked what some of the parables meant. This approach of public discourse followed by private explanation was a common Jewish method enabling the disciples to clarify parable meaning and go further.[1] Following rabbinic patterns, the near context strictures the polyvalent meaning of the parables to specific application in heading toward the kingdom.[2]

The Parable of the Sower could be better known as the Parable of the Soils, since the issue of focus is the variety of responses to the message of the kingdom (Matt 13:1–9, 18–23; Mark 4:3–20; Luke 8:5–15).[3] In the parable, the sower is unidentified. The seed is the message of the kingdom, which should be understood as largely defined by Jesus' previous kingdom teaching such as in the Sermons on the Mount and on the Plain.[4] Matthew and Luke get right to the significance of the soils as those who decide (Matt

---

1. This is a similar pattern to that of first-century teacher Johanan ben Zacchai; Daube, "Public Pronouncement and Private explanation in the Gospels," *ET* 57 (1945–46) 175–77.

2. Explanation and justification of this method for interpreting parables is in Kennard, *Messiah Jesus*, 214–18; *Epistemology and Logic in the New Testament*, 83–85.

3. Similar parables are told in: *m. 'Abot* 5.10–15 (especially v. 12, which describes four kinds of hearers: (1) slow to hear and swift to lose, (2) slow to hear and slow to lose, (3) swift to hear and swift to lose, and (4) swift to hear and slow to lose); *Pesikta Rab.* 11.2; *ARNa* 40.9; *Gos. Thom.* 9; Davies and Allison, *Matthew*, 2:386.

4. These are developed in Kennard, *Messiah Jesus*, 69–155.

13:19; Luke 8:11 compared to Mark 4:14). There are some who hear the word of the kingdom but they do not understand it, and the evil one takes the word away.[5] Even though these may contemplate the kingdom message ("in his heart"), the kingdom message is no longer accessible to them. There are others who hear the word and receive it with joy but, because it gains no root in its rocky environment, when persecution comes the outcome is stumbling (σκανδαλίζεται), which in Matthew's terminology is damnation in everlasting hell (Matt 11:6; 13:41–42; 18:7–9). There are others caught up in the worry of the world and the deceitfulness or pleasures of riches. The message of the kingdom is not received but gets choked out by these cares so that the message remains unfruitful (ἄκαρπος). This imagery of unfruitfulness remains ambiguous in not defining where the person is between a clearer life of good or bad fruit, who can clearly be delineated as included or excluded from Jesus' kingdom (Matt 7:17–18). Luke may imply further ambiguity by the description that the fruit does not bring about maturity (τελεσφοροῦσιν; Luke 8:14). This ambiguity raises a lack of clarity about whether these unfruitful will make it into the kingdom or not. The final soil is good in that this man hears the word of the kingdom, understands it, and himself epitomizes this message so that he (not merely the word) brings forth the abundant fruitfulness[6] that clearly identifies these people with the kingdom. Jesus concludes the parable with the gospel exhortation for his audience to *understand the kingdom message and thus join the last group of kingdom-responsive people.*

The Lukan and Markan contexts fold the Parable of the Soils into the Parable of the Lamp (Mark 4:21–25; Luke 8:16–18). Oil lamps that are lit are used to shine light to their whole environment, not to be under a basket (Matt 5:14–15; Mark 4:21; Luke 8:16; 11:33).[7] This parable is used by Jesus in at least two different situations. Matthew records it as an exhortation to do good works, thereby glorifying God (Matt 5:14–16). That is, the disciple is to let this light quality of his life be visible to others by doing good works reflective of the beatitudes narrow way (Matt 5:16). Luke used the parable more as a warning that anything secret will become known. The exhortation of the Parable of the Soils in Luke calls disciples to *listen to and apply* the kingdom message because whoever possesses kingdom benefits will have more given to him. In contrast to the one who does not have, even what

---

5. Jesus' identification of the birds with Satan (Matt 13:19) comports with Jewish tradition that reflects Azazel manifesting himself as an unclean bird (*Apoc. Abr.* 13; *Jub.* 11.11).

6. Varro, *R.R.* 1.42.2 claims that seed in Syria could yield a hundredfold; *Sib. Or.* 3.263–264; Theophrastus, *Hist. Plant.* 8.7.4; Strabo 15.3.11; Pliny, *N.H.* 18.21.94–95.

7. The same point is made in *Gos. Thom.* 33b.

he thinks he has will be taken away from him.⁸ For example, Jesus' mother and brothers came to try and reach Jesus surrounded by the crowd (Luke 8:19–21). In this situation Jesus belongs to the disciples because it is they who hear and obey the word of God. Thus the disciples become Jesus' intimate family. Jesus' mother and brothers thought that they had Jesus, but he is taken from them and the intimate relationship with Jesus is given instead to those who hear and obey the word of God. Thus obeying the kingdom message is akin to aligning with Jesus. The same historical incident appears immediately before Matthew's and Mark's description of the Parable of the Soils, giving the impression that Jesus' immediate family and the multitude are being weighed in the balance as to which soil they are (Matt 12:46–50; Mark 3:31–35). His family is in a precarious place of losing him, whereas for the multitude the judgment may still be open, until the next paragraph. They are wondering if Jesus is the Davidic Messiah (Matt 12:23). Will the multitude hear the word of God and do it? Also in the Matthew and Mark context, the scribes and Pharisees reject Jesus as empowered by Satan in his exercising demons (Matt 12:14–45; Mark 3:22–30). Jesus excoriates these religious leaders as evil in their blaspheming the Holy Spirit. They condemn themselves because what they say shows the evil they are within. These rejecting religious leaders sound rather similar to the soil by the road.

While Jesus teaches the multitude by the sea, the disciples asked why he taught the multitude in parables (παραβολαῖς; Matt 13:10–17, 34–35). Jesus' sage ministry reveals hidden things and fulfills prophecy by teaching in parables. However, Jesus indicated that his disciples, who ask these questions, are those who have been granted the mysteries of the kingdom, but the multitude has not been granted this privilege. He explained himself by the same kind of statement he made about the Parable of the Lamp: whoever has, more will be given to him, up to an abundance; but whoever does not have, what he has shall be taken away from him. This shows the multitude to be precariously at risk because while hearing the parables, they do not understand. It is as though Isaiah's prophecy of hardening the people so that they would go into captivity is revisiting the multitude yet again. In the Hebrew text of Isaiah 6, the prophet's ministry performs an active hardening role, whereas the LXX, which Matthew uses, permits the multitude to harden themselves. Everything the multitude hears from Jesus hardens them more into an ignorant blindness if they do not respond with obedience unto the kingdom. So this judgment is the bad news of rebellion. Davies and Allison summarize this role of the Parable of the Soils.

---

8. The same point is made in 4 *Ezra* 7.25; *Gos. Thom.* 41; *b. B. Qam.* 92a.

> The course of salvation-history is not predetermined, for while God may extend his love towards his people, he does not force them to respond. Hence if Jesus' ministry has not brought about what one might have anticipated [coming kingdom], the fault lies neither with him nor with God but with human sin and hardened hearts. In this way, then, the parable of the sower comes to function as an apologetic, even a sort of theodicy, explaining the evil that has befallen Israel.[9]

There is the need to be careful at this point not to make this description of the effect of Jesus' parabolic ministry a universal principle, such as: Jesus' teaching in parables hides the kingdom from the rejecting religious leaders and multitude. Jesus' earliest teaching incorporates parables (Luke 5:27–39; Matt 5:13–16) and elsewhere parables communicate clearly to many who reject him (Luke 7:41–50; 10:25–37; 15:4–32). For example, in Luke 15 Jesus urges grumbling scribes and Pharisees to rejoice when sinners are found instead of grumbling. In early Jewish parallels these parables emphasize Moses, Law, and the need to allow sinners to repent and be found by God without judging them.[10] The last early Jewish meaning from the Jewish Parables of the Prodigal Son and the Lost Coin may have the same point that Luke emphasized in this context. In Luke's textual context, the three parables are all the same and should be preached to self-righteous grumblers who need to *rejoice when sinners are recovered for the kingdom*. The repetition of the message to rejoice when the lost are found (Luke 15:6–7, 9–10, 32) makes Jesus' teaching blatantly clear; the grumblers should rejoice when sinners are recovered for the kingdom. So these warnings to rejoice do not present Jesus' gospel but are clear warnings.

The Parables of the Two Sons and the rented vineyard clearly communicate warnings to the religious leaders as they reject John the Baptist's and Jesus' authority, but the contrast in the parable may be sufficient to claim a legitimate gospel message is present here (Matt 21:28–46; Mark 12:1–11;

---

9. Davies and Allison, *Matthew*, 2:375.

10. A similar parable to the Prodigal Son of Luke 15:11–32 was told by Rabbi Absalom the Elder *Mek. Beshallach* 4.35–41 and Rabbi Meir in *Deut. Rab.* 2.24; *Pesikta Rab.* 44.9; *Ex. Rab.* 46.4. Likewise, similar parables to the Lost Coin were told by Rabbi Phineas ben Jair in *Song Rab.* 1.1.9; Rabbi Nehemiah in *Gen. Rab.* 39.10; and *Ruth Rab.* 8.1. Furthermore, the Parable of the Lost Sheep was also told in Matt 18:12–14, disciples are to recover straying disciple; Luke 15:4–7, grumblers are to rejoice when lost are found; *Ex. Rab.* 2.2, Moses is the appropriate leader; *Gen. Rab.* 86.4, Jews are to stay out of Gentile regions; *Gos. Thom.* 107, Jesus rescues the ones he loves the best; and in *Gos. Truth* Jesus seeks lost, providing them with gnostic knowledge. Context determines meaning.

Luke 20:9–19).[11] The Parable of the Two Sons sets up a question as to who really obeys: those who promise, or those who do the work asked by their father. The chief priests and elders recognized that the gospel contains: *the truly obedient are those who do the father's will.* Jesus responded with, "Truly I say to you that the tax-gatherers and harlots will get into the kingdom of God before you. For John came to you in the way of righteousness and you did not believe him; but the tax-gatherers and harlots did believe him; and you seeing this, did not even feel remorse afterward so as to believe him" (Matt 21:31–32). In light of the Jewish parallel accounts, the judgment is even harsher on those who are well informed and do not comply than on those who may be more ignorant in their sin.[12] Jesus now follows with a parable about renting out a vineyard (Matt 21:33–44; Mark 12:1–11; Luke 20:9–18). At harvest time slaves were sent to collect the owner's share of the produce. However, the renters beat and killed these slaves. Then the son was sent, but they killed the son supposing that they would then inherit the vineyard. Jesus asks them, "What will he do to the vine growers?" The religious leaders know and answer that the owner "will bring those wretches to a wretched end, and will rent out the vineyard to other vine growers, who will pay him the proceeds at the proper seasons" (Matt 21:41). Jesus applied this parable to the Jewish religious leaders as the tenants; those who reject the Son reject the chosen cornerstone to their own destruction. This was reminiscent of a parable of the condition of Judaism before the Babylonian conquest and captivity (Isa 5:1–7). This means, upon comparison, that the destruction of Jerusalem by the Romans (in A.D. 70 and 135) and their removing the religious leaders from power is predicted by Jesus. The chief priests and Pharisees realized Jesus had spoken this parable against them. While they recognized the parable warned them, the parable also implied that *those who align with the authority behind Jesus and John did the right thing.* Is that sufficient as a gospel message? The chief priests and Pharisees tried to lay hands on him that very hour because they knew he spoke this parable against them (Matt 21:45; Mark 12:12; Luke 20:19). The parable was blatant and it communicated, even though they were still prone to rebel. So Jesus' parabolic ministry communicates; his intent is not concealment. Unfortunately, major groups of people reject Jesus' message.

As such, the nature of Jesus' use of parables concerning the kingdom in the Sermon on the Seashore is one of separating his audience into different response groups as the Parable of the Soils indicated. In this context,

---

11. Some similarities are in Isa 5:1–7; *Deut. Rab.* 7.4; and *Ex. Rab.* 27.9; *Gos. Thom.* 55, 65–66.

12. *Deut. Rab.* 7.4; *Ex. Rab.* 27.9.

the multitude is precariously at risk of being hardened into ignorant blindness. In contrast, the disciples are blessed because they have the privilege of hearing these parables and understanding Jesus' explanation of the parables' meaning (Matt 13:16–17). Prophets and righteous men desired this privilege but the disciples realize the benefit of understanding the message of the kingdom and thus gain the kingdom in their responsiveness to Jesus (Matt 13:18, 23). This clearly identifies the disciples with the fruitful soil in the Parable of the Soils. In this Robert Gundry reminds us that "the typically Matthean οὖν . . . helps turn Mark's question into an authoritative command based on the forgoing beatitude, as though to say, 'Since you are so blessed to hear, hear!'"[13]

Jesus describes a series of parables that communicate that the kingdom grows. Jesus' describes seeds that grow and produce crops automatically (αὐτομάτη; Mark 4:26–29). Following this automatic growth and maturity comes harvest time. Mark follows this with the Parable of the Mustard Seed, which highlights that the kingdom starts small in Jesus' present discipleship context and grows to be large (Matt 13:31–32; Mark 4:31–32; Luke 13:19).[14] Matthew also has the Mustard Seed Parable surrounded by the Parable of the Weeds (Matt 13:24–43), whereas Luke leads off this discussion of the kingdom with this parable (in contrast to judging Jesus' healing on Sabbath). Matthew and Luke follow this parable with the Parable of the Leaven, which starts small in Jesus' discipleship context but then permeates everything with its kingdom effect in time (Matt 13:33; Luke 13:21). This kingdom growth has already begun with many pressing their way into the kingdom (Matt 11:12; Luke 16:16).[15]

Matthew surrounds these small parables by the description and interpretation of Jesus' Parable of the Wheat and Tares (Matt 13:24–30, 36–43). For this parable, the land-owning sower is identified as the Son of Man (unlike the Parable Of The Soils, where the sower is ambiguous). The field is the world. The good seed are the sons of the kingdom sown and growing to maturity in the world; the people of the kingdom are the present expression of the growing kingdom.[16] There is also an enemy, the devil, who sows his

---

13. Gundry, *Matthew*, 258.

14. *B. Taanith* 4a contains a simile of "a young scholar may be likened to seeds under a hard clod; once he has sprouted, he soon shoots forth." However, the individual nature of this Jewish parable on growth leads in a different direction from the macro kingdom growth in these biblical mustard seed parables.

15. Justin, *Dial.* 51.3.

16. Such a present expression of the kingdom is corroborated by Second Temple sources that identify the present expression of God's kingdom as where God's people are (*Paris Ms* 110; *Sifre* on Deut 32:10).

evil sons into the same world to grow up to maturity concurrently in the world. No meaning is given to the "men sleeping" so none should be conjectured.[17] The Son of Man does not judge the devil's evil sons prematurely, out of risk of harming those who are the sons of the kingdom. So the opposition remains as the kingdom grows, because Jesus is compassionate for the welfare of his sons of the kingdom. When the end of the age comes, the Son of Man sends his angels to gather the devil's evil sons (stumbling blocks and those identified as Law violators) out of his kingdom. This has the implication that the Son of Man's kingdom is present from at least the Son of Man's ministry in the world and identified with the sons of the King in our present day (Matt 13:41, "his kingdom"). In the apocalyptic "end of the age,"[18] angels are used to eschatologically gather the judged (Matt 13:41; 16:27; 24:31; 25:31; Mark 13:26; Luke 21:27-28; Rev 14:15-19).[19] The devil's sons are gathered *out of* (ἐκ) this kingdom and are judged into the furnace of fire with its weeping and gnashing of teeth. The Jewish parallels to this parable identify that the focus is on the separating of two peoples (the parable of intertwined tree separates Jews from Ishmaelites; grain and ryegrass separate Jews from idolaters; and grain and stubble separate the grain as that which is truly valuable).[20] The Jewish pattern is that good and evil must stand together side by side until the eschatological judgment.[21] Likewise, in this parable and it's near textual parallel (Matt 13:47-50), the separation of the damned from the kingdom bound is critical. That is, the damned are the devil's evil sons and the Parable of the Soils has identified some of their characteristics. When this removal into judgment is done then the expression of Christ's kingdom, which has been here since Jesus' ministry, moves into another phase when the righteous will shine brilliantly in God's kingdom. This has implication that Christ's kingdom and God's kingdom are the same kingdom; here there is no distinction between the Davidic and sovereign kingdom. Thus the gospel here is that *those who make up the kingdom are birthed by God and characteristically righteous in their lives*. In that

---

17. Contrary to patristic interpreters that allegorize this (Jerome, *Comm. on Mt.*). *Gos. Thom.* 57 neglects mentioning this in its version of the parable.

18. *1 En.* 16.1; *T. Levi* 10.2; *T. Benj.* 11.3; *As. Mos.* 12.4; *4 Ezra* 7.113; *2 Bar.* 13.3; 19.5; 21.8; 27.15.

19. Angels often accompany a theophany (Deut 33:2; Isa 6:2-7; Ps 68:17). Angels aid in the gathering of damned and elect (Jer 51:53; *1 En.* 54.6; 62.11; 63.1 *Apoc. Elijah* 3.4; *1 En.* 1.6-9; *Asc. Isa.* 4.14; *4 Ezra* 4.26-37; 9.17; *2 Bar.* 70.1-2; *b. B. Mes.* 83b; *Midr. Ps.* on 8:1). Additionally, Gabriel blows the *šophar* for gathering into the kingdom (*Quest. Ezra B* 11; *Gk. Apoc. Ezra* 4.36).

20. Similar parables are in *Gen. Rab.* 61.6 and 83.5; *Num. Rab.* 4.1; 11.2.

21. *T. Abr. A* 10.

later stage of the kingdom, the virtuous character of the righteous kingdom occupants brings their righteous character into dominating that new era. The interpretation of this parable ends with an exhortation to understand and apply the parable.

Matthew adds two unique parables, the Parables of Treasure and Pearls (Matt 13:44-46). The kingdom is like a treasure found by chance, which a man joyously sells all to buy the field and the treasure.[22] Likewise, the kingdom is like a sought-for pearl of great value that costs everything.[23] Each parable has the gospel implication that *the kingdom message costs entirely what one has but it is well worth it*. These parables conclude with the exhortation to understand and apply the previous parable. The message has the volitional import of *obtain the kingdom regardless of the cost*.

Matthew adds a unique Parable of the Kingdom being like a dragnet, which parallels the Parable of Wheat and Tares (Matt 13:47-50). Both parables bring this message: the present kingdom grows until judgment, when the wicked will be removed leaving the righteous in the kingdom. It is possible that the Jewish disciples and readers would have thought of good versus bad fish through a kosher lens of clean and unclean fish (Lev 11:9-12), rather than edible and inedible. However, both these parables (Wheat and Tares, and Dragnet) and their Jewish parallels emphasize this separation of the damned from the righteous, as developed above.[24] The issue of damnation is probably more acutely mentioned here, since bad fish tended not to be burned but used as fertilizer,[25] while these bad fish are damned in tormenting fire. The *Gospel of Thomas* 8 includes a fish-sorting parable in which the sorting takes place on the basis of size: large and beautiful, as opposed to too puny to eat. There the issue of damnation is not so acute. Additionally, another Jewish fish-sorting parallel parable underscores the quality of a disciple, as though the Dragnet Parable and Parable of the Soils were merged, which further underscores the separation of the damned from the righteous.[26] These two parables in this context (Wheat and Tares, and Dragnet) also structure the Sermon on the Seashore in Matthew as follows: this message (Wheat and Tares), two parables on kingdom growth (Mustard Seed and Leaven), this message (Wheat and Tares interpreted), two parables

---

22. Similar to *Gos. Thom.* 109.

23. Also in *Gos. Thom.* 76.

24. As a parallel parable to that of the Wheat and Tares (Matt 13:24-30, 36-43) these Jewish parables are likewise parallel: *Gen. Rab.* 61.6 and 83.5; *Num. Rab.* 4.1; 11.2.

25. Davies and Allison, *Matthew*, 2:442.

26. *ARNa* 40.9 has Rabban Gamaliel the Elder (ca. A.D. 40) tell of four types of disciples: "unclean fish, clean fish, Jordon fish and the Great Sea fish." Only the last is fully praised.

on kingdom cost (Treasure and Pearl), and this message (Dragnet). This structure presents a gospel message that identifies that *kingdom life birthed by God is lived righteously with the specter of judgment; make sure you have bought into the kingdom!*

With the closure of the Sermon on the Seashore, Jesus asks the disciples if they understand these things, which connects with the exhortations to understand and apply the message of the kingdom (Matt 13:51–52). The disciples say they understand these things. Jesus then turns the disciples' role into a scribal role of bringing forth new things of the kingdom amid the old. The scribal role to which Jesus calls the disciples is somewhat of a self-portrait, which Jesus' emulated. The disciples' understanding the kingdom now brings with it responsibility to communicate and apply the kingdom into life.

8

Forgiveness in the Synoptics

THE SYNOPTICS PRESENT FORGIVENESS as something God and Christ accomplish from their authority without an exchange of an action, such as Christ's death. By extension, divine eschatological forgiveness is the opposite of divine damnation. Jesus' disciples should follow Jesus' example in forgiving others. Divine forgiveness is given to those who forgive in the same measure as they forgive fellow humans. Whereas, people are damned as they reject the Holy Spirit's involvement in miracles and forgiveness. Likewise, people will be damned who do not forgive.

The crowd in Capernaum had filled a house (probably Peter's house, Mark 1:29–31; 2:1) where Jesus was staying so that four friends carrying a paralytic could not get to Jesus (Matt 9:2–8; Mark 2:1–12; Luke 5:18–26).[1] So these friends removed part of the roof and dug an opening through the clay and branches so that they could let the paralytic's pallet down in front of Jesus.[2] Instead of excluding the lame and paralyzed as some Jews were inclined to do (Lev 21:17–23; LXX 2 Sam 5:8),[3] his friends and Jesus included the paralytic into kingdom benefits of healing and forgiveness. When Jesus saw the faith of those who brought him, he said, "My son, your sins are forgiven." Here divine forgiveness is obtained through the corporate faith of the paralytic and his friends. Some of the Pharisees and scribes

---

1. Multiple attestation supports the authenticity of this miracle.

2. There is no evidence that this healing coming through the roof was an attempt to confuse the demons as to where the door was (contra. Jahnow, "Abdecken des Daches [Mc 2,4/Lc 5,19]," *ZNW* 24 (1925): 155–58), since the demoniac did not live in the house, and the text explains it was because of the crowd that they came through the roof, and then the healed man walked out the door carrying his pallet.

3. 1QM 7.4; 1QSa 2.5–6; 4QDb.

sitting there reasoned that Jesus was blaspheming,[4] because forgiveness was reserved for the role of God alone.[5] So it is taken by these in the crowd that Jesus is claiming to have this divine ability, and they do not believe him. Jesus asks them, "Which is easier to say: (1) your sins are forgiven, or (2) rise and walk?" Each would be difficult because both forgiveness and healing are from the realm of God, though each were expected in the messianic age[6] and both are related since early Judaism often saw paralysis as a product of sin[7] and healing was a sign of forgiveness and repentance.[8] However, in order to show that the Son of Man (an ambiguous metaphor for Jesus' kingship and divinity) has authority to forgive sins, Jesus said, "Rise, take up your pallet and go home." The paralytic got off the stretcher, gathered up his things, and walked home. Those gathered were amazed at the wonderful act beyond explanation,[9] feared the power, and glorified God who had given Jesus this authority.

At times Pharisees criticize Jesus for allowing the unclean to touch him (Luke 7:39). One instance of this particular criticism was in the house of a Pharisee, when a sinful woman broke an alabaster vial and began to anoint Jesus' feet with perfume and wipe it with her hair (Luke 7:37-38). The Pharisee who had invited Jesus said to himself, "If this man were a prophet he would know what sort of person this woman is who is touching him, that she is a sinner." The Pharisees were overly restrictive to not be touched by sinners so that they would not defile themselves. For example, the *Assumption of Moses* 7:9-10 describes these Jews as "their hands and hearts are all corrupt, and their mouths are full of boasting-and yet they complain: Do not touch me lest you make me unclean." Jesus responded

---

4. Blaspheming in the first century is broader than the Mishnah's narrow definition that requires the name of God to be used (*m. Sanh.* 7.5), and other texts speak of three ways to blaspheme: (1) speaking ill of Torah (*Sipre* 112 on Num 15:30 [=Neusner, *Sifre to Numbers*, 2:168-70]), (2) engaging in idolatry (*Sipre* 112 on Num. 15:31 [=Neusner, 2:170]), or (3) bringing shame on Yahweh's name (*b. Pesaḥ.* 93b; Bock, *Blasphemy and Exaltation in Judaism*).

5. Forgiveness is a divine prerogative (Exod 34:6-7; 2 Sam 12:13; Pss 32:1-5; 51:1-2, 7-9; 103:3; 130:4; Isa 43:25; 44:22; Dan 9:9; Zech 3:4; 1QS 2.9; CD 3.18; 20.34) and Matthew and Mark hint that the Messiah is included within this privilege (Matt 6:12, 14-15; 9:9-13; 18:19-35; Mark 2:10-12) but Luke emphasizes this claim (Luke 5:29-32; 7:34, 36-50; 15:3-7, 11-32; 18:10-14; 19:8-10; 23:40-43).

6. Forgiveness is expected in the messianic age (CD 14.19; 11QMelch. 4-9) and asked for in prayer (4QPrNab.; LXX 2 Chr. 30:18-19). Healing is also expected as the first section of this chapter demonstrates.

7. 1 Macc 9:55; 2 Macc 3:22-28; 3 Macc 2:22; John 9:2-3; Evans, *Luke*, 301.

8. *T. Sim.* 2.12-13.

9. Luke 5:26 describes this miracle as beyond explanation (παράδοξα), the only instance of this word in the NT.

to this Pharisee with a parable about a certain moneylender who forgave a debtor who owed five hundred denarii, and another who owed fifty denarii (Luke 7:41–42). Simon the Pharisee recognized that the one forgiven more would love more (Luke 7:43). Jesus applied the parable by reminding the Pharisee of his lack of hospitality (no foot washing, no kiss, no anointing), which was made up by the woman who had washed Jesus' feet with her tears and hair and provided the rest as well. "For this reason I say to you, her sins, which are many have been forgiven, for she loved much; but he who is forgiven little, loves little" (Luke 7:47). The reason or the result of her forgiveness (as expressed by the ἵνα clause) is that she loved much. It is difficult to be dogmatic from grammar as to whether her love for Jesus was the disposition grounding the forgiveness or whether her love expressed her gratitude to Jesus in the wake of her forgiveness, as the debt-forgiveness parable better fits.[10] Her forgiveness was described by Jesus in the perfect tense, so it would be easier to consider that Jesus announced her past and continuing forgiveness, prompting her love as a result, which Jesus and the Pharisee evidentially see. However, it is grammatically possible that Jesus announced her continuing forgiveness as a result of her passionate love for him. We need to admit that the ἵνα clause retains this ambiguity.

Jesus clarified that his exorcisms and healings were by the power of God and not from Satan. Jesus knew that religious leaders in some synagogues were thinking that he healed as a satanic trick, so he countered their reasoning, showing that a commitment to reject the Holy Spirit's empowerment to heal will end up damning these religious leaders (Matt 12:22–45; Mark 3:20–30; Luke 11:14–32).[11] Matthew 12 emphasized five times that every careless word brings such a hypocritical judge into eschatological condemnation. So these critical religious leaders were strongly condemned. However, the gospel is the opposite of this condemnation.

Jesus, as a sage, called his disciples to not judge lest they be judged in return (Matt 7:1–2; Luke 6:37–38). Perhaps this is said implicating the Pharisees in the synoptic tradition as so often wrongly passing judgment on others (Matt 9:10–13; 12:1–8; Luke 7:39; 15:1–2; 18:9–14). However, Jewish rabbinical instruction reminds us that we should "not assume the place of God by deciding you have the right to stand in judgment over all, do not do it, I say in order to avoid being called to account by the God whose place you usurp."[12] The Jewish wisdom retribution principle, you reap what you sow, was applied by Jesus to remind his disciples that they will be judged

---

10. Wallace, *Greek Grammar*, 473–74.
11. Multiple attestation supports the authenticity of this discussion.
12. B. Šabb. 127b; 151b; m. Soṭah 1.7; b. Baba Metzia 59b; b. Roš. Hoš. 16b.

after the same measure that they do to others (Job 4:8; 5:1–16; Prov 11:18; 22:8; Matt 7:1; Luke 6:37).[13] According to the rabbis, God judged the world by two measures: mercy and justice.[14] The merciful will receive mercy and those concerned about righteousness will receive satisfaction (Matt 5:6–7).[15] Luke more strongly warned "do not condemn or you shall be condemned." However, Luke then encouraged generosity in the forms of pardoning and giving, "for whatever measure you deal out, it shall be dealt to you in return" (Luke 6:38). Jesus in Matthew and Luke applied this issue with colorful imagery much like the rabbis did: "Why do you get fixated on the speck[16] in your brother's eye and do not notice the log in your own eye?" (Matt 7:3–4; Luke 6:41–42).[17] The issue is hypocrisy, which is a greater "log" in one's own eye (Matt 5:5; Luke 6:42). However, when a brother in a meek and self-judging spirit removes the log from his own eye, he has the responsibility for helping his brother remove his speck (Matt 7:5; Luke 6:42).

Imbedded within teaching on the retribution principle in Luke is a warning that a blind man cannot guide a blind man, for both will fall into a pit (Luke 6:39).[18] Likewise, a student "is not above his teacher; but after he has been fully trained he can be like his teacher" (Luke 6:40). This reminds us that Jesus called his disciples to the very practice of non-judging mercy that he emulates.

Jesus reminded his disciples that they should only help those who they think will be receptive to their instruction (Matt 7:6).[19] This is reflective of Proverbs 9:8, "Do not reprove a scoffer, lest he hate you, reprove a wise man, and he will love you."[20] Matthew 7:6 continued in this Jewish proverbial tradition: "Do not give what is holy to dogs, and do not throw your pearls before swine, lest they trample them under their feet, and turn and tear you to pieces." The "holy" and "pearls" are the valuable and sacred in contrast to the "dogs" and "swine," which are wild unclean animals capable of savage ac-

---

13. Sir 16:14; 2 *En.* 44.5; *Mek.* on Exod 13:19, 21; 14:25; 15:3, 5, 8; 17:14; *m. Soṭa* 1.7; *t. Soṭa* 3.1; *Tg. Ps.—J.* on Gen 38:26; *b. Šabb.* 105b; *b. Sanh.* 100a; *b. Soṭa* 8b; *T. Zeb.* 5.3; *Tg. Isa.* on 27.8.

14. *Lev. Rab.* 29.3.

15. *T. B. Qam.* 9.30; *y. B. Qam.* 8.10.6c.

16. The word κάρφος means a small piece of foreign matter, Gen 8:11 LXX.

17. Similar to Rom. 2:1; *b. Arakh.* 16b; *Baba Bathra* 15b; *Sextus, Sent.* 90; *b. Qidd.* 70a; *b. B. Meṣ.* 107b; *b. Sanh.* 18a, 19b; *Gos. Thom.* 26b.

18. Matt 15:14 takes this saying to be one of judgment on the Pharisees who resist Jesus' kingdom ministry.

19. *Gos. Thom.* 93.

20. Also said in: Prov 23:9; *b. Sanh.* 90b; *m. Tem.* 6.5; *b. Bek.* 15a; *b. Pesaḥ.* 29a; *b. Šebu.* 11b; *b. Tem.* 117a, 130b.

tions (1 Sam 17:43; 2 Kgs 8:13; Job 30:1). If you try to correct the fool or the scoffer, they may become violent and try to harm you (Matt 7:6, "tear you to pieces"). Likewise, the Jewish tradition urged, "Let not sacred words enter a place of uncleanness."[21] Therefore, be wise about whom you instruct and try to correct. That is, *receptivity to correction indicates likelihood of heading towards the kingdom.* So correction should be limited to these heading toward the kingdom and not those on the broad way toward destruction.

The section concluded with the golden rule (Matt 7:12).[22] Probably the "therefore" is summarizing the whole sermon. There are many statements of a negative form of the golden rule in early Judaism.[23] For example, in about A.D. 20 Rabbi Hillel was challenged to summarize the Law in the time it would take a Gentile to stand on one leg. Hillel responded, "What is hateful to you, do not do to anyone else. This is the whole Law; all the rest is commentary. Go and learn it."[24] Jesus showed his continuity with this point of view, but went further by putting the golden rule into the positive. "Therefore, however you want people to treat you so treat them, for this is the Law and the Prophets" (Matt 7:12). Such a golden rule motivates forgiving others.

In the midst of the Lord's Prayer, personal petitions spell out particulars reflecting God's will on earth, which fit within Jewish patterns of adding personal petitions following the *Eighteen Benedictions*.[25] The repeated "and" in the Lord's Prayer links the last three requests of the Lord's Prayer together as outworking expressions of God's will on earth. For example, "forgive our debts" is reminiscent of the Jubilee or Sabbatical Year, which Jesus announced as the center of his freeing ministry and thus was to be expected in Jesus' disciples' prayer (Luke 4:18–19). The word "debts" (ὀφειλήματα) is a rare word present in the LXX Jubilee account, but Jesus extends it to refer to sins as well (Deut 24:10; Luke 11:4 parallel to Matt 6:12).[26] The prayerful response is not to justify oneself in prayer before God and others, for such speech is essentially only to oneself, but the sinner's pattern is to humbly ask

---

21. This is a quote of *b. Šabb.* 127b, which might raise the impropriety of such critique being said to a Gentile who does not know the Law, cf. *b. Ḥag.* 13a; *b. Ketub.* 111a.

22. *Gos. Thom.* 6.

23. *B. Šabb.* 31a; *T. Naph* 1.6; *2 En.* 61.1–2; *Tg. Yer.* 1 to Lev. 19:18; *ARN* 15; *Sent. Syr. Men.* 250–251; cf. Sextus, *Sent.* 89; *Did.* 1.2; Eusebius, *Praep. ev.* 8.7.6 (358d).

24. *B. Šabb.* 31a.

25. The third paragraph of the *Eighteen Benedictions* emphasized forgiveness; *b. ʿAbod. Zar.* 7b; also claimed by Tertullian, *De orat.* 10; Finkel, *Pharisees and the Teacher of Nazareth*, 115.

26. *1 Esd.* 3.20; 1 Macc 15:8.

for forgiveness from God (Luke 18:9–14). Such *humble requesting of forgiveness will be exalted by God.*

However, the shocking thing for evangelicals about the extent of the forgiveness requested of God in the Lord's Prayer is that it is *in the same pattern and to the same extent* that (ὡς) "as we also have forgiven our debtors" (Matt 6:12). Thus, *the request for divine forgiveness is made in a context in which human forgiveness is already accomplished toward one's debtors*, as evident by the aorist tense within this prayer so dominated by eschatological requests. To make sure that his disciples understood this point, Jesus emphasized it further through his teaching after the prayer: "For if you forgive men for their transgressions, your heavenly Father will also forgive you; but if you do not forgive men, then your Father will not forgive your transgressions" (Matt 6:14–15).[27] Additionally, Mark 11:25 identifies that disciples forgiving others in prayer is imperative "so that" (ἵνα) your Father in heaven may forgive your transgressions. Such prayers for forgiveness reflect the Jewish pattern[28] from at least the second century B.C. as *ben Siraḥ* 28:2–5 enumerates:

> Forgive your neighbor the wrong he has done, and then your sins will be pardoned when you pray. Does a man harbor anger against another, and yet seek healing from the Lord? Does he have no mercy toward a man like himself, and yet pray for his own sins? If he himself, being flesh, maintains wrath, who will make expiation for his sins?

Jesus joins this Jewish perspective, making the disciple's forgiveness of others the pattern for God forgiving the disciple in the final judgment and the kingdom.[29] So, if you wish God to generously forgive your sins and you pray the Lord's Prayer, then you need to generously forgive other's sins (Matt 6:12, 14–15). Likewise, if you skimp on forgiving others and you pray the Lord's Prayer, you ask God to skimp on forgiving your sins (Matt 6:12). Can you afford this?

---

27. The same point is made by a Byzantine addition of Mark 11:26.

28. Other parallels include: *b. Šabb.* 151b; *T. Zeb.* 5.3; 8.1–2; *T. Jos.* 18.2; *m. Yoma* 8.9; *t. B. Qam.* 9.29; *b. Meg.* 28a; *Polyc.* 6.2; in contrast, the prayer for forgiveness in the *Eighteen Benedictions* does not have a condition.

29. Polycarp, *Phil.* 2.3; 6.2; Clement of Rome, *1 Clem.* 13.1–2; Clement of Alexandria, *Strom.* 2.18.91; Meier, *Marginal Jew*, 2:301; Theissen and Merz, *Historical Jesus*, 263; Aune, "The Forgiveness Petition in the Lord's Prayer: First Century Literary, Liturgical and Cultural Contexts," in *Jesus, Gospel Tradition and Paul*, 66, 70–71.

Jesus' prayer ends[30] with, "And do not lead us into temptation, but deliver us from the evil one[31]" (Matt 6:13; Luke 11:4).[32] When the Holy Spirit came upon Jesus at his baptism, anointing him for the kingdom, the Spirit lead Jesus out into the wilderness to be tempted by the devil (Matt 4:1; Luke 4:1–2). For the disciples contemplating and praying for the coming kingdom, such temptations would become particularly acute in the messianic woes, which encroach into this life through persecutions for Christ's sake (Matt 5:10–12; 24:5–31).[33] One of the disciples' temptations is that they might not forgive. Even a moment before, Jesus had urged his disciples to pray for their persecutors, which is Jesus' pattern as he forgives his crucifiers (Matt 5:44; Luke 23:34).

Jesus commanded the disciples to recover and forgive each other through church discipline unto the kingdom (Matt 18:15–17). Scribal decisions including or excluding practices and people are binding also in heaven, which has great implications for one wishing to be involved with the kingdom. Whoever and whatever was "bound" by the assembly as out of bounds are people and practices excluded from the kingdom. Whoever and whatever was loosed by the assembly are people and practices included for the kingdom. In this context of compassionate recovery to the kingdom, prayer becomes extremely valuable. For when two agree in prayer for the recovery of a straying brother, they are eliciting the Father's aid in the recovery process. The promise is that the Father will do what his family members ask of him in this process of recovering kingdom family members. Furthermore, Jesus promised his enabling presence when two or three gather together, as when two or three witness to the straying brother, or when the church is trying to decide these issues to recover a brother. Such a promise of aid in prayer and forgiveness recovery is analogous to the rabbinic expectation of God's *shekhinah* presence when *Torah* is discussed, intimating Jesus is God present to recover the straying through forgiveness.[34] So kingdom living is to be humble, compassionate, interdependent, mutually accountable, and demonstrate divinely enabled living.

---

30. The longer endings of the prayer are not supported by the earliest and best manuscripts.

31. The addition of the article before "evil" normally indicates a person.

32. 11QPs 24.10; *b. Ber.* 60b.

33. *Berk.* 60b; Pate and Kennard, *Deliverance Now and Not Yet*, 302–25, 401–69; Davies and Allison, *Matthew*, 1:594.

34. M. *'Abot* 3.2; Sievers, "'Where Two or Three . . .'"; Hays, *Echoes of Scripture in the Gospels*, 168.

In this context, Peter asked about the extent of required forgiveness (Matt 18:21–22).[35] Peter realized that church discipline requires forgiving his brother (whether it is Andrew or another kingdom family member). Peter thought maybe a magnanimous seven times of forgiving was sufficient, but Jesus virtually says to continue to forgive an indefinite number of times without counting (which is the meaning of seventy times seven). Then Jesus tells a kingdom parable about forgiveness (Matt 18:23–35). The kingdom may be compared to a certain king who wished to settle accounts with his slaves. One slave owed ten thousand talents[36] or virtually the national debt (since a talent is about 58–80 pounds of precious metal, such as gold). This slave did not have the means to repay so the lord commanded that he, his wife, his children, and all that he had be sold to recoup a slight part of the loss. The slave fell down, prostrating himself before his lord, saying, "Have patience with me, and I will repay you everything." The lord of the slave felt compassion and released him and forgave him the debt.[37] The slave went out and found a fellow slave who owed him a hundred denarii, or roughly a hundred days' wages for a day laborer, and seized him. Putting a choke hold[38] on him, he said, "Pay back what you owe." So his fellow slave fell down and began to entreat him, saying, "Have patience with me and I will repay you." The first slave was unwilling, however, and instead had him thrown in prison until he should pay back what was owed. Such a debtor's prison does not pay the debt; it merely removes the person from being able to earn money so that family and friends might step forward to pay his debt. his fellow slaves were deeply grieved over what had happened so that they reported it to their lord. The lord summoned the slave, saying, "You wicked slave, I forgave you all that debt because you entreated me. Should you not also have had mercy on your fellow slave, even as I had mercy on you? His lord, moved with anger, handed him over to the torturers[39] until he should

---

35. Corroborated by *Gos. Nazareans* 10 as reported by Jerome, *Against the Pelagians* 3.2, though here Peter asks if he should forgive "seven times in a day."

36. 10,000 is the largest single number Greek could express and talent is the largest unit of currency (Keener, *Matthew*, 458). Josephus, *Ant.* 12. 175–76 describes a tax farmer as offering to collect for Ptolemy up to 16,000 talents. Jerome gives the revenue from Egypt to Ptolemy to be 14,800 talents. Darius tried to purchase peace from Alexander the Great for 10,000 talents (Plutarch *Mor.* 180B; *Alex.* 29). So this servant is probably a highly placed political appointment or an outrageous amount to make an exaggerated point (like the cutting off of hands or eyes; Matt 18:8–9). Cf. Davies and Allison, *Matthew,* 2:798. The combined annual tribute of Galilee and Perea just after the death of Herod the Great was 200 talents (Josephus, *Ant.* 17.318).

37. The parable in *Ex. Rab.* 31.1 describes a lender who forgave a large debt.

38. Same action described in *B. Bat.* 10.8 and *b. 'Abod. Zar.* 4a.

39. Herod the Great employed torture (Josephus, *J.W.* 1.548). Such torture was a

repay all that was owed him, which, of course, was an everlasting torment in debtor's prison, since there was no way possible that he could pay the equivalent of the national debt. We sometimes think how inappropriate the lord is in forgiving and reobligating a slave for this debt, but in the ancient Near East such a master had the right to do this. The really shocking thing about this parable is not what the individuals do in the parable, but what Jesus says in the next verse: "So shall my heavenly Father also do to you, if each of you does not forgive his brother from your heart." Jesus developed that an *everlasting destiny of being relationally forgiven by the Father is contingent upon being forgiving people.*[40] We Christians, who tend to see things from such a positional justification standpoint, tend to doubt that Jesus is committed to the everlasting forgiveness of God being patterned on our having the virtue of forgiving others, as in the Lord's Prayer (Matt 6:12) and in *ben Sirah* 28:2–5. However, divine forgiveness is patterned after and to the same extent as our human forgiving of others (Matt 6:14–15). Jesus says, "For if you forgive men for their transgressions, your heavenly Father will also forgive you. But if you do not forgive men, then your Father will not forgive your transgressions." Such forgiveness involves everlasting destiny as the parable makes clear, therefore it is necessary to be forgiving people.

---

practice cruel rulers used to extort money from tardy officials (Josephus, *J.W.* 2.448; Livy 3.13.8; 25.4.8–10; 39.41.7; 43.16.5; Appian, *R.H.* 2.8.2; Aulus Gellius, *Attic Nights* 16.10.8).

40. Polycarp, *Phil.* 2.3; 6.2; Clement of Rome, 1 *Clem.* 13.1–2; Clement of Alexandria, *Strom.* 2.18.91; Meier, *Marginal Jew*, 2:301; Theissen and Merz, *Historical Jesus*, 263; Aune, "The Forgiveness Petition in the Lord's Prayer: First Century Literary, Liturgical and Cultural Contexts," in *Jesus, Gospel Tradition and Paul*, 66, 70–71.

9

Matthew 19:16—20:16: Standard and Poor

JESUS' STANDARD ETHICAL PATTERN is to love God and love one's neighbor as one loves oneself (Matt 22:36-40; Mark 12:29-34; Luke 10:26-27), whereas some American evangelicals operate as though they could love God and money at the same time. Jesus said that such a love and pursuit of money is mutually exclusive of a legitimate love for God (Matt 6:24; Luke 16:13). Matthew 19:16—20:16 (and its parallels) argues that such a love and pursuit of money excludes both a love for God and love for one's neighbor, and is thus worthy of damnation. Kingdom-oriented Christianity calls the disciple back to the standard of loving God and loving one's neighbor as one loves oneself. Such a love must be expressed in a practical manner.

Jesus addressed issues of wealth and the kingdom in a context in which he urged God's designed best option in contrast to a Pharisaic concern for a less ideal but legally permitted option (Matt 19:3-12 and Mark 10:2-12 show commitment in marriage in contrast to divorce, while Luke 18:9-14 shows humble prayer asking for forgiveness instead of a Pharisee defending himself before God). Jesus has already emphasized that disciples need to buy in to the kingdom whatever it costs, as evident by parables of Treasure and Pearl (Matt 13:44-46). Such zealous alignment with the kingdom should define the disciple.

The kingdom is the rule of God from heaven that the praying disciple will realize on earth as it is in heaven (Matt 6:10, [13]). Jesus grants to his disciples the privilege to understand and be included within this kingdom (Matt 13:11, 19). Jesus and his disciples proclaim the nearness of the kingdom and they demonstrate this encroachment with healing (Matt 3:2; 4:17,

23; 6:33; 9:35; 10:7; 12:25–26, 28; 19:12; 24:14). The present expression of the kingdom (shown in the verb tenses) is especially evident through virtues that align one with Christ and Christlikeness (Matt 5:3, 10; 13:24, 31, 33, 38, 41, 43–45, 52; 18:4, 23; 19:14; 20:1; 21:43). Becoming a son of the kingdom is graciously caused by Christ seeding them into his kingdom (Matt 13:38). However, a son of the kingdom must show evidence of being like Christ in order to get into the future expression of the kingdom (Matt 5:19–20; 7:21; 8:11–12; 11:11–12; 13:31, 33, 43, 47; 16:19, 28; 18:3; 19:23–24; 20:21; 21:31; 22:2; 23:13; 25:1, 34; 26:29). Therefore, the kingdom is a salvation metaphor with implications for living virtuously.

In this context, Jesus showed his sensitivity to vulnerable children, who appropriately fit within humility unto the kingdom and are blessed by him (Matt 19:13–15; 18:1–5; Mark 10:13–16; Luke 18:15–17). Jesus' kingdom concern also extends to meeting the needs of the poor (Matt 11:5; Mark 12:42–43; Luke 4:18; 6:20; 7:22; 14:13, 21; 16:19–31). Additionally, all the synoptics regularly show Jesus is there to heal those in need.

The structure of the account of the rich young man begins with an alternating conversation between the rich young ruler and Jesus. Then there is a shift to Jesus alternating with the disciples. Finally, there is a personal alternating interchange between Peter and Jesus. Jesus keeps setting up the next account and then he brings closure with the kingdom Parable of the Landowner hiring workers.

It is in this light that Jesus' comments to the rich young man practically support what has been taught in the Sermon on the Mount (Matt 19:16–26; Mark 10:17–30; Luke 18:18–30).[1] Luke alone adds that the rich man is a "ruler," perhaps of the Sepphoris Council due to inherited land holdings (Luke 18:18).[2] The rich young man[3] addressed Jesus as "Teacher."[4] Jesus is

1. Also corroborated by *Gospel of the Nazareans* 1, as recounted by Origen, *Comm. Matt.* 15.14; John Chrysostom, *Hom. Matt.* 63.2.

2. Luke 18:18 identifies the man as a ἄρχων "a ruler" among others and yet he is a νεανίσκος ("a young man"), perhaps twenty-something (Matt 19:20; Philo, *Migr.* 105; Josephus, *Ant.* 6.179), which would indicate that he was not a ruler in a synagogue for that would require him to be an elder, so he has likely inherited a position with his wealth within one of the local councils at Jerusalem, Gadara, Amathus, Jericho, or Sepphoris originally arranged by Syrian governor Gabinius in 57 B.C. and continuing to provide governance through the Jewish War in A.D. 67 (Josephus, *Ant.* 14.90–91; *J.W.* 1.170; Meyers, *Galilee Through the Centuries*, 113; Freyne, *Jesus Movement and Its Expansion*, 50).

3. Later texts assimilate synoptic Greek descriptions concerning the young man.

4. After early and good Alexandrian and Western texts leave ἀγαθέ absent, later texts add "good" to teacher in Matt 19:16 and in Matt 19:17 ("Why do you call me good?"), following Mark 10:17–18 and Luke 18:18–19. Most exegetes that retain the discussion about good do so by pointing to only God is good, though a few identify

asked, "What good thing shall I do that I may obtain everlasting life?" Here obtaining everlasting life is analogous to entering the kingdom and being saved (Matt 19:16, 23, 24, 25; Mark 10:17; Luke 18:18, 24–25).[5] Jesus shifts the focus from a good deed to be done to that of the good God to be obeyed (Matt 19:16–17).

Jesus' salvific answer for this young Jewish man is the covenant nomist option to keep God's commandments of the Law. Jesus does not say to try to do the Law until you find out you can't and then throw yourself on the mercy of God; Jesus says keep the Law. N. T. Wright identifies, "The Torah was the boundary marker of the covenant people: those who kept it would share the life of the coming age."[6] This should not surprise us because it was what Jews repeatedly expected and Christian Jews for several centuries tried to live.[7] Since God alone is good (Matt 19:17),[8] Jesus' answer points to

---

the statement as affirming the goodness of the Law similar to *'Abot* 6.3; Murray, "Rich Young Man"; Cope, "'Good Is One'"; Collins, "Matthew's ΕΝΤΟΛΑΙ," 2:1327.

5. Early Jewish sources support this point as well (1QS4.6–8; CD3.20; 4Q1811.3–4; *1 En.* 37.4; 40.9; 58.3; 4 Macc 15:3; *Pss. Sol.* 3.12).

6. Wright, *Jesus and the Victory of God*, 301.

7. Kennard, *Messiah Jesus*, 107–52; Jer 31:31–34 and Ezek 36:24—37:28; Jdt5:17–21; 8:18–23; 10:5; 12:2, 9–19; 13:8; *Pr. Azar.* 6–14; *Jub.*1:22–25; 2:17–33; 15:11–34; 1Q3 4, 5; 1QH 4, 5, 18; 4QShirShalb; Tob 1:10–12; 4:12–13; 1 Macc 1:48; 2:15–28; 2 Macc 6:18–31; 7; 3 Macc 3:4–7; 4 Macc 5:1—6:30; *T. Jud.* 26; *Jos. Asen.*; Josephus, *J.W.* 1.145–147, 157–60, 651–655; 2.169–74; *Ant.* 13.252; 14.237; 17.149–67; 18.55–59, 261–4, 267, and 271; *mek. Bachodesh* 5.81–82; Augustine, *Serm.* 35.1; Wright, *Jesus and the Victory of God*, 301; Sanders, *Paul and Palestinian Judaism*; *Paul, the Law, and the Jewish*; *Jewish Law from Jesus to the Mishnah*; and *Judaism*; and Dunn, *Jesus, Paul and the Law*; *Jews and Christians*; and *Paul and the Mosaic Law*, especially interesting is Wright's chapter "The Law in Romans 2," 131–50. Furthermore, biblical texts like James, Matthew, and Acts indicate that Jews and Jewish Christians were zealous for the Law. However, especially at focus is Matt 5:17–48 and 19:16–22; Saldarini, *Matthew's Christian-Jewish Community* and Kennard, *Biblical Covenantalism*, 3:15–160; Klijn, "Study of Jewish Christianity"; Taylor, "Phenomenon of Early Jewish Christianity"; Velasco and Sabourin, "Jewish Christianity of the First Centuries"; Klijn and Reinink, *Patristic Evidence for Jewish-Christian Sects*; Strecker, "Appendix 1: On the Problem of Jewish Christianity," in Bauer, ed., *Orthodoxy and Heresy in Earliest Christianity*, 257; Strecker, "The Kerygmata Petrou," in Hennecke and Schneemelcher, eds., *New Testament Apocrypha*, 2:102–27, especially 210–22 and 270–71; Strecker, *Judenchristentum in den Pseudoklementinen*; Schoeps, *Paul* and his later abbreviated synthesis, *Jewish Christianity*; Van Voorst, *Ascents of James*; Park, "Covenant Nomism and the Gospel of Matthew."

8. Philo, *Mut.* 7; *m. Ber.*9.2; *b. Ber.*45b, 46a, 48b, 49a, 59b, 60b, *Pesah.*50a; *p. Ta'an*, 2.1, 10; 4.5, 10; *Gen. Rab.*13.15; 57.2; Justin, *Dial.*101; 1 *Apol.*16; Irenaeus, *Adv. Haer.* 1.20.2. Some Jewish texts permit human teachers to be referred to as good (*m. Ber.* 9.2; *B. Menaḥ* 53b; Abrahams, *Studies in Pharisaism and the Gospels*, 2:186).

God's commands. Judaism affirmed that the Law is by extension also good.[9] Even Mark and Luke (who do not emphasize the keeping of the Law as does Matthew) declare on Jesus' lips that keeping the Law is the narrow way to everlasting life (Mark 10:17–19; Luke 10:25, 28; 18:18–20). Or as N. T. Wright describes it, the kingdom is obtained by following "Jesus in finding a new and radicalized version of Torah-observance" which fits within early Jewish expectations.[10] Jesus further clarified that the commandments he had in mind were those like the sixth, seventh, eighth, ninth, and fifth of the Ten Commandments, and Leviticus 19:18, all of which are focused on others and have financial overtones.[11] With regard to the Ten Commandments, not mentioning the first four (focused on allegiance to God) and the last (internal covetousness) places the emphasis on doing that others can notice. Placing the fifth out of order brings emphasis to one's parents as a pair of others especially impacted by these types of decisions and introduces positive honor toward others (namely, parents). Jesus' statement of the ninth command omits that the bearing of false witness was "against your neighbor" (Exod 20:16; Deut 5:20), but the inclusion of Leviticus 19:18 affirms the love of neighbor that was omitted from this command statement (Matt 19:18–19). This inclusion of Leviticus 19:18 shifts the focus from that of restraining harm (sixth through ninth commands) to that of positive practical love to do good to others. This command clarified that the standard by which one should love one's neighbor is one's own love for oneself (Matt 19:19; Lev 19:18), which was also recognized in Jewish rabbinic teaching.[12] The Law applied this command to all vulnerable, such as sojourners (Lev 19:19, 33–34).[13] Jesus concurred, even extending such

---

9. 1 Chr 16:34; Pss 34:8; 73:1; 86:5; 119:30, 68; Rom 7:12, 13, 16; Philo, *Leg.* 1.47; Josephus, *Ant.* 9.1; *m. 'Abot* 6.2; *m. Ber.* 9.2; *b. Ber.* 28b.

10. Wright, *Jesus and the Victory of God*, 307; consistent with early Judaism: *T. Jos.* 18.1; *Jub.* 5.10; 10.17; 22.22; 2 *Bar.* 14.12; 48.22b; 51.7; Wis 5:15; 6:18; *Pss. Sol.* 9.3–5; 1QS 3–4; CD 3.11–16, 20–21; 7.5, 9; 13.11; 20.17–20, 25–27; 4Q228 frag. 1 1.9; 4Q266, frag. 11; 4QMMT C; 1QS 3.7–12; *4 Ezra* 6.5; 7.34–36, 77; 8.33, 36; 13.39–40; *Hymn Scroll* 19.12–14; Bird, "Salvation in Paul's Judaism?," in Beiringer and Pollefeyt, eds., *Paul and Judaism*, 16.

11. These commandments are from the broadly Protestant numbering of the Decalogue. All the Synoptic Gospels list the fifth command last after the others, however, Luke 18:20 reverses the first two (giving the order as: seventh, sixth, eighth, ninth and fifth) and Mark inserts "do not defraud" (which might be a restatement of the tenth command on covetousness) after the ninth and before the fifth command. Neither Mark nor Luke has Lev 19:18 as does Matthew.

12. *Sifra Qed.* 4.200.3.7; *Gen. Rab.* 24.7; *b. Šabb.* 31a.

13. Other OT and early Jewish texts that concur: Exod 23:4–5; 1 Sam 24:17–19; 2 Sam 19:6 LXX; 1 Kgs 3:11; Job 31:29 (cf. Eusebius, *Dem. ev.* 1.6); Ps 7:3–5; Prov 24:17–18 (cf. *m. 'Abot* 4.19); 24:29; 25:21–22; Jer 29:7; Jonah 4:10–11; *T. Iss.* 7.6; *Jub.* 7.20; 20.2;

love to one's enemies (Matt 5:44; 22:39; Luke 6:27–28; 10:29–39; 23:34).[14] Jesus recognized that the Law's primary focus was on the loyal relationship to the Lord (Matt 22:37–38), however, Jesus focuses on the human side of the Law, emphasizing that one's love relationship to others demonstrates practically whether one truly loves the Lord (Matt 22:39). Practicing this radical love commitment identifies one's inheritance of everlasting life and the kingdom (Matt 5:45; 12:34; Luke 10:25, 28). Jesus' citation of commands has in mind here particularly those commandments that others can see and benefit from, or at least not suffer under their violation. The last command, Leviticus 19:18, sums up all the minutia of relationships one to another in the Law (Matt 19:19; 22:39–40).

The young man affirms that under a legally tight reading of the Law he has kept all these commands (Matt 19:20), which is not atypical in early Judaism.[15] However, he senses that in some way he is still failing through a lack in his life (Matt 19:20),[16] whereas in the Mark and Luke accounts Jesus is the one who declares that the rich young ruler still lacks (Mark 10:21; Luke 18:22).

Jesus offers him completion or maturity[17] (which Jesus had commanded in Matt 5:48), and obtaining the goal of the kingdom by means of a radical extrapolation of Leviticus 19:18; loving one's neighbor as oneself means sharing the proceeds of the sale of his possessions with those in need, the poor.[18] For example, Rabbi Chiyah identifies that the righteous come into the kingdom by loving others with practical good deeds.[19] Tobit 12:9 identifies, "It is better to give alms to the poor than to lay up gold, for almsgiving saves from death and purges away every sin." Origen appealed to the sectarian *Gospel of the Hebrews* to better understand the Gospel of Matthew at this point by accentuating that such love for one's neighbor (in giving up

---

36.4; Philo, *Decal.* 108–10.

14. Jewish parallels include: *Ep. Arist.* 207, 227, 232; Philo, *De. virt.* 116–18; *T. Gad.* 6.1–7; *T. Zeb.* 7.2–4; *T. Iss.* 7.6; *T. Benj.* 4.2–3; *2 Bar.* 52.6; *2 En.* 50.4; *b. Ketub.* 68a; *m. 'Abot* 1.12; 2.11; 4.3; 5.16. Early Christian literature echoes this love of enemies: Acts 7:60; Rom 12:14, 17–20; 1 Cor. 4:12–13; 1 Thess 5:15; 1 Pet 3:9; Polycarp, *Ep.* 12.3; Irenaeus, *Adv. haer.* 3.18.5; *Ps.-Clem. Hom.*3.19; *Ep. Apost.*18; *2 Clem.*13.4; Justin, *1 Apol.* 14.3; Athenagoras, *Supp.* 12.3.

15. *SB* 1:814; *b. Sanh.*101a; Phil 3:6.

16. A similar question in *b. Soṭa* 22b.

17. The word τέλειος means "maturity" not sinlessness (Matt 5:48; 1 Kgs 11:4; Tob 3:14; *Jub.* 23.10; 27.17; *Pr. Man.* 8; 11QPsDavComp 1.3; *T. Iss.* 7.1–7; *T. Abr.* A 10.13–14; *2 Bar.*9.1; *T. Mos.* 9.4; *t. Sanh.*13.3; *b. Qidd.*40b).

18. A similar spirit is shared and complied with by *Jos. Asen.* 13.2.

19. *Semachot de Rabbi Chiyah* 3.2.

wealth for the welfare of the poor) is required to fulfill the Law.[20] Jesus does not develop the attitude of being willing to give to the poor; his emphasis is on doing: keeping the commandments, selling and giving to the poor (Matt 19:16–17, 21).

Perhaps behind Jesus' sentiment lies Proverbs 10:2, "treasuries of wickedness," as understood by Bruce Waltke, meaning accumulating wealth for personal use as opposed to giving it away to those in need; "the wicked . . . store up physical assets for themselves and lose their lives, and the righteous use their resources to serve others and store up life for themselves."[21] This sentiment is echoed by *ben Sirah* 5:8a: "Do not trust in wealth that lies." Furthermore, *ben Sirah* 31:1–11 warns about the different effect of pursuing wealth by rich and poor, damning the wealthy who are not generous benefactors of the needy.

> A rich man loses weight by wakeful nights,
> When the cares of wealth drive sleep away;
> Sleepless worry keeps him wide awake,
> just as serious illness banishes sleep.
> A rich man toils to amass a fortune,
> and when he relaxes he enjoys every luxury.
> A poor man toils to make a slender living,
> And when he relaxes he finds himself in need.
> Passion for gold can never be right;
> The pursuit of money leads a man astray.
> Many a man has come to ruin for the sake of gold
> And found disaster staring him in the face.
> [They cannot be saved from evil
> Nor delivered on a day of wrath.][22]
> Gold is a pitfall to those who are infatuated with it,
> And every fool is caught by it.
> Happy the rich man who has remained free of its taint
> And has not made gold his aim!
> Show us that man, and we will congratulate him;
> He has performed a miracle among his people.

---

20. Tob 4:5–11; Sir 31:5–7; *b. B. Bat.*10a; Origen, *Comm. Matt.* 15.14; Augustine, *Serm.* 35.1 and 36; John Chrysostom, *Hom. Matt.* 63.1.

21. Waltke, *Proverbs*, 1:453; also echoed by Prov 11:4 and *T. Jud.* 25.4.

22. Anderson (*Charity*, 58–59) pointed out the textual addition added by a later scribe.

> Has anyone ever had it in his power to sin and refrained,
> Or to do wrong and has not done it?
> Then he shall be condemned in his prosperity,
> And the whole people will hail him as a benefactor.

Individual and corporate greed to increase personal or corporate wealth to the neglect of others is damnable.

Generosity of the benefactor reflects the core beatitude virtue of showing mercy; Jesus oriented his disciples toward, "Blessed are the merciful for they shall receive mercy" (Matt 5:7). Jesus' teaching reflects the sentiment of rabbis elsewhere.[23] The merciful are the benefactors who attempt to meet other's needs.[24] The dominant expression of mercy in the synoptics is the Son of David healing others in need (Matt 9:27; 15:22; 17:15; 20:30–31; Mark 5:19; 10:47–48; Luke 1:58; 17:13; 18:38–39).[25] Whereas, in Jewish tradition, the primarily merciful one is God (1 Sam 23:21; Ps 72:13; Prov 14:21; Mic 6:8).[26] According to Jesus, mercy (as one of the weightier matters of the Law) was unfortunately neglected by the scribes and Pharisees (Matt 23:23). One form of the Jewish neglect of mercy was their restrictiveness to their own Jewish group.[27] Jesus' disciples must have mercy in ministering to sinners and forgiving others without judging them (Matt 6:12–15; 7:1–5; 9:13; 12:7; 18:21–35; Mark 11:25). The good Samaritan exemplifies mercy in meeting his neighbor's and even enemy's needs (Matt 5:44–47; Luke 10:37). This sentiment of showing mercy universally was also a factor in some forms of Jewish tradition.[28] The merciful shall receive mercy (Matt

---

23. This is parallel in *b. Šabb.* 151b, "He who has mercy on people obtains mercy from heaven;" also *t. B. Qam.* 9.30, "As long as you are merciful, the Merciful One is merciful to you;" *T. Sim.* 4.4; Josephus, *Ant.* 10.41. Additionally, the rabbis identified that God judged the world by two measures: justice and mercy (*Lev. R.* 29.3), so that following a verse about righteousness it is appropriate to develop the theme of mercy. This sentiment continues in early Christendom (*1 Clem.* 13.2; Polycarp, *Ep.* 2.3; Tertulian, *Or.* 4.2; 5.1; *Paen.* 6.4; *Exh.cast.* 2.3; *Marc.* 2.6.7; 4.31.1; Cyprian, *Eleem.* 1, 2,5; Rhee, *Loving the Poor, Saving the Rich*, 73–102).

24. *T. Jud.* 18.3–4; *Epict. Disc.* 1.18.4.

25. Kennard, *Messiah Jesus*, 23–67.

26. *T. Zeb.* 5.1, 3; 7.1–8.6; Philo, *Spec. leg.* 4.72, 76–77.

27. For example, Qumran, the Essenes, and other Jews maintained mercy within the community but urged hate to outsiders (1QS 1.4, 10–11; 2.4–9; 9:21–23; 1QM 4.1–2; 15.6; 1QH 5.4; *b. Ber.* 33a; *b. Sanh.* 92a; Josephus, *J.W.* 2.139).

28. A commitment to universal mercy is present in rabbinic Judaism (*Sipra* on Lev. 19:18 and *Mek.* on Ex. 21:35) and outside the Jewish tradition (Polybius 18.37.7; Hesiod, *Op.* 342–3, Solon, frag. 1.3–5; Plato, *Tim.* 17d–18a; *Rep.* 375c; *Meno* 71e; Tacitus, *Hist.* 5.5–6).

5:7).²⁹ The future mercy to be received could be in this life or the kingdom beyond.³⁰ Worshippers praise God for his merciful salvation plan (Luke 1:50, 54, 72, 78). Through Luke 16:24, Jesus warns his disciples that those who do not give mercy, such as the rich man's abuse of Lazarus, will not receive mercy in the afterlife, for such lack of love for the needy identify the would-be damned. Jesus' Parable of the Sheep and Goats echoes generous aid to the needy as identifying the righteous who will be saved, whereas such lack of generosity identifies the damned (Matt 25:31–46).

Jesus commanded the rich man to sell his possessions and give to the poor (Matt 19:21). Such giving away all wealth to the poor went against rabbinic teaching.³¹ However, Jesus had some followers who as patrons supported his ministry while not giving all their money to the poor (Matt 27:38–42, 57; Luke 8:1–3; 10:38–42; John 3:1). Among these patrons (such as Matthew) there was a concern for generous restitution and for hosting of sinners so that they might have access to Jesus (Matt 9:9–13; Mark 2:14–17; Luke 5:27–32; 19:5–10). Such generous restitution and hosting evidenced that salvation included these patrons (Luke 19:9). Furthermore, those who had wealth and wished to itinerantly follow Jesus, such as Matthew, left his wealth and tax collection franchise to others in order to follow Jesus (Matt 9:9–17; Mark 2:14–22; Luke 5:27–39). Matthew accomplished what the rich man rejected for his future.

This rich man had many possessions (Matt 19:22). Jesus joins the rabbinics in acknowledging that "where your treasure is, there will be your heart also" (Matt 6:21; Luke 12:34).³² "In fact it is impossible to serve both God and money" (Matt 6:24; Luke 16:13).³³ The word for "possessions" (κτήματα) occurs only here in Matthew but it also is evident in the book of Acts, where Christians were willingly giving possessions away to meet the needs of Christian poor (Acts 2:45; 5:1). Luke records Jesus' teaching more broadly that seeking the kingdom entails selling possessions and giving them to the poor (Luke 12:30, 33).

---

29. This theme is echoed salvifically by Leo the Great, *Sermon* 10.
30. 2 Tim 1:18; Jude 21; *1 Clem.* 28.1.
31. *B. Ketub.* 50a; Hagner, *Matthew*, 2:558.
32. *B. Ber.* 61b.
33. *T. Job* 33.4–5; Tob 4:8–9; Sir 29:10–13; 31:7; *Ps. Sol.* 9.5, 9; *2 Bar.* 14.12; 24.1; 44.8; *T. Levi* 13.5; *1 En.* 94.6–8; 95.4–7; 96.4–8; 97.7–8; 98.9–16; 99.1–16; 100.4, 9; 102.5; *Pss. Sol.* 5.2, 11; 10.6–7; 15.1; 18.2; 1QS 4.3–11; Philo, *Praem.*104; *Spec. Laws* 1.24.3; *4 Ezra* 7.77; *m. Pe'a* 1.1; *b. B. Bat.* 11a; *Tosefta Peah* 4.18; *Gos. Thom.* 47, 64, 76. From this perspective Clement of Alexandria considers that the rich man is damned and the generous are saved (*Quis div.* especially 1.6–7; 16.5). Hoag, *Wealth in Ancient Ephesus and the First Letter to Timothy*, 100–130.

Giving up these possessions would enable the young man to follow Jesus in his itinerant ministry as Peter and the disciples had done (Matt 19:21, 27). Perhaps Matthew includes Jesus' statements of giving to the poor for purposes of the itinerant ministry, to address issues in his readers' lives such as poverty from famine or dispersion as persecuted Jewish Christians. If the young man had complied, he would have had kingdom treasure as the disciples were to receive (Matt 19:21, 29). Unfortunately, the young man was unwilling to pay the price of Jesus' radical Law demands. His departure provided an opportunity to instruct the disciples in the near impossibility of a rich person pursuing the kingdom. The primary focus of the Law is evident as serving God rather than money (Matt 6:24). The fact that the young man went away with his riches shows that ultimately he was unwilling to serve God and love his neighbor as he loved himself. In this case the kingdom was missed for failure to keep the Law, namely, *loving one's neighbor as oneself*.

There is no evidence that the rich young man enters the kingdom, for he does not follow Jesus but instead leaves grieving (Matt 19:22). Jesus responds that it is hard for a rich man to enter into the kingdom of heaven, illustrating it by a rabbinic hyperbolic simile of the largest animal in Israel, namely, a camel, going through the eye of a sewing needle (the smallest hole in Israel) as being easier than for a rich man to enter the kingdom.[34] The disciples recognize the impossibility of this and wonder, "Then who can be saved?" (Matt 19:25). Such a specific statement of "impossibility" (Matt 19:26) makes it clear that a sewing needle is in view instead of the inconvenience of unloading a burdened animal to enter a small wicket gate.[35] Furthermore, there is no early Jewish evidence that such human-sized gates

---

34. Later Greek texts read "rope" but earlier texts present "camel" with strong textual support. Both words would sound alike so it is easy to imagine a scribe writing the slight misspelling he thought he heard. Rabbinic parallels are consistent with Jesus' statement: *b. Ber.* 55b and *b. B. Mes.* 38b portray the impossible by the largest animal of Babylon (an elephant) going through a sewing needle, and *b. Yebam.* 45a describes the impossibility of a camel dancing in a tiny area. So these might identify Jesus' statement as an existing proverbial statement. The proverb is followed by the clear statement of human "impossibility" (ἀδύνατόν, Matt 19:26; Mar 10:27; Luke 18:27; Acts 14:8; Heb 6:4, 18; 10:4; 11:6). Augustine, *Serm.* 35.2 and John Chrysostom, *Hom. Matt.* 63.2 recognize that Jesus discusses the impossibility of a camel going through a sewing needle.

35. The view that a "needle" is a small wicket gate is very common among exegetes (eg. Barclay, *Matthew*, 217) since the fifteenth century, when forts and castles utilized human-sized doors (restricting how many could enter) within a larger door or next to a larger door that would pass riders and wagons, but there is no ancient Near Eastern archeological evidence for such a gate. Chalmers, "Influence of Cognitive Biases on Biblical Interpretation," 477 utilized this as an example of an illusory truth effect that occurs when an in-group bias confirms a view through a false consensus within a group with no archeological evidence.

were called "needles" or utilized to fund this later interpretive conjecture. Wealthy humans trying to save themselves cannot be successful no matter what else their money can buy. The wealthy show by their excess wealth that they do not really love God or their neighbor, thus they will not be saved.[36]

In recognizing the impossibility of the wealthy being saved, the disciples respond, "Then who can be saved?" (Matt 19:25). Such "salvation" is seen as eschatological salvation, realized at the last judgment (Matt 1:21; 10:22; 16:25; 18:11). Jesus corrects them by saying that such human attempts at salvation are impossible, but with God all things are possible (Matt 19:26). So the impression that the context brings is not that the rich will necessarily be reduced to a low position in the kingdom, but that they tend to not even make it into the kingdom in the first place, and are thus usually damned. Perhaps also, with God graciously transforming individuals, even some who were wealthy would be able to love and live this way by loving others as they love themselves.

Mark 10:29 and Luke 13:30 do not have a subsequent parable and reiteration of the idea of the last being first, so they tend to reinforce that this text is emphasizing that the disciples will gain a great place and the rich will be last. In Luke 13:30 the enigmatic statement is removed from the rich young man (Luke 18:18–30) but is reflective of the narrow way to eschatological throne-room judgment (Luke 13:23–30). The outcome word "last" (ἔσχατοι) in Luke 13:30 is best seen in that context as those Jesus casts away as damned evildoers who weep and gnash their teeth (Luke 13:23–30). Subsequently, Mark 10 identifies that Jesus fulfills his own standard by leaving everything for his kingdom ministry and heading toward his death. In Mark 10, Jesus' teaching is spun for disciples to follow in this narrow kingdom way. Only those who enter by the narrow door gain entrance into the kingdom, though others may try and be damned (Matt 7:13–14).

At this point in Matthew, Peter chimes in and says, "Behold, we have left everything and followed you; what gain will there be for us?" (Matt 19:27). Jesus reassures the disciples that they have complied with this radical paying the cost of the Law and that they will have a unique role of judging Israel (Matt 19:28). In fact, everyone who has left house and family members[37] for

---

36. Origen, *Comm. Matt.* 15.14; Clement of Alexandria, *Quis div.*; Commodianus, *The Instruction* 29; Augustine, *Serm.* 35.5 damn the wealthy and 35.4 calls all to be rich in good works.

37. Actually, the text sandwiches family members between houses and lands, showing the issue is cost lost. The inclusion of "father" and "mother" within the middle of the list of family members clarifies that at this point the fifth of the Ten Commandments is not primarily in view, but rather Christ's kingdom generously overwhelms any cost the disciples have paid out on their way (Matt 19:29). Some later texts add "wife" (γυναῖκα) after "mother" but this is likely a scribal assimilation to the Lukan parallel 18:29.

Christ's sake will receive many times as much[38] and will inherit everlasting life (Matt 19:29).

Jesus told a kingdom parable in response to Peter's and the disciples' claim that they have left everything to follow him (Matt 19:27). For most of the disciples, this is a modest loss of time away from family, and perhaps giving up house, fishnet, and boat (Matt 4:18–22; 8:14–15). For tax-collector-turned-disciple Matthew, there was more wealth than the other disciples had (Matt 9:9–13; Mark 2:14–15; Luke 5:27–29; 19:2–9; similar pattern with tax collector Zaccheus). So when Matthew became a disciple, he hosted Jesus, the disciples, and many sinners as a patron of Jesus' ministry. This Matthean response was similar to what Jesus asked the wealthier ruler to do (Matt 19:21). Jesus reassured the disciples in their giving up family, houses, and farms that they will be truly rewarded with responsibilities and benefits in the kingdom.[39] When the regeneration phase of the kingdom has the Son of Man sitting on his throne, then these Jewish disciples will also sit upon twelve thrones, judging the twelve tribes of Israel, which is an extreme privilege for them (Matt 19:24, 28).[40] Though the disciples gave up different amounts of wealth, they all enjoy the privilege and responsibility of judging Israel. The kingdom is described as of heaven and of God and salvation and where Christ reigns (Matt 19:23–25, 28). Within this kingdom, the disciples also have the benefits of everlasting life and many times more reward than the cost of those things and family which they left to follow Jesus.

Jesus then said an enigmatic phrase, which he says again in reverse order after the next parable, "the first will be last; and the last first" (Matt 19:30; 20:16).[41] Obviously, in this context, the disciples are one or the other of these groups, and in this instance the emphasis of the context would be an encouragement to them, as it was in Mark 10:31 and Luke 13:30. One needs to resist importing Jew and Gentile issues[42] (perhaps following Luke 13:29 from a different context) into this Matthew statement of parable and phrase, since everything in the near context is presented without any Gentile allu-

38. Mark 10:30 reads "hundredfold" and Luke 18:30 reads either "manifold" or "sevenfold" but these are all comparable and reflect dissimilarity among multiple attestation.

39. Mark 10:30 reflects symmetry of benefits in the same pattern of costs given up; Marcus, *Mark*, 2:737; in the last days those who gave up their wealth for others will be rewarded with abundant wealth (*1 En.* 104.6; *2 En.* 50.5; 1QpHab 6.1; 9.4–6; *T. Jud.* 25.4; *Jos. Asen.* 12.12; *B. Bat.* 10a).

40. Such judging of the twelve tribes is also apparent in: *Pss. Sol.* 17.26, 29; Philo, QE 1, 2.114; *T. Jud.* 25.

41. Matt 20:16 adds a few more words than 19:30 but with the same meaning following strong textual support.

42. Augustine, *Sermon* 37 and *On Holy Virginity* 27; Kissinger, *Parables of Jesus*, 23.

sion. There is no extended kingdom ministry of the prophets in the context so this phrase likely grows out of the preceding issue and events, meaning: the wealthy (first) will be last place in the kingdom or possibly damned, and those who have given up everything (last) will be first place in the kingdom with responsibilities and benefits (encouraging the disciples).[43] Jesus' enigmatic statement is echoed by rabbinic and popular Jewish eschatological reversal, identifying that those who present themselves as last place in humble poverty will be eschatologically elevated to first place in the kingdom (Luke 1:51–52; 6:20–26).[44] Such a view of damning the wealthy and encouraging generous disciples was how the phrase "first will be last and last will be first" was taken in the parallel synoptic gospel accounts (Matt 19:30; Mark 10:31; also Luke 13:30, which concludes Jesus' narrow-way teaching). So here the enigmatic phrase "last shall be first" encourages the disciples with kingdom generosity and salvation.

In this Matthew context, Jesus told a parable to explain this enigmatic statement ("for" [γάρ] in Matt 20:1). The simile identifies the kingdom to be like a landowner (or technically "a master of a house" [οἰκοδεσπότῃ]) who hired laborers for his vineyard (Matt 20:1–16). The workers hired were not standing idle but were simply those who were without work (Matt 20:3 ἀγορᾷ ἀργοὺς, Matt 20:6 ἀργοί), explaining that they had not been hired by an employer. They are not "the undesirables—the boozers, the goof-offs, the careless," or minorities as Buttrick claims.[45] They simply had not been hired; they were unemployed (Matt 20:7).

Since the owning of a vineyard requiring several harvesters required substantial investment, such a landowner was wealthy in society, comparable to the rich young man of Matthew 19.[46] This landowner hired his day laborers at the usual day wage of a denarius (Matt 20:2).[47] This fits the usual

---

43. Luke 16:19–31; a similar parable particularly in regard to the rich man's afterlife conversation is present in *Ruth Rab.* 3.3 and *Eccl. Rab.* 1.15.1. In *y. Ber.* 2.5c, 15 there is an account in which the last into a vineyard are harder working and earned as much so that they were remunerated comparable to their labor. There is also an Egyptian story of a man with royal linen and a poor man on a mat who reversed fortunes in the afterlife; Creed, *Luke*, 209–10; Bock, *Luke*, 2:1362.

44. 1 *En.* 104.6; 2 *En.* 50.5; 1QpHab 6.1; 9.4–6; *T. Jud.* 25.4; *Jos. Asen.* 12.12; *B. Bat.* 10a; rabbinic parallel, "Some obtain and enter kingdom in an hour, while others reach it only after a lifetime" (b. 'Abod. Zar.17a; Ebel Rabbati 3); Schmidt, *Hostility to Wealth in the Synoptic Gospels*, 46–47; Carter, *Households and Discipleship*, 127, 138; Talbert, *Matthew*, 238–39; Eubank, *Wages of Cross-Bearing and Debt of Sin*, 95–96.

45. Buttrick, *Speaking Parables*, 114.

46. Herzog, *Parables as Subversive Speech*, 85.

47. The common price for a day laborer (Tob 5:14; Pliny, *N.H.* 33.3; Tacitus, *Ann.* 1.17; Davies and Allison, *Matthew*, 3:72).

Jewish practice of hiring workers early at about dawn and finishing at about dusk.[48] Likewise, this wage of a denarius would provide the usual Jewish family with food for between three to six days, which was a living wage.[49] The workers agreed that the payment was fair (Matt 20:2). He then hired laborers at noon, three, and five p.m. for "whatever is right." The workers trust the integrity of the landowner so his reputation would likely support that he could be trusted. By five p.m. there is little need for more labor, so Thomas Long suggests that the landowner is generously hiring extra labor because the text does not explicitly develop any need for more labor.[50]

The payment time fits within the Jewish pattern as at the end of the day (Lev 19:13; Deut 24:15). The last group chronologically hired got paid first, on to the first hired. They all received the same wage regardless of when they commenced their work. Notice the wage is not merely grace, because it is a wage earned even if the owner is generous to many of his workers. When the first group hired noticed that the wage was the same, they protested about the excessive burden they bore, which plays on the word for "work": "These last worked [ἐποίησαν] one hour, and you have made [ἐποίησας] them equal to us" (Matt 20:12). Interestingly, the text identifies that both the workers and the landowner were working (ἐποίησας). The landowner addressed the worker as "friend," which in Matthew's presentation of Jesus has him only use this term elsewhere in an ironic manner (Matt 20:13; 22:12; 26:50). The landowner clarified that he had done no wrong and that they had the contracted amount, and the landowner was within his rights to pay others as generously as he desired. Other parallel Jewish parables also make the point that a landowner may be as generous with his pay as he desires and early Jewish wisdom encourage such valuing of workers with generosity.[51]

Many generations of interpreters viewed the landowner as a symbol for God because the landowner claims that he is himself good (Matt 19:17; 20:15 ἀγαθός).[52] Such a view shows God in "extraordinary forgiveness and

---

48. M. Baba Meṣ. 7.1.

49. Oakman, "Buying Power of Two Denarri"; textual variety could reflect dissimilarity among multiple attestation but strong external support backs this text; some interpreters understand the denarius to be an egalitarian "eternal life" (Augustine, *Sermon* 37 and *On Holy Virginity* 27; Aquinas as referred to by Kissinger, *Parables of Jesus*, 43).

50. Long, *Matthew*, 225.

51. Sir 7:20–22; Ps.-Phoc. 153–74; Bek. 2.7; *Sifra* on Lev. 26.9; *Eccl. R.* 5.11.5 and *Midrash Tanhuma Ki Tissa* 110 tell of a generous employer who paid an exceptional amount in response to an exceptionally able laborer who had worked a long time for the employer. So these parables emphasize the landowner's generosity to the later workers so everyone obtains a living wage.

52. Irenaeus, *Haer.* 4.20–26.7; Augustine, *Sermon* 37.1 and *On Holy Virginity* 27; Calvin, *Harmony of the Evangelists*, in *Calvin's Commentary*, 16:410–11; Kissinger,

grace"⁵³ at the eschatological judgment. This shifts a daily wage of a denarius to be a symbol for everlasting life within a cultural pattern of eschatological judgment before God in which what one does in life matters.⁵⁴ If the wage of a denarius is a symbol of everlasting life, then that would make everlasting life fully or partially earned by the works of especially those early into the vineyard, because the landowner's mercy increased for the later hires. If this is the meaning then Matthew would be floating that it is possible that Jesus is telling the disciples this parable to keep them from envy over his generosity,⁵⁵ but that would shift the meaning of the enigmatic statement from being an encouragement in Matthew 19:30 to that of a chiding warning when it is repeated in 20:16. If it is taken that way, Blomberg claims that this parable with more than two groups involved develops three points to be obtained as follows:

> (1) From the earlier groups of workers, one learns that none of God's people will be treated unfairly . . . (2) From the last group of workers comes the principle that many seemingly less deserving people will be treated generously, due to the sovereign, free choice of God. (3) From the unifying role of the master stems the precious truth that all true disciples are equal in God's eyes.⁵⁶

Here the last (ἔσχατοι; Matt 20:12, 14, 16) are chronologically the last group into the labor force, who gain a generous payment and may be paid first, whereas the first labored earlier and are paid chronologically last. This first group (perhaps the disciples) needs to watch out and excise envy. However, such a view changes the encouraging statement of Matthew 19:30 into a warning in 20:16. Wouldn't consistency of the meaning of these statements be desirable?

Perhaps a better way to maintain consistency of the enigmatic statements of Matthew 19:30 and 20:16 would be that some Jewish prophets or workers were the early laborers and the disciples become the later ones encouraged by their judging the twelve tribes.⁵⁷ However, such a view would not have Jesus accentuate egalitarianism in kingdom benefits, since only a

---

Parables of Jesus, 3, 23, 52; Dodd, *Parables of the Kingdom*, 94–95.

53. Maldonatus, *Commentary on the Holy Gospels: Saint Matthew's Gospel Chapters XX to the End*, 162–73; Snodgrass, *Stories with Intent*, 362.

54. *4 Ezra* 8.33; *T. Abr.* A 12–13; Gk. *Apoc. Ezra* 1.14; *m. 'Abot* 3.15; *t. Qidd*.1.14; *b. Qidd.* 39b.

55. Such envy was understood in Israel as having an evil eye (Prov 23:1–6; 28:22; Matt 20:15).

56. Blomberg, *Interpreting the Parables*, 224.

57. Augustine, *Serm.* 37.5.

moment before Jesus had also emphasized the disciples' unique privilege in judging the twelve tribes of Israel (Matt 19:28). This unique privilege fits within the Matthean context where Peter is granted privilege in his affirmations (Matt 16:17–19), and a core group of disciples (consisting of Peter, James and John) were granted exceptional access (Matt 17:1). Likewise, Jesus identifies that greatness in the kingdom is shown through humility, with which all the disciples struggle (Matt 18:1; 19:13).

Such a soteriological view of equal pay for unequal work is also in early Jewish texts, so the idea is not foreign to the sociological context. For example, *Semachot de Rabbi Chiyah* 3:2 asks:

> How do the righteous come into the world; through love, because they uphold the world through their good deeds. They depart also through love. Rabbi Simeon ben Eliezar told a parable. To what may the matter be compared? To a king who hired two workers. The first worked all day and received one denarius. The second worked only one hour and yet he also received one denarius. Which one was the more beloved? Not the one who worked one hour and received a denarius! Thus Moses our teacher served Israel one hundred and twenty years and Samuel only fifty two. Nevertheless, both are equal before the omnipresent.[58]

However, early Judaism does not have a problem recognizing a role for works to salvation in a narrow way unto the kingdom, even though most evangelicals would have problems (as they permit a wage to stand for everlasting life).

Matthew 19:30 and Mark 10:31 have the order "the first will be last and the last will be first" since they both follow Jesus' encouragement to the disciple to give oneself away as last to be eschatologically first, receiving a hundredfold more than it costs in this life (Mark 10:30). The parallel statements in Matthew 20:16 and Luke 13:30 with perhaps only a few being saved in the narrow way (Luke 13:23–24; Matt 7:14) have the order reversed, "the last shall be first and the first will be last," as a Lukan encouragement to continue on the narrow way to be eschatologically included as rewarded among the "last who will be first." So, on the basis of synoptic comparison, all "last will be first" statements present encouragement for the disciples and for any who generously give themselves and their money away. So, the master of the house placed himself as last by giving generously a living wage

---

58. *Semachot de Rabbi Chiyah* 3.2; similar accounts occur in *Eccl. Rab.* 5.17; *Sifra on Lev* 26:9; *P. Berakoth* 2.8; *Song Rab.* 6.2.6; *Midrash Tanhuma Ki Tissa* 110; Augustine, *Serm.* 37.6 takes it this way.

even to part-time workers, such that he becomes another model for loving one's neighbor as one loves oneself.

Furthermore, keeping all statements in this Matthew context of "the first will be last and the last will be first" with the same meaning would make them encouragements to the disciples for inclusion rather than a chiding warning (Matt 19:30; 20:16; Mark 10:31; Luke 13:30). The disciples have impoverished themselves in kingdom itinerancy and in serving others, so Jesus' encouragement in the context would have relevance for how to understand this enigmatic statement launching Jesus' encouragement for them (Matt 19:29–30).

Richard Ford proposed that the parable "may well be exploring a pervasive conflict present in the first-century Roman-occupied Jewish Palestine" in which a "chronic aristocratic expropriation had forced many land-owning peasants into the marginal under-class of day laborers."[59] Such a class-dividing view (present in *1 En.* 97.8–10) is quickly dismissed by Levine and Shinall: "If we begin with the presupposition that all landowners are exploitative and all laborers are victims, we have already skewed the reading."[60] In fact, *m. 'Abot* 2:15 indicates that during this time before the Jewish War there was plenty of work and workers were paid ample wages, showing Ford's Marxist approach is foreign to the context. Furthermore, archeology does not support that severe economic distress occurred in Galilee during the early decades of the first century.[61] Additionally, vineyards are not exclusive crops of the wealthy but also harvested and utilized by non-wealthy growers.[62] So just vineyards that require a lot of hired labor were owned by the wealthy, as is the case in this parable. Furthermore, Mark 6:36 shows that the disciples were concerned for the welfare of the crowd but thought that it would be little trouble for most of them to buy their

---

59. Ford, *Parables of Jesus*, 115, following Herzog, *Parables as Subversive Speech*, 79–97; Oakman argues for exploitation of ordinary structures of agrarian society without specific textual evidence in "Debate: Was the Galilean Economy Oppressive or Prosperous? A. Late Second Temple Galilee: Socio-Archeology and Dimensions of Exploitation in First-Century Palestine," and Overman argues for economic health without any specific evidence of exploitation in "B. Late Second Temple Galilee: A Picture of Relative Economic Health," in Fiensy and Strange, eds., *Galilee in the Late Second Temple and Mishnaic Periods*, 1:348 and 357–63, respectively.

60. Levine and Shinall, "Standard and Poor: The Economic Index of the Parables," in Stewart, ed., *Message of Jesus*, 100.

61. Reed, "Reappraising the Galilean Economy" and Levine's interaction with it (*Short Stories by Jesus*, 220); Overman, "B. Late Second Temple Galilee: A Picture of Relative Economic Health," in Fiensy and Strange, eds., *Galilee in the Late Second Temple and Mishnaic Periods*, 1:357–63.

62. Levine, *Short Stories by Jesus*, 224.

food if they were released early enough in the day to travel to the cities. Furthermore, Matthew sets out a positive model for "a master of a house" (οἰκοδεσπότῃ), often identifying the disciples in this responsible role (Matt 13:52; 24:43; Mark 14:14; Luke 12:39; 22:11). The parable continues this positive picture of a master of a house (οἰκοδεσπότῃ) in employing others as an illustration of kingdom generosity (Matt 20:15), thus not sociopolitically as their enemy. The workers' trust in the master of the house for a wage of "whatever is right" shows that this house master likely has a reputation for being fair. Additionally, the parable does not show economic stress from the lack of employment or lack of wealth. Furthermore, there is no evidence for day laborers in the parable organizing, as was done among weavers, dyers, bakers, donkey drivers, and trade guilds.[63] In fact, Jesus grew up during the years of substantial employment of day laborers under Herod Antipas and others in the capital Sepphoris, before Herod shifted his capital to Tiberias and thus construction shifted from Sepphoris to Tiberias about the time Jesus is baptized (Luke 3:1–2).[64] Neither is there evidence in early Judaism that workers were expendable, because manual labor was valued.[65]

Instead, Amy-Jill Levine follows Robert Fortna in considering this parable as "The Humane Capitalist" or "The Conscientious Boss."[66] From this perspective, the house master would then provide a positive example for a wealthy person, in contrast to the rich young ruler, for the house master wished to demonstrate alignment with the kingdom in his employment of others. Hire more people than one needs because you care about people and pay them all a living wage, even the part-time workers, no matter how much time they spend within one's workforce. Such a kingdom employment strategy would be erring toward generosity to insure all receive a living wage. This generosity fits the pattern realized in the temple when the construction work was completed and 18,000 workers were laid off but were paid for a full day's wage even if they only worked for an hour.[67] Likewise, David instituted that all warriors would share alike in the spoils of battle (1 Sam 30:24). Furthermore, pious Jews even valued giving wages to those who

---

63. Tosefta, *Baba Meṣ.* 11.24–26.

64. Tacitus, *Ann.* 1; 15.44; Josephus, *Ant.* 17.1.4; *J.W.* 1.33.8.

65. M. *'Abot.* 1.10; *ARN* B 21.23a; and it was important to teach one's son a trade (*m. Qidd.* 4.14; *t. Qidd.* 1.1 1; *b. Qidd.* 29a).

66. Fortna, "Exegesis and Proclamation"; Levine, *Short Stories by Jesus*, 215; Levine and Shinall, "Standard and Poor: The Economic Index of the Parables," in Stewart, ed., *Message of Jesus*, 95–115; this view is illustrated by the filmstrip *The Good Employer*; Kissinger, *Parables of Jesus*, 325.

67. Josephus, *Ant.* 20.219–20.

were not expecting such a wage.[68] Perhaps that is what is meant by the house master's claim that he is good, in that he is there to be generous toward others, mirroring the generosity in which God excels (Matt 20:13). The focus should not be on profits because one cannot serve God and money. The focus should be in loving others as one loves oneself. If the poor are included as we love ourselves, all will be cared for generously.

Levine and Shinall summarize this parable as: "If the landowner pays everyone a living wage and if the workers can be content with what is right, rather than what they perceive to be fair."[69] Thus, kingdom employment is generous and includes as many as possible in paying all a living wage. Thus, the parable shows another pattern for kingdom-bound wealthy than at one point in time giving their wealth away.

Taken together, the passage shows several patterns for the kingdom-bound serving others with their resources. The standard pattern of the gospel is to love God, and your neighbor as oneself; namely, place yourself last after God and others so God will place you first. Such love of neighbor could be realized by the wealthy giving their wealth away to meet the needs of the poor, or following Jesus in itinerant ministry giving up one's wealth for Jesus and others, or generously employing more workers than needed and paying them all a living wage, even the part-time ones. Either of these strategies for the wealthy identify that they are putting themselves last, and thus they will be amply included in the kingdom (Matt 19:19–21; 20:16). However, the majority of the disciples are not wealthy, but leave what they have to join Jesus in itinerant ministry. Such leaving is still costly as it identifies the disciples with putting themselves last for other's kingdom benefit (giving up houses, family, and land), and they are encouraged they will be amply rewarded in the kingdom (Matt 19:27–30).

---

68. *T. Job* 12.3–4; *p. B. Meṣ.* 6.1, 2.

69. Levine and Shinall, "Standard and Poor: The Economic Index of the Parables," in Stewart, ed., *Message of Jesus*, 112.

10

Eschatological Reversal

IN LUKE'S PRESENTATION THE Jewish wisdom theme of eschatological reversal is emphasized. In this theme the rich and the elevated rulers are brought low in judgment (Job 5:11; 12:19; 15:29; Ps 37; 1 Sam 2:7; Jer 17:11; Luke 1:52–53; 6:24–26; 12:19–20; 16:25; 21:1–4).[1] Likewise, the poor, oppressed, and neglected are elevated to blessing, especially in Christ's kingdom (Pss 37; 107:9; 146:7; 147:6; 1 Sam 2:5–7; Isa 61; Luke 1:52–53; 4:18–19; 6:20–22; 16:19–23).[2]

When Mary met with pregnant Elizabeth, Mary praised God for exalting the humble in the kingdom program begun with the impending births of John and Jesus. Mary saw herself as a humble servant experiencing mercy to realize Abrahamic covenant blessing in exaltation and in being freed from the peril of hunger (Luke 1:52–55). This testimony personalized eschatological reversal in her son's kingdom.

Jesus began his ministry of teaching in the synagogues by identifying that the Spirit has empowered him to proclaim and effect Jubilee freedom as evident in healing (Luke 4:14–30). Jesus was aware that he was God's anointed Savior at the center of eschatological events to bring an expression of God's kingdom to earth. To present this point, Jesus quoted Isaiah 61:1–2 and inserted Isaiah 58:6d from the LXX as a way of continuing his kingdom theme in the quote.[3] According to the quote, Jesus' ministry was to bring

1. Sir 10:14; Jdt 9.3; 1QM 14.10–11.

2. Sir 10:14; *Pss. Sol.* 5.10–11; *Sib. Or.* 8.208; *Gos. Thom.* 54, 64; *Ruth Rab.* 3.3; *Eccl. Rab.* 1.15.1; *y. Ḥag.* 77d or 2.27d; *y. Sanh.* 6.23c; *b. Bat.* 10a; *midrash on* Ps 25:9 in McArthur and Johnston, eds., *They Also Taught in Parables*, 186; rabbinic parallel, "Some obtain and enter kingdom in an hour, while others reach it only after a lifetime" (*b. ʿAbod. Zar.*17a; *Ebel Rabbati* 3).

3. The substitution of Isa 58:6d for a line in 61:2 may not be apparent in the English

major benefits of a Jubilee kingdom into the present, especially proclaiming good news to the poor and release to captives, which are kingdom instances of eschatological reversal entering the present.

Jesus began the Sermon on the Plain addressing his disciples with beatitudes that reflect eschatological reversal. Those disciples who experience some threat now will be blessed (Luke 6:20–22). The poor are benefited because they already are located within God's kingdom. However, this poor is personalized to the disciples through use of the second-person plural address "yours" with the present-tense "is the kingdom" (Luke 6:20). These disciples who experience the kingdom now are further blessed in their relationship to eschatological reversal in the grander form of the kingdom to come. For example, the disciples' hunger (missing meals) indicates that they will be blessed in the eschatological kingdom by being satisfied with food then. The disciples are declared to be blessed in their present weeping, perhaps in the peril of hunger or persecution, because joy and laughter await those who are persecuted for their affiliation with Jesus. This joy is the appropriate response to the guaranteed certainty of future reward in heaven, as indicated by the first γὰρ clause. This guarantee is further grounded by the second γὰρ clause, which recollects the pattern that persecution came to the prophets from the Jews previously as the prophets longed for and spoke about the kingdom.

In contrast to these blessings, Luke presented woes that show the eschatological reversal goes the other way as well (Luke 6:24–26). Speaking to the disciples and using second-person plural references means that if these conditions become true of those who wish to follow Jesus' teaching, then they are strongly warned about devastating consequences. For example, those who are rich currently receive their full comfort now and should not anticipate a beneficial kingdom to come. Additionally, those who laugh and are well fed now should expect that when the kingdom comes they will be excluded to famine and mourning. Jesus warned his disciples that if all men speak well of you now then you are likely selling out to conditions similar to the false prophets because that was the ambiance around them. These are circumstances common among those around the disciples, based on the third-person "their" in Luke 6:23 and 26, but they should not be named

---

text but it is readily recognizable by comparing the LXX with the Greek text of Luke 4:18, which follows the LXX of Isa 61:1–2 until this line. Luke could have paraphrased the Hebrew text on this line but it is likely that he followed the LXX on this line like he did in the rest of the quote. Furthermore, the parts of the pericope of Isa 61:1–3 that Jesus does not quote include divine vengeance upon Israel's enemies and an enabled replanting of Israel in the land of Zion. Such a strong Jewish emphasis of Jesus' kingdom task works against Luke's purposes of Gentile inclusion into salvation in Luke-Acts.

among the disciples. So these descriptions do not describe an authentic disciple even though it is possible that they describe some who view themselves as disciples. So the rich have a brief consolation now but it is short-lived and will be excluded by the eschatological kingdom when it comes.

Even when the wealthy give their alms, they do so from their excess so it costs them little (Luke 21:1–4). Which in contrast means that if a poor widow gives even a very small amount in alms then the fact that she gives from her poverty means that her gift is far more generous and costly, depriving her of something she has committed to do without. Her livelihood is put at risk in her generosity as she depends upon God. God and Jesus take note of such generous actions.

At another time, Jesus urged the disciples to utilize the money that they had to make friends for the kingdom and to prepare for themselves everlasting dwellings in the kingdom (Luke 16:9–10). This teaching to the disciples came to a head with Jesus insisting that *a true disciple cannot serve God and money*. "No servant can serve two masters; for either he will hate the one and love the other, or else he will hold to one, and despise the other. You cannot serve God and mammon" (Luke 16:13).

In this context, a group of Pharisees were listening and scoffing so he addressed them, presumably to offer them a gospel message and not just warnings (Luke 16:14–18) because Jesus identified that in the present setting "The *gospel* of the kingdom of God *is preached*" (εὐαγγελίζεται, Luke 16:16). Jesus began to warn these scoffing Pharisees not to try to justify themselves because God knows their hearts. Jesus identified that foundational to his kingdom message is the Law and the Prophets, which will all come to pass because "it is easier for heaven and earth to pass away than for one stroke of a letter of the Law to fail" (Luke 16:16–17). This Mosaic Law framework addressed issues such as money, scoffing, divorce, and adultery (Luke 16:15–16, 18). So Jesus told this group of Pharisees a parable about money and its consequences to underscore that Moses and the Prophets are binding in such matters (Luke 16:19–31).

A rich man habitually dressed in purple,[4] with linen undergarments, had a gated[5] house and feasted[6] daily (Luke 16:19–20). The feasting

---

4. Purple indicates wealth of a king: Prov 31:22; 1 Macc 8:14; 1QapGen 20.31; Fitzmyer, *Luke*, 2:1130–31; the use of the imperfect here for "dressed" probably indicates a daily indulgence (Levine, *Short Stories by Jesus*, 272).

5. Such gates are usually at entrances for cities or temples (Luke 7:12; Acts 3:10; 9:24; Heb 13:12) so it indicates much wealth.

6. The word εὐαγγελίζεται indicates feasting as in Luke 12:19; 15:23–32; LXX Esther 5:9; Sir 19:5; 25:7.

indicates at least "modest excess" because there were crumbs or food that *fell* (πιπτόντων) from his table.[7]

A poor man named Lazarus (meaning "God helped"),[8] covered with sores,[9] had been *thrown as a cripple* (ἐβέβλητο) at the rich man's gate.[10] This homeless poor man longed to be fed with the food that fell from the rich man's table. Nothing is said about what happened with the remains that fell from the table but they were not made available to poor Lazarus, who hungered without food. There is no obvious divine help except that wild dogs came and licked the poor man's sores, which probably provided some healing for him.[11] There is no development that this poor man was affiliated with Jesus or a *Torah* scholar, as some rabbinic texts develop into similar stories.[12]

Both the rich man and Lazarus died. Lazarus had no burial so he was carried away by angels[13] into paradise onto Abraham's lap of privilege,[14] indicating eschatological reversal from his living condition. Hospitable Abraham welcomed Lazarus.[15] In a Jewish concept of paradise and Hades, both sides can see the other side (Luke 16:24–31).[16] Upon the rich man's death he was buried and became instantly aware in the afterlife, crying out from Ha-

---

7. Noland, *Luke*, 2:828 claims from "crumbs" (τῶν ψιχίων) but this word is not actually in the Greek text and was introduced from Matt 15:27 by scribes to explain what *fell* (πιπτόντων), but it might be more than crumbs. There is no mention that the dogs ate up the crumbs, contrary to Noland, *Luke*, 2:829.

8. This is not the Lazarus of John 11 who has some wealth as a host for Jesus and his disciples, nor is this Eliezer (name in Hebrew) of Gen 15 who is a very responsible steward with many resources, for this Lukan Lazarus is poor with sores. Several ossuaries in Jerusalem tombs have this name inscribed (Fitzmyer, *Luke*, 2:1131).

9. B. Beṣa 32b indicates that a person has no life if their body is "full of sores" and dependent upon another for food. "Full of sores" is used as euphemism for leper; Fitzmyer, *Luke*, 2:1131.

10. The word ἐβέβλητο literally means "thrown" but the word often means "bedridden" or "crippled," Fitzmyer, *Luke*, 2:1131; Matt 8:6, 14; 9:2; Rev 2:22; Josephus, *J.W.* 1.32.3 sect 629; *Ant.* 9.10.2 sec. 209.

11. Dogs were viewed negatively (1 Kgs 14:11; 16:4; 21:19, 23–24; 22:38; 1 *En.* 89.42–43, 47, 49) but since they are outside the gate they likely come from elsewhere than the rich man. Philostratus, *Life of Apollonius*, 24 indicates that dogs licking sores provides healing.

12. *Y. Ḥag.* 77d or 2.27d; *y. Sanh.* 6.23c.

13. *T. Job* 47.11; 52.2, 5; *T. Abr.* 20.11–12; Shepherd of Hermes, *Vis.* 2.2.7; *Sim.* 927.3.

14. Abraham's lap is seen as in paradise (*T. Abr.* 20.14; *b. Qidd.* 72a–b; *Echa rabb.* 1.85; *Pesquita rabb.* 43 sect 108b; Abraham welcomes martyrs: 1 Macc 13:17; *b. Qidd.* 72a; *b. Giṭ* 57b; *Pesikta Rabbati* 43.4).

15. Abraham's reputation of hospitality (Gen 18:1–15; Philo, *Abr.* 22–23, sec. 107–108; Josephus, *Ant.* 1.11.2, sec. 196; *T. Abr.* 20.15.

16. 2 Esd 7:85, 93; 2 *Bar.* 51.5–6.

des with other unrighteous people in agony from the flame,[17] "Father Abraham, have mercy on me, and send Lazarus, that he may dip the tip of his finger and cool off my tongue; for I am in agony in this flame" (Luke 16:24).[18] Abraham reminded the rich man that during his life he had good things but Lazarus bad things and thus the eschatological reversal means that Lazarus is comforted in paradise and the rich man is in agony (Luke 16:25). Additionally, Abraham described a great gulf between the two realms that prevented travel between them (Luke 16:26).[19] In response, the rich man asked if Lazarus could be sent to warn his brothers so that they might not come to Hades' torment (Luke 16:27–28).[20] Such a warning indicated that the rich man was aware of his moral culpability.[21] Abraham responded that the rich man's brothers have the warnings of the Law and the Prophets and that is sufficient to provoke the brothers to mercy, and if they do not listen to Moses and the Prophets then they will not listen to someone who rises from the dead (Luke 16:29–31). While in the account such a resurrection is contemplating poor Lazarus rising from the dead, in the Gospel of Luke the message also echoes that Jesus' resurrection will not provoke those who love money to repentance either.

Is this parable only a warning for the lovers of money so that they might see the outcome of such a life, thus the bad news? Or is this a continuation of Jesus' gospel (Luke 16:16) and the Law and the Prophets (Luke 16:17, 29–31), showing that people need to repent from their love of money so that they will mercifully care for those in need (such as Lazarus) and be included in paradise?[22] Or is this an eschatological reversal showing the danger of damnation from being wealthy so that we might give up our possessions sufficiently for kingdom purposes as disciples of Jesus (Luke 16:9)?[23]

17. The unrighteous enter torment in Hades (Wis 3:1–10; Josephus, *Ant.* 18.1.3, sec. 14; *J.W.* 2.8.14, sec. 163; 3.8.5, sec. 375; 4 Macc 13:15; *1 En.* 22; *2 Clem.* 10.4; 17.7); flame in Hades (Isa 66:24; Mark 9:48; Rev 19:12; Sir 21:9–10; 1QH 17.13). *1 En.* 10.13–14; 63.10; 103.5–8 warns that wealthy Sadducees will descend to Sheol.

18. Jewish documents present occupants in the afterlife with the ability to see each other and converse (2 Esd 7.36–37, 79–85, 91–93; *Jub.* 23.30–31; *2 Bar.* 51.5–6; *1 En.* 95.3; 96.1; *Eccl. Rab.* 1.15.1; *y. Ḥag.* 77d[2.2]; Bock, *Luke*, 2:1371).

19. *1 En.* 18.11–12; 4QEnc 1 8.27–30.

20. Hellenistic culture contemplated messengers from the dead (Plato, *Resp.* 10.614D; Lucian, *Demon.* 43, similar to Jacob Marley in Charles Dickens' *A Christmas Carol*) but such specters were quite surprising and not anticipated in Jewish culture (1 Sam 28:12–19).

21. Noland, *Luke*, 2:831.

22. Bock, *Luke*, 2:1364, 1378; Levine, *Short Stories by Jesus*, 294–96.

23. Crossan, *Power of Parable*, 94; Bauckham, "Rich Man and Lazarus," 104; a similar sentiment is expressed in Sir 29:9–12.

Give alms from your possessions, and do not let your eye begrudge the gift when you make it. Do not turn your face away from anyone who is poor, and the face of God will not be turned away from you. If you have many possessions, make your gift from them in proportion; if few, do not be afraid to give according to the little you have. So you will not be laying up a good treasure for yourself against the day of necessity. For almsgiving delivers from death and keeps you from going into the Darkness.[24]

---

24. Tob 4:7–10.

11

Sheep and Goats

MATTHEW'S OLIVET DISCOURSE CLOSES with a parable concerning the eschatological coming of the Son of Man to bring judgment in the Jewish pattern through which God judges everyone (Matt 25:31–46).[1] Jesus identified that when the Son of Man comes in glory, and all the angels with him, then the Son of Man will sit on his glorious throne. This statement reminds the reader of the previous statement of the coming of the Son of Man during which his angels are sent out to collect the elect (Matt 24:30–31; 25:31). All the ethnic groups (ἔθνη) will be gathered before him and he will separate them into two groups like a shepherd separates sheep from goats. In this account the sheep stand for the people of God.[2] These two groups have essential defining characteristics that mark them as two distinct animal groups with their two distinct ways of life within a two-ways soteriology (Matt 7:13–27; 13:24–50; 25:14–32). In this parable, the Son of Man is the King in judgment from his glorious throne. He will say to those righteous on his right, "Come you who are blessed of my Father, inherit the kingdom prepared for you from the foundation of the world." Their preparation identifies that they are the elect from the foundation of the world. However, eschatological judgment always utilizes the life evidence of works,[3] because one's whole life matters.

1. Dan 7:9–10, 18, 26; 12:2; Rev 20:11–15; *1 En.* 9.4; 60.2; 62.2–16; 63:1–12; 90:20–36; 47.3 with 46.2; *2 En.* 63.1–2; 4Q246 col. 2; 11Q Melch. 2.13; *2 Bar.* 72. 2, 6; 73–74.4; *Ps. of Sol.* 17; *T. Abr.* A 11.11; 12.1–18; 13.12; 14A; *Sib. Or.* 2.183–84, 239–54, 283–338; *4 Ezra* 7.37; *b. Ned.* 39b–40a; *Midr. Ps.* 118.19. Much of this material is nicely laid out in chart form in Davies and Allison, *Matthew*, 3:419.

2. *1 En.* 90.20, 32–33; *Pesiq. R.* 9.2; 26.2.

3. This judgment according to deeds fits the Jewish narrow way pattern: 1 Kgs 8:32; Job 34:11; Pss 28:4; 62:12; Prov 24:12; Jer 16:18; 17:10; 21:14; 32:19; Ezek 7:4; Hos

The righteous will be recognized by King Jesus for their works, benefiting Jesus himself and aligning with him. "For I was hungry, and you gave me to eat; I was thirsty, and you gave me drink; I was a stranger and you invited me in; naked, and you clothed me; I was sick, and you visited me; I was in prison, and you came to me." These are classic Jewish expressions of righteousness in many eschatological judgment texts and thus represent the saved.[4] The righteous may not even remember when they did these deeds, for their motivation was not to gain Jesus' favor by their actions.[5] Instead, the righteous acted out of concern for the welfare of those around them; they were merely consistent with their character. Perhaps Jesus develops an early expression of the "body of Christ" imagery in his substitutionary good deeds imagery, as it extends a Jewish idea that good deeds done for others are good deeds done toward God.[6] King Jesus pointed out, "to the extent that you did these deeds to one of these brothers of mine, even the least of them, you did it to me." Thus the gospel can be said as: *care about others in practical ways and you align with Jesus, obtaining everlasting life in the kingdom* (Matt 25:34, 46; Dan 12:2).

Then he will say to those on his left, "Depart from me, accursed ones, into the everlasting fire which has been prepared for the devil and his angels." That is, this everlasting punishment was designed primarily for the devil and his angels[7] but these unrighteous condemn themselves to this fate by identifying with the devil's side, by neglecting good deeds because they

---

4:9; Mic 7:13; Dan 7:9–10, 18, 26; Matt 16:27; 25:41–46; Rom 2:6; 14:12; 1 Cor 3:5; 2 Cor 5:10; Eph 6:8; Col 3:25; Rev 2:23; 20:11–15; 22:12; Sir 11:26; 16:12, 14; 32:24; *Jub.* 5.11, 15; 20.2; 23.20–21; *1 En.* 9.4; 47.3 with 46.2; 60.2; 62.2–16; 63:1–12; 82.4; 90:20–36; 95.5; 100.7; *2 En.* 63.1–2; *Pss. Sol.* 2.7, 7, 16, 25, 34–35; 17.8–9; *Jos. Asen.* 28.3; 1QS 2.7–8; 9.18–21; 10.21; 11.13; 1QSa 1.2; 1QHa 12.18–25; 14.10, 23–24; 1QX 10.11, 17–18; 1QH 4.18–19; 5.5–6; 14.24; 1QM 11.3–4; 18.14; CD 1.11, 13, 16; 2.3; 3.4–5; 5.15–16; 7.9; 20.24; 1QpHab 12.2–3; 1Q22 2.8; 4QpPs 37.4–9; 4Q185 1.1–2; 2.1–2, 4; 4Q246 col. 2; 4Q260 5.1; 4Q400 1.1, 14; 4Q405 23.1.11; 4Q429 4.1.10; 4Q473 1; 4Q511 2.1.6; 11Q5 22.10; 11Q Melch. 2.13; 11QT 54.17; *L.A.B.* 3.10; 44.10; 64.7; *2 Bar.* 54.21; 72. 2, 6; 73–74.4; *4 Ezra* 5.1; 7.37, 76–77; *T. Abr. A* 11.11; 12.1–18; 13.12; 14A; *Sib. Or.* 2.183–84, 239–54, 283–338; *b. Ned.* 39b–40a; *Midr. Ps.* 118.19. Yinger, *Paul, Judaism and Judgement According to Deeds*; Kim, *God Will Judge Each One According to Works*.

4. Job 22:7; Isa 58:7; Ezek 18:7, 16; 2 Macc 12; Philo, *Sacr.* 118–26; *T. Ab.* 14; *T. Jos.* 1.5–7; *T. Jacob* 2.23; 7.24–25; *2 En.* 9.1; 10.5; 42.8; 63.1; *Pss. Sol.* 9.5; *4 Ezra* 7.37 Gentiles are judged by how they treated Israel; *Mek.* on Exod 14.19; *b. Soṭa* 14a; *m. 'Abot* 2.2; *m. Qidd.* 1.10; *t. Qidd.* 1.13; *b. Ned.* 39b–40a; *Midr. Ps.* 118.19; *Tg. Ps.-Jn.* on Deut 34:6; *Eccl. Rab.* on 11.1; Justin, *1 Apol.* 67. Much of this material is nicely laid out in chart form in Davies and Allison, *Matthew*, 3:426.

5. Reiche, "New Testament Concept of Reward," 203; Jeremias, *Neotestamentliche Theologie*, 209; Grindheim, "Ignorance Is Bliss."

6. *Midr. Tann.* on Deut 15:9; Jeremias, *Parables of Jesus*, 208.

7. 2 Pet 2:4; Tob 6:17; Wis 9:8; 1QM 13.11–12; 15.13–14.

don't care about others in practical ways. "For I was hungry, and you gave me nothing to eat; I was thirsty, and you gave me nothing to drink; I was a stranger, and you did not invite me in; naked, and you did not clothe Me; sick, and in prison, and you did not visit Me." The unrighteous may not even remember these neglected opportunities to do good deeds because it is their very character to be insensitive to others and neglect them. However, the same substitutionary principle for deeds applies. King Jesus will answer them, "To the extent that you did not do these good deeds to one of the least of these, you did not do it to Me." Thus, good deeds identify that a person aligns with Christ and the neglect of good deeds show that a person does not love others, nor ultimately Christ. The unrighteous group is banished by Christ to everlasting punishment without end or annihilation, but the righteous enter into everlasting life without end. The everlasting quality evident in αἰώνιον guarantees the same everlasting without end for everlasting punishment as for everlasting life (Matt 25:41, 46; LXX Dan 12:2).[8]

---

8. This everlasting feature contrasts to the normal early Jewish view of temporality in hell then released (*Num. Rab.* 18.20; some texts are often taken this way but are unclear: Sir 7:16; *Sipre Num.* 40.1.9; *Sipre Deut.* 311.3.1; 357.6.7; *'Abot R. Nat.* 16 A; 32.69 B; 37.95 B; 12 months in hell is a familiar duration in Jewish Second Temple texts [*b. Šabb.* 33b; *Lam. Rab.* 1.11–12]) or destroyed (2 Macc 12:43–45; 1QS 4.13–14; *Gen. Rab.* 6.6t. *Sanh.* 13.3–4; *Pesiq. Rab Kah.* 10.4; *Pesiq. Rab.* 11.5). In the biblical text there is no dwelling on the punishment like the kind of sadism one finds in: *Apocalypse of Peter*; *Acts of Thomas* act 6; *Sib. Or.* 2.252–312; Tertullian, *De. spect.* 30; Dante Alighieri, *Divine Comedy*, sec. 1, "Hell," cantos 1–34.

12

John 3:
Believing Jesus Begets Everlasting Life

IN THE JOHN 3 context, Nicodemus realized that God enables Jesus' miracles, so he approached Jesus with respect attributed toward an effective rabbi (John 3:1–21). This encounter occurs in the darkness of night probably because of Nicodemus's fear (John 3:2; 7:50–52), but John's Gospel plays off this real darkness in the account by metaphorically presenting Jesus as the light that shines in darkness (John 3:19–21). Jesus responded to Nicodemus by saying that only those who are born "again" or "from above"[1] will be able to see the kingdom of God. Nicodemus was confused about how new birth could take place. Jesus identified that our first birth brought about our human embodiment, but the new birth to spiritual being is created by the Spirit of God and illustrated by baptism (which is the initiation rite unto the kingdom).[2] Jesus was surprised that Nicodemus did not understand

---

1. The word ἄνωθεν can mean: (1) "from above" as from God or the Spirit, which is an emphasis in the context (John 3:6, 13), or (2) "again" as either: (2a) born unto the kingdom, instead of into this world (John 3–5, 16); or (2b) as a Spirit birth in contrast to a human flesh birth (John 3:4–6).

2. "*Born by water* and the Spirit" could mean: (1a) semen (as in born initially); (1b) water sack (as in born initially); (2) water as metaphor for the Spirit (Titus 3:5); (3) born from above, with baptism as the initiation rite unto the kingdom, which baptism in the context is associated with the Spirit (John 1:26–33; 3:23; proselyte baptism among the Jews: *m. Pesaḥ* 8.8; *t. 'Abod. Zar.* 3.11; 1QS 2.25–3.12; Epict. *Diatr.* 2.9.20; probably Juv. *Sat.* 14.104; *Sib. Or.* 4.162–65; *Yeb.* 2.29). 4). Some also claim the water is kingdom purifying immersion (with John 2:6–7, 14–16; 1QS 4.21; *p. Qidd.* 3.12.8; *Num. Rab.* 7.10 reading Ezek 36). Views 1a and 1b are unlikely since they have occurred and Jesus presents what is necessary to happen to enter the kingdom. View 2 is unlikely because there is already a closer metaphor for the Spirit in this context with that of wind. View 3 is the likely way to take this metaphor of water for baptism because of the near context

and believe these earthly things. Jesus clarified that he referred to a spiritual (πνεύματος) birth brought about by the causality of the Spirit (πνεῦμά), like the causality of wind (πνεῦμα) functions; you can't see the Spirit or wind but you can see their effect (John 3:6–8).

Jesus responded that he is uniquely qualified to reveal heavenly truth because he is simultaneousness in heaven and earth—the Chalcedonian christological position. The majority of Bruce Metzger's United Bible Societies' editorial committee rejected this reading of "in heaven" as too advanced a development of Christology and let John 3:13 be parallel to 1:18; 3:31; 6:38, 42, which teaches that Jesus "has come from heaven" to reveal God and implement the Son of Man's role into an already established mystical judgment and the kingdom. Such a meaning would be profound in its already mystical realization of the Son of Man's judgment and kingdom consequences. Metzger makes the claim that the "in heaven" reading is "supported almost exclusively by Egyptian witnesses," which is contrary to the case,[3] whereas in the second edition he acknowledges that his own reading is the reading almost exclusively supported by Egyptian sources.[4] A minority on the team argued that "there is no discernable motive that would have prompted copyists to add the words 'who is in heaven,' resulting in a most difficult saying"[5] and thus a likely original textual reading. Additionally, some of the support for the minority reading comes from third and fourth century sources, before and not normally identified with Chalcedon (like Origen). I join the minority of the UBS editorial committee who consider Jesus' "present-ness" in heaven as a more difficult textual statement to be preferred as the earlier text, and as a reading it does have stronger and broader textual support than the other options. Thus, I conclude in this verse for a two-natures view of Christ that permits a simultaneous Jewish monotheistic divine presence in heaven while his earthly human presence is visually before Nicodemus. Such a meaning would still convey that the

---

use in John (1:6–8, 19–36, 40; 4:1) and in the culture, and the early church clearly embraced this view as well (Acts 2:38, 41; 8:12; Rom 6:3; 1 Cor 12:13; 1 Pet 3:21). View 4 is unlikely because it would occur as the kingdom begins, so it would be redundant to entering the kingdom and thus not a requirement to enter the kingdom as Jesus presents it to Nicodemus.

3. Byzantine textual support for the "in heaven" reading: A, E. F, G, H, K, M, S, V, Γ, Λ, Π, *Byz. Lect.*, Basil, Chrysostom, Didymus Nonnus, Theodoret. Western textual support: Old Latin, Syriac (Harclean), Hippolytus Novation, Hillary. Alexandrian textual support: 892 Coptic (mss. of the Bohairic), Dionysius, Origin. Caesarean textual support: Θ, *f*1, *f*13, 28, 565, Armenian Georgian. This reading "in heaven" is indicated in the margin for the English Standard Version.

4. Metzger, *Textual Commentary on the Greek New Testament*, 174.

5. Ibid.

Son of Man has come for judgment and the kingdom but, simultaneous to that, this view would also underscore the Chalcedonian position of Jesus as the God-man.

Jesus clarified that his simultaneity in heaven (John 3:13)[6] and presence before Nicodemus (John 3:3, 5, 10) as the Son of Man enables him to become the healing object of faith, like the bronze serpent on a pole (Num 21:9). Instead of obtaining healing for snake bite by looking to God through means of the bronze serpent, *the follower of Jesus is to look to Christ as the God-man, who through the Holy Spirit brings them to the kingdom.* Jesus himself is the bridge from earth to heaven because he occupies both. In this present incarnational role Jesus reveals that his followers must see him as the present bridge object of their *ongoing faith* (John 3:15, present active participle πιστεύων). This idiolect Johannine ongoing faith as a progressive present tense reflects the present-tense emphasis of half the verbs in the context, especially the *presentness of faith* in John 3:12 (present active indicative πιστεύετε) and the present possession of *having* (present active ἔχῃ) everlasting life in John 3:15. Having everlasting life is a continual progressive experience that does not end and, likewise, such present faith would be continual progressive faith that lasts as long as everlasting life (John 3:15). Dan Wallace concludes that this present emphasis points to "*continual* belief as a necessary condition of salvation."[7]

Jesus' death and glorification are fused by the Gospel of John as the Son of Man is lifted up, so that those who believe him in this role do not perish but have everlasting life. Normally in the NT the concept of "lifted up" (ὑψωθῆναι) is that of exaltation, either of inappropriate pride, or of the salvific rescue accomplished for the humble, or of Jesus' exaltation to the right hand of the Father in glory (Matt 11:23; 23:13; Luke 1:52; 10:15; 14:11; 18:14; Acts 2:33; 5:31; 13:17; 2 Cor 11:7; Jas 4:10; 1 Pet 5:6). However, John identifies Jesus' "lifting up" (ὑψωθῆναι) with his death (John 3:14; 8:28;

---

6. The claim to be presently in heaven is a significant textual variant with strong and broad manuscript support (much more than the omission option that has support from A and B), and the simultaneous claim to be present in heaven while he is also present before Nicodemus is clearly the most difficult reading even if it is no shorter. The other options of "coming from heaven" have significantly less textual support and other Johannine texts to explain why they might have been harmonized to soften this option. The omission option would also internally soften this issue. Metzger, *Textual Commentary on the Greek New Testament*, 203–4; Black, *New Testament Textual Criticism*, 49–56 sides with the minority that prefers the reading of Jesus presentness in heaven.

7. Wallace, *Greek Grammar*, 523 n. 26 "customary present" and also 621 argues for this conclusion from the broad use of soteriological verbs using the present tense in the NT. Campbell, *Verbal Aspect*, 50–53 argues for present as presentational proximity, which would support Wallace's view.

12:32–34). It includes something that the Jews will do to him (John 8:28). Such a "lifting up" makes Jesus the object of the believer's faith, much like the bronze serpent "lifted up" on a pole was for the wilderness snake-bitten Israelite. In looking to the lifted up object of faith they obtain healing (John 3:14–16; Num 21:9). In this "lifting up" the Jews will know that Jesus is the "I am" (John 8:28). Likewise, this "lifting up" is necessary for Jesus to draw all men to himself (John 12:32–34). John has fused the raising up movement of his death with that of glorification. While the synoptic gospels and Acts describe his ascension to the divine throne room, with his kingship and divinity as glorification (Matt 19:28; 24:30; 25:31; Mark 10:37; 13:26; Luke 9:26, 32; 21:27; 24:26; Acts 7:55), John identifies that Jesus' death is his hour of glorification (John 7:39; 12:16, 23–24; 13:31; 16:14; 17:1, 5). The death becomes a glorification in that like a seed it enables Jesus to bear much salvific fruit (John 12:23–24). So lifting up and glorification come together in John's theology of Jesus' death because of the salvific gain we have from him.

Jewish texts promised continued life in Deuteronomic *Torah* blessings (Deut 30:6, 15–16, 19),[8] until early Judaism deepened this blessing into everlasting life and personal resurrection, where the dead will awake from their sleep among the dust to either everlasting life or everlasting contempt (Dan 12:2–3).[9] Such everlasting life cannot be merely realized eschatology, for it continues without end as an expression of the kingdom (Dan 12:2–3; John 3:15–17; 1 John 5:11–13).[10] This sort of eschatological resurrection hope into the kingdom is strongly instanced in early Judaism.[11] Additionally, a

---

8. Bar 3:9; 4:1–2; *Pss. Sol.* 14.1–2; *L.A.B.* 23.10; 2 *Bar.* 38.2; *m. 'Abot* 2.7; *b. 'Abot* 6.7, bar.; *'Abot R. Nat.* 34A; 35B; *Sipre Deut.* 306.22.1; 336.1.1; *b. Ḥag.* 3b; *Roš Haš.* 18a; *p. Ber.* 2.2, section 9; *Ex. Rab.* 41.1; *Lev. Rab.* 29.5; *Num. Rab.* 5.8; 10.1; 16.24; *Deut. Rab.* 7.1, 3, 9; *Tg. Eccl.* 6.12.

9. 1QS 4.6–8; CD 3.20; 4Q181 3–4; *1 En.* 37.4; 40.4; 58.3; 4 Macc 15:3; *Ps. Sol.* 3.12; *Sib. Or.* 3.49 frag. 3; Baldwin, *Daniel*, 204–6; Wright, *Resurrection of the Son of God*, 108–10.

10. 1QS 4.6–8; CD 3.20–21; 1QH 3.10–22; 6.34; 11.12; 1QM 12.1–4.; 2 Macc 7:9–14, 22–23.

11. 1QH 3.10–22; 6.34; 11.12; 1QM 12.1–4; *1 En.* 58.3; 62.14–16; 91.10; 92.2; 108.11–14; 2 *Bar.*[Syriac] 30.1–5; 2 Macc 7:9–14, 22–23; 14:43–46; 4 Macc 7:19; 16:25; 4 Ezra 7.32; *Sib. Or.* 4.180; *T. of Benj.* 10.6–8; *T. Levi* 18; *T. Jud.* 24; *T. of Hos.* 6:2 interprets this text to be resurrection whereas the text speaks of the reviving of Israel on the third day; *Tg. Jon.* on Isa 27:12f describes salvation as being accomplished on the third day; *b. Sanh.* 90b where Gamaliel claims that God would give the resurrected patriarchs land, not merely their descendants and Johanan Numbers 18:28 the portion of YHWH given to Aaron is taken that he will be alive again, likewise Num 15:31 is claimed that the remaining guilt of the offender will be accountable in the world to come; 91b–92a; *B. Ta'an.* 2a; *B. Ket.* 111; *m. Sanh.* 10.1, 3; *T. Mos.* 10.8–10; *Gen. Rab.* 14.5; 28.3; *Lev. Rab.* 14.9; *Messianic Apocalypse* adds resurrection to a modification of Ps 146:5–9 as a messianic expectation to be done to others; *T. Jud.* 25.4 claims this messianic resurrection

minority Pharisaic view, which Jesus embraces, anticipates resurrection life for the faithful Jew resurrecting upon death, thus affirming the monotheistic God as the God of the living Abraham, Isaac, and Jacob even though they have died (Exod 3:6; Luke 16:19–30; 20:39).[12] God is the God of the living!

Going beyond early Judaism, John develops a climactic sign miracle in raising Lazarus from the dead to elucidate Jesus' teaching that he is the resurrection and the life (John 11:25). Responding to Martha's hope for better than resurrection unto the kingdom, Jesus announced, "*I am the resurrection and the life*; he who believes in me shall live even if he dies, and everyone who lives and believes in me shall never die" (John 11:25–26). *Jesus as the embodiment of resurrection life is bringing her a present power to meet her need.* In John 11:26, one article governs the two present active participles, "lives and believes," indicating that they are intimately connected on the same plain; a realized eschatology both now and everlasting. That is, the one who continuously believes in Jesus continuously lives with everlasting life already (John 3:16; 11:26). This is not a past faith; it is entering into a life of continuing believing and continuing everlasting life. In Johannine writing, this everlasting life is a mystical reality that is already true of the one who believes (John 3:16–18). Jesus then asked Martha if she believes, to which Martha responds that she believes that he is the Messiah, the Son of God. To demonstrate his claim, Jesus resurrects Lazarus and then after a few weeks even Jesus resurrects. Jesus' affirmation that he is the resurrection and the life is like Peter's statement that Jesus is the "Prince of Life," which indicates that it was completely incongruous for the Prince of Life to be killed, so God

---

would begin with Abraham, Isaac, and Jacob; *T. Benj.* claims that after these are raised the whole of Israel will be raised; *Pss. Sol.* 3.11–12; 4Q521 frag. 2, col. 2.1–13; frags. 7 and 5, col. 2.1–7; 1QH 14.29–35; 19.10–14; *Targum Songs* 8.5; the benediction in the *Amidah*, the *Shemoneh Esre*. However, Wis 3:1; 8:19–20; 9:15 and Josephus' description of the Pharisees (*Ant.* 17.152–154; 18.1.3–5; *J.W.* 2.151–153; 2.8.14; *Ap.* 2.217–8) follow more a Platonic immortality of the soul view, but even here the soul eventually is given a body to match (Wis 9:15; Josephus, *J.W.* 2.163). Also the biblical authors (Matt 22:23–33; Mark 12:18–27; Acts 23:6–7) and the *Eighteen Benedictions* present the Pharisees as believing in the bodily resurrection of the dead; Gillman, *Death of Death*, 101–42; Wright, *Resurrection of the Son of God*, 129–206 for the post-biblical Jewish view. The early church from patristic through medieval eras embraced bodily resurrection instead of Platonic immortality of the soul with regard to personal eschatology (Bynum, *Resurrection of the Body in Western Christianity*; Wright, *Resurrection of the Son of God*, 480–552).

12. Jesus' view (Luke 16:19–31) is consistent with Jewish tradition (*Abr.* 50–55; 4 Macc 7:18–19; 13:17; 16:25; Philo, *Sacr. CA* 1.5; *T. Abr.* 20.8–14; *Qoh. Rab.* 9.5.1; *b. Sanh* 90b; *Ex. Rab.* 1.8; *Deut. Rab.* 3.15; *LAB* 4.11; *T. Isaac* 2.1–5; *T. Benj.* 10.6; *Apoc. Sed.* 14.3; *3 En.* 44.7). The sages could also read "living God" as "God of the living" (*Pesiq. R.* 1.2).

vindicated him by raising him from the dead (Acts 3:15–16). Thus Jesus embodies the everlasting life message. Any follower of Jesus in her ongoing faith also joins Jesus in embodying the everlasting life healing provided to those who believe.

These Johannine contexts using the present-tense "believe" (πιστεύων in John 3:15, 16, 18) draw the follower of Jesus into the point that John 11:26 developed: that people need to enter a life of continual faith to enter a life of continual everlasting life. The person who continually believes in Jesus as the God-man able to bring her to the kingdom continually *has* everlasting life (John 3:15–16 ἔχῃ) and has passed from judgment already (John 3:18). Likewise, those who do not believe are also currently already judged with a judgment that is everlasting (John 3:18).

In incarnation, Jesus is the light shining into the world. The Revelational Light draws practitioners of the truth to the light, exposing their deeds as created by God. In contrast, as a person might turn on a light and cockroaches scurry for dark corners, so the doers of evil hate the light lest their deeds should be exposed (John 3:19–20; 1 John 2:15).[13] Nicodemus later shows obvious allegiance to Jesus as his faith, confession, and hope matures (John 7:50–51; 19:39).

---

13. *1 En.* 108.11–14; *Com. Rule* cols. 3 and 4.

13

Messiah unto Everlasting Life

WHEN JESUS AND A Samaritan woman come to Jacob's well at Sychar, Jesus told her the gospel (John 4:1–42). As the disciples left to buy food,[1] Jesus asked the woman for a drink.[2] She was surprised that a Jew was talking to her because Jews had no dealings with Samaritans (John 4:9)[3] and she came at noon to avoid others. Jesus responded, "If you knew the gift of God, and who it is who is talking with you, you would ask and he would have given you living water."[4] "Living water" could just mean flowing spring water (LXX: Gen 26:19), but as a blessing living water is associated with God, wisdom, and the eschatological kingdom that produces life (Jer 2:13; 17:13; Ezek 47:9; Zech 14:8; Prov 13:14; 18:4).[5] However, here Jesus utilized living water to image everlasting life (John 4:14). The woman wondered if Jesus was greater than Father Jacob, who dug and gave the Samaritans this well.[6] Jesus pointed out the contrast that one

---

1. Rabbis usually have disciples obtain supplies (b. 'Abod. Zar. 35b; Keener, *John*, 1:596).

2. This is a reasonable request by a stranger at a well (Gen 24:14; b. Qidd. 9a; Euripides *Cycl.* 96–98). However, Jewish men usually avoided conversation with a woman (m. 'Abot 1.5; t. Šabb. 1.4; b. 'Erub. 53b) because often being in private with a woman would draw suspicion of adultery (p. 'Abod. Zar. 2.3.1; Soṭah 1.1.7; m. 'Abod. Zar. 2.1).

3. B. Yebam. 68a; m. Nid. 4.1; t. Nid. 5.1; b. Šabb. 17a.

4. A good teacher is sometimes compared to a well of water (*Sipre Deut.* 48.2.7) and good disciples do not lose a drop (m. 'Abot 2.8).

5. Living water in Second Temple Judaism is used as a metaphor for *Torah* (Sir 24:23–29; CD 3.16; 6.4–11; 19.34). Some Jews consider Samaritan women as perpetually unclean (m. Nid. 4.1; t. Nid. 5.1). However, such living or flowing water would be a new *mikveh* for cleansing away menstrual impurity (m. Miqw. 8.5; b. Nid. passim; Šabb. 84a). Furthermore, 1QS 4.21 identifies that the spirit of truth will purify beneficiaries with purifying water.

6. This is a reasonable claim for Jesus (Matt 12:41–42; Luke 11:31–32).

drinking from this water will end up thirsting again but the living water (Jesus gives) springs up to everlasting life (John 4:14; 6:35). The woman asked for this living water, so Jesus demonstrated he was a prophet[7] by identifying that she had had five husbands and the man she was with now was not her husband. Acknowledging Jesus was a prophet in a Samaritan context approached a messianic claim as the prophet following Moses' pattern, since Samaritans did not credit the Pharisaic prophet tradition until the ultimate restorer would provide Mosaic prophetic restoration (Deut 18:18–22).[8] The woman wished to release the moral tension by distracting the issue to Samaritans' worship at Gerizim[9] while Jews insisted that worship be done in the Jerusalem temple.[10] Jesus challenged both the Jewish and Samaritan traditions by identifying that the hour had come to move beyond both the Jewish and Samaritan biases for worship sites. When the monotheistic God is granted to be Spirit (John 4:24; Ps 139:7), then true worship is not based on location, but true worshippers worship God in[11] spirit and truth, for such people the Father seeks to be his worshippers (John 4:23). The woman acknowledged that when the Messiah comes he will declare all things to them. This Samaritan concept of Messiah or *Taheb* is a restorer as a new Moses who teaches the Law.[12] Jesus identified that he is this Messiah, which means that the worship that God seeks is only for those who identify themselves in the sphere of the truth that Jesus is the Messiah (John 4:25–26, 29; 1:14, 17; 8:32; 14:6) and the Holy Spirit as the context for worship (John 4:23; 3:8; 14:26; 16:13–15). She returned to the village and gave testimony that Jesus was the Messiah, who provided prophetic insight into her life. Jesus told the disciples that the process of reaping fruit for everlasting life was about to begin with the villagers pouring out to hear him (John 4:36). Having heard Jesus, many of the Samaritans believed Jesus to be the Savior of the world and thus aligning with Jesus. These believing Samaritans received everlasting life salvation (John 4:42, 14, 36).

---

7. A view shared by the crowds (John 6:15; 7:40; Matt 16:14; Mark 6:15; Luke 9:8).

8. Josephus, *Ant.* 18.85–87; Bruce, *New Testament History*, 37–38; *Time Is Fulfilled*, 39; Freed, "Did John Write His Gospel Partly to Win Samaritan Converts?," 248; Brown, *Gospel According to John*, 1:172.

9. Samaritan Pentateuch: tenth commandment requires worship to take place exclusively on Mt. Gerizim in verse following Exod 20:17 and Deut 5:21; Josephus, *Ant.* 18.85; *b. Yomma* 69a. Alexander the Great permitted the Samaritans to build their temple on Mt. Gerizim but John Hyrcanus I destroyed it to its functioning ruin in Jesus' day.

10. Conflict over proper worship site was intense between Jews and Samaritans (Luke 9:51–53; 4Q372 frg. 1, line 12; 4Q371 frg. 1, 8, 11; Josephus, *Ant.* 13.74–79; *Gen. Rab.* 64.10).

11. The preposition ἐν retains its locative sense: not *in* Gerizim or *in* Jerusalem but that worship is done *in* the sphere of spirit and truth.

12. Brown, *Gospel According to John*, 1:172.

14

Believe in Jesus as Sent from God to have Everlasting Life

JESUS WAS IN JERUSALEM for a[1] feast of the Jews (John 5:1). At such feasts, some Jews would exclude the lame and paralyzed as though they were dead (Lev 21:17–23; 2 Sam 5:8 LXX).[2] However, regularly many sick would be gathered around pools, anticipating healing at the Pool of Bethesda or Sheep Pool (John 5:3–4).[3] On the Sabbath, Jesus healed a paralyzed man at the Pool of Bethesda and the paralyzed man began to carry his pallet into the temple (John 5:2–18).[4] The Jews sought to kill Jesus for breaking the Sabbath because he healed the paralyzed man.[5] Some Jews were further offended because Jesus called God his Father, which was understood as a claim making Jesus equal to God. Jesus' response was that he only did

---

1. Strong external evidence favors an anarthrous noun and thus an unidentified feast rather than a particular one (Metzger, *Textual Commentary on the New Testament*, 178).

2. 1QM 7.4; 1QSa 2.5–6; 4QDb.

3. John 5:4 is a scribal gloss only present in later manuscripts but it supports the fact that healings took place at this pool (Metzger, *Textual Commentary on the New Testament*, 179), as does the Pompeia Lucilia inscription and votive offering left by the pool (Keener, *John*, 1:638). However, pools were commonly healing sites and sick were placed there (Josephus, *J.W.* 1.657; 2.614; 4.11; *Life* 85; Pliny, *Nat.* 2.95.208; 5.15.71–72; *Pesiq. Rab. Kah.* 11.16; *Eccl. Rab.* 10.8).

4. Some Jews joined Jesus in viewing the Sabbath as a release day where good could be accomplished (Deut 14:28—16:17 especially 15:7–11; 1 Macc 2:29–41; *Šabb.* 18.3; *T. Šabb.* 15.14; *Šabb. M. Eduyoth* 2.5; *m. Šabb.* 6.3; 22.6; *Yoma* 8.6; 84b; *b. Yoma* 85b; *m. Yoma* 8.6; *T. Yoma* 84.15; *Mek.* On Exod 22:2 and 23:13; 4Q265 frag. Lines 6–8).

5. *M. Yoma* 8.6; *T. Šabb.* 12.12–13; 17.14; *p. ʿErub.* 10.11; *Maʿaś Š.* 2.1.4; Kennard, *Messiah Jesus*, 128–32.

work that the Father did and the Father did this miraculous work as an act of love for the Son and so that observers might marvel at the miracles (John 5:19-20). Jesus' miracles were witnessed to by John the Baptist, the Father who facilitates the miracles, and the Scriptures that predict such messianic healing (John 5:30-39; 1:7, 15, 23, 26; Isa 53:5). The fact that the Father resurrects the dead means that the Son will also resurrect the dead miraculously (John 5:21, 26). Thus all should honor the Son like they honor the Father who sent him (John 5:23). Notice that the concept of "sent from God" is not Jesus' atonement, but that *Jesus is doing the same miracles as God the Father within the ministry that the Father has sent the Son to accomplish.* That is, whatever the Father does, the Son also does (John 5:19-20). Such miracles were recorded in the Gospel of John to prompt faith that Jesus is the Christ and that in believing they might have everlasting life (John 5:24-25, 29; 20:31). Embracing this affirmation, which recognizes that Jesus was sent from God, is the good belief in God that provides the believer with everlasting life (John 5:24-25, 29). Such a believer has already passed out of death into everlasting life, which indicates inclusion in the resurrection (John 5:28-29).

Later as Passover approached, Jesus compassionately and miraculously fed the five thousand. Some perceived that this miracle indicated that Jesus was the messianic King (John 6:1-15; Matt 14:14-21; Mark 6:34-44; Luke 9:12-17).[6] Many were motivated by eating this food (reminiscent of exodus manna) to declare Jesus to be the Messiah by attacking the Jewish and Roman leaders (John 6:15). Jesus tried to dissuade these Jews from a zealot strategy[7] so that they would believe in the God who sent Jesus and thereby have everlasting life (John 6:27, 29). Jesus invited the Jews who followed him to *work* (ἔργον) for everlasting life (John 6:27-29).[8] The *work* Jesus needed them to do was to *believe in Jesus sent by God* (John 6:29). That is, Jesus wanted the Jews to believe in what God and he were accomplishing at that time rather than ignoring it by being distracted by something else that they wished Jesus to be about. The Jewish people demanded more feeding signs in the pattern of manna from Moses, perhaps because through it they anticipated that the eschatological kingdom would be underway (John

---

6. *2 Bar.* 29.3-8; *4 Ezra* 6.52; Kennard, *Messiah Jesus*, 49-50.

7. Similar to comments describing zealots by Josephus, *Ant.* 18.4-6, 9-10, 23-24; *J.W.* 7.418-19.

8. Works were central for early Judaism's ethic (Wis 9:12) and the Semitic expression "to work works" (ἐργάζεσθε ... ἔργον, John 6:27-28) is common for "the task that needs to be accomplished (Hab 1:5; Matt 26:10; John 9:4; Acts 13:41; 1 Cor 16:10; Köstenberger, *John*, 207).

6:30–32). However, Jesus focused on a *midrashim*[9] that went beyond Moses' manna miracle (for manna allowed people to die); Jesus is himself the bread of life that comes down from the Father so that any who believe in the Son with regard to this role also believe the Father who sent him (John 6:38–40, 46–48, 58). That is, in Israel bread is the primary sustenance that keeps people alive and Jesus was claiming that he is the food that provides everlasting life. As with food, what the Son was about needed to be internalized by those who followed him. These believers in Jesus have everlasting life and Jesus himself will raise these believers on the last day (John 6:40, 47, 50, 54, 58; 10:28; 17:2–3; 20:31). The crowd grumbled, tripping over the fact that bread was not being given and that Jesus was trying to stretch them to a deeper analogy, like he had done with the Samaritan woman. Jesus made the point blatant that they needed to internalize him by munching on his flesh and drinking his blood (John 6:51–58). In response to this blatant cannibalistic language, many left and did not continue to follow Jesus.[10]

Jesus responded to this departure of disciples by asking the Twelve, "You do not want to go away also, do you?" (John 6:67). Simon Peter answered him, "Lord, to whom shall we go? You have words of everlasting life. And we have believed and have come to know that you are the Holy One of God" (John 6:68–68).

Both accounts, of working as the Father and the bread of heaven, identify that disciples need to deeply believe in Jesus Christ as sent from and empowered by God the Father. *Believing in the Son as sent from the Father includes the believer in everlasting life now and the Son will resurrect these believers into the kingdom.*

---

9. A reapplication of an analogy or text to a present concern. The pattern is developed by Brown, *Gospel According to John*, 1:262, 265–66.

10. Some traditions develop this eating of Jesus' flesh and blood as the Eucharist but there is no sacramental development in this chapter (Keener, *John*, 1:689–91).

15

Jesus Is the Resurrection and the Life

IN JOHN'S GOSPEL, A climactic sign miracle was developed in raising Lazarus from the dead, elucidating Jesus' teaching that *Jesus is the gospel in being the resurrection and the life* (John 11:25). Lazarus was on his death bed when friends sent for Jesus. However, Jesus delayed coming because, as he said, "This sickness is not unto death[1] but for the glory of God, that the Son of God may be glorified by it" (John 11:4). That is, the outcome will be a miracle that brings forth glory to Jesus and God. After two days, Jesus announced to his disciples that they were going to respond to Martha and Mary's request to come to Judea for their brother Lazarus. The disciples were alarmed, knowing that the Jewish leadership was seeking Jesus' life. Jesus reassured his disciples that missteps do not have to be devastating, but Lazarus was dead so it was time to go to him (John 11:7–16). Thomas pessimistically concluded that they were all going to go and die with Lazarus.

This miracle takes the Jewish idea of a resurrection as foreshadowing the general Jewish resurrection[2] and specifically applies it to Jesus, who is the resurrection source for eschatological life. As Jesus was coming to Bethany, Martha met him with an expression of faith: "Lord, if you had been here, my brother would not have died. Even now I know that whatever You ask of God, God will give You" (John 11:21–22). She was hoping for resurrection as Jesus had done for others (Matt 9:18, 23–25; Mark 5:35–42; Luke

---

1. This phrase is used in 1 John 5:16–17 regarding sin that leads to death, namely condemnation. Morris (*John*, 538–40) conjectures that Lazarus is already dead when the friends make the appeal to Jesus, with Bethany a one-day journey away and Jesus staying two more days and then traveling the one day to Bethany, thus Lazarus was dead for four days.

2. *Pesiq. Rab Kah.* 9.4; *1 En.* 62.14–15 identify that when the Son of Man resurrects the elect will resurrect also.

7:12–16; 8:49–56). However, Jews had little hope of the spirit remaining near the body for four days. Jesus responded with, "Your brother shall rise again." Martha took this statement as an affirmation of the Pharisaic view of final resurrection in the last days. Jesus responded to her, "*I am the resurrection and the life*; he who believes in me shall live even if he dies, and everyone who lives and believes in me shall never die" (John 11:25–26). This statement promising resurrection life identifies that Jesus is the gospel. *Jesus as the embodiment of resurrection life is bringing Martha a present power to meet her need.* In verse 26, one article governs the two present active participles, "lives and believes," indicating that they are intimately connected on the same plain, most likely describing a person's present condition. That is, the continuous believer lives with everlasting life already. In Johannine writing, this everlasting life is a mystical reality and relationship that is already true of the one who believes (John 3:16–18). Jesus then asked her if she believes this gospel, to which she responded that she believes that he is the Messiah, the Son of God. So Martha called Mary to come to meet Jesus.

Mary greeted Jesus much as Martha had done. Jesus asked where Lazarus had been laid. Upon showing him, Jesus wept. Jesus was deeply angry with the ravages death brings. Jesus asked for the stone to be removed. Martha protested that by this time he will stink. Jesus asked, "Did I not say to you, if you believe, you will see the glory of God." So the stone was removed. Jesus then prayed, thanking the Father for hearing him but saying that the miracle that was about to be accomplished was for those standing there so that they might believe that the Father had sent him. Following this prayer, he shouted, "Lazarus, come forth." And Lazarus came walking out of the tomb bound in his burial wrappings. Jesus said, "Unbind him and let him go." Many of the Jews who saw this believed in him but some told the religious leaders, who then plotted to kill Lazarus along with Jesus (John 11:45–57).

Since Jesus himself is the resurrection life, this miracle of resurrection for Lazarus hints at the subsequent miracle that would take place in the next few weeks: that of Jesus' own resurrection. These miracles of Lazarus' and Jesus' resurrection further confirm that Jesus is the resurrection and the life as he claimed. Jesus' affirmation means that it is completely incongruous for the believer in Christ to not currently live in resurrection life and thus have confidence for eschatological resurrection hope.

16

Jesus as Gospel[1]

JESUS IS THE GOSPEL in the book of Acts and the Gospels. Luke's gospel message from his gospel and the book of Acts is that *Jesus is the Lord who will eschatologically judge, so align with him*. Peter and Paul describe their salvation messages in Acts as gospel (εὐαγγέλιον: Acts 15:7; 20:24).[2] Dibelius describes these sermons as follows: "An introduction suggested by the actual situation is normally followed by the kerygma of Jesus' life, passion and resurrection, usually with the disciples' witness; to this is subjoined a scriptural proof and an exhortation of repentance."[3] Luke clearly remains within an exclusivist strategy for salvation in Jesus: "there is salvation in no one else" (Acts 4:12). N. T. Wright captures the essence of this gospel as, "*Jesus, the crucified and risen Messiah, is Lord.*"[4] The vicarious atonement is not developed in Luke's statements of gospel. Luther identified that "the gospel is a story about Christ, God's and David's Son, who died and was raised and is established as Lord. This is the gospel in a nutshell."[5] The Lukan emphasis of gospel proclamation may be summarized as follows:[6]

1. Material is reworked from Kennard, *Messiah Jesus*, 439–70 and *Epistemology and Logic in the New Testament*, 101–20, used with permission by Peter Lang and Wipf and Stock.

2. Stuhlmacher, "The Theme: The Gospel and the Gospels," in Stuhlmacher, ed., *Gospel and the Gospels*, 22.

3. Dibelius, "Speeches in Acts and Ancient Historiography," 165.

4. Wright, *What Saint Paul Really Said*, 46.

5. Luther, "A Brief Instruction on What to Look for and Expect in the Gospels," in *Luther's Works*, 35:118.

6. Conzelmann, *Acts*, xliv; and Schweizer "Concerning the Speeches in Acts," especially 210 have similar lists affirming my numbers: 1, 6, and 7 (Conzelmann's "Christological kerygma"). Their lists make more of stylistic rhetorical devices like connecting

1. The focus of gospel messages is that Jesus is the Davidic King (lordship), whom you will have to deal with in end-times judgment.

2. The core salvation benefits have to do with the kingdom being realized now in: forgiveness and the Spirit being poured forth. However, additional kingdom benefit also ensues, like: healing, Jubilee, eschatological reversal, special Spirit manifestations, and freedom from one's previous entanglements of the Law or idolatry.

3. The gospel message to Gentiles may have a preliminary focus emphasizing the Creator God as well.

4. Jesus' death provides an example for Jesus' disciples to imitate and it shows the responsibility of rebellion; it is never referred to by Luke as a vicarious atonement.

5. Jesus' resurrection shows God's vindication, identifying that Jesus is the Davidic King.

6. Every gospel sermon appeals to evidence to confirm the message, such as prophecy and miracles.

7. For Peter in Acts, repentance is what Jews in rebellion need to do, while Gentiles need to come to faith, whereas Paul and Luke use the terms interchangeably (Acts 20:21).

8. Baptism is tightly connected to this initial salvation response (Acts 2:38, 41; 8:12, 36–8; 9:18 10:47–8; 11:16; 16:15, 33; 18:8; 19:3–5; 22:16).

9. This salvation message brings the converts into the way of salvation, extending Jesus' Way unto the kingdom (Acts 9:2; 13:10; 16:17; 18:25–6; 19:9; 22:4; 24:14, 22).

---

the speech with the situation and the role for OT quotes as beginning and demonstrating the message (Conzelmann's call for a hearing from miracle or prophecy, connection with the situation, use of OT quotation, *kerygma* attempted to be scripturally proven), supporting my #6. Conzelmann's response is more strongly slated toward "repentance the condition for salvation (where appropriate)." Instead see my more balanced assessment in my #7. McKnight (*King Jesus Gospel*, 113–31, 166–75) placed the focus of the Acts sermons on the narrative of Jesus' life and ministry as a miniature of the Gospel of Luke, though the life and ministry emphasis in Acts sermons mainly serve as a forum to recount Jesus' confirming miracles (number 6 on list) and to connect with the audience's awareness of Jesus' ministry. Earlier studies include: Stanley, "Conception of Salvation in Primitive Christian Preaching"; Guilbert, "Message of Salvation in the Acts of the Apostles"; Jones, "Christology of the Missionary Speeches in the Acts of the Apostles."

This topic is usually studied in more microscopic detail.[7] As such, it is rather rare for works to explore and compare the gospel speeches as a group, but this has been done before by a few.[8] Marion Soads has the best summary as follows:

> When one views the speeches together, one observes a remarkable coherence. The consistency occurs in terms of the form and the contents of the speeches. There are 1) regularly repeated elements-for example, the manner of address, the tendency to speak beyond the immediate situation, the declaration of truth claims, the use of the past in explanation or support of

---

7. Usually each feature of the respective sermons is mentioned verse by verse in a commentary but occasionally closer looks of a particular sermon are undertaken such as: Balch, "Areopagus Speech"; Barrett, "Paul's Speech on the Areopagus"; Gärtner, *Areopagus Speech and Natural Revelation*; Dibelius, "Paul on Areopagus" and "The Speeches in Acts and Ancient Historiography"; Hemer, "Speeches in Acts II"; Kilgallen, "Acts 13,38–39"; Montague, "Paul and Athens"; Neyrey, "Acts 17, Epicureans, and Theodicy"; Porter, "Thucydides 1.22.1 and Speeches in Acts" re-evaluated the issue in favor of Bruce's previous works; Schubert, "Final Cycle of Speeches in the Book of Acts" and "Place of the Areopagus Speech in the Composition of Acts"; Shields, "Areopagus Sermon and Romans 1.18ff"; Zehnle, *Peter's Pentecost Discourse*. Other sermons include: Klijn, "Stephen's Speech—Acts 7,2–53"; Zehnte, *Peter's Pentecost Discourse*.

8. Soards, *Speeches in Acts* is the most profitable here in analyzing content with a special sensitivity to rhetorical device but he does not correlate the speeches together like I am doing in this paper; Ridderbos, *Speeches of Peter in the Acts of the Apostles* nicely summarizes the content in each speech, especially with a focus on: eschatology apostolicity, Christology (especially my point #1), and paraenesis; Schweizer, "Concerning the Speeches in Acts" appraised the contents of the sermons; Dodd, *Apostolic Preaching and Its Developments* mostly develops a continuity of the gospel through the whole NT, with a few pages on the Spirit, messianism, and eschatological nature of the gospel *kerygma*, and a nice overview chart covering the whole NT gospel statements; which gems are foreshadowed in "The Framework of the Gospel Narrative," which primarily examines the Gospel of Mark; Cadbury, "Speeches in Acts"; Bruce, *Speeches in the Book of Acts* and "Speeches in Acts"; and Kennard, *Messiah Jesus*, 439–70 surveys the speeches in Acts with an emphasis on showing the gospel particulars, and in *Epistemology and Logic in the New Testament*, 101–20 analyzed the epistemic and logical concerns of the gospel sermons. Luke responsibly handled these sermons after the pattern of the historian Thucydides; Hemer, *Book of Acts in the Setting of Hellenistic History*, 75–79, 415–27; Padilla, *Acts*, 75–197, and Kennard, *Epistemology and Logic in the New Testament*, 86–101 defend the historicity of the speeches by comparing them to other Greek historians with the surrounding Acts context and then summarizes their theology; Horsley, "Speeches and Dialogue in Acts" primarily shows that Acts is consistent and more generous with the placement of speeches in Greek classical narrative; Kennedy, *New Testament Interpretation through Rhetorical Criticism*, 114–40 surveys the speeches in Acts for some of the gems through rhetorical criticism; a narrative approach is framed by McKnight, *King Jesus Gospel*, 113–31, 166–75 and Kuhn, "Kingdom Story through Speech and Theme in Luke 24 and the Acts of the Apostles," in *Kingdom according to Luke and Acts*, 147–78.

the claims made, and the act of offering God's now-available salvation to the hearers for acceptance or rejection; 2) regularly repeated motifs–for example, divine necessity, a Christological contrast scheme, the Holy Spirit, the early Christian witness, and salvation; and 3) regularly repeated basic vocabulary... What is "the meaning to be attributed to the speeches in the work as a whole"? One finds that the speeches unify the Acts account, and through them Luke advances his theme of divinely commissioned unified witness to the ends of the earth.[9]

In the spirit of this synthetic approach, I intend to delineate the basic content that Luke (and perhaps his speakers) thought constituted the gospel message as expressed in Acts. This chapter is then a biblical-theological study, but it will have implications for how Christians should or could present the gospel. I intend to explore this topic in several ways: (1) I begin with some preliminary studies in Luke's soteriological expectations. (2) Next, I briefly explore Jesus' gospel unto the kingdom, from a Lukan perspective. (3) I then develop the emphasis of Peter's gospel in Acts. (4) I briefly develop Phillip's gospel in Acts. (5) I conclude with the emphasis of Paul's gospel in Acts.

Narrative account (like Luke and Acts) has profound theological meaning and value provided the author prescribes these ideas and does not merely describe them as past events. Any author is selective and chooses material to include in his document. If the material is unique in any expression, then it has the potential to become part of the accurate description that the author is making. In this Luke is known to be a very competent historian and theologian.[10] However, further, it is widely recognized that Greco-Roman rhetoric (including narratives and speeches) was written to emphasize paradigms for imitation by readers.[11] Henry Cadbury especially

---

9. Soads, *Speeches*, 14–14.

10. Marshall, *Luke* concludes Luke to be both a precise historian and adept theologian; on the issue of historicity, there many to support this point as are especially developed in articles that either reflect Luke 1:1–4, or specific passages connection with the place and culture described, Hemer, "Speeches in Acts II"; as to Luke being a theologian, Cadbury ("Speeches in Acts," 402, 410–22) defends the continuity of Luke's language in these speeches that further support that Luke is a deft theologian like other NT writers, as Dibelius, "Speeches in Acts and Ancient Historiography" proposed, even if Luke invented them they are Luke's writings with clear Lukan literary evidence; then there are several theologies of Luke that are worth consulting and confirm Luke as an able theologian with his distinctive agenda, for example: Conzelmann, *Theology of St. Luke*; Green, *Theology of the Gospel of Luke*; Harrington, *Luke*; Jervell, *Theology of the Acts of the Apostles*; Karis, *Luke*; Kee, *Good News to the Ends of the Earth*; O'Toole, *Unity of Luke's Theology*.

11. Kurz, "Narrative Models for Imitation in Luke-Acts"; Fiore, *Function of Personal*

points out that it is the speeches in Acts that bring vibrant interpretation with prescription as of a theologian to the book of Acts.[12] That is, when the authorial thrust emphasizes a trait in the text, the author lifts that idea from mere description to that of prescription for his audience. The narrative develops the character of great models of Christianity to be emulated by repeatedly showing how they respond in common situations, which the first-century Christians faced.[13]

In such a narrative, Luke has several ways in which he emphasizes the gospel content. First, the narrative tends to set up and accentuate the content of statements and especially intentional speeches as prescriptive, provided the speaker is speaking commands or warning to his audience and is seen as an authority for the community (as Jesus, Peter, and Paul are clear authorities for the church). Additionally, those speakers who associated positively with such an authority also tend to have their message elevated to the level of authority, as in those contexts where they are making such a positive identification with an authority (such as John the Baptist and those of Luke 1–3 in their affirmation of Jesus). In contrast, the things that opponents (like the Sanhedrin) say are not taken as authoritative for Christians. Secondly, the gospel speeches take on an authoritative role to the readership of the document if the speeches repeatedly say the same thing. Such repetition accentuates that the content of the sermon is what the textual author (Luke) wishes to communicate and prescribe for his audience, and not merely a coincidence of agreement among his characters (Peter and Paul) for their respective audiences. Likewise, the content comes to the audience with prescriptive emphasis if those sermons repeatedly *warn their audiences with consequences that the narrative develops as occurring*. So, the reader should become identified within the Spirit benefits of salvation by heeding the exhortations of these sermons. That is, the narrative development that realizes the consequences shows that this gospel is an intentional issue that the author, Luke, prescribes. So the study that follows is not merely a descriptive one exploring the Lukan Gospel, but, by Luke's emphasis, Luke's statement

---

Example in the Socratic and Pastoral Epistles, especially ch. 3, "Example in Rhetorical Theory, Education, and Literature"; De Boer, *Imitation of Paul*; Crouzel, "L'imitation et la 'suite' de Dieu et du Christ," especially 7–30; Cothenet et al., "Imitation du Christ"; Gutierrez, *Paternité spirituelle selon S. Paul*; Pate and Kennard, *Deliverance Now and Not Yet*, 369–72; Trompf, *Idea of Historical Recurrence in Western Thought*.

12. Cadbury, "Speeches in Acts," 402.

13. This is a similar point for how Hellenistic culture functions in these authors: Talbert, "Biographies of Philosophers and Rulers as Instruments of Religious Propaganda in Mediterranean Antiquity," 1643; Trompf, *Idea of Historical Recurrence in Western Thought*, 97–101; Fornara, *Nature of History in Ancient Greece and Rome*, 104–20.

of the gospel is a legitimate statement we could repeat as the gospel in our day as well.

LUKAN SOTERIOLOGICAL WORDS

Luke uses "gospel proclamation" (εὐαγγελίου) only twice, both in the book of Acts. In Acts 15:7 Peter refers to his sermons as the gospel message to be believed for salvation. In this context, the issue is the content that is to be included within this gospel, so the idea of evaluating the content of the gospel is within Luke's thought forms. The Judaizing sect wished for Gentiles to have the Law of Moses included among the gospel, but the Jerusalem council declared that God had authentically accepted the Gentiles by the Holy Spirit, without this Law being included, so that the Law should not be considered as part of the gospel. The other instance is in Acts 20:21–24, where Paul summarizes his gospel as the good news of God's grace for Jews and Gentiles (εὐαγγέλιον τῆς χάριτος τοῦ θεοῦ). The repetition of his phrase "solemn testimony" (διαμαρτυρόμενος v. 21, διαμαρτύρασθαι v. 24) identifies that the statements in verse 21 and 24 are both referring to the concept of gospel. Paul envisions the response to this gospel to be repentance to God and faith to our Lord Jesus Christ.

The parallel εἰς clauses in Acts 20:21 (εἰς θεὸν μετάνοιαν καὶ πίστιν εἰς τὸν κύριον ἡμῶν Ἰησοῦν) draw repentance and faith together as largely underscoring a synonymous response in aligning the believer with God. That is, in the Acts gospel proclamations, Peter maintains repentance (μετάνοιαν) as the turning from rebellion that Jews must do as they respond to the gospel (Acts 2:38; 3:19; 5:31) and faith (πίστις) as the response for a Gentile who is already predisposed to the gospel (Acts 10:43), but Paul sees these terms as interchangeable in this context, where both Jews and Gentiles are described by both of them (Acts 19:2, 4; 20:21; 26:20). Luke also uses these terms interchangeably (μετάνοιαν [Luke 13:1–5; 24:47; Acts 11:18], πίστις [Acts 15:9; 20:21; 24:24; 26:18] and πιστεύω [Acts 2:44; 4:4, 32; 5:14; 8:12–13, 37; 9:42 etc.]). This is parallel to Josephus' use when he confronted Jesus the Galilean brigand leader "to repent and believe in me."[14] In other words, this person must give up his agenda of trying to throw the Romans out of Israel and become a loyal follower of Josephus' agenda instead.[15] John the Baptist, Jesus, and Peter used the term *repentance* only for the Jews in

---

14. Josephus, *Life* 110.

15. Josephus, *Life* 110 in the LCL ed, by Thackery, where he translates this text (1.43) as "if he would . . . prove his loyalty to me."

signifying *what Israel must do if Yahweh is to restore her fortunes at last.*[16] Peter sees that first-century Israel must especially repent from their culpability in killing Christ, whereas Paul (as recorded by Luke) also uses the term "repentance" of Gentiles to communicate their need to depart from their idolatry and entrapment to Satan (Acts 26:18). Paul and Luke use the term "faith" more often and at times without "repentance" being mentioned as well (Acts 13:48; 16:31; 17:34; 18:8). N. T. Wright reminds us that both repentance and faith (in Acts) appear in contexts linking them inescapably with eschatology and the narrow way to obtain that outcome.[17]

The verbal expression of proclaiming gospel is communicated by two words (εὐηγγελίζω and κηρύσσω) that largely overlap in their semantic field for proclaiming the good news. Κηρύσσω is the broader word, with the possibility of an indefinite or Mosaic Law message having been proclaimed (Luke 12:3; Acts 15:21). Likewise, in Luke only εὐηγγελίζω is used when the announcement of good news comes from angels to Zacharias or to the shepherds (Luke 1:19; 2:10). However, apart from these instances the semantic field is the same. For example, John the Baptist proclaimed good news to the people (εὐηγγελίζω [Luke 3:18], κηρύσσω [Luke 3:3; Acts 10:37]). Likewise, quoting Isaiah 61:2, Jesus announced that his Spirit-anointed mission is to fulfill the Sabbatical and Jubilee Year release, allowing the poor, debtors, prisoners, downtrodden, and even the blind and demonized to go free (εὐηγγελίζω [Luke 4:18, 43; 7:22; 8:1; 9:6; 20:1], κηρύσσω [Luke 4:18–19, 44; 8:39]). This freedom extends to real practical ways of release, including those of fiscal diminishment, legal entrapment, overwhelming attitude, social oppression, physical impairment, and spiritual bondage. With this extensiveness of generous freedom, this proclamation of Jesus is one of proclaiming the kingdom of God (only εὐηγγελίζω [Luke 8:1; 16:16]). In this the disciples emulate their master in preaching the kingdom of God (εὐηγγελίζω [Acts 8:12], κηρύσσω [Luke 19:2; Acts 20:25; 28:31]). This gospel that the disciples communicate centers on Jesus as the messianic King, which their audience will have to deal with in the eschatological judgment (εὐηγγελίζω [Acts 5:42; 8:12, 35; 10:36; 11:20; 13:32; 17:18], κηρύσσω [Acts 8:5; 9:20; 10:42; 19:13]).[18] As such, this message is to turn Gentiles from their idolatry (Acts 14:15). There is a great degree of continuity from John the Baptist to Jesus and to the disciples, who follow the great commission in proclaiming the gospel (Luke 24:47; Acts 10:42). This gospel to

---

16. Wright, *Jesus and the Victory of God*, 249.

17. Wright, *Jesus and the Victory of God*, 249–51.

18. Such a message is the word preached, only referred to by κηρύσσω (Acts 8:4, 25, 40; 14:7, 21; 15:35; 16:10).

be proclaimed highlights a repentance that brings the disciples in line with the parallel εἰς clauses imbedded within the great commission (Luke 24:47 μετάνοιαν εἰς ἄφεσιν ἁμαρτιῶν εἰς πάντα τὰ ἔθνη). Namely, the gospel is repentance to the outcome of forgiveness of sins and to the extent of the whole range of the Gentiles. This gospel proclamation is to begin in Jerusalem (Luke 24:47; Acts 1:8).

"Salvation" is expressed in Luke verbally by σῴζω and nominally by σωτηρία. In the Gospel of Luke these salvation words refer to healing 30 percent of the time (Luke 7:50; 8:36, 48, 50; 17:19; 18:42; Acts 4:9; 14:9) while 40 percent of the time they refer to preserving one's life during a time of risk (Luke 6:9; 9:24; 17:33; 23:35, 37, 39; Acts 7:25; 16:30?; 27:20, 31, 34). In the introduction to Luke's Gospel, σωτηρία emphasizes entrance into the kingdom, including the destruction of Gentile enemies (Luke 1:69, 71, 72).[19] Probably continuing this same idea is the Lukan emphasis of these words as saved in repentance (Luke 8:12; 13:23; 18:26; 19:9–10; Acts 2:21, 40, 47; 4:12; 11:14; 15:1, 11;16:30–31; 13:26, 47). This later approach is expressed as the way of salvation (Acts 23:33, 35, 39) much like Luke's Gospel had developed the narrow way unto the kingdom. It is in this broad sense that Jesus is identified as the Savior (Luke 1:47; 2:11; Acts 5:31; 13:23).

"Redemption" in Luke refers to the establishment of the kingdom. Redemption is expressed in Luke by λύτρωσιν in 1:68 and 2:38 with reference to the coming kingdom in which Gentile enemies will be destroyed and Jerusalem will be free. Jesus refers to his second coming as a redemption for his Jewish disciples, likely meaning the same thing (ἀπολύτρωσις, Luke 21:28).

PREPARATION FRAMEWORKS FOR GOSPEL

The expectation of salvation informs Luke's concept of gospel to be a Spirit-produced kingdom in which Jesus, the Davidic King, reigns. For example, the angel Gabriel's announcement to Mary that Jesus will be born from the Spirit through her to be the Son of the Most High, that is, the Davidic King (Luke 1:32–35). His kingdom is to have no end. Likewise, in response to Elizabeth's filling by the Spirit, Mary praised God for the eschatological reversal in the kingdom, which fulfills the promises made to Abraham and the fathers (Luke 1:50–55). This eschatological reversal benefits the poor, humble, and those who fear God. It includes an everlasting defense for Israel over their enemies. Additionally, the Spirit prompts Zacharias to praise

---

19. Conzelmann, *Mitte der Zeit*, 216; Ross, "Concept of σωτηρία in the New Testament."

God for the eschatological redemption of Israel, in which the Davidic King is raised up to provide salvation from Israel's enemies (Luke 1:61-79). The dominant way that Luke uses σωτηρία refers to this kingdom perspective (Luke 1:69, 71, 77; and perhaps Acts 7:25). This kingdom is also seen as fulfilling the Abrahamic covenant. This kingdom realization should bring about the desired effect of serving God without fear and with holiness and righteousness. Zacharias announces that John's role will be to give knowledge of salvation by the forgiveness of sins. Next in the narrative, the angel announced to the poor shepherds that the Savior the King was born (Luke 2:11). On Jesus' presentation day Simeon announced that Jesus is the Lord's King and salvation to provide Israel with glory, which extends to become a light of revelation to the Gentiles (Luke 2:26, 29-32).

John the Baptist's gospel message (Luke 3:18, εὐηγγελίζετο) requires Jews to be baptized as an expression of anticipation of the kingdom and a recognition of one's repentance for sins. The distinctive way that avoids God's eschatological wrath of fire is one of generosity and justice aligned with the King who is coming (Luke 3:3, 7, 9, 11, 13-18). The coming King will baptize with a single baptism, which will immerse in two different directions reflective of the two ways people live. Those kingdom-bound will experience baptism in the Spirit while the damned will experience baptism into eschatological wrath fire. The fire (πῦρ) of Jesus' baptism is to be understood by how fire (πῦρ) is used in the immediate context, that of unquenchable destruction fire (πῦρ, Luke 3:9, 16-17).[20]

Jesus shows himself to be this King, aligned with God. The kingship is clearly announced by Luke in identifying Jesus as the Son of God, in the midst of extending John's ministry and dogged by the grand conflict with Satan (Luke 3:38; 4:3, 9). Jesus aligns himself with God and his word rather than Satan's quick solutions. Jesus then embodies in his incarnation the noble way to the kingdom.

JESUS' GOSPEL IN LUKE

Jesus announced his ministry purpose by quoting Isaiah 61:1-2 (Luke 4:17-21). This ministry purpose is that: the Spirit has empowered him to proclaim the gospel, with a jubilee of eschatological reversal attesting to it.

> The Spirit of the Lord is upon me, because he anointed me to preach the gospel to the poor. He has sent me to proclaim release to the captives and recovery of sight to the blind, to set free

---
20. Therefore, this fire imagery is no allusion to the Pentecost tongues of fire, for that is quite foreign to this context.

those who are downtrodden, to proclaim the favorable year of the Lord.

The issue is the public acknowledgement of the Son of Man for who he is as the Spirit-endowed King. The one who publicly acknowledges Jesus before men, Jesus will acknowledge before the angels of God (Luke 12:8-9). Likewise, the one who denies Jesus before men, Jesus will deny before the angels of God. This has ramifications for the acceptance or denial of the Spirit's empowerment of the Son's miracles. Those who blaspheme the Spirit will be damned without forgiveness in this life and in the afterlife as well (Luke 12:10-12). Unfortunately, some people responded to his amazing announcement with rage and rejection; they tried to kill Jesus (Luke 4:28-30). Furthermore, the religious leaders rejected Jesus for his persistent healing and doing good on the Sabbath (Luke 6:1-5, 11; 13:10-17; 14:1-6).[21] However, the more basic issue that Jesus proposed and these people rejected is: who is Jesus? The right response is to align with Jesus as the King (Luke 19:37-38; 20:17-18). The people were warned to repent or perish, for exclusion will bring destruction for Israel and hell for the individuals (Luke 13:3, 5, 23-30). Unfortunately, the religious leaders reject Jesus and head for their destruction (Luke 19:27, 39; 20; 22:47—23:49).

Luke reiterated that Jesus' primary purpose was to preach the gospel of the kingdom of God (Luke 4:43-44; 8:1; 9:11). This is reflected in the mimetic role in which the Twelve are sent out to also preach the kingdom of God (Luke 9:1-6). They carry Jesus' message and extend his ministry.

Therefore, the gospel gets framed by Jesus' preached content as he directs his disciples toward the kingdom. Luke frames Jesus' message to the kingdom in a classic two-ways strategy. The salvific way is a narrow way to life, while the broad way ends in damnation. Luke identifies that these two ways are grounded upon wisdom (wise or fool, Luke 7:35 with 8:4-15) and the Law (blessed or cursed, Luke 10:25-28). The way toward the kingdom is to identify with Jesus and his way of life.[22] This way holds out the kingdom blessing for the poor, weeping, and ostracized who identify with Jesus (Luke 6:20-27). One's commitment to Jesus is shown by loving your enemies and doing good as they try to abuse you (Luke 6:27, 35, 45). The defining issue is: do you hear the word of Jesus to do it (Luke 8:15, 21; 10:42; 11:28)? It is in this way that Jesus' kingdom teaching extends the Law's blessing strategy for his Jewish disciples; the kingdom is the era of Deuternomic blessing (Luke 10:25-28). Those who internalize the Law love others as they love them-

---

21. Also, the religious leaders raised difficulties with Jesus over fasting (Luke 5:33-39) and the lack of ceremonial washing before meals (Luke 11:30-52).

22. Robinson, "'Way of the Lord.'"

selves. Such an approach is also a wisdom strategy because by following Jesus' teaching "wisdom is vindicated by all her children" (Luke 7:35). One such child is the sinful woman who expressed her great love for Jesus by washing, kissing, and anointing Jesus' feet with her tears (Luke 7:36-50). Furthermore, the wisdom strategy of parables shows that in the Parable of the Soils it is the honest and good application of the word that will bear fruit with perseverance unto the kingdom (Luke 8:4-15). That which is hidden, such as those who are kingdom oriented, will be revealed by deeds (Luke 8:16-17). However, this is not a works-salvation; it has to do with aligning with Christ. Even a criminal on a cross may align with Christ and enter into paradise with Jesus on that very day (Luke 23:40-43).

The other side of this two-way gospel is that if Israel does not identify with Jesus as the Christ, they will be destroyed.[23] The cursing of the fig tree in Luke 13:1-9 argues for the Deuteronomistic curses to be implemented upon unrepentant Israel. However, this is the bad news, not the gospel, and Marv Pate and I developed this extensively in our book so there is no need to do so again.[24]

The kingdom encroaches into the present kingdom way. The most obvious way to see this present encroachment of the kingdom is in the miracles that surround the King. The jubilee of eschatological reversal, as seen in Jesus' miracles, is provided as attesting evidence to identify Jesus as this King. For example, in the midst of Luke's emphasis on miracles, when John's disciples come to Jesus to ask him if he is the King, he quotes Isaiah 61:1-2 and then turns their focus on the miracles (Luke 7:21-22). The issue here is the identification of Jesus, because a person is blessed if he can keep from stumbling over him. Jesus demonstrated through his miracles that he had divine authority as the King, the Holy Son of God sent from God. The variety of miracles[25] show his dominant authority as an expression of the kingdom wherever the King is present. Immediately following Luke's emphasis on the miracles, Jesus asks the disciples who they consider that he is. They identify that the people at that time understand him to be a prophet,

23. Sanders, *Jews in Luke-Acts*, 189-90.

24. Pate and Kennard, *Deliverance Now and Not Yet*, 304-9, 312-19, 402-20, 433-61.

25. His authority is demonstrated by: (1) he cast out demons (Luke 4:33-36; 6:18, 33; 9:42-43; 11:14); (2) he healed the sick (Luke 4:40-41; 5:24; 6:8-10, 18-19; 7:8-10; 8:43-48; 13:13; 18:41-43); (3) he cleansed lepers (that is, going beyond healing to cleansing them from their uncleanness as well, Luke 5:12-13; 17:11-14); (4) he accomplished nature miracles like a catch of fish, calming a storm, and feeding the multitude (Luke 5:6-9; 8:24; 9:13-17); and (5) he resurrected others (Luke 7:16; 8:52:-56). A good discussion of these issues from the view of the historical Jesus is presented in Meier, *Marginal Jew*, 2:509-970.

but Peter at least recognizes Jesus to be the King (Luke 9:19-20). At the triumphal entry the people also recognize him to be the King because of his miracles (Luke 19:37).

A further expression of the eschatological reversal encroaching into time is that the status of intimate family with Jesus is taken from Jesus' mother and brothers and given to those who hear and apply the word of God to do it (Luke 8:18-21).

The two-ways strategy shows itself most blatantly in the mimetic atonement of *imitatio Christi*.[26] The first mention of Jesus' death in the Gospel of Luke is quickly followed by the charge to the disciples that they cannot try to save their lives, for authentic discipleship puts them at risk for daily martyrdom, even by a scandalous cross (Luke 9:22-26). The cost of discipleship under Jesus became severe with: itinerancy, endurance of tribulation, daily heading for martyrdom, and being unswayed by one's family (Luke 14:25-35; 21:19). If a disciple is ashamed of Jesus and his words, then Jesus will be ashamed of him when the Son of Man comes in his glory as the King to reign (Luke 12:8-9). Instead, the disciple should seek the kingdom and strive to enter by the narrow door; this way brings intimacy of being known by the Lord (Luke 12:31-34; 13:23-35).

Within this two ways, authentic conversion shows itself by identifying whole heartedly with Christ. For example, when Jesus called Matthew to follow him, Matthew hosted a great feast for a great number of tax collectors (Matt 9:9-13; Luke 5:27-32). Jesus explains to the Pharisees why he joined such festivities with tax collectors and sinners, as he is calling those who understand that they need Jesus as a physician for their condition. In contrast, one Pharisee hosted Jesus for a meal but he provided no foot washing, greeting, or kiss (Luke 7:36, 44-45). However, a sinful woman[27] crashed the meal to weep and anoint Jesus' feet with her tears, expensive dowry oil, and kisses, wiping Jesus' feet with her hair. Jesus identified that she loved Jesus much so her sins, which were many, were forgiven (Luke 7:47, 50). Likewise, Zacchaeus, the short chief tax collector of the Jericho region, wished to see Jesus so he climbed a tree on Jesus' route (Luke 19:1-10). Jesus noticed him there and announced that he must stay at his house. When the crowd complained that Jesus had chosen to stay with a sinner, Zacchaeus spoke up, "Lord I give half of my goods to the poor; and if I have taken wrongly from anyone, I restore fourfold." Jesus responded, "Today salvation has come to

---

26. Pate and Kennard, *Deliverance Now and Not Yet*, 461-67 continuing the dominant Jewish tradition of mimetic atonement during Second Temple Judaism (29-57).

27. Mary Magdala is introduced in Luke 8:2; she is not this unidentified forgiven woman of Luke 7:36-50 as Gregory the Great first proposed in A.D. 591.

this house, because he also is a son of Abraham; for the Son of Man has come to seek and save that which was lost."

Two-ways salvation is also shown by how one identifies with the disciples' ministry. Only those who follow Jesus and identify with those following Jesus are fit for the kingdom (Luke 9:10, 57–62; 11:23). The acceptance of the disciples' ministry is an acceptance of Jesus and God (Luke 10:9–16). So Luke's Gospel ends with a great commission for disciples to proclaim in Jesus' name repentance for the forgiveness of sins (Luke 24:47). This very message sets up the second volume, the book of Acts, which continues the saga.

PETER'S GOSPEL SERMONS IN ACTS

Luke has recorded four of Peter's gospel presentations in Acts, and I have correlated these to surface the Petrine pattern of the gospel (Acts 2:14–39; 3:12–26; 3:8–12; 10:34–43). It is amazing how similar the pattern is in light of these messages emerging from very different situations, with different amounts of time, and being heard by rather different groups. This either shows that Peter was consistent with his presentation of gospel or it shows Luke's selectivity, only recording that portion of what Peter said that Luke wishes to emphasize as gospel. Either way, these sermons become authoritative gospel statements (on Peter and Luke's authority or merely on Luke's authority). The chart on the following page summarizes these sermons.

The gospel begins with an introduction transitioning from the circumstances at hand to the person of Jesus. These circumstances are as varied as the Spirit has poured out, or a man has been healed, or they are on trial, or the fact of Jewish exclusivity, when a Gentile requests Peter's salvation message. This introduction with its variety bridges to the person of Jesus.

The focus of the gospel message is that the person of Jesus is the one who you will have to deal with in kingdom salvation. Each sermon develops this theme a little differently, but the commonality places the focus on Jesus and whether the audience aligns with him. For example, Acts 2 develops that Jesus is the promised Davidic King (Acts 2:30 quoting 2 Sam 7:12–13) announced as the Anointed One to be King by God (Acts 2:36), and functioning in this exalted Christ role as receiving and giving the Holy Spirit (Acts 2:33). While in this context "lord" (κύριος) stands for the Davidic King and Deity, as a term it was also appropriated by the Caesars (Augustus, Tiberius, Caligua, Nero and Domitian) and the Jewish rulers (Herod the Great, Agrippa I and Agrippa II).[28] Contrary to these others, Acts 2 demon-

---

28. Bietenhard, "Lord, Master," in *DNTT*, 2:511; Cullmann, *Christology of the New Testament*, 197–99; Suetonius, *De Vita Caesarum* 13.2; the title was also used to describe

strates Jesus is the Lord (Davidic King and God). The Lord concept of this Acts 2:36 reference is elevated by the quote from Psalm 110:1 in Acts 2:34, which takes the אֲדֹנִי/*Adonai* as "Lord" (κύριος) in referring to Christ. However, in Acts 2:34 the κύριος also translates Psalm 110:1 יְהוָה/*Yahweh*, which draws Jesus' divinity within a Jewish monotheism as part of the gospel as well, whereas in Acts 3 Jesus serves many roles, including healer, forgiver, ἀρχηγὸν (the prince or leader of life), the prophet after Moses' pattern, and the one who will bring in the kingdom. For a more hostile audience, on trial Jesus is presented as the only savior for physical and spiritual healing (use of σῳζω in Acts 4:9 and 12). For a receptive Gentile audience, Jesus is presented as the Lord and Judge of all, who also heals (Acts 10:38, 42). So the focus of Peter's gospel statement is the person of Jesus Christ (as the one that they have to deal with in their salvation), rather than an event that this person does. Reception of the gospel entails aligning oneself with this Jesus as King and Savior.

The kind of salvation that Peter offers the Jews is forgiveness of their sins and the gift of the Holy Spirit, with the outcome that the kingdom would then come[29] (Acts 2:38; 3:19–21). This retains the kingdom relationship that John the Baptist and Jesus maintained of the kingdom, forgiveness, and the Spirit. The main sin that Peter identified that these first-century Jews were involved with is that of killing Christ (Acts 2:23; 3:18–19). Presumably, it is this sin of killing Christ that they must repent from as they align themselves with Christ. When they repent, Luke reports that they believe the message (Acts 4:4). When the Jewish leaders are addressed by Spirit-filled Peter, they are offered a salvation that includes physical as well as spiritual salvation (use of σῳζω in Acts 4:9, 12). This also identifies Peter's gospel with the kingdom message that Jesus had maintained in Luke's Gospel.

Salvation offered to the Gentile proselytizers in Cornelius' house had the same outcome of forgiveness and the Holy Spirit (Acts 10:43–44). However, no specific sin was mentioned, so they are not called to repent but rather to believe in Jesus as the Christ. So Luke's record of Peter's preaching reserves repentance for those who had shown some rebellion previously, while those, like Cornelius, who are heading toward God, responsive to his revelation, are called to believe in the gospel message that helps them to know it a bit more specifically.

These salvation messages do not develop any efficaciousness of the death of Christ for sins. Rather, in Peter's gospel presentations the death

---

gods (1 Cor 8:5); Deissmann, *Light from the Ancient East*, 352–53.

29. For the defense of the interpretation of this clause see Kennard, *Classical Christian God*, 202.

Peter's Gospel Sermons in Acts

	Made to Jewish populace		To Jewish leaders	To Gentiles
Introduction	Acts 2:14–40 Spirit poured forth	Acts 3:12–26 God healed the man	Acts 4:8–12 If on trial for healing	Acts 10:28–43 Neither God nor I am partial
Focus	Jesus is declared to be Davidic King	Jesus is the healer, forgiver, prince or leader, the prophet, and the One Who brings in kingdom	Jesus is savior (physical and spiritual healing)	Jesus, the Lord and Judge of all, enabled by Spirit did good and healed all sick
Attestation	God attested to Jesus by signs and predetermined His death	God glorified Servant by miracle	Miracle done in Jesus name	God anointed him with powerful Spirit to do miracles
Death	You Jews killed Jesus by Lawless (Romans) men	You Jews ignorantly disowned him to death	You Jews crucified him	Jews killed him
Resurrection	God raised him	God raised him	God raised him	God raised him
Evidence	Prophecy required Jesus resurrection because he is the Davidic king	All prophets spoke of Jesus suffering and reign in kingdom, which includes healing	Prophecy of your Jews rejection and God's choosing him	Prophets witness to salvation thru Jesus and we witness to the fact of His resurrection
Salvation	Repent for forgiveness of sins and the gift of the Spirit, and each be baptized	Repent so kingdom may come	Salvation only in the name of Jesus	Believe and receive forgiveness of sins
	Cut off by Sadducees and temple guard			Cut off by Spirit and salvation

of Christ is a historical fact of which many in the audience are aware and it also shows the culpability of the Jews of that generation as killing Christ (Acts 2:23; 3:14–15, 17; 4:10; 10:39). Notice that I am not saying that Peter does not believe Jesus' death to be efficacious for sins; he clearly does (1 Pet 2:24), however, he does not see the need to mention this fact in his statement of the gospel as Luke has clearly repeatedly shown. This means that the efficaciousness of the death of Christ is not an essential component to be mentioned when the gospel is stated (for Peter and Luke do not mention it). They treat the death of Christ as indicating first-century Jewish culpability. In Acts 2:23 there is an admission that "lawless men" were involved in Christ's death, which probably shows culpability as violators of the Law but probably alludes to Roman involvement. Also, God determined Christ's death as well.[30] Additionally, in Acts 3:17 Peter identified that the Jewish people and their rulers acted in ignorance, not knowing Jesus to be the Prince of Life, whom they will have to deal with in their salvation. However, this ignorance does not remove their culpability for their rebellion and killing of Christ. Notice that I am not saying the anti-Semitic statement that all Jews of all time are Christ-killers; I am merely saying that a particular group within a generation of Jews is clearly indicated to be culpable for their rejection and killing of Christ. Peter sees that this is an important thing to say in all of his gospel statements that Luke records, even when Peter is not talking to Jews (Acts 10:39).

In Acts 3:13 and 26 the word παῖδα refers to Jesus as "Son" or "Servant." Traditionally, many import vicarious atonement into this text by connecting this term with Isaiah's Servant Songs.[31] In verse 13 the meaning of παῖδα could be either "Servant" or "Son," though the context refers to Jesus' death without any development except Israel's culpability. Rather, what is developed in this context is that God glorified his παῖδα Jesus, whom Israel had culpably killed. God's assessment of Jesus is that he is the Holy and Righteous One, the Prince of Life. There is no atoning Servant development; rather there is regal honor, which would be better associated with a translation of παῖδα as "Son." In verse 26 παῖδα is referred to as the resurrected one to bless Israel by turning them from their wicked ways. Resurrection is not clearly developed in Isaiah 53, but there is some ambiguous continuing of the Servant so that he could be allotted a portion with the great and divide booty with the strong after the Servant's atoning death (Isa 53:12). However, nowhere in this or any other Petrine gospel statement in Acts is there a clear

---

30. At least since the commentary of Holtzmann, *Apostelgeschte*, 34–37, commentators have commented upon the sharp juxtapositioning of the human free will and the divine determinism to kill Christ.

31. Pate and Kennard, *Deliverance Now and Not Yet*, 433–81.

connection of Jesus' death as Isaiah's Servant atonement. Here παῖδα can be understood as in verse 13 as better referring to Jesus as God's Davidic Son, who in his reign will bless Israel in turning them from their wicked ways (Acts 3:26). In fact, if we let the previous Petrine sermon influence our hermeneutical choice, παῖδα should be understood as "Son," in that "Jesus is the Davidic Messiah" is the core of the previous sermon (Acts 2:22–36). At this point Bruce chimes in and appeals to: (1) Phillip's encounter with the Ethiopian eunuch and (2) the Acts 4 prayer.[32] In Acts 4:25 παιδός is often translated as "Servant" because David is faithfully providing revelation, but it could be understood as an allusion that he is the King, "God's Son." The critical παῖδά reference comes in Acts 4:27 as referring to Jesus as "God's Son" the King, to whom Psalm 2:1–2 refers. Psalm 2 defines παῖδά as Son, referring to the messianic Christ rather than connecting it with Isaiah 53. Thus, the point in Acts 3:13 is the same as the core of the previous Acts 2 sermon and the following prayer παῖδά reference, namely, that Jesus is glorified as the Davidic King, thus Israel is culpable in their killing of their Messiah. Likewise, the elevated role to bless Israel in Acts 3:26 fits wonderfully within this theme of Jesus ascending in honor as the Davidic Messiah to bless with salvific blessings like the giving of the Spirit (Acts 2:33–36). Therefore, I take παῖδα in Acts 3:13 and 26 as referring to "Son" in a messianic sense here, since there is no near-context development for Isaiah's Servant imagery, and there is in both sermons near-context evidence for Jesus as Davidic Messiah. In a broader biblical theological argument, there is also a dominant emphasis of Jesus as the King with whom they will have to deal in Petrine and Lukan salvation sermons as well. So, once again, neither Peter nor Luke develop any soteriological accomplishment in Jesus' death, rather, they merely say that first-century Israel is culpable.

The statements of Christ's death are quickly followed by a resurrection statement vindicating Jesus as the Christ, for God raised him up (Acts 2:24–32; 3:13, 15; 4:10; 10:40). Taken together, the Jewish culpability shows their rebellion, and God's victory through resurrection shows that this generation of Jews are in a very precarious condition of cursing themselves under the Abrahamic and Mosaic covenants (Acts 3:22–26).[33]

32. Bruce, "Speeches in Acts," 60–61. On 61–62 Bruce continues his appeal with the phrase "hanging on a tree" (ξύλου) in Acts 5:30 and 13:29, which he sees must carry a vicarious atonement meaning, but this does not follow from his good point from Deut 21:22 that Jesus death is an experience of curse by hanging on a tree. Most other individuals who experienced this Deuteronomic curse were criminals with no development of an efficaciousness of Christ's death developed. Jesus is certainly viewed by the Jews who killed him to be a criminal (guilty of heresy) and thus to be cursed in this way.

33. Pate and Kennard develop this Deuteronomistic curse on Israel in the first century and in the Great Tribulation in our book *Deliverance Now and Not Yet*.

Each of Peter's gospel statements is also accompanied by two forms of evidence to prompt faith: that of (1) the Spirit-orchestrated healings and (2) the prophetic fulfillment for Jesus. The Spirit-orchestrated healings include the recollection of the miraculous attestation from Jesus' ministry (Acts 2:22; 10:38–39) as well as the continuing empowerment of healing among the apostles (Acts 3:1–12, 16; 4:9). This healing from Jesus' ministry is taken to be an aspect of the fulfillment of prophecy (the repetition τέρατα [from LXX Joel 3:3 {English: Joel 2:30}] and σημεῖα [not in the LXX of Joel but added by Peter or Luke in their quoting of Joel] in Acts 2:19, 22). However, the fulfillment of prophecy extends to a range of other evidence, including that: (1) Jesus would be the Mosaic prophet and the Davidic King, (2) Jesus would be rejected by the Jewish leadership, (3) Jesus would resurrect, (4) the Spirit would be poured out and cause the tongues phenomena at Pentecost, and (5) the whole world would be blessed by Jesus' kingdom ministry (Acts 2:16–22, 24–36; 3:21–25; 4:11; 10:43). There is no gospel statement that Peter mentions without including a mention of both healings and fulfillment of prophecy.

A favorable response to the gospel message is shown not just in faith or repentance, but also in immediately being baptized if they are able (Acts 2:41; 10:47). This follows the pattern of proselytizing into Judaism[34] and John the Baptist's baptism for repentance and the identification with a Judaism aligned with the kingdom (Luke 3:3–6). In the gospel presentation of Acts 3, Peter and John are taken captive by the temple guard, so that this response does not occur. In fact, in Acts 2:38 Peter develops the response to the gospel as follows: (1) you all repent (μετανοήσατε, second-person plural); (2) each be baptized (βαπτισθήτω, second person singular) in the name of Jesus Christ (3) for your all forgiveness of sins (εἰς ἄφεσιν τῶν ἁμαρτιῶν ὑμῶν, second-person plural); and (4) you all shall receive the Holy Spirit (λήμψεσθε, second-person plural). The order leaves it quite clear that their responsibility is to repent and be baptized as they identify with Jesus and this gospel. The third and fourth features are divine benefits given to them in response to their repentance and baptism. The εἰς clause indicates that baptism also heads toward the outcome of their forgiveness of sins. That is, the first two are their responsibility and the second two are the divine benefits. However, the fact that the first, third, and fourth are plural while the command to be baptized is singular tends to pull the plurals together as referring to the same thing: repent for forgiveness and the Holy Spirit. The

---

34. Josephus, *J.W.* 2.150; *Ant.* 14.285; 18.93–94; 18.117; *T. Levi* 2.3.1–2; *Sib. Or.* 4.162–70; Epictetus, *Dissertationes* 2.9.19–20; *Apoc. Moses* 29.6–13; *b. Yebam.* 46a-48b; *Midrash Sifre Num.* 15.14; *m. Tohar* 7.6; *t. Yoma* 4.20; *t. Pesaḥ* 7.13; 1QS 3.3–9; 4QTLevi ar; *m. Para* 8.10; S.v. "βαπτίζω," *NIDNTT* 1(1975) 144–145; Witherington, *Acts*, 155.

second-person singular of the command to be baptized makes this feature an attending circumstance to these others: indicate your repentance and involvement with this salvation by baptism. Additionally, the statements come in pairs: the first command is the essence but it is seen or evidenced in the second command. So repentance is seen in a person's baptism. Likewise, their forgiveness is evidenced in the manifestation of the Spirit of God upon them. In Cornelius' household Peter calls them to believe for their reception of forgiveness, and the Spirit manifests the kind of tongues that he had done at Pentecost. This Spirit manifestation shows that they had embraced the authentic salvation (Acts 10:43–46; 11:14–17). It follows then from this that baptism is not critical like a work to obtain forgiveness, but Peter had them quickly baptized as a further evidence of their faith, seeing that the divine authentication of their salvation had been given through the Spirit's manifestation. So whether baptism occurs before or after salvation begins is not as critical as to keep it close to this beginning. Luke records another instance in which Phillip had expressed the gospel and the people of Samaria had believed and been baptized, identifying them with this gospel message, but these Samaritans did not receive the Holy Spirit until Peter came and laid hands upon them (Acts 8:12–17). In these instances, the baptism of the Holy Spirit evidences that authentic salvation includes them, while their water baptism pictures this inclusion as an act of obedience identifying them with the authentic salvation.

In the Petrine portion of Acts, the narrow way continuing toward salvation is anecdotally present, unlike the clear statement of the way toward salvation and the reverse way toward damnation in 2 Peter 1:5–11 and 2:1–22, or as the Gospel of Luke developed the two ways. On the positive side, Peter refers to Jesus as the ἀρχηγὸν, the role of "pioneer" or "Prince," who leads the way and blazes the trail for others to follow into salvation life (Acts 3:15).[35] However, in the Petrine section of Acts this two-ways or *imitatio Christi* salvation way is more apparent through the broad way of curse. For example, Peter's curse of Judas with two imprecatory psalms in Acts 1:20 is best seen as an apostasy on Judas' part toward damnation (Luke 22:22; also the passing of Judas portion [κλῆρον] to Matthias in Acts 1:17, 26; cf. Matt 26:24–25; Mark 14:21; and his association with Satan in John 13:27). Likewise, Ananias and Saphira apostatized to the love of money and personal honor rather than practically loving others, and the Spirit killed them (Acts 5:1–11). In this perspective, these three (Judas, Ananias, and Saphira) did not continue toward salvation but were damned. Similarly,

---

35. Elsewhere in the NT taken in this same way in Heb. 2:10; 12:2; Lampe, "Lucan Portrait of Christ," 167; Bruce "Speeches in Acts," 61.

Peter threatened Simon the magician with damnation when he tried to buy the power to bestow the Holy Spirit (Acts 8:20, where Peter says, "May your silver and you go to hell" [τὸ ἀργύριόν σου σὺν σοὶ εἴη εἰς ἀπώλειαν]).[36] This last situation adds an interesting spin since Simon is said by Luke to have believed and been baptized (Acts 8:13), and yet here Peter threatened him with destruction. This view is even more acute if Ireneaus' and Hippolytus' traditions of Simon are true, since in these extra-biblical traditions Simon opposes Peter and the gospel and Simon dies trying to show that he could also bring himself back from the dead.[37] The narrow-way quality for Peter's gospel will be developed further in a later chapter on Petrine redemption as the way to the kingdom. This two-ways view is more apparent in Jesus' teaching in the Gospel of Luke and in the Lukan comments around Paul's gospel presentations.

PHILIP'S EVANGELISM

The gospel that Philip communicates is summarized as "proclaiming Christ" and "the good news about the kingdom of God and the name of Jesus Christ" (Acts 8:5, 12, 35). Notice again the kingdom emphasis of the gospel here. Such a gospel came with miracles to corroborate it (Acts 8:12) and was followed by baptism as well (Acts 8:13, 36). However, Philip could not provide the Holy Spirit like the apostles did when they came to see his new converts. Thus, with Peter giving the Spirit, Philip's gospel is completed in the Lukan pattern.

When Philip is sent to the Gaza road, the Ethiopian eunuch is reading from Isaiah 53, so Philip preaches Jesus to him (Acts 8:26–36). This whole Servant Song wonderfully unpacks the meaning of Christ's vicarious atonement probably more fully than any other biblical passage. However, Luke does not quote or develop any of those portions of the Servant Song. Luke quotes instead a section on the silent martyrdom of Jesus in his death so that one can recognize Isaiah's Servant. In this context, Philip preached Christ, but with no development of the efficacy of Jesus' death. Instead, this gospel expression merely connects Jesus with a recognizable martyrdom death. The dominant Jewish interpretation available at this time was the view of mimetic atonement.[38] However, if we let the few strands that we have of Philip's gospel fill in the message, it does so by focusing on the kingdom

---

36. Bruce, *Acts*, 184 n. 37.

37. Irenaeus, *Haer.* 1. 23.1–5; Hippolytes, *Homily of Clement* 7.9; *Acts of Peter* 4–28.

38. Kennard, *Messiah Jesus*, 269–91; Pate and Kennard, *Deliverance Now and Not Yet*, 29–58, 433–468.

(Acts 8:12). Additionally, if we let Luke's emphasis fill in the gospel message, the vicarious atonement is not emphasized but rather a martyrdom that demonstrates Jesus the Servant was killed by rebellious Jews but God raised him because he is the King. Either way, we are left with Luke intentionally not developing the vicarious atonement present in the Isaiah context. That is, Luke goes out of his way to avoid developing vicarious atonement here.

PAUL'S GOSPEL SERMONS IN ACTS

Luke develops Paul's gospel seven times in the book of Acts (Acts 13:16–48; 14:15–17; 16:31; 17:22–32; 18:3–6; 19:1–7; 20:21). Two of these statements are merely summaries. For example, in Acts 16:31 Paul's gospel is summarized as, "Believe in the Lord Jesus and you shall be saved." Likewise, in Acts 20:21 Luke records that Paul solemnly testifies to "repentance toward God and faith in our Lord Jesus Christ." Both these summaries join with the sermons in emphasizing that the focus of Paul's gospel is to *believe in Jesus as the Christ*. These sermons are summarized in chart form, presented on the following page.

Each gospel presentation begins with a transition to move Paul's audience to consider the good news. To Jews in a synagogue, this entailed a brief history of Israel from exodus to the Davidic King to the one proclaimed by John the Baptist (Acts 13:16–25). To Jewish followers of John the Baptist the transition was more direct, finding out whether they had received the gift of the Holy Spirit (Acts 19:2–3). To Gentile audiences, the transition connected with their ignorant practice of idolatry and tried to move them first to a worship of the monotheistic God who creates everything (Acts 14:15; 17:22–24).

To a Gentile audience the gospel partakes of two foci: (1) *God is the book of everything*; and (2) *Jesus is the one with whom you will have to deal for salvation*. For example, at Lystra Paul healed a man lame from birth and the people informed by the Phrygian tradition, the gods Zeus and Hermes being among them,[39] wished to offer sacrifices, presuming Paul to be the spokesman Hermes and Barnabus to be the king god Zeus (Acts 14:8–18). Trying to restrain them from this pagan practice, Paul and Barnabus identified that they were merely human and there to preach the gospel to turn their audience from vain pagan sacrifice to the God who created everything and sustains everything by his providence. The audience would not listen to the rest of the gospel and instead, agitated by Jews, stoned Paul (Acts 14:18–19).

---

39. Ovid, *Metam.* 8.618–724 identifies how Zeus and Hermes rewarded Baucis and Philemon for their hospitality and destroyed everyone else in Phrygia through a flood.

	To Jews & God fearers	To Gentiles	Summary
Acts	13:16–48	14:15–17	16:31
Introduction	Israel's history from exodus to Davidic King	We are not gods	Summary
Focus	Jesus declared to be the Davidic King and Savior	God creates all	
Attestation	John announced him as Davidic King	Rain and seasons attest to God	
Death	Rebellious Jewish rulers killed Jesus		
Resurrection	God raised him		
Evidence	We saw him repeatedly & prophecy of Davidic King guarantees resurrection		
Salvation	Believe Jesus as King & Savior brings about salvation, forgiveness of sins & freedom beyond which the Law provided		All who believe in Lord Jesus will be saved
Warning of Judgment	Prophecy warns scoffers will perish		
Jewish Response	Jews repudiate gospel, judging selves as unworthy		
Gentile Response	We turn to Gentiles; all elect Gentiles to everlasting life believe		

JESUS AS GOSPEL

To Gentiles	To Jews	Disciples of John	Summary
17:22–32	18:3–6	19:1–7	20:21
In ignorance, you made monument to an unknown God		Did you receive H.S.?	
God is book of all & doesn't need our service. He sets boundaries so we would seek him	Jesus is the Davidic King	Is the one to which John pointed	
Temples are not needed & don't reflect the Divine Nature who created & surrounds us			
God gives faith by this resurrection			
Repent in light of end time judgment		Baptized in Jesus name	Repentance toward God & faith in Jesus as Lord
	Warning		
	Now going to Gentiles		

In a later, more fruitful occasion at Athens, the whole gospel was heard (Acts 17:16–34).[40] The Athens context transitions from reasoning in the marketplace to that of the Agorapagus. These Agora men were known as the unemployed day laborers, loafers, and agitators in the culture.[41] There were also rival Epicurean and Stoic philosophers in the group. This was very much like a postmodern environment where rival philosophies prevailed side by side: the Epicureans were committed to the passion of happiness and the party life, while the Stoics were equally committed to the rational impassionate life that held the emotions in check.[42] Both worldviews hold that history is cyclical: the Epicurean with a circle-of-life view and the Stoic with an internal idealistic fire evident in an atomism that cycles through an evolving creation, beginning again after a cataclysm. They were interested in the novel sense of the gospel but, while viewing Paul as a "hick" (σπερμολόγος), they could not quite make out what sort of strange "deities" (δαιμονίων) he expressed. Luke reminds us that these Athenians enjoyed talking about the novel.[43] Paul shows himself to be better versed in these philosophies than the Athenians initially grant, even quoting from the

---

40. Balch, "Areoagus Speech" confirms Luke as using credible historical practices of his day by comparing it with Poisdonius and these later historians; Barrett, "Paul's Speech on the Areopagus" primarily appreciates the role of Hellenism as he compares Paul's and the Epicurean appreciation for popular religion; Gärtner, *Areopagus Speech and Natural Revelation*; Dibelius "Paul on Areopagus" analyzes the speech for a common ground in creation and providence with Hellenistic religious and philosophical views; Hemer, "Speeches in Acts II" primarily tries to show that this sermon is Pauline by connecting it with Athenian culture; Montague, "Paul and Athens"; Neyrey, "Acts 17, Epicureans, and Theodicy" compares Paul with Epicurean theodicy and has a particularly good section on providence in Paul's sermons; Porter, "Thucydides 1.22.1 and Speeches in Acts" re-evaluated the issue in favor of Bruce's previous works; Schubert, "Place of the Areopagus Speech in the Composition of Acts" helps to confirm the legitimacy of the gospel going to the Gentiles; Shields, "Areopagus Sermon and Romans 1.18ff" explores creation based theology from the positive and the negative trajectory of these texts.

41. Plato, *Protoporus*; Xenophon, *Hellenica* 6.2.23; Plutarch, *Aemilius Paullus* 38; Aristophanes, *Ranae* 1015; Theophrastus, *Char.* 4.2; Herodotus, *Persian Wars* 2.141.

42. Epicurus, frag 374; *Letter to Herodotus*, 37, 50; Hicks, *Epicurus Principle Doctrines*, 23 accessed April 16, 2014, http://Classics.mit.edu/Epicurus/princdoc.html; Diogenes Laertius, *Lives of Eminent Philosophers*, 10.33. Diogenes Laertius, *Vit.* 7.87–89; Marcus Aurelius Antoninus, *Med.* 3.11; 4.4, 40; 7.55; 11.1; Chrysippus in Cicero, *De Natura Deorum*, 1; Graver, *Stoicism and Emotion*; Allen, *Philosophy for Understanding Theology*, 66–69; Kennard, *Critical Realist's Theological Method*, 10–11; "πῦρ," in TDNT 6:928–45.

43. This statement in Acts 17:21 is similar to what the 5th-century politician and general Cleon said, "You are the best people at being deceived by something new that is said," Thucydides, *Hist.* 3.38.5; Demosthenes, *Phil.* 1.10.

Stoic poet Aratus of Soli (Acts 17:28)[44] and the Epicurean doctrine that God needs nothing from men (Acts 17:25).[45] Paul shows his ample awareness of these philosophies by also polemicing them. However, Paul begins with their common ground, that of their public religion. Since the Areopagus was next to the dominating Acropolis, the temples to Athena and Zeus were visible, but Paul does not start with their public idolatry since some of these philosophical types downplayed this popular religion. Paul instead calls attention to about a dozen small monuments about three feet high that had been left from when a plague had been averted by extreme measures. Diogenes Laertius tells the story[46] that the plague could not be lifted by offering sacrifices to any of the known gods of Athens, so Nicholas was sent to Crete to get Epimenides for advice. Epimenides obtained a flock of white and black sheep, which he released all over Mars Hill, with men marking where any sheep laid down after a night with no food. He interpreted this to be a god's willingness to help. So they sacrificed every sheep on an altar where it had lain and the plague was lifted.[47] So as Paul appealed to this bit of popular culture it already showed the impotence of the Athenian gods and the greatness of this unknown God. It was part of their culture owned by them but the fact that it was admittedly unknown allowed for Paul to fill out the concept. He begins with the major Gentile gospel foci: God creates everything and thus does not dwell in temples. This terminology polemics the Stoic pantheistic concept of God with that of a personal theistic God, who creates and judges all.[48] Paul treats the concept of God to entail part of the design plan recognized from empirical knowledge of the creation, so humans are culpable if they do not honor him as God, and this very condition of dark futile thinking by those who deny God is in fact part of the present experience of the wrath of God upon them (Rom 1:19–21, 24, 26).[49] This shows that Paul's Jewish-Christian concept of God is personal

44. Aratus of Soli, *Phaenomena* 7; Hemer, "Speeches in Acts II," 243–44.

45. Euripides, *Heracles*, 1345–6; Plato, *Euthyphro* 14c; Bruce, *Acts*, 357.

46. Diogenes Laertius, *The Lives of Eminent Philosophers*, 1.110; Plato, *Laws* also prophesied that ten years into the future a Persian army would attack and return home frustrated, after suffering more wars than they inflict. As a result of this prophecy, Epimenides asked as his payment to be a treaty between Athens and Knosses. Additionally, the inscribed altars to an unknown god are also mentioned in: Pausanias, *Description of Greece*, 1.1 and 4; cf. Philosttus, *Appolanius of Tyana*.

47. Neyrey ("Acts 17, Epicureans, and Theodicy") compares at length this sermon's treatment of theodicy and those of Epicurean philosophers.

48. Paul uses the very stoic terminology (τὸν θεόν) for the Divine (Epictetus 2.20.22) but transforms it into a Personal God who creates and judges; Hemer, "Speeches in Acts II," 244.

49. Most early Judaisms do not maintain natural knowledge of God, so this is a

and cares about humans as his offspring rather than being an unmoved impersonal idol (Acts 17:28–29).[50] This concept also polemics a god who is unconcerned about human affairs as the Epicureans held,[51] because the Christians' God cares about humans in that he created humans and rescued them from the plague. God created every kind of person, and set our times and our boundaries, so that we would have a purpose of seeking him. This orients a person to a soteriological way of searching for God even though this transcendent God is also immanent to each of us. The divine imminence and superintending is shown even by their own poets, who admit "We are his offspring." From the realization that humans are the offspring of God, idolatry does not make sense, for the divine nature must be superior to idols since human nature surely is. "Therefore having overlooked the times of ignorance God is now declaring to men that all everywhere should repent" (Acts 17:30). This is about as far as Paul can go with common ground. Next, Paul woos the cyclical worldviews of Epicureanism and Stoicism toward his testimony for a Judeo-Christian linear history consisting of creation unto the kingdom (Acts 17:26, 31). This life heads toward judgment before this Creator God and his mediator, Jesus. With this shift, the second foci of the gospel emerges within the gospel to Gentiles: that Jesus is the one that they will have to deal with in this judgment. In this, God furnished proof or, more literally, "prepared faith" (πίστιν παρασχὼν) for all men by raising

---

novel Pauline idea in his context (Bietenhard. "Natürliche Goetteserkenntnis der Heiden?: Eine Erwägung zu Röm 1"; Jewett, *Romans*, 154; design plan fits Plantinga, *Warrant and Proper Function*, 6–17; Scott, *Paul's Way of Knowing*, 15–23, especially 18). Unfortunately Ian universalizes moral lack of knowing God as a noetic effect of the present human condition, rather than treating it as one of several culpable conditions (such as violating conscience and violating the Law in Rom 2–3; Jewett, *Romans*, 148–267; Fitzmyer, *Romans*, 283; Mayordomo, *Argumentiert Paulus logisch?*, 181, 228). A Stoic appeal for harmony among rivals based on creation similar to Paul's (Acts 17:26) was also made by Dio Chrysostom (*Or.* 40.35–39), including setting of seasons and boundaries (*Or.* 12.27–30; frag. 368 Th.; Balch, "Areopagus Speech," 56–57).

50. Statement that humans are the gods' offspring made by: (1) Epimenides of Crete (Clement of Alex, *Strom.* 1.14.59; (2) Aratus, *Phenomena* 5; (3) Cleanthes, *Hymn to Zeus*; (4) after Paul by Dio Chrysostom, *Or.* 12.27, 29, 39, 43, 47, 61, 75, 77; this statement is consistent with Judaism (Wis 11:15–16; 13:121–2, 10–19; 14:8–11, 27) and Christianity (Rom 1:18–25). Thus God is not far from humans (Acts 17:27; Dio Chrysostom, *Or.* 12.28). Such philosophical statements polemic an Epicurean view of gods as having human shape (Lucretius, *De Rerum Natura* 2.16583; 1090–1104; 5.146–234; Plutarch, *Stoic Rep.* 1034B; Cicero, *Nat. D.* 1.15.71; 1.27.75–77). Some Stoics also polemicized the futility of idols as empty such as Paul does (Acts 17:29; Plutarch, *Superst.* 167DE; Strabo, *Geog.* 16.2.35–39; frag. 133 Th.; Dio Chrysostom, *Or.* 12.80–81; Lucian, *Iup. Trag.* 7–12; *Gall.* 24; Balch, "Areopagus Speech," 69, 74, 78).

51. For the Epicurean view of the gods see Lucretius, *De Rerum Natura* 2.165–183; 1090–1104; 5.146–234.

Jesus from the dead. At this point the Epicurean, Stoic philosophers, and common Athenian populous held a view of the afterlife that is more ethereal in its immortality of the soul than that the bodily resurrection familiar to Paul's Christianity, so they broke off the discussion.[52] Few of these listeners came to Christ, and some, like Tertullian, reject this Athens message as not a legitimate gospel message as Peter's in Jerusalem had been.[53] However, Luke considers it to be a legitimate gospel statement and reminds us that some men and women did believe in Christ, including Dionysius the Areopagite, Damaris, and others (Acts 17:34).[54] In Luke's framework, if people can come to faith in Christ on the basis of this message then this is an authentic gospel statement.

To an audience of Jews and God-fearers in a synagogue, the focus of the gospel is directly on Jesus as the Davidic King and Savior (Acts 13:27–39; 18:5). There is no need to develop a monotheistic Creator that sustains everything, since that idea is already part of the audience's worldview. The Davidic King emphasis is especially built off the fact that God raised Jesus as a vindication, indicating that Jesus is that Davidic King (Acts 13:30–37).[55] When Paul's ministry is summed up at the end of Acts it especially underscores this christological kingdom emphasis as "preaching the kingdom of God, and teaching concerning the Lord Jesus Christ" (Acts 28:31).[56]

Prophecy permeates the gospel to Jews and God-fearers for they have the worldview to make sense of it. For example, Paul acknowledges that Moses and the Prophets predicted Jesus to suffer (Acts 26:22–23). However, Jesus' resurrection is especially the divine fulfillment of prophecy as well (Acts 13:27, 32–37). Likewise, the offer of forgiveness, everlasting life, and freedom beyond what the Law could provide is an extension of this prophetic gospel word (Acts 13:38–39, 46, 48). Furthermore, Paul appealed to prophecy to warn them not to fulfill the prophetic word as scoffers, for such scoffers live in a precarious condition (Acts 13:40–41). Unfortunately, a major group of Jews did return the next Sabbath as scoffers and blasphemers, prompting Paul to again respond with prophecy, indicating the gospel will

---

52. Hemer, "Speeches in Acts II," 244 and especially 246 discusses that classical Greek literature was not unfamiliar with resurrection (providing examples in Aeschylus *Oresteia* and *Eumides* 647–48), however, it was not a common belief.

53. Tertulian, *Praescr.* 7.22–25.

54. Eusebius, *Hist. eccl.* 3.4.10; 4.23.3. Paul Moser (*Jesus and Philosophy*, 6) presents Jesus (Luke 18:8) and Paul (Acts 17) as recognizing that humans have a volitional role in knowing and being sincerely willing to participate in God's powerful life .

55. This point is especially strong in Kilgallen, "Acts 13,38–39."

56. The conclusion of Schubert, "Final Cycle of Speeches in the Book of Acts," 16; Stanton, *Jesus and Gospel*, 46.

now be directed to a Gentile audience (Acts 13:47–49). The culpability of the Jews indicated it was time to go to the Gentiles (Acts 13:46–47; 18:6–7). Paul and Luke cite the Servant Song of Isaiah 49:6[57] and extend it from the singular (σε) to the plural (ἡμῖν) as a command from the Lord Jesus Christ in grounding Paul and Barnabus' Gentile ministry. The last line of the quote is reminiscent of Acts 1:8, "to the end of the earth." However, this line is broadly parallel to a Gentile gospel ministry. From this focus of the gospel going to Gentiles, many Gentiles responded with joy and worship, believing as God had appointed them.

This Gentile trajectory fits with Luke's trajectory in the book of Acts as a whole, in justifying that the gospel is authentically for Gentiles as well. In Paul's gospel presentations the death of Christ is almost completely absent. To a Jewish audience Paul points out that first-century Jews in Israel were culpable of putting Jesus to death (Acts 13:27–28). That is, only the first-century Jews in Israel were culpable, not the Jews he was talking with, for they become culpable on the basis of what they will do with Jesus when they hear the message (Acts 13:40–41). However, to a Gentile audience the death of Christ is mentioned only as a condition to be undone, as God resurrected Jesus (Acts 17:31). In a non-gospel defense before Agrippa, Paul describes Jesus' death and resurrection as predicted by Moses and the Prophets (Acts 26:23). However, Luke does not record any development of the gospel here, merely Paul and Agrippa's banter about the possibility of persuading Agrippa to become a Christian. In all the other gospel presentations that Luke records by Paul in Acts, the death of Christ is not mentioned at all, let alone as an efficacious element of the gospel. This is shocking to me but Luke (and maybe even Paul) must not see the death of Christ to be an essential facet of every gospel statement.[58] This is not to claim that Christ's death is not effective, for Luke records Paul as describing in a non-gospel presentation that Christ purchased the church with his blood (Acts 20:28). However, such a statement is never in Luke's statement of Paul's gospel sermons.

To a group of John the Baptist's disciples who had believed in the hope of the coming Messiah, Paul identified that Jesus is this Messiah (Acts 19:3–4). They responded by being rebaptized in Jesus' name. Paul bestowed the

---

57. The quote comes from Isa 49:6 rather than similar 42:6, because Τέθεικά is used.

58. Notice I am *not* saying that the death of Christ is not soteriologically important; it clearly is. Paul develops it elsewhere as a mystical grounding that justifies (Rom 5); Pate and Kennard, *Deliverance Now and Not Yet*, 119–267. Additionally, Luke's view has already been developed in the excurses as mimetic atonement, which is significant soteriologically in a two-ways tradition to then imitate. However, they don't find it necessary to mention the death of Christ in their repeated statements of the gospel in Acts.

Spirit upon them and they began to speak in tongues and prophecy, which in Lukan concepts identifies that they received the authentic salvation.

The most important thing included in authentic Lukan-Paul salvation is that the believer identifies with Jesus, who is the Messiah and Judge (Acts 9:5; 13:33–34; 16:31; 17:31; 19:4; 20:21; 22:8; 26:15). This has implications for seeing Jesus as Lord and permitting Jesus' lordship to be the core of the gospel. The gospel issue then becomes: *Will you submit to Jesus and his way?* Authentic salvation also entails: (1) forgiveness of sins, (2) freedom from the things that the Law could not free you from, (3) freedom from the domain of darkness and Satan, and (4) everlasting life (Acts 13:38–39,[59] 46, 48; 26:18). However, most of Paul's gospel statements in Acts do not develop these additional benefits. It is as though promising them is not as critical as identifying with Jesus. At times salvation also includes tongues and prophecy, which in these Lukan patterns identifies it as the authentic salvation (Acts 19:6).

Paul and Luke see that the appropriate response to this salvation message is to identify with it, but they use the terms for "faith" and "repentance" interchangeably as synonyms (Acts 20:21; 19:2, 4; 26:18, 20). This is parallel to Josephus' use when he confronted Jesus the Galilean brigand leader "to repent and believe in me."[60] John the Baptist, Jesus, and Peter used the term "repentance" only for the Jews in signifying *what Israel must do if Yahweh is to restore her fortunes at last*,[61] whereas Paul also used the term "repentance" of Gentiles to communicate their need to depart from their idolatry and entrapment to Satan (Acts 26:18). Paul also used the term "faith" more often and at times without "repentance" being mentioned as well (Acts 13:48; 16:31; 17:34; 18:8). N. T. Wright reminds us that both repentance and faith (in Acts) appear in contexts linking them inescapably with eschatology and the narrow way to obtain the kingdom.[62] Additionally, Paul even used the term "calling on Jesus" in prayer as the initial response in his own testimony (Acts 22:16). Occasionally, God is presented as strongly sovereign in designating this faith as dependent upon divine election (Acts 13:48).

There is a strong emphasis of this sovereign direction in Paul's salvation, for in it he is already called by the Lord to take the gospel to the Gentiles (Acts 9:15; 22:21; 26:17–20).

---

59. Kilgallen, "Acts 13,38–39."

60. Josephus, *Life* 110 in Thackery, ed., LCL, where he translates this text (1.43) as "if he would . . . prove his loyalty to me."

61. Wright, *Jesus and the Victory of God*, 249.

62. Ibid., 249–51.

Baptism is tightly connected to this initial salvation response (Acts 9:18; 10:47–48; 11:16; 16:15, 33; 18:8; 19:3–5; 22:16). This baptism is the external expression of the unseen divine reality of forgiveness, for Paul identifies that the baptism occurs *with* the washing away of sins (Acts 22:16). There is no development of chronology, only that baptism and washing away of sins are conjunctively tied, as the listeners arise and call upon Christ's name. This baptism is in Christ's name and thus might warrant a rebaptism that had not clearly identified the believer in this way (Acts 19:3–5). Paul can mention individuals identifying with salvation without mentioning baptism (Acts 13:48; 17:34; 20:21).

This salvation message brings the converts into the way of salvation, extending Jesus' way unto the kingdom from Luke's Gospel (Acts 9:2; 13:10; 16:17; 18:25–6; 19:9; 22:4; 24:14, 22). That is, in this metaphor the focus is not on a past accomplished salvation but rather on continuing toward the goal of the kingdom. This fits within the two-ways salvation previously developed in Luke. The most critical aspect that identifies one as on this the kingdom way is one's identification with Jesus as the King.

CONCLUSION

Luke's Gospel could be summarized as: (within theism) *identify with Jesus, who is* demonstrated to be *the Davidic King,* and be baptized *and you will have: forgiveness, the Holy Spirit, and the way to the kingdom.* The italicized type is the essence of Luke's gospel. The non-italicized text is resilient in many of the Lukan statements of gospel. The parenthetic statement sets up the condition within which the statement is understandable.

17

Christ's Vicarious Atonement[1]

PAUL INCLUDES CHRISTIAN BELIEVERS in Abrahamic blessing, including: justification, bestowal of the Spirit, and heirs according to the promise (Gal 3:6–8, 14, 29). Justification has some basis in the context of the Abrahamic covenant but in the Genesis 15:6 context it probably should be viewed as a *characteristic status* (Abram has believed God for many miles in his travels from Ur to the promised land and God views Abram as righteous in status; Gen 15:6; Gal 3:6; Rom 4:3, 22).[2] The promise of righteousness was realized by Abraham, the model of faith. In Genesis 15:6 Abram's response was characteristically to believe God (similar to the people in Exod 4:31 and 14:31)[3] and God "reckoned it to him as righteousness." Gerhard von Rad pioneered a new way to interpret the phrase "reckoned" as a "declaration of acceptance," meaning "acceptable status within the binding covenant configuration" (Pss 15:2; 24:4–5; Ezek 18:5–9).[4] Such a response of declaration of acceptance would reflect the context in which a priest offers a sacrifice for atonement and cleansing, and then announces to the worshipper the

---

1. Some of this chapter is a rearranging of Kennard, *Biblical Covenantalism*, 3:43–108, reprinted with permission by Wipf and Stock.

2. At this point, Jewish tradition understands Abraham to be "faithful" (Sir 44:19–20; *Jub.* 19.8–9; 23.9–10; 1 Macc 2:52; Philo, *Migr.* 127–30; *Abr.* 275–6; *Her.* 6–9; Josephus, *Ant.* 1.233–34; 4Q225 1.4; 2.1.9–11, 14; 2.7–8; 4Q226 7.1–2; CD 3.2–4; *m. Qidd.* 4.14; *m. Ned.* 3.11; de Roo, "God's Covenant with the Forefathers," in Porter and de Roo, eds., *Concept of the Covenant in the Second Temple Period*, 195–96).

3. Remember that Abraham has already traveled well over a thousand miles as an expression of faith by this time and the *waw* (ו) beginning Gen 15:6 is simply a narrative connector, rather than a conjunction of response "then."

4. Von Rad, "Faith Reckoned as Righteousness," in *Problem of the Hexateuch and Other Essays*, 125–30; Van Seters, *Abraham in History and Tradition*, 257; Jewett, *Romans*, 311.

benefits of her atonement. Such a Jewish sacrificial atonement was available before Paul's conceptions (Isa 53:5–6, 10–12; John 1:29), because Paul identifies that Christ's vicarious atonement framework for sins is something that Paul received in his context (1 Cor 15:3).[5]

Such atonement depends upon God's choice (Rom 9:11) and Abraham is simply trusting God to justify (Rom 3:27–28, 30; 4:3–5). That is, the Scriptures clarify that "Abraham believed God and it was reckoned (ἐλογίσθη) to him as righteousness" (Rom 4:3, 22; Gal 3:6; Gen 15:6).[6] Therefore, Abraham is not justified by works but by faith (Rom 4:1–3).[7] That is, Abraham is not earning (λογίζεται) his place, like a wage, through the Law (Rom 3:31; 4:4, 7, 10). This concept of reckoning is either metaphorically "taking it into account" (LXX: 2 Sam 19:44; Isa 53:3) or functions as a replacement to a commercial term, "calculate" or "put it on the account of someone" (Rom 4:4– 5; LXX: Ps 105[106]:31; Isa 53:12).[8] The term is not primarily legal in a forensic courtroom sense, but commercial or relational, "included among" in a covenantal manner.

A Reformational Pauline view would understand these pronouncements as forensic, but no law court would be making these statements in Abraham's context of obediently laying out sacrificed animals. Additionally, no law court should change the status of a sinner to that of declared righteous, producing a "legal fiction." For only an unrighteous judge violating the Law of God would pervert justice in that manner (Deut 25:1–2). Additionally, with the Law identifying the sinner as worthy of death in capital punishment (Rom 5:12; 6:23; 7:6, 9–11; 1 Cor 15:22), no judge would have the right to legally substitute another forensic representative to take the sinner's place, for even if others died in such a capital punishment within a forensic model the guilty sinner would still be under death sentence (Deut 25:2; 27:19).[9] Furthermore, Yahweh brought a covenant lawsuit upon Israel,

---

5. Dunn, "When Did the Understanding of Jesus' Death as an Atoning Sacrifice First Emerge?"; Kennard, *Messiah Jesus*, 293–332 for Jesus' messianic sacrifice.

6. 1 Macc 2:52 claims that Abraham gained credit as a righteous man by successfully negotiating trials and thus the Genesis texts aligns with Jas 2:22–24. However, such an argument is foreign to Paul.

7. The traditional understanding of this in contrast to legalistic Judaism is nicely argued by Seifrid, *Justification by Faith*.

8. Moulton and Milligan, *Vocabulary of the Greek Testament*, 377 citations of P. Oxy. 12. Nr. 1434.8 and P. Flor. 2 Nr. 123.7–10.

9. No ancient Near Eastern, Greek, or Roman law text permits a substitute to die for an individual found guilty of a capital crime. Sometimes a significant fine could be paid by the guilty person to replace capital punishment if the victim's family requested it, but such a fine would still be paid by the criminal: Exod 21:29–30; 4Q251 frag. 8 5; Beckman, *Hittite Diplomatic Texts*, p. 109, no. 18B "Treaty Between Hattusili 3 of Hatti and

casting them out of the land unto Babylonian captivity, partially for those who deserved capital punishment not being brought to justice (Isa 1:15; Jer 7:8–9). Only if the guilty could not be found could the nearest community to a murder offer a young heifer sacrifice to remove themselves beyond blood guiltiness and obtain covenantal communal forgiveness in their innocence (Deut 21:1–9). However, in Paul's framework the criminals are every human (Rom 3:23) and we are all culpable to capital punishment (Rom 5:12; 6:23; 7:6, 9–11; 1 Cor 15:22). Unlike a payment of a fine assessed in a forensic context, a death sentence is not a legal sentence another can pay to release the culpable sinner from the demands of the Law regarding his active deeds of sin. Furthermore, a law court makes its forensic declaration on the basis of the evidence of past deeds accomplished to indicate freedom from guilt within a crime. However, such an evidential approach is resisted by Paul in Romans 4:2 and 4 and replaced by a religious strategy of faith, foreign to a forensic evidential context. Such a religious or covenantal justification better fits as a priestly sacrificial atonement that cleanses a sinner.

Shifting to a covenantal priestly context, Paul contextually develops such justification interlaced with covenant and sacrificial language (Rom 3:4, 25; 4:6–8; Ps 32:1–2; 1 Cor 5:7). For example, God is "justified" as David and subsequent worshippers in the tabernacle or temple context confess their sin (Rom 3:4 citing Ps 51:4). Paul also presents that such activity involves going through (διὰ) Jesus as a priest (Rom 1:8).[10]

In Romans 4:7, Paul quotes the language of forgiveness (ἀφίμι) from penitential Psalm 32:2, in which forgiveness is repeatedly a benefit from an appropriate Levitical sacrifice (LXX: Lev 4:20, 26, 31, 35; 5:6, 10, 13, 16, 18; 16:26). The LXX extends this forgiveness of sins into the release from debt in the sabbatical year, Jubilee, and the kingdom (ἄφεσις LXX: Lev 27:18; Deut 15:1, 3; Isa 61:1; Jer 41:8, 15, 17). Paul does not emphasize forgiveness (ἄφεσις) for he only twice elsewhere identifies the new covenant redemption already accomplished in Christ as forgiveness of sins, harkening back to that accomplished in sacrifice (Eph 1:7; Col 1:14). However,

---

Ulmi-Teshhup of Tarhuntassa" 1 obv. 7'–14'; p. 119, no. 18C "Treaty Between Tudhaliya 4 of Hatti and Kurunta of Tarhuntassa" 20 ii 95–iii 20; p. 145, no. 23A "Letter from a King of Hatti to an Anatolian Ruler" 4 obv. 31–35; Roth, *Law Collections from Mesopotamia and Asia Minor*, 82; *Laws of Hammurabi* 5. Or later in Roman law a criminal under death sentence might make an appeal to the whole populous to have banishment substituted for capital punishment in *provocation ad populum*, but if granted the criminal would suffer banishment from the community. No evidence of any ancient Near Eastern law provides for an innocent person dying in place of a criminal of a capital crime to legally expunge the criminal's guilt. Furthermore, no person could stand in the place for another person (Kant, *Religion within the Limits of Reason Alone*, 66).

10. Origen, *Comm. Rom.* 14.854; Longenecker, *Romans*, 104–5.

Paul harkened forward to the new covenant realization in the kingdom in which God "takes away" (ἀφέλωμαι) Gentiles' sin (Rom 11:27 citing Isa 27:9 LXX).[11] Paul also used the gift (χαρίζομαι) of forgiveness which Christ accomplished among new covenant benefits for believers in Christ (Eph 4:32; Col 2:13; 3:13) to motivate our forgiveness of others as well (Eph 4:32; Col 3:13; 2 Cor 2:7, 10).

Similarly, "reckoning righteousness" expression occurred in response to Phinehas' priestly activity killing pagan Israeli Baal worshippers in their idolatrous sexual act (Num 25:4–8). Phinehas demonstrated righteousness (especially within the Mosaic Covenant) by accomplishing the priestly activity of atoning (כִּפֶּר; ἐξιλάσατο) for Israel's sin such that Yahweh established the everlasting priestly covenant with Phinehas' lineage (Num 25:10–13; also LXX Ps 105[106]:30). In a covenantal liturgical context, Psalm 105[106]:30–31 identified that Yahweh responded to this priestly atoning sacrifice by Phinehas as being "reckoning righteousness for all generations" (וַתֵּחָשֶׁב לוֹ לִצְדָקָה לְדֹר וָדֹר עַד־עוֹלָם; LXX Ps 105[106]:31 καὶ ἐλογίσθη αὐτῷ εἰς δικαιοσύνην εἰς γενεὰν καὶ γενεὰν ἕως τοῦ αἰῶνος). Such a priestly atonement is the same reckoning expression especially in the Greek texts comparing LXX with NT. Using this priestly imagery, "Yahweh reckoned Abraham as righteousness" (Gen 15:6 וַיַּחְשְׁבֶהָ לּוֹ צְדָקָה; καὶ ἐλογίσθη αὐτῷ εἰς δικαιοσύνην; also Rom 4:3, 9, 22 and Gal 3:6). That the same phrase[12] is used in a priestly atoning sacrifice (Ps 105[106]:31 LXX) renders it more likely that the expression "God reckoning him as righteousness" should likewise be understood in a priestly framework (Gen 15:6 LXX; Ps 105[106]:31 LXX; Rom 4:3, 9, 22 and Gal 3:6).

Such priestly pronouncements of "reckoned righteous" would be expected to be made about a worshipper who presents an appropriate sacrifice at the altar or performs some religious service (Lev 7:18). Although the discussion that followed von Rad's proposal identified that priestly use of "reckoned" usually utilized the niphal form of the verb rather than the qal form used in Genesis 15:6, Achin Behrens demonstrated that the qal form also has this meaning of "acceptable status" within the governing covenant in 2 Samuel 19:19 and Psalms 32:2.[13] Such a psalm expression (as in Psalm 32) would usually occur within the temple cult where a priest would make

---

11. This mechanism is reminiscent of the use of the word εὐαγγελίου ("good news") in the spiritual cleansing and the priest through sacrifice declaring the worshiper righteous (LXX Ps 39[40]:9).

12. In Greek the same words are used but in Hebrew similar words are also used and can fund the same basic argument. Farmer, "Patriarch Phinehas."

13. Oeming, "Ist Gen. 15.6 ein Beleg für die Anrechnung des Glaubens zur Gerechtigkeit?"; Behrens, "Gen. 15.6 und das Vorverständnis des Paulus," 329.

pronouncement to encourage the worshipper[14] (1 Sam 1:17). If proper cultic sacrifice is performed, this priestly pronouncement of "reckoned righteous" can change the status of the sinner to that of *accepted righteousness* in the prevailing covenant. Such an act of changing one's status is being developed in Paul's use of this "reckoning" metaphor. As such, Paul, in Romans 4:7–8, contextually developed the meaning of this phrase by appealing to the parallel qal statement in Psalm 32:2 reflecting this cultic context and meaning (Rom 4:3–8, 22–23; Gal 3:6). Such a sacrificial view fits within the Jewish pattern of rabbinic assessment that the priestly sacrifices offered during the Day of Atonement provide forgiveness for the worshipper concerning sins against God.[15] So we have Abraham as a pattern for all who as Gentile sinners also believe, and so we too will have righteousness "reckoned" to us on the basis of the effectiveness of the covenantal sacrifice (Rom 4:22–24, ἐλογίσθη 2 times, λογίζεσθαι). We, who did not have covenantal inclusion, being among the unrighteous because of our sins, are now included in covenantal blessings (or reckoned) among the righteous because of God's choice, Christ's priestly sacrifice, and our believing him.

Otfried Hofius argued that the first line of Romans 4:25 "παρεδόθη διὰ τὰ παραπτώματα ἡμῶν" ("who was delivered over because of our transgressions") closely aligns with LXX Isaiah cβ and also recalls LXX Isa 53:5a, both of which convey messianic atonement.[16] Hofius also argued that the second line of Romans 4:25, "He was raised because of our justification" follows the Hebrew of the MT in Isaiah 53:11, identifying justification with the Messiah's transformative righteousness for new covenant participants. This view further places justification within a covenantal sacrificial context.

In this priestly approach to justification, the believer does not earn her status by works but comes to the cult as a believer and the priest declares her acceptable on the basis of her allegiance of faith within the covenant and perhaps whatever the appropriate sacrifice would provide. Eventually an elaborate system of sacrifices developed in the Mosaic covenant but

---

14. LXX Isa 40:2 identifies "priests (ἱερεῖς) speak to the heart of Jerusalem" to identify that they are forgiven for their sins; LXX Ps 39[40]:9 priest declares good news of covenantal righteous condition; *b. Ber.* 34b; *Tg. Onq.* Lev 10:17 identifies priests bring forgiveness, which atones Israel; Anderson, *Out of the Depths*, 101–2; Bautch, *Developments in Genre between Post-Exilic Penitential Prayers and the Psalms of Communal Lament*, 1; Hägerland, *Jesus and the Forgiveness of Sins*, 164; priests declare worshipper righteous in context of sacrifice and prayer: Kraus, *Psalms 1–59*, 149; Brueggemann and Bellinger, *Psalms*, 41, 70, 86, 103, 233, 259, 290, 302, 326, 546, 560–61; deClaissé-Walford et al., *Psalms*, 79, 218, 457, 929.

15. *M. Yoma* 8.9; *y. Yoma* 8.9, 45c; *b. Yoma* 65 ab; *Sifra Ahere Mot* 8.5.

16. Hofius, "The Fourth Servant Song in the New Testament Letters," in Janowski and Stuhlmacher, eds., *Suffering Servant*, 180–81.

Christ's sacrifice provides for believers in the new covenant utilizing Mosaic covenant patterns.

Christ's sacrifice is described as "propitiation" (ἱλαστήριον, Rom 3:25), identifying what is accomplished on behalf of the people at the "mercy seat" on the Day of Atonement (ἱλαστήριον, LXX: Exod 25:17-22; 31:7; 35:12; 38:5-8; Lev 16:2, 13-15; Num 7:89; Ezek 43:14-20).[17] Framing Christ's corporate atonement accomplishment through the lens of the Day of Atonement is a profoundly *priestly accomplishment rather than a forensic declaration*[18] (especially as developed in Hebrews 9:1—10:18). Christ's atonement in a pattern of the Day of Atonement means that the whole group of believers in Christ obtain real cleansing and forgiveness as a group. Justification and atonement are not legal fiction but a priestly restoration of corporate covenantal relationship. Hebrews, John, Paul and the early church viewed Christ's death through this Jewish covenantal sacrificial model rather than a legal one, so such metaphors are not to be seen as inventions of the new perspective in Paul (Heb 9:7-28; John 1:29, 36; Rom 3:25).[19] Remember

17. 1QIsa 52:14 replaces the MT "marring" (מִשְׁחַת) with a Qal singular "I have anointed" indicating that God established the sacrifice role for his Messiah, and 1QIsa 51:5 replaces the MT first-person "my righteousness" with a third-person "His arm" also indicating messianism, also 4Q541 9.1.1.2 "he will atone" (Hengel and Bailey, "The Effective History of Isaiah 53 in the Pre-Christian Period," in Janowski and Stuhlmacher, eds., *Suffering Servant*, 101, 103, 108, 146; Fryer, "Meaning and Translation of *Hilastērion* in Romans 3:25"; Kruse, *Romans*, 187-89).

18. Kraus, *Tod Jesu als Heiligtumsweihe*, 21-32 lists six instances in pagan sacrifice (the most telling is Josephus, *Ant.* 16.182 in which a votive offering placates the wrath of God) and thirty-nine in Jewish sacrificial atonement texts (21 Torah, 5 in Ezek 43, one in Amos, 6 times in Philo, and one in the Rahlfs edition of 4 Macc 17:22, twice in Symmachus, one in *T. Sol.*); Tiwald, "Christ as Hilasterion (Rom 3:25): Pauline Theology on the Day of Atonement in the Mirror of Early Jewish Thought," in Hiecke and Nichlas, eds., *Day of Atonement*, 189-209 argues for this Jewish atonement meaning and that the temple still functioned not being abrogated by this Romans text.

19. Barn. 7-8 Jesus' death parallel to Day of Atonement and red heifer cleansing; Justin Martyr, *Dial.* 13.1-9, 40.1-4, 72.1, 111.2-3 develop Jesus' death as parallel to paschal lamb, Day of Atonement, and Isaiah 53 sacrificial lamb (Markschies, "Jesus Christ as a Man before God: Two Interpretive Models for Isaiah 53 in the Patristic Literature and Their Development" and Baley, "'Our Suffering and Crucified Messiah' [*Dial.* 111.2]: Justin Martyr's Allusions to Isaiah 53 in His Dialogue with Trypho with Special Reference to the New Edition of M. Marcovich," in Janowski and Stuhlmacher, eds., *Suffering Servant*, 332-33 and 378-79; Cyprian, *Test.* 15 Jesus' death is parallel to Jewish sacrifice, Isaiah 53, and Passover lamb; *Letter* 63.14.4 in Filium, ed., *Corpus Scriptorum Ecclesiasticorum Latinorum*. 3c: 410-11; Origen, *Comm. Jo.* 6.32-38 and Augustine, *Trin.* 4.14 or 19 and *On Forgiveness of Sins, and Baptism* 54-55 identify Jesus' death parallel to Jewish daily sacrifices; Theodoret of Cyrrhus, *Interpretation of the Letter to the Romans*, in Migne, ed., *Patrologia graeca*, 82; John Chrysostom, *Hom. Rom.* 7 in Schaff, ed., *Nicene and Post-Nicene Fathers*, 11:378; both mentioned in Thomas Oden, *Justification Reader*, 62; Origen, *Commentary on the Epistle to the Romans* 2:110

that in a Levitical sacrifice, the animal sacrificed is not declared to receive covenant curse but it averts covenant curse in atonement. Around A.D. 200, the Mishnah first identified that the scapegoat was to be pushed off a cliff,[20] whereas before this the scapegoat was simply led into the wilderness and released to fend for itself, having borne Israel's iniquities out of their camp (Lev 16:22 similar to purification/sin offering "bearing iniquity" [Lev 10:17] in atonement and forgiveness [Lev 4:20, 26, 31, 35]). So before the Mishnah comments, this atonement is vicarious but not penal. That is, even though the scapegoat had not been earlier identified to die, the sacrifice becomes part of the means to avert covenant curse to recover believers in covenant.

Such an identification of Christ's sacrifice with the Day of Atonement and a Jewish covenantal sacrificial atonement does not argue for this "propitiation" (ἱλαστήριον, Rom 3:25) to be merely an expiational covering, as was argued by C. H. Dodd.[21] Dodd's view was built on the nineteenth- and twentieth-century misunderstanding that כָּפַר/kpr was identified with Arabic *kafara*, "to cover" sin.[22] However, meaning is not determined by etymol-

---

cited in Oden, *Justification Reader*, 65; Cyril, *Catechetical Lectures* 13.3 develops Jesus' death parallel to the Day of Atonement; Eusebius, *Theoph.* 3.59, *Comm. Isa.* 2.42 on Isa 53:5-6 and 11-12, and *Dem. ev.* 3.2.61-2 develop Jesus' death as a Jewish sacrifice and sin offering (Markschies, "Jesus Christ as a Man before God: Two Interpretive Models for Isaiah 53 in the Patristic Literature and Their Development," in Janowski and Stuhlmacher, eds., *Suffering Servant*, 305, 308, 312-13); Gregory Nazianzen, *In Defense of His Flight to Pontus* 1.3-4 develops Jesus' atonement parallel to Passover; Ambrose, *Fid.* 3.11.67 parallel to Melchizedek sacrifice; Leo the Great, *Sermons* 55.3; 56.1; 59.5, 7; 68.3 parallel to daily Jewish sacrifice and Passover; Presbyterian Church of England, *Articles of the Faith, 1890*, art. 13, "Justification by Faith," in Schaff, ed., *Creeds of Christendom*, 3:918; also the abundance of early church iconography presenting Jesus as a sacrificial lamb show the profusion of Jesus' death conceived through the lens of Jewish sacrifice, for example: a third-century Roman catacomb lamb image for Christ, Jesus as lamb with cruciform halo in the apex of the dome in a 6th-century church of Ravenna, the 6th-century basilica of Saints Cosmos and Damian in Rome shows the Lamb of God on a rock surrounded by the twelve apostles as lambs indicating mimetic atonement, a 7th-century Roman altar portraying the Lamb of God on the altar with the cross, the 82nd canon of the A.D. 692 Council of Trullo affirmed Jesus was incarnate in human flesh by banning the very common practice of representing Jesus' death as a lamb, "we decree that henceforth Christ our God must be represented in his human form but not in the form of the ancient lamb," Schaff, ed., *Nicene and Post-Nicene Fathers*, 14:401; Sanday and Headlam, *Romans*, 122-24.

20. M. *Yoma* 6.4; *Bar.* 7.7, 9; perhaps by analogy from *Oedipus Rex* 1290-93.

21. Dodd, "HILASKESTHAI, Its Cognates, Derivatives, and Synonyms in the Septuagint," 360; Thornton, "Propitiation or Expiation?," 54-55; Campbell, *Rhetoric of Righteousness in Romans 3:21-26*, 188-89.

22. Kurtz, *Sacrificial Worship of the Old Testament*, 67-71; Janowski, *Sühne als Heilsgeschehen*, 20-22; Stamm, *Erlösen und Vergeben im alten Testament*, 61-66; Elliger, *Leviticus*, 71.

ogy; meaning is determined by use.[23] Richard Averbeck claims that such an etymology is confused when compared to other options, like the Hebrew piel stem and Akkadian D stem.[24] For example, in Genesis 32:20 כִּפֶּר/*kpr* does not mean "cover" the face, since the face of Esau is immediately seen by Jacob. Instead, כִּפֶּר/*kpr* or *kipper* is probably better related to כֹּפֶר/*kpr* or *kopper*, which means "ransom" (Exod 30:12–16; Lev 16:10, 21–22; 17:11; Deut 21:1–9)[25] and also carries the meaning of "atonement."[26] Ransom is clearly seen in the use of כִּפֶּר/*kpr* concerning both (1) census and (2) the law of homicide, which permitted a certain amount of money to be paid "to ransom a life" (Exod 21:29–30; 30:12–16; Num 31:50; 35:31–33; while there is a prohibition banning ransoming in response to the sin of adultery in Prov 6:34–35).[27] These are payments made as "vicarious atonement" *on behalf of* the beneficiaries.

Additionally, the purification and guilt offerings (which describe Christ's atonement in Isa 53:10 MT and LXX) both vicariously bear the uncleanness or guilt away from the sancta and the one or group for whom they are offered. Each of the purification and guilt offerings accomplish vicarious *atonement* (כִּפֶּר: Lev 14:18–19; Num 5:8) or *propitiation* (LXX: ἱλασμόν; Num 5:8; Ezek 44:27).[28] Averbeck also develops that the ritual of the scapegoat is of great significance in that it symbolizes the vicarious removal of all iniquity and transgressions from Israel, cleansing the tabernacle (Lev 16:19) and also the people (Lev 16:30).[29] Both the purification offering and the scapegoat contribute to the Day of Atonement, accomplishing atonement or propitiation (כִּפֶּר: Lev 16:6–34; LXX: ἱλασμοῦ: Lev 25:9) from Israel's uncleanness and sin.[30] The scapegoat bears the guilt away from the nation (Lev

---

23. Saussure, *Cours de linguistique générale*; Barr, *Semantics of Biblical Language*; Feder, "On *Kuppuru, Kippēr* and Etymological Sins That Cannot Be Wiped Away."

24. Averbeck, "כִּפֶּר," in VanGemeren, ed., *NIDOTT*, 2:689–710, especially 692.

25. Hermann, *Idee der Sühne im Alten Testament*, 99, 101–2; "ἱλάσκομαι, ἱλασμός," in *TDNT*, 3:301–10, especially 303; Brichto, "On Slaughter and Sacrifice, especially 26–27 and 34–35; Levine, *In the Presence of the Lord*, 67; Schenker, "*Kōper* et expiation"; Milgrom, *Leviticus 1–16*, 1082–83; Sklar, *Sin, Impurity, Sacrifice, Atonement*, 46–72.

26. Janowski, *Sühne als Heilsgeschehen*, 185–276; Gese, "Sühne" and "Atonement."

27. Milgrom, *Numbers*, 370 identifies that atonement prevents Yahweh's wrath. In a similar ransom situation 11QT 21.7–9; 22.15–16 has first fruits offering to ransom the rest of the crop for common purposes.

28. Dan 9:9 uses the word to identify "forgiveness"; in 2 Macc 3:33 the high priest offers atonement using ἱλασμόν.

29. Averbeck, in VanGemeren, ed., *NIDOTT*, 2:344 and Gane, *Cult and Character* follow Milgrom on tabernacle atonement but also add individual atonement and forgiveness, which Milgrom ignores (Lev 4:26; 14:19; 15:15; 16:30, 34a; Num 6:11).

30. Further confirmed as atoning by rabbinics (*m. Šebu.* 1.6; *Sipra Aḥare* 5.8).

10:17; 16:22). In this way the nation of Israel was able to continue for another year in Mosaic covenantal relationship of peace with Yahweh because their corporate unclean condition had been atoned for at the yearly Day of Atonement. Through such atonement Israel nationally continues with Yahweh in a relationship of peace, as evidenced by the continuing Mosaic covenant benefits.

Such propitiation (ἱλαστήριον, Rom 3:25) obtains real forgiveness (ἀφέθησαν, Rom 4:7) and covenantal righteousness (Rom 4:3, 5-6, 9, 13). Such forgiveness and righteousness are understood to be justification in the Pauline context (Rom 3:24, 28, 30; 4:5; 5:1, 9). Christ's justification of sinners is a gracious accomplishment on the basis of his vicarious atonement on behalf of the sinner. Because the same imagery is utilized in the same context, it is better to identify justification with the same covenantal imageries that bring about atonement.

Likewise, the Pauline emphasis placed the word "sanctification" as an atonement[31] benefit strongly emphasizing the initial aspect of the Spirit's rendering believers holy in Christ (ἁγιάζω in perfect tense: Acts 20:32; 26:18; Rom 15:16; 1 Cor 1:2; 7:14; also Heb 10:10; in aorist tense: 1 Cor 1:30; 6:11; Eph 5:26; also Heb 10:14 present tense but accomplished at the cross in verse 10; 2 Thess 2:15 beginning means of salvation with faith and truth; 1 Pet 1:2 accomplished when a believer initially obeys and is atoned for by Christ) after the pattern of the Mosaic covenantal concept of set apart persons,[32] objects, and places for covenantal purposes (LXX: Lev 6:9, 20, 23; 7:6). Christ became sanctification so that in Christ Christians are declared holy (1 Cor 1:30; 6:11). Thus believers are already declared to be saints[33] (ἁγίοις: Rom 1:7; 15:25, 31; 1 Cor 1:2; 16:15; 2 Cor 1:1; Eph 1:1, 18; 3:5, 18; 5:3; Phil 1:1; Col 1:2, 26; 2 Thess 1:10), even if they still have many sins working in their lives. In the LXX, the concept of saint or holy (ἁγίοις) primarily describes the temple (Exod 29:30; Num 4:12; Isa 57:15; Ezek 44:5-11; Pss 73:3; 150:1), though it also describes the holy God (Isa 11:16; 57:15; Ps 21:4; also Heb 2:11), and occasionally separated Israel (Dan 7:22, 27; Ps 16:3; also Heb 2:11). Thus, as saints, believers are like a temple separated (or

31. Gese, "Sühne" and "Atonement"; Hofius, "Sühne und Versöhnung"; "The Fourth Servant Song in the New Testament Letters," in Janowski and Stuhlmacher, eds., *Suffering Servant*, 174-75.

32. Atonement is parallel with forgiveness in Lev 4:20, 26, 31, 35; 5:10, 13, 18; 6:7; 10:17; 16:30 and Ps 79:9, indicating that forgiveness is included within כָּפֶר. Additionally, כָּפֶר deals with people's sins such that forgiveness is included within its semantic field (Lev 16:32-34; Num 15:25, 28; Deut 21:8; Pss 65:3; 78:38; 79:9; Isa 6:7; 27:9; Ezek 16:63); Gane, *Cult and Character*, xx, 47-49, 299; Gammie, *Holiness in Israel*, 39; Kennard, *Biblical Covenantalism*, 1:289-313.

33. Seebass, "Holy" 2 (a), in *NIDNTT*, 2:229.

sanctified) for God by the appropriate covenantal sacrifice[34] (1 Cor 3:16–17; 6:19; 2 Cor 6:16; Eph 2:21; also Heb 9:13; 10:10, 14, 29; 13:12). Because Christ's atonement accomplishes this sanctification, believers are in Christ *declared holy in status*. So the Pauline emphasis identifies that *sanctification is an initial work of Christ's atonement declaring the believer holy in status*, akin to justification's initial *declared-righteous status*. Such a concept is built upon Mosaic sacrifice and one's internal disposition rendering food, temple objects, and the Lord as sanctified (ἁγιάσαι) and thus beyond the bounds of common people (LXX: Exod 19:23; 29:1, 33, 36; Num 20:12; 27:14; 2 Chr 2:3; Prov 20:25). People who are sanctified (ἁγιασμόν) are separated akin to a Nazarite's separation for God's purposes (Amos 2:11 LXX). With this Pauline emphasis, theologians should not use "sanctification" as a synonym for the Christian life, because they are playing to a minor implication of the idea rather than Paul's emphasized core meaning already accomplished by God. Believers are to remain within Christ's established sanctification (1 Thess 3:13 dative following preposition ἐν to indicate sphere of holiness; 1 Thess 4:4, 7 and 1 Tim 2:15 continuing in ἁγιασμῷ datives of sphere of holiness). Therefore, sanctification has implications for the believer to live a holy life by righteous living, word, and prayer (Rom 6:19, 22 ἁγιασμόν; 2 Cor 7:1 maturing consistent purity; 5:23 ἁγιάσαι in aorist optative; 4:5 ἁγιάζεται in present tense; also 2 Tim 2:21 cleansing; also Heb 12:14), as justification also implies that the believer lives a righteous life (Rom 6:11–22). The initially sanctified should continue in and mature their sanctification in their life.

However, Paul's concept of Jesus' atonement has been proposed to be considered as "penal" in that Paul once mentions that Christ becomes a curse for us, at least in the manner in which Jesus dies hanging on a tree (Gal 3:13). Vicarious substitutionary atonement is indicated through the preposition phrase ὑπὲρ ἡμῶν, which identifies that Jesus' death is "on our behalf." Notice the curse aspect is not the soteriological accomplishment of his atonement for us, but rather only the circumstantial manner in which Jesus dies. In a penal atonement view the guilty receive God's wrath and the elect are spared God's damming wrath because Jesus Christ provides a vicarious substitute that takes God's wrath due us in our place. Paul clearly taught that disobedient humans are due God's wrath (Rom 1:18; 2:5, 8; 9:22; Eph 5:6; Col 3:6; 1 Thess 2:16). Likewise, Paul taught that Christ's vicarious sacrifice saves those who are his from the divine wrath to come (Rom 5:9; 1 Thess 1:10). Such a vicarious atonement mystically removes us from

---

34. Procksch, "ἁγιάζω," in *TDNT*, 1:112.

eschatological wrath while still permitting persecution in this life.³⁵ So, the one final aspect that would make this vicarious atonement penal would be whether Christ receives our wrath in our place. There is only one Pauline passage that might address the subject, and that is Galatians 3:13, where Paul identified that Christ became a curse for us. However, Paul explains himself by quoting Deuteronomy 21:23 to identify that the manner of Christ's *death hanging on wood* marks him out to be cursed (also Lev 18:5),³⁶ not that the wrath due humans is given to Christ. So if Christ is cursed simply because he dies hanging on a tree and is not buried quickly, then he is cursed due to the circumstances of his death and not as a penal substitute for a sinner's curse. Notice, that the author does not exclude penal substitution from describing Christ's death but merely raises the question as to how clearly it is presented in Paul. Furthermore, if a covenantal sacrificial view is a more compelling metaphor in Paul, then why shift to a courtroom metaphor such as the term "penal"? Additionally, Peter also says that Christ dies on a tree without spinning it toward curse, so penal is not a required description here (1 Pet 2:24).

A more ambiguous passage includes Paul's claim that God made the impeccable Christ "sin on our behalf" (2 Cor 5:21, ὑπὲρ ἡμῶν ἁμαρτίαν). Several commentators treat the phrase to refer to penal substitution in identifying that Jesus, who did not know sin, was being treated by God as if he were a sinner destined for God's wrath.³⁷ Others get to this penal substitution conclusion by viewing that Christ is being treated as sin itself and thus worthy of God's wrath.³⁸ However, a more Jewish interpretation of this text views Christ as the substitutionary sin bearer: Christ becomes like

---

35. Pate and Kennard, *Deliverance Now and Not Yet*, 119–270.

36. Hahn, *Kinship by Covenant*, 254 connects this use of "wood" with Gen 22:9 LXX, *Gen Rab.* 56.4 and Tertullian, *Adv. Iud.* 10.6 to show Jesus as similar to the near-sacrifice of Isaac but the Galatians context does not support this. Deut 21:23 and Lev 18:5 probably refer to impaling hanging as occurred to the baker, king of Ai, Saul impaled on a wall, and others (Gen 40:19, 22; 41:13; Philo, *Joseph* 98; Josh 8:29; 10:26–27; 1 Sam 39:9–13; 2 Sam 4:12; 21:12; LXX Esth 2:23; Josephus, *Ant.* 11.246, 267, 289) but extended to include the possibility of death by crucifixion (earliest in LXX Esth 7:9; 4QpNah 3–4.I.6–8; 4Q282i; Josephus, *Ant.* 11.289; 13.380; *J.W.* 1.97), though the curse references the circumstances of an exposed death not buried quickly (1 Kgs 11:15; Ezek 39:11–16; 11QT LXIV.7–13= 4Q524 14.2–4; 4Q285; Philo, *Spec. Laws* 3.151–52; Josephus, *Ant.* 4.202; *J.W.* 4.317; *m. Sanh.* 6.5–6; *Sem.* 13.7; Evans, *Jesus and the Remains of His Day*, 109–30).

37. Bultmann, *Second Corinthians*, 165; *Theology of the New Testament*, 1:277; Guthrie, *New Testament Theology*, 466; Garland, *2 Corinthians*, 302.

38. Robertson, *Word Pictures in the New Testament*, 4:233; Zerwick and Grosvenor, *Grammatical Analysis of the Greek New Testament*, 2:545; Harris, *Second Corinthians*, 452–54.

the scapegoat bearing sin away on the Day of Atonement. In positioning Christ within Mosaic sacrificial imagery, any allusion to the penal aspect of substitution is removed as Christ deals with our sin on our behalf.³⁹ This last option is preferable since the phrase begins with the prepositional phrase emphasizing that this Christ-as-sin construct is "on our behalf" (2 Cor 5:21, ὑπὲρ ἡμῶν). Furthermore, this statement comes within an extended context of "reconciliation" (καταλλαγὴν; 2 Cor 5:18–21), which as a biblical metaphor is dominantly framed from within Jewish covenant renewal and atonement contexts (LXX: Jer 6:14; 8:11, 15; 12:12; 14:19; 16:5; 14:13; 23:17; 28:9; 33:6, 9; Lam 3:17).⁴⁰ With this Jewish covenant renewal emphasis from the context, it is better to take this Christ-as-sin reference as consistently within the more dominant Jewish metaphor. Thus, Christ becomes the "sin sacrifice on our behalf" without reference to penal imagery. Furthermore, this construct is consistent with how Paul presents Christ's death as a covenantal vicarious atonement, which in propitiation delivers his people from the threat of the wrath of God (Rom 5:9; 1 Thess 1:10) so that we might be the righteousness of God in Christ (2 Cor 5:21).

In Paul's context, the sacrifice is provided by Christ, framing the penitent's faith and a community of beneficiaries to be parallel. It is the commonality of this faith that serves Paul's purpose for providing a salvation for the whole community in Christ (Rom 3:29–30; 4:10–18).

Such a "declaration of righteousness" at times appears as an ascribed *status of acceptable within covenant*, though this also must be *reflective of an intrinsic virtuous quality* (Deut 24:10–13; 25:1–2).⁴¹ That is, the individual who makes *Torah* practically true in her life is recognized for her *virtuous attitude*. Such a person in early Judaism obtains the declaration that it "will be reckoned to you as righteousness, since you will be doing what is righteous and good in his eyes, for your own welfare and for the welfare of Israel."⁴² Here "reckoned as righteousness" identifies an acknowledgement of the *status of those who keep the Law*. Just before this text in the context is a call to reflect on past examples of righteousness and how they were com-

---

39. Bernard, "The Second Epistle to the Corinthians," in Nicoll, ed., *Expositor's Greek New Testament*, 3:73; Riesenfeld, "ὑπὲρ," in *TDNT*, 8:510; Martin, *2 Corinthians*, 157.

40. 2 Macc 1:5; 5:20; 7:33; 8:29; Josephus, *Ant.* 3.315; 6.143; 7.153, 295; Philo, *Praem.* 166; Dunn, *Romans*, 1:259.

41. Rottzoll, "Gen. 15.6—Ein Beleg für den Glauben als Werkgerechtigkeit," especially 26; Behrens, "Gen. 15.6 und das Vorverständnis des Paulus," 331.

42. 4QMMT C 26–32; 4Q397 frag. 23; 4Q399 frag. 1; frags. 14–17 col. 2; developed by Dunn, *New Perspective on Paul*, especially chs. 1, 8, 10, 14, 17, 19, which were articles from 1992 to 2008.

mitted to *Torah*, as evident in their works of the Law, and forgiven in the midst of their sins.

Such a status of "reckoned as righteousness" was already ascribed to Abraham by 1 Maccabees 2:52 as though it was a payment for "faithful" (πιστός) good deeds.[43] It could be that Paul is directly reacting to this 1 Maccabees statement or similar Jewish teaching describing Israel in 4QMMT as eschatologically reckoned righteous at the eschatological judgment or of Abraham's successful completion of ten spiritual tests in *Jubilees* 19.[44] Instead, Paul identifies that such status can't be earned (Rom 4:4-5). That is, Paul recognized such an expression of "reckoned as righteousness" in Genesis 15:6 should not be understood as earning a wage evidentially; rather, God granted Abram his acceptable status (of righteousness) through faith within a sacrificial covenantal context (Gen 15:9, 18; Rom 3:25; 4:3-8). Thus Jewett concludes, "Genesis 15.6 therefore declares Abraham's faith in God's promise sufficient to declare him righteous, that is, acceptable to God."[45]

Abraham responds by faith to God's repeated initiation with promise and covenant. This faith challenges the extremity of hope in Abraham and Sarah's long-term infertility and advanced age. Paul used the expression "in hope against hope" to express an "in hope" expectation of sharing the benefits where most would reasonably be "beyond hope" (Rom 4:18).[46] Abraham was fully convinced in faith to what God had promised (Rom 4:20).

When Abraham was uncircumcised, he set the pattern in which believers are justified in the Abrahamic promise by faith without regard to circumcision (Rom 4:1-12). Abraham was an ideal model in early Judaism for the obedient proselyte, showing such initial proselyting obedience through submitting to circumcision.[47] For Paul, circumcision is a seal showing Abraham's precircumcision righteous status through faith, thus further identifying that "righteousness" is a covenant concept as circumcision its covenantal sign is as well (Rom 4:11). The salvific Abrahamic promise is changed from the broad blessing of Paul's use in Galatians to Paul's use in Romans as the national blessing (Gen 15:5; Rom 4:17-18). However, the essence of the salvific Abrahamic promise remains the same. Obtaining the offspring Isaac out of a context of faith within a righteous status serves as the

43. Also meritorious obedience of Abraham in *Mekilta* on Exod 14:15 [35b]; 40b.

44. Ward, "Works of Abraham"; Wall, "The Intertextuality of Scripture: The Example of Rahab (James 2:25)," in Flint, ed., *Bible at Qumran*, 224.

45. Jewett, *Romans*, 312.

46. In Rom 4:18, Paul has put together a mixed metaphor, παρ' ἐλπίδα ("beyond hope"), also used by Philo (*Mos.* 1.250) to describe a *hopeless* battle, and ἐπ' ἐλπίδι is used in 1 Cor 9:10, citing Sir 6:19 about farmers ploughing and reaping *in hope*.

47. CD 3.2-3; 16.4-6; Philo, *Cher.* 31; *Mut.* 7b; *Samn.* 161; *Spec.* 1.52.

pattern for Abraham obtaining believing justified offspring not genetically related to him (Rom 4:16-25). The fact that Gentiles are included in this group (now called Christians) is not new since others beyond Israel were beneficiaries of the promise (for example, Ishmael and Esau contributed to the descendants and nations in the Genesis context). The new feature has to do with the fact that descendants of the singular "promise" (ἐπαγγελίαν) can be obtained through faith without regard to circumcision. Paul believes the Abrahamic covenant with its "promises" (ἐπαγγελίαι) is still in effect for Israel by their relationship to God through the fathers (Abraham, Isaac, and Jacob) to whom those Abrahamic promises were made (Rom 9:4-5). Neither Paul nor any other biblical author ever removes circumcision as a condition for the extensive Abrahamic promises and benefits for Jews, since God placed that requirement as an everlasting requirement and sign of the Abrahamic covenant (Gen 17:10-14).[48] However, as Gentiles proselyte to Christianity, not Judaism (where circumcision is the mark of proselytism), this one salvific promise has no regard for circumcision, with only its context being that of faith (Rom 4:9-12; Col 2:11-14; Acts 15:5, 19); believers in Christ are saved, circumcised or uncircumcised. Neither circumcision nor uncircumcision contributes anything relevant to faith, salvation, or new creation (1 Cor 7:18-19; Gal 5:2-3; 6:15).

Abraham, as a model, is reckoned righteous by faith before he is circumcised and retains this same righteous description of his life after he is circumcised because he retains the same consistency of faith (Rom 3:31; 4:5, 9; Gal 3:6-7). Therefore, the exclusiveness of Israel's blessing based on covenant nomism in early Jewish sources is no cause for boasting by Abraham or anyone else who might be tempted to boast (καύχησις) in the Law or good works (Rom 3:27-28; 4:2).[49]

Perhaps the best example of a boasting Second Temple Jewish text is the one Simon Gathercole marshals from *ben Siraḥ* 31[34].5-11 as he translates it.

---

48. *Jub.* 15.11-14, 23-34; Sir 44:20; *m. Kilʾayim* 1.7.

49. Early Jewish statements are presented as testimony of living righteously with no awareness of sinning, but this is not necessarily sinless perfection because the issue is living virtuously not that every deed is free from sin (Gen 26:5; *Jub.* 15.1-2; 16.20, 28; 21.2-3; 23.10; 24.11; 35.2-3; Sir 44:19-21; CD 3.2; 2 *Bar.* 57.2; *m. Qid.* 4.14; *T. Zeb.* 1.2-5; *T. Jos.* 1.2-3; *L.A.B.* 20.10; 62.5-6; Tob 1:3; Josephus, *Life* 15.82-83; Phil 3:5-9; Bradley Gregory, "Abraham as the Jewish Ideal"; Gathercole, *Where Is Boasting?*, 225-26, 323-42; Dodd, *Romans*, 84-85; Nygren, *Romans*, 162). In A.D. 344 Aphrahat of Persia also criticizes Jews of boasting as being "the nation of God and Sons of Abraham" (Syriac *Demonstrations* 16). Some Jews thought Abraham had a written copy of the Law passed down from righteous Enoch (1QapGen 19.24b-26a).

> We will call him blameless, for he has done wonderful things among his people.
> Who has been tried in this, and found perfect? Then let him boast [καύχησιν].
> Who has had opportunity to transgress, and not transgressed?
> To do evil and not done it?
> His good deeds will be established, and the congregation shall declare his alms.[50]

Stepping out of Gathercole's ideolgical agenda, the *New English Bible* translates this same *ben Sirah* text as follows, showing more of the context that indicates that no one can live righteously with issues of wealth, so there is likely no boaster to be expected.

> Passion for gold can never be right; the pursuit of money leads a man astray. Many a man has come to ruin for the sake of gold and found disaster staring him in the face. Gold is a pitfall to those who are infatuated with it, and every fool is caught by it. Happy is the rich man who has remained free of its taint and has not made gold his aim! Show us that man, and we will congratulate him; he has performed a miracle among his people. Has anyone ever come through this test unscathed? Then he has good cause to be proud. Has anyone ever had it in his power to sin and refrained, then he shall be confirmed in his prosperity, and the whole people will hail him as a benefactor.[51]

So, in spite of Gathercole's claiming this as an example of Jewish boasting, I am left with the conclusion that it is not. Thus, I have no clear early Jewish text to indicate Jewish boasting in their righteousness. So the closest text to a boasting of Jews in early Judaism is Jesus' criticism of the religious disposition of some Pharisees who wished to keep their lives pure and to celebrate their purity at the expense of concern for the needy and unrighteous. The gospels present Jesus as teaching against such twisted "holiness" that does not care about the other, even if it is motivated out of gratitude to God. The best emblem of such unrighteous boasting behavior is "the Pharisee . . . praying to himself [not actually to God], 'God I thank Thee that I am not like other people, swindlers, unjust, adulterers, or even this tax-gatherer. I fast twice a week; I pay tithes of all that I get'" (Luke 18:11–12).

---

50. Sir 31[34]:5–11, cited by Gathercole, *Where Is Boasting?*, 241 and subsequently by Jewett, *Romans*, 309.

51. Sir 31:5–11, New English Bible. I could have provided my own translation but by using available translations I show that I am not biasing a text as I am claiming Gathercole's contextual limitations and selective translation is biased.

No early Jewish document, to my knowledge, encourages or legitimates such unrighteous behavior as boasting in purity. Such prideful attempts at prayer probably happened for Jesus to call it down as unjustifiable, with the wise counsel "for everyone who exalts himself shall be humbled, but he who humbles himself shall be exalted" (Luke 18:14). So with no obvious boasting texts in early Judaism, we are left with the impression that such boasting was not a prescribed Jewish pattern. Rather, such boasting likely occurred on the fringe of Judaism as a corruption of authentic Judaism and such a vice was attacked in Christian texts. Thus with no evidence except from Christian critics, such boasting is better considered as an occasional aberrant practice among some Jews. With no Jewish text advocating such boasting, such a response has no proper place in Judaism and should not be used to slant Pauline passages as antagonistic against supposed Judaic legalism. Paul should be understood allowing the near context itself to determine meaning in interpretation. With Paul developing that all are found guilty under the Law, there is no place for such boasting in the Law or in "works of the Law" (Rom 3:19-20, 27-28). Such occasional boasting is excluded for those who appreciate that such salvation is divinely gracious through faith, not of our own accomplishments.

Paul extends this issue of boasting into Abraham for his Jewish ancestors; "For if Abraham was justified by works, he has something to boast about" (Rom 4:2). In this instance, the first-class conditional sentence expects the actuality of Abraham boasting.[52] Additionally, some Second Temple documents identify that Abraham, as the father of many nations, kept the Mosaic Law (following Gen 26:5) and in this obedience God reckoned him as righteous. But while Israel may boast of Abraham's justification by works, there is no boasting from Abraham in these descriptive texts.

> Abraham was a great father of many nations, and no-one was found like him in glory, who kept the Law of the Most High, and entered into covenant with him, and established in his flesh, and was found faithful in testing.[53]

---

52. As a first-class conditional sentence such boasting on Abraham's part is expected, even if it is not before God (Jewett, *Romans*, 309; Cranfield, *Romans*, 1:227); in contrast Lambrecht, "Why Is Boasting Excluded?," 366-67 argues that the "if" clause designates an unreal condition while the "not before God" clause states the real situation. In contrast, Hübner (*Law in Paul's Thought*, 116) argues that those who boast in Christ boast only in "being in Christ" (1 Cor 1:26-31).

53. Sir 44:19-20; *Jub.* 19.8-9; 23.9-10; 4Q225 2.7-8; de Roo, "God's Covenant with the Forefathers," in Porter and de Roo, eds., *Concept of the Covenant in the Second Temple Period*, 195-96.

> Was not Abraham found faithful in temptation and it was reckoned to him as righteousness.[54]

> Abraham did not walk in it [evil], and he was accounted a friend of God because he kept the commandments of God and did not choose his own will.[55]

Such a virtuously righteous person as Abraham would not need to turn from this course of faithful action because he is already living rightly, as the *Prayer of Manasseh* claims.

> Thou therefore, O Lord, that art the God of the just, hast not appointed repentance to the just, to Abraham, and Isaac, and Jacob, which have not sinned against thee; but thou hast appointed repentance unto me that am a sinner.[56]

I don't read these as a claim that Abraham and the patriarchs always were sinlessly perfect; Genesis shows otherwise. Rather, as a whole, Abraham's life aligns with God and the Law revealed to Moses, such that any repentance they had done occurred earlier (in leaving Ur or the sins of their earlier years). This narrow-way approach identifies Abraham's continued dependency upon Yahweh's instruction and provision. So Abraham does not boast of self-sufficiency, even though Israel may boast of him as indicative of how God's provision enables a man of God to continue in the narrow way. So Abraham becomes a model for divinely driven synergism in which his human faith and obedience reflects the divinely accomplished growth in his life. Therefore, Abraham and the patriarchs stand as a pattern for the Christian to emulate in faith and obedience. Gathercole and Jewett present *Jubilees* as portraying a theoretical boast of Abraham, but it could just be testimony of a commitment that Abraham showed for Jewish emulation.

> Behold, I am a hundred and seventy-five years old, and throughout all of the days of my life I have been remembering the Lord, and sought with all my heart to do his will and walk upright in all his ways. I hated idols, and those who serve them I rejected. And I have offered my heart and spirit so that I might be careful to do the will of the one who created me.[57]

---

54. 1 Macc 2:52; 4Q225 2.7–8.

55. CD 3.2–4; Philo, *Migr.* 127–30; *Abr.* 275–6; *Her.* 6–9; Josephus, *Ant.* 1.233–34; *m. Qidd.* 4.14; *m. Ned.* 3.11.

56. *Pr. Man.* 8.

57. *Jub.* 21.1–3; cited by Gathercole, *Where Is Boasting*, 241 and subsequently by Jewett, *Romans*, 309.

If such a text was taken as boasting, it could set up a perspective that diminishes the gracious aspect of the two ways, with a person viewing the narrow way as their effort. Such a contortion would then replace God's gracious transformation in the person with a legalistic quality trying to earn God's recognition of righteousness. I don't read the early Jewish documents as encouraging such a self-righteous abuse, rather I read this text as the testimony of a faithful man encouraging others to follow such faithfulness. That is, maybe there is an occasional instance of Jewish boasting but I have found no Jewish text encouraging such an unrighteous practice. Furthermore, Paul clearly presents Abraham as a person that the Christian should imitate (Rom 4:3–25; Gal 3:6–18).

What righteousness of God is manifested in faith is that from Christ, who is "the righteous" himself and the means by which the believer becomes righteous (Rom 3:22, 24–28; 1:17; 4:5, 9, 13). Not that they must believe the whole process of salvation as the content of faith, but that they believe "upon" (ἐπὶ) the *God* of the righteousing process (Rom 4:5 masculine article with the participle read "him who"). God is the content and focus of the believer's faith, not the details of the salvation he graciously provides. So, as the example, Abraham *believed God*, not that all the details of the outworking of the covenant were fully known or comprehended (Rom 4:3).

Paul grounds the righteousness of God for Jews and Gentiles alike to be by faith rather than by the Law or "works of the Law" (Rom 3:26–31). The phrase "righteousness of God" (δικαιοσύνη δὲ θεοῦ) is best understood as subjective, similar to the righteous deeds of God witnessed to by the Law (Gen 18:19–32; Ps 97:7–9).[58] This divine righteousness is revealed publically in Christ's death deed, accomplished for any Jews or Gentiles (without distinction) that identify with it by faith (Rom 3:21–26). For we all are in need, having fallen short of God's glory in sin (Rom 3:23). Furthermore, the Law identifies that in such violation there is wrath (Rom 4:15). Therefore, such contrasting righteousness is divinely gracious as a gift.

The fact that Abraham was reckoned as having righteous status while uncircumcised identifies that he becomes the pattern for Gentiles as well as for Jews (Rom 4:9–13). As an expression of this, a few rabbinics view Abraham as called to covenant for the nations,[59] which made Abraham the first Gentile proselyte[60] and missionary to Gentiles.[61] Such an opening to Gentiles along with Jews opposes the dominant early Jewish teaching of

---

58. Also in 1QS 1.21.
59. *T. Benj.* 10.9–10.
60. Philo, *Cher.* 31; *Mut.* 76; *Somn.* 161; *Spec.* 1.52.
61. *B. Ḥag.* 3a; Josephus, *Ant.* 1.161–67.

Jewish exclusivity[62] to side with a minority of early Jewish teachings on God's gracious atonement extending to Gentiles.[63] This enabled Abraham to become "the father of us all" (with a nice repetition of *pa* sound in πατέρα πάντων) who follow in the steps of faith (Rom 4:11, 16).[64] Their righteous status is through the "righteousness of their faith."[65] As such, the Law is not the means by which Christians obtain their righteous status, denying covenant nomism (Rom 4:13-14).

However, Paul does not exclude the Law altogether because he identifies that the Jewish and Gentile salvation is by a "law of faith," a righteousness not dependent upon the Law but witnessed to by the Law and the Prophets and thus establishes the Law by faith (Rom 3:21, 27, 31). That is, by faith the Christian will be prompted by the Spirit to live a transformed life of love, righteousness, and other virtues of an appropriate Law lifestyle (Rom 8:4; Gal 5:23).[66]

The issue of "faith or faithfulness of Christ" (πίστεως Ἰησοῦ) in the genitive permits: (1) a subjective option, which in the patristics was "Jesus' faith" but in recent decades is usually translated as "Jesus' faithfulness" in contrast to the Law's condemnation; (2) an objective option, which is the believer's "faith in Jesus" or the Spirit's work to produce believers to be "faithful in Jesus"; or (3) hybrids like a plenary genitive or a mystical genitive, in which the believer joins Jesus in his faith and faithfulness.[67] While certain texts are more open to a subjective or a mystical option, such as Galatians 3:14, 26 in contrast to the Law, or 1 Timothy 1:14 and 2 Timothy 3:15 as within virtues found in Christ. Other verses emphasize usually the phrase to be taken in those contexts as an objective genitive for the believer's subjective faith in the object Christ. For example, Romans 3:22 and Galatians 3:22 identify late in these verses that the discussion is the believer's faith. Romans 3:26 occurs in a context developing the believer's faith (Rom 3:22, 25). Romans 5:1 occurs in a context in which the believer's faith is likened to

62. Gal 2:15; *Pss. Sol.* 11.8-11; 12.6; 17.15, 23; *Jub.* 23.24; *L.A.B.* 7.3; 10.2; 11.1; 12.4; 14.5; 19.8; 30.4; 35.2; *2 Bar.* 82.5; *4 Ezra* 6.56; *Pesiqta* 45.185b.

63. *L.A.B.* 11.1-2; also Philo, *Mos.* 2.36.

64. While the argument here is about Jews and Gentiles united in faith, Jewett (*Romans*, 332 citing Rom 9:3-5) points out that Abraham is also father of non-believing Jews as well.

65. Rather than Gentiles being identified as "righteous" by the Law as in *2 Bar.* 41.3; Josephus, *Ant.* 20.44-45; *t. Demai* 2.5; *m. 'Abot* 1.12; 3.5; *b. Šabb.* 31a; *T. Sanh.* 13.2.

66. Stegman, "Paul's Use of Dikaio-Terminology" argues for a real transformative righteous beyond the forensic.

67. Deissmann, *Paulus*, 127; *St. Paul*, 163; Hooker "πίστις Ἰησοῦ," 341; also helpful discussions are in Bird and Sprinkle, *Faith of Jesus Christ* and Hays, *Faith of Jesus Christ*.

be parallel to Abraham's faith. Furthermore, Galatians 2:16 identifies by the plural verb "believed" (ἐπιστεύσαμεν) that the discussion is believers' faith rather than Christ's. Additionally, the believer's faith or faithfulness occurs within lists of the believer's virtues (Eph 6:23; 1 Thess 1:2). So, on emphasis, the phrase will usually indicate the faith that a Christian places in Jesus.

Abraham's faith was in God, who promised that Sarah and he would have a son, and ultimately uncountable descendants (Rom 4:5, 16–22; Gen 18:10; 15:5; 17:6). Abraham responds to God's repeated promise and covenant by faith. This faith challenges the extremity of hope in his own and Sarah's long-term infertility and advanced age. Paul used the expression "in hope against hope" to express a hoped expectation of sharing the benefits where most would reasonably be "beyond hope" (Rom 4:18).[68] Thus again God's gracious generosity is shown. As such, Abraham was fully convinced in faith to what God had promised (Rom 4:20). In this, Abraham becomes the father of those who believe in God (who raised Jesus from the dead) because God ascribed to Abraham that he is righteous by faith in the same pattern by which God ascribes righteousness by faith to us (Rom 4:16, 24). In this way, Abraham is the father of both Jewish believers as well as Gentile believers.[69] As such, the law that speaks of God's righteousness is "established" (ἱστάνομεν) as we believers follow Abraham in the way of believing unto God's reckoned righteousness (Rom 3:21, 31; 4:11, 24). Such an "establishment" (ἱστάνομεν) of the Mosaic Law renders the Law as a standing description of life by faith.[70] This is another hint at the establishment of aspects of the Abrahamic covenant in the Mosaic covenant and aspects of the Mosaic covenant in the new covenant. However, the kingdom inheritance is not obtained by compliance with the Law (as many Second Temple Jewish authors claimed)[71] but by faith in the central message (Rom 4:13–14). Additionally, Abraham's pattern encourages the Christian to join Abraham in growing strong in faith, focused on our central message and giving God

---

68. In Rom 4:18 Paul has put together a mixed metaphor παρ' ἐλπίδα ("beyond hope") used by Philo (*Mos.* 1.250) to describe a *hopeless* battle and ἐπ' ἐλπίδι is used in 1 Cor 9:10, citing Sir 6:19 about farmers ploughing and reaping *in hope*.

69. Donaldson, *Paul and the Gentiles*, 51–78.

70. Compare other instances of ἵστημι (Rom 5:2; 10:3; 11:20; 14:4; 1 Cor 7:37; 10:12; 15:1; 2 Cor 1:24; 13:1; 2 Tim 2:19). ἵστημι has an ethical quality to live up to an established framework, exhorting a person to stand in that way (Eph 6:11, 13, 14; Col. 4:12).

71. *Jub.* 20.6–10; 21.21–24; 30.21–22; *1 En.* 94.1–5; 98.6–8; *Charter of a Jewish Sectarian Association* (1QS; 4Q255–264a; 5Q11)1.9–10; 2.11–17; 3–4; 4.20–22; 4Q228; 4Q473 frag. 2; 4Q176 frags. 12–13 16, frags. 10+11+7+9+20+26 verse 7; 4Q504 3.4–13; 4Q548 frag. 1 2.2–16; Philo, *Pot.* 1.67–68 obedience identifies good; *Her.* 9, 161–93, 313–16; *2 Bar.* 85.12–15; *Sib. Or.* 8.399–401; *T. Ash.* 1–7; *T. Abr.* 11; these are similar to Matt 7:7; 13:43; 25:46.

the glory (Rom 4:20). Thus, this pattern of God considering Abraham appropriate encourages believers who will be eschatologically[72] identified as righteous (Rom 4:24). In this instance, Paul identifies this reckoning of righteousness as still in the future.

Simply put, the gospel is: *believe that Jesus' death provides justification, everlasting forgiveness, and sanctification after the pattern of Abraham's covenantal sacrifice and a Jewish sacrifice on the Day of Atonement.*

---

72. Μέλλει with a future in Paul maintains a future description to the point of view of the context, which here is present faith of believers (Rom 5:14; 8:13, 18, 38; 1 Cor 3:22; Gal 3:23; Col 2:17; 1 Thess 3:4), thus not just future to Abraham context (contra Kühl, *Brief des Paulus an die Römer*, 135) so that the future reckoning is broadly recognized to be the eschatological judgment by God or Christ (Michel, *Brief an die Römer*, 127; Schlier, *Römerbrief*, 134; Käsemann, *Romans*, 128; Schlatter, *Romans*, 117; Barrett, *Romans*, 99; after the pattern of 1QS 11.2–3, 12–15 and 4QMMT C31; Wright also argues this stance in "4QMMT and Paul" and *Pauline Perspectives*, 332–55).

18

Gospel as Jesus' Death and Resurrection

PAUL IDENTIFIES THAT GOSPEL (εὐαγγέλιον) is a message of good news having to do with God (Rom 1:1, 16) and Christ (Rom 1:9; 16:25; 1 Cor 9:12), which will judge human secrets (Rom 2:16; 11:28).[1] This gospel message is something that Paul is committed to having proclaimed (Rom 1:9, 15; 15:20; 1 Cor 1:17; 9:14, 16, 18; 15:1; 2 Cor 10:16; 11:7; Gal 1:8; 2:2; 4:13; Phil 4:15; 1 Thess 1:5; 2:9). Acceptance of this message saves the recipient (1 Cor 15:1–2), brings immortality (2 Tim 1:10; 1 Cor 15), and fosters hope (Col 1:23). Those who accept Paul's gospel became sons of Paul (1 Cor 4:15). To not accept the gospel message makes one an enemy of those who accept and obey gospel (Rom 11:28; 2 Thess 2:14). For example, those committed to the gospel are often persecuted (2 Tim 1:8; Phlm 13).

However, Paul only once identifies in his letters the content of this gospel as Jesus' death and resurrection according to the Scriptures (1 Cor 15:1–8):

> The gospel which I preached to you, which also you received, in which also you stand, by which also you are saved, if you hold fast the word which I preached to you, unless you believed in vain. For I delivered to you as of first importance what I also received, that Christ died for our sins according to the Scriptures, and that he was buried, and that he was raised on the third day according to the Scriptures, and that he appeared to Cephas, then to the twelve. After that he appeared to more than five hundred brethren at one time, most of whom remain until

---

1. Harnack, "Gospel: History of the Conception in the Earliest Church," 326; Stuhlmacher, "The Pauline Gospel," in Stuhlmacher, ed., *Gospel and the Gospels*, 150; *Paulinische Evangelium*, 325.

now, but some have fallen asleep; then he appeared to James, then to all the apostles; and last of all, as to one untimely born, he appeared to me also.

This good news message then initiates an extended discussion about the fact that Jesus' resurrection sets the pattern for the Christian's resurrection hope.

Jesus' death was developed predictively from the Scriptures as Isaiah's Servant. So the meaning that "Jesus died for our sins according to the Scriptures" can be assumed to have this previous meaning of atonement through ritual Jewish guilt or sin offering. In fact, Isaiah 53 even identified features for how to recognize the Servant's burial, which guarantees that he died. So the particular emphasis that this 1 Corinthians 15 text contributes in context is a resurrection hope according to the Scriptures.

In a precarious time, David prayed the lament Psalm 16, with its bold confession of trust in the protecting relationship with Yahweh for this life and beyond (Ps 16:1, 8–11; Acts 2:25; 13:34–36). David's confidence was that Yahweh would "not abandon my life to *sheol*; neither will Thy holy one to undergo decay" (Ps 16:10). The synonymous parallelism indicates that David was confident that he would not suffer a premature death,[2] whereas Luke records Peter as fusing this psalm with 2 Samuel 7:12 to proclaim the necessity that David's greatest Son, Jesus, must have risen (Acts 2:25–32).[3] Luke records Paul getting to the same conclusion through a fusion of the Psalm 2 affirmation of David's messianic Son being empowered by God through resurrection indicated by Psalm 16:10 (Acts 13:33–36). This rationale is built on the confidence that David remained in his tomb in Peter and Paul's day and that Peter and Paul identified Jesus to be the Davidic King by his resurrection. Therefore, the Scriptures identify Jesus must have risen as Davidic King.

Likewise, by similar rationale, Isaiah 53:11–12 hints at a continuing life of satisfaction, benefit, and intercession of the Servant of Yahweh because he has borne other's iniquities in atonement. Furthermore, Hosea 6:2 may have been extended from its encouragement of God to revive the nation Israel on a third day to be viewed as a promise to bring about the national resurrection on the third day.

Jesus predicted that he would be killed by the religious leadership of Israel and that he would resurrect on the third day (Matt 12:40; 16:21; 17:9,

---

2. Anderson, *Psalms*, 1:145–146; Eichrodt, *Theology of the Old Testament*, 2:524; von Rad, *Old Testament Theology*, 1:405; Wright, *Resurrection of the Son of God*, 104–5.

3. Bock, *Proclamation from Prophecy and Pattern* develops that OT quotes are used by Luke for their proclamation value in these sermons; Marshall (*Acts*, 77–78) claims that like Ps 132 and 2 Sam 7:10–16 (which is present in Acts 2:30) being interpreted by 4Q Florilegium as messianic, so to Peter takes Ps 16 as referring to the Messiah.

12, 22–23; 20:18–19; 27:63; Mark 8:31; 9:12, 31; Luke 9:22, 44; 17:25; 18:32; 24:7; John 2:19). Paul claims that Jesus' resurrection occurred on the third day, fulfilling the Scriptures (1 Cor. 15:4). No OT text claims the timing of a third-day resurrection of the Messiah, but the sentiment grew among Pharisaic early Judaism that began to see the biblical text describe the general resurrection and even a messianic resurrection on the third day.[4] However, Paul may have meant merely that the fact of resurrection fulfills Scripture (maybe, Isa 53:11–12; Ps 16:8–11), and Jesus' resurrection happened to occur on the third day, as Jesus had prophesied (Matt 12:40; 16:21; 20:19; 27:63; Mark 9:31; Luke 24:7; John 2:18–22). In some of these discussions, the disciples did not understand what Jesus was saying until later when he resurrected (Luke 9:44).

Jesus predicted his resurrection will be a sign of Jonah and of his temple. Jesus' resurrection will be a sign like that of Jonah so that others will later (when it happens) know who Jesus is as one greater than Jonah (Matt 12:38–41; 16:4, 17).[5] Likewise, John also reflects an enigmatic prediction from Jesus, "destroy this temple and in three days I will rebuild it" (John 2:18–22), indicating that his resurrection as a sign was misunderstood as opposition to the Jerusalem temple (Matt 26:61; 27:40; Mark 14:58; 15:29). Instead, Jesus referred to the raising of the temple of his body.

One statement of Paul's gospel is that *Jesus died for our sins according to the Scriptures and that he rose on the third day according to the Scriptures.* The believer in this gospel will resurrect after Christ's pattern.

---

4. The scriptural rationale for why Jesus' resurrection is predicted to occur on the third day must be seen through the slight *targum* evidence interpreting the Scriptures as describing the general resurrection of the elect occurring on the third day (*T. Hos.* 6:2 interprets this text to be resurrection whereas the text speaks of the reviving of Israel on the third day; *Tg. Jon.* on Isa 27:12f. describes salvation as being accomplished on the third day, implying a resurrection); there is also mention of third-day resurrection in *Midrash Rab.* on Gen 22:4; 42:18; Exod 19:16; Josh 2:16; Jon 2:1; Ezra 8:32. There may be some recapitulation of this third-day resurrection in Jesus' resurrection as the first fruits. Cf. Wright, *Resurrection of the Son of God*, 321–22; Thiselton, *First Corinthians*, 1196–97.

5. Peter, the son of John (John 1:42) will become the son of Jonah (Matt 16:17) by identifying Jesus as the Messiah through his resurrection (Matt 16:4); Gundry, *Matthew*, 242–45.

19

Christ's Imputation

IMPUTATION OF SIN ADDS condemning consequences from Adam's sin to human sin indebtedness (Rom 5:13–14).[1] This is the bad news that sets up the framework for Christ's imputation to his Christians as the good news.

Paul draws upon the early Jewish idea of a heavenly ledger in which sins and righteousness are recorded as debt and credit.[2] Once the Mosaic Law is put in place, this imputation to the heavenly ledger is enlivened with a covenantal mechanism of an imputation of guilt and a multigenerational curse, much as the Hittite suzerainty treaties utilized (Exod 20:5–6; 34:6–7; Deut 5:9–10; Josh 7:19–26; Jer 25:4–11 and 29:10 with 2 Chr 36:21).[3] That

---

1. This Pauline statement is contrary to 2 *Bar.* 54.19, a warning in the vein of Pelagius against blaming Adam for any subsequent generation's sin. However, several early Jewish texts identify a position welcomed among Augustinianism that Adam immediately brought condemning death on his descendants (2 *Bar.* 23.4; 48.42–43; 54.15; 2 *Esdr.* 7.118–19; 4 *Ezra* 3.7).

2. *Jub.* 30.17–23; 1 *En.* 104.7; 2 *Apoc. Bar.* 24.1.

3. Beckman, *Hittite Diplomatic Texts*: p. 14, no. 1A, "Treaty Between Arnunda 1 of Hatti and the Men of Ismerika" 3 (obv. 12–18); pp. 40–41, no. 5, "Treaty Between Suppiluliuma 1 of Hatti and Aziru of Amurru" 17 (A rev. 12'–16'); p. 48, no. 6A, "Treaty Between Suppiluliuma 1 of Hatti and Shattiwaza of Mittanni" 15–16 (A rev. 58–75); p. 52–54, no. 6B, "Treaty Between Shattiwaza of Mittanni and Suppiluliuma 1 of Hatti" 9–11 (rev. 25–62); p. 58, no. 7, "Treaty Between Suppiliuma 1 of Hatti and Tette of Nuhashshi" 17 (A 4.44'–57); p. 64, no. 8, "Treaty Between Mursili 2 of Hatti and Tuppi-Teshshup of Amurru" 21–22 (A 4.21–32); pp. 65, 69, no. 9, "Treaty Between Mursili 2 of Hatti and Niqmepa of Ugarit" 1 and 20–21; p. 73, no. 10, "Treaty Between Mursili 2 of Hatti and Targasnalli of Hapalla" 15; pp. 92–93, no. 13, "Treaty Between Muwattalli 2 of Hatti and Alaksandu of Wilusa" 21 (A 4.31–46); p. 99, "Treaty Between Hattusili 3 of Hatti and Ramses 2 of Egypt" 19 (A obv. 65–70); p. 112, no. 18B, "Treaty Between Hattusili 3 of Hatti and Ulmi-Teshshup of Tarhuntassa" 9–11 (rev. 5–14); no ancient Near East law code has multigenerational imputation or curse like the biblical law code has in its similarity to

is, such imputation is a covenantal strategy completely absent from all non-biblical ancient Near Eastern law codes. This fusion of a covenant strategy when Paul writes "law" identifies a level of covenant nomism in imputation of sin, which view continues in rabbinic writings.[4]

Paul's word for "imputation" (ἐλλογεῖται) is a commercial concept applying one person's debt against the ledger of another (Rom 5:13; Phlm 18).[5] Paul parenthetically comments that such a representative "imputation" or "commercial transaction" does not occur when there is no law or, more technically, suzerainty treaty as covenant law (Rom 5:13).[6] However, once the Mosaic Law[7] is in place, imputation of Adam's sin becomes an additional mechanism to condemn humanity. However, there is nothing in the Mosaic Law or early Judaism that develops such a mechanism of imputation of Adam's sin.[8] The closest approximation is the modest extent at which Yahweh's jealousy will judge iniquity of a father's idolatry on four generations of children who hate Yahweh (Exod 20:5; 34:7; Deut 5:9). Such a situation transpired during the Babylonian captivity; several generations suffered covenant curse and dispersion provoked by the sins of a prior generation. A similar discussion in Deuteronomy 23:2-8 picks up selective groups who experience covenant curse from the previous generation's sin. The lineage of an illegitimate birth is excluded from the assembly up to the tenth generation. Additionally, Amori-

---

these Hittite suzerainty treaty texts. *Hittite Proverbs* 1.80 v. 5 identifies imputation of sin from father to son (Hallo, ed., *Context of Scripture*, 215). Second Temple texts did not pick up on this imputation of sin but did identify humanity as universally condemned in sin and death since the sin of Adam (*4 Ezra* 3.7, 21; 7.1, 118; *2 Bar.* 23.4).

4. *Mekhilta* 52.1.8-9.

5. In papyri ἐλλογεῖται is a commercial term "to charge to someone's account" (*P. Ryl.* 2 Nr. 243.11; *P. Grenf.* 2. Nr. 67.18; *P. Lond.* 2. Nr. 359.4; Friedrich, "ἁαρτία οὐκ ἐλλογεῖται, Röm. 5,13").

6. Sin is learned and expanded upon by subsequent generations with divine consequences of death similar to Gen 3-6 and *2 Bar.* 54.15. The Law is not a reissuing of an Adamic covenant; the Law contrasts with the Adamic sin condition in that the Law adds imputation (Murray, "Adamic Administration," in *Collected Writings of John Murray*, 2:50; counter to VanDrunen, "Israel's Recapitulation of Adam's Probation under the Law of Moses," 322-23).

7. In Rom 5:13 νόμου is best taken to be Mosaic Law since it changes the way sin impacts humanity in Moses' day (Rom 5:14).

8. Much of early Judaism blames Adam, Eve, and Satan for beginning the deed and habit of sin but there is no development of imputation among Second Temple documents (Sir 14:17; 25:24, where Eve alone is blamed; Wis 2:23-24; *L.A.E.* 44; *Apoc. Mos.* 14, 32; *4 Ezra* 3.7, 21-22; 4.30; 7.11-12, 116-18; *2 Apoc. Bar.* 17.2-3; 23.4; 48.42-43; 54.15, 19; 56.5-6). However, the inevitability of sin deed for humans (Philo, *Mos.* 2.147; 1QS 3.18-4.1; *4 Ezra* 8.35) is in tension in early Judaism with personal responsibility (*4 Ezra* 8.35; *2 Apoc. Bar.* 54.15, 19). Additionally, *2 Bar.* 64.15-19 identifies Adam almost in a Pelagian manner as merely an example for how anyone could initially sin.

tes and Moabites are excluded from the assembly up to at least ten generations for their sin of inhospitable antagonism during Israel's wilderness wanderings (though Ruth is not banished as she proselytes into Judaism). In contrast, Edomites and Egyptians are merely excluded up to the third generation. Each of these instances of exclusion transfers a judgment multigenerationally, but no one is as open ended and universal as Paul's imputation of Adam's sin to humanity. Paul claims that one of God's purposes of the Mosaic Law is to impute Adam's sin, something the Mosaic Law never addresses. However, prior to the Law being given, there was an epidemic of condemnation and death from Adam which was realized because humanity joined Adam in his deed of sinning (Rom 5:12-14). Before the Law came humanity might not have violated the Law's standard in transgression, but now that the Mosaic Law has been given there is a more direct transaction of Adam's sin deed to humans' heavenly ledger in imputation, leaving us with an epidemic of death through a direct commercial means (Rom 5:13, 15-16). A federal model of imputation of sin describes this commercial transaction the best. It is as if Adam took the family credit card and charged up the national debt, leaving all humans to pay. No human has the resources to pay the national debt, thus all humans directly receive the resultant consequences from our representative Adam's sin, namely, condemnation and death (Rom 5:16, 18).

In this commercial imputation, Adam and Christ occupy leadership of distinctly different realms of humanity within a framework of an Adamic Christology (Pss 8:6; 110:1; Matt 22:44; Mark 12:36; 1 Cor 15:25-27; Eph 1:20-22; Heb 1:13—2:8; 1 Pet 3:22). Expressing their distinctive realms in a similar manner as Qumran uses "the many" and "all,"[9] so Paul appropriates these terms to describe Adam's group (humanity) and Christ's group (new covenant humanity). Through Adam's one transgression Adam makes all in his humanity become sinners, resulting in condemnation and death (Rom 5:15-16). We humans are actively damned and Gollumized into the walking dead by Adam's sin. In contrast, through Christ's death as a gift of grace, all his new covenant humanity become considered righteous, with everlasting life (Rom 5:8-9, 15-21).[10] So the positive accomplishment for Christ's humanity is a legitimate gospel in which Christians are justified in Christ (1 Cor 1:30; 2 Cor 5:21; 6:11).

---

9. A few examples from Qumran of "the many" (1QS 4.1, 7; 6.13, 15, 17-18, 20[2 times]; CD-A 13.7) and "all" (1QS 1.7, 19, 24; 2.24; 3.21-22; 4.24, 26).

10. If an interpreter understands the armor in Eph 6 to be an extension of Yahweh's into the NT as Christ's, then the breastplate of righteousness (Eph 6:14) pictorializes this benefit in Christ. The other option would be to take this metaphor as righteous deed, and they are related to this condition in Christ. The graciousness is further supported by Das, *Paul and the Jews*, 147; 1QHa 19[=11].29-32; 1QS 11.12.

If Adam and Christ are taken as parallel, then a representative model best reflects the mechanism of the imputation; the representative (Adam or Christ) did the deed and their respective humanities get the consequences of the respective status of condemned or righteous in new covenant. Adam left humanity owing the national debt until Christ credited his positive amount to our account, overwhelming the Adamic debt and leaving a strongly positive ledger amount of righteousness. The commercial transaction from our representative Christ includes a rare word, δικαίωσις, which likely incorporates an "act of executing righteous judgment," "justification," or "vindication" (Rom 5:18).[11] Many commentaries take this term as a forensic status of "not guilty" before God's court of judgment.[12] However, in this text this term qualifies "life," so Jewett understands the meaning to be a vindication through the state of righteous living produced by Christ's grace.[13] Jewett's view fits within Edward's religious affections showing authentic Christianity within a Reformed Christian life. Dunn sees that this vindication is forensically eschatological on the basis of a changed life.[14] Dunn's view frames a narrow way within a two-ways salvation strategy. Either option (by Jewett or Dunn) makes sense of the living quality of Christ's gracious righteousness lived out in the believer. Thus, the believer is transformed by far more than a forensic status into a new vital everlasting life creation, mystically reflecting Christ's righteous life quality.

This condition of righteousing life is akin to a marriage covenant that has forensic legal status but goes much deeper into the transformation of the couple's whole being in which they live. To emphasize the forensic marriage certificate is to remain superficial with Christ, though true. To deny the forensic quality of our marriage is to be completely out of touch with the initiation that Christ begins with us in him. However, the transformative quality of imputation does not remain bounded by simply legal forensic status. So, in marriage one's spouse interpenetrates all of life. Likewise here, Adam sin dominates all aspects of our life. However, now in Christ we are married to Christ as his bride in which we grow with greater intimacy and consistency, because Christ mystically interpenetrates all aspects of our life (Rom 8:10; Gal 2:20; Eph 3:17). Our lives are transformed by Christ's imputational righteousness, which initiates us in the new covenant.

Furthermore, the bad news of "death reigning" is more than a commercial or legal transaction; it is a controlling domination by the power

---

11. Schrenk in *TDNT*, 2:223; Thucydides, *Hist.* 1.141; Dionysius Halicarnassus, *Antiq. Rom.* 1.58; 7.59.

12. Murray, *Romans*, 198.

13. Jewett, *Romans*, 386; perhaps Schreiner, *Romans*, 286.

14. Dunn, *Romans*, 1:225, 283.

and consequences of death (Rom 5:14, 17, ὁ θάνατος ἐβασίλευσεν parallel to the same verb where "grace reigns," Rom 5:21, or "the Lord reigns," Rev 19:6).[15] Such a reign of death dominated and controlled "over" (ἐπί) humans held guilty for Adam's offense (Rom 5:14 parallel to Judg 9:8, 10; 1 Kgs 8:7; Rev 5:10; 17:18).[16] Whether through imputation (Rom 5:17) or before such Law-based imputation (Rom 5:14), death reigned mystically through Adam (Rom 5:17). This rule of death before imputation is a spread of death (Gen 5:5–31; Rom 5:12; 7:9–11) because the flesh character of the person is weak and personified sin takes advantage of the person in such a condition (Gen 4:7; Rom 6:19; 7:9–11, 14, 17–18, 20). As God warned Cain, beastly "sin is crouching at the door and its desire is to master you but you must master it" (Gen 4:7). Unfortunately, this results in personified sin reigning as lord in the non-Christian life (Rom 5:21; 6:12–14 κυριεύσει), rather than Jesus Christ, who is our Lord (Rom 5:21 κυρίου; 6:23 κυρίῳ). This rule of sin and death is what Placeus described concerning Adam's sin deed infecting and dominating human sin nature.[17] Agreeing with Placeus on this sin and death reigning does not exclude the federal imputation elsewhere in the passage.[18] This death reigning is akin to that of indwelling sin reigning as a dominating master that characterizes the life before mystically dying with Christ to covenantally enter in Christ (Rom 6:12–14, βασιλευέτω ἡ ἁμαρτία). Such a sin reigned life Gollumizes the person into a contorted walking-dead existence whispering after our precious sins.[19] Such an individual following the broad way of impurity and lawlessness obtains his wages[20] of death (Rom 6:23). However, once alive

---

15. In the LXX ἐβασίλευσεν usually means rule as a human king over his realm (Gen 36:32–39; Josh 13:10–12), though in the Psalms it indicates that God reigns over creation (Pss 46:9; 92:1; 95:10; 96:1; 98:1); Augustine, *Bapt.* 1.13 or 11; Lampe in Balz and Schneider, eds., *Exegetical Dictionary of the New Testament*, 1:208.

16. The non-imputational Adam-caused character change is similar to the original and universal depravity spoken of in *4 Ezra* and *2 Baruch*, which burdened humans "with an evil heart," yet we are still responsible for our own sins (*Ezra* 3.2021; 7.118–26; *2 Bar.* 54.15, 19).

17. La Place, *De Imputatione Primi Peccati Adami*, in *Opera Omnia*.

18. La Place, *De Imputatione Primi Peccati Adami*, in *Opera Omnia*, not so much for his exclusion of federal transmission of sin in response to the Synod of Charenton (1645), but for the argument in chapter 8 that explores the addition of a lived quality, which can be hybridized with federalism as done by Garret, *Systematic Theology*, 1:493 and also 488–89; Schweitzer, *Mysticism of Paul the Apostle*, 115–27, 144, 166–67, 219; Sanders, *Paul and Palestinian Judaism*, 453–523, 548–9; Dobbeler, *Glaube als Teilhabe*, 166–70, 239–80.

19. The metaphor is especially the dialog, domination, and warfare that Gollum and Sméagol have within himself in the *Two Towers* volume of Tolkien's *Lord of the Rings*.

20. This phrase is elsewhere used of a soldier's pay (Luke 3:14; 1 Cor 9:7; *1 Esd* 4.56; 1 Macc 3:28; 14:32; Ignatius, *Pol.* 6.2).

in Christ, the Christian has the new life sufficiently to resist and banish the reign of sin, so he should "not let sin reign in his mortal body" (Rom 6:12).

Parallel to Adam's sin being imputed, Christ's righteousness is imputed as a commercial transaction (Rom 5:16–19 with 5:13, Law now in place). Christ's righteousness commercially transacted as a free gift is the result or the goal (εἰς, Rom 5:16). However, such righteousness also carries mystical new covenant consequences.

The good news includes that this gift and goal "reigns in life" through Jesus Christ (Rom 5:17). Grace and righteousness "reigning" dominates and rules the new covenant Christian life much as sin and death had done for the non-Christian, only now righteousness contributes for our good and with the means (διὰ) being righteous living mystically in Christ and the outcome that of righteousness life (Rom 5:17, δικαιοσύνης . . . ἐν ζωῇ βασιλεύσουσιν διὰ . . . Ἰησοῦ Χριστοῦ, 5:18, εἰς δικαίωσιν ζωῆς, 21, χάρις βασιλεύσῃ διὰ δικαιοσύνης εἰς ζωὴν). Because this imputation is that of a new covenant reality in Christ, this imputation results in more than an accounting or forensic pronouncement but extends to an internal mystical transformation (of a circumcised heart and Law-transformed heart), prompting subsequent obedience (Rom 5:18–19; 6:17 with 2:15, 29; 2 Cor 3:2). Placeus, Sanders, and von Dobbeler develop this as participative and transformative righteousness.[21] This transformative righteousness was developed mystically by Albert Schweitzer, A. Feuillet, Mary Sylvia, Alfred Wikenhauser, Wilhelm Bousset, and Kennard's studies of Qumran with Paul.[22] So this gospel righteousness is not merely *federal forensic and commercial righteousness but also a mystical lived-out righteousness of being "in Christ."* However, only when the last enemy, "death," is conquered will grace reign undiminished (Rom 5:21; 6:9–10; 1 Cor 15:26).

---

21. La Place, *De Imputatione Primi Peccati Adami*, in *Opera Omnia*, ch. 8; Garret, *Systematic Theology*, 1:493 and 488–89; Schweitzer, *Mysticism of Paul the Apostle*, 115–27, 144, 166–67, 219; Sanders, *Paul and Palestinian Judaism*, 453–523, 548–49; Dobbeler, *Glaube als Teilhabe*, 166–70, 239–80.

22. Schweitzer, *Mysticism of Paul the Apostle*, 115–27, 144, 166–67, 219, 225; Feuillet, "Mort du Christ et mort du Chrétien"; Sylvia, *Pauline and Johannine Mysticism*; Wikenhauser, *Pauline Mysticism*; Bousset, *Kyrios Christos*, 193–94; Kennard, *Messiah Jesus*, 315–19; Dunn, *Theology of Paul the Apostle*, 390–412; Kuula, *Law, the Covenant and God's Plan*, 1:37–45 and 2:chs. 2–3, 9; and Bielfeldt, "Response to Sammeli Juntunen, 'Luther and Metaphysics,'" in Braaten and Jenson, eds., *Union with Christ*, 165, argue the Finnish school on Luther agrees with an inner transformational view; Torrance, "Justification" argues that Calvin joins the inner transformational view similar to the Finnish school and opposed to an exclusive forensic perspective; *1 En.* 9.6; 103.2; 1QS 115–118; *4 Ezra* 14.5.

20

Mystical Justification by the Spirit

IN THE MIDST OF the struggle for consistent Christian living, the Holy Spirit becomes the guarantor of growth, indwelling the Christian. This indwelling and empowerment is reminiscent of early Judaism's new covenant transformation as empowered by God's Spirit, prompting Israel to obey the Mosaic covenant (Ezek 34:25 with 36:26-27; Joel 2:28-29; Jer 31:33).[1] While the Spirit identifies that the Christian is in the new covenant, such a ministry of the Spirit also fulfills the essential obligation of the Mosaic covenant as well (Rom 8:4; 13:9; Gal 5:22-23).[2]

The non-Christian[3] is recognizable as the person who thinks and acts according to the things of the flesh, including hostility to God and

---

1. *1 En.* 61.7; *Jub.* 6.17; *Charter of a Jewish Sectarian Association* (1QS; 4Q255-264a; 5Q11) 3.7, 15-4.1; 4.5, 18-23; 1QpHab col. 11.13; *The War Scroll* (1QM, 4Q491-496) 1.1-20; 16.11; 1QH 4, 5, 18; 4Q548 frag. 1 col. 2 9-16; 11Q13 22-25; VanderKam, "Covenant," in Schiffman and VanderKam, eds., *Encyclopedia of the Dead Sea Scrolls*, 1:152; Blanton, "Spirit and Covenant Renewal," 137.

2. *Jos. Asen.* 8.9; 19.11.

3. The contrast of flesh and Spirit in Rom 8 is taken by advocates of Keswick and Augustinian-Dispensational Christian life teachings to be that of the carnal and spiritual Christian; whereas the contrast of flesh and Spirit in Rom 8 is taken by advocates of Reformed, two-ways, and Lutheran Christian life teachings to be that of a non-Christian and vital Christian. A decision between these views is best weighed by considering the descriptions of the affect from the Spirit's enablement. Because Paul provides encouragement of the assurance of salvation in contrast to being a better Christian, it is better to take this text as a contrast between non-Christian and Christian (Rom 8:9-10, 15-17). By listing the flesh and Spirit descriptions one can notice that the flesh has death as the mindset and outcome of flesh existence (Rom 8:6, 13), while life is: the mindset, spiritual condition at present, and ultimate resurrection description of life according to the Spirit (Rom 8:6, 10-11, 13). Such a contrast better fits that of non-Christian and Christian. Additionally, Paul is convinced that the Christians to whom he writes are not in the flesh,

the Mosaic Law (Rom 8:5–8). For them, the Law became "sick" or "weak"[4] on account of their flesh (Rom 8:3; 7:5–6, 14–24). The deeds of the flesh are evident as immorality, idolatry, and fragmenting of community (Gal 5:19–21). Any person who habitually practices such deeds will not inherit the kingdom of God, which in Paul's thought identifies such a person as not belonging to Christ, excluded from God's family, and not inheriting with Christ (Gal 5:16–21; 6:8; Rom 8:7, 9, 15, 17; 1 Cor 6:9–10).

In contrast, the Christian is one who is broadly characterized by the Holy Spirit such that her life and mind reflects the Spirit's concerns. This process is begun by Christ mystically connecting his embodiment (Rom 8:3, "in the likeness[5] of sinful flesh") to our own (Rom 7:25, "sinful flesh"), so that our outcome might have Christ condemning sin in our flesh by Christians living the Law through the Spirit (Rom 8:3–4; 2 Cor 6:11; Gal 5:22–23; Phil 1:11).[6] That is, Christ can be considered to be the agent pouring forth the purifying Spirit, who cultivates the Christian's inheritance in the kingdom and everlasting life (Titus 3:5–7). Such a life lived through the agency of the Spirit bears the fruit of the Spirit through the believer's life, aligning him with the kingdom, namely: love, joy, peace, patience, kindness, goodness, faithfulness, gentleness, and self-control (Gal 5:22–23; Rom 14:17).[7] Notice that such a Spirit-fruitful life condemns sin in our flesh by bringing about the outcome of having the requirement of the Law fulfilled in us (Rom 8:4 ἵνα τὸ δικαίωμα τοῦ νόμου πληρωθῇ ἐν ἡμῖν; Gal 5:23). For

---

probably best taken as the realm of the flesh (Rom 8:9). Paul is inclined to grant that his audience has the Spirit indwelling them, which evidences that they belong to Christ (Rom 8:9, 11). This assurance of belonging to Christ better fits an assurance context, contrasting Christian and non-Christian. Additionally, the Spirit's testimony that we are adopted as sons, that we are children of God, that we are fellow heirs with Christ all better describe the assurance a Christian should have in contrast to non-Christians (Rom 8:15–17) rather than spiritual and carnal Christian lifestyles.

4. The verb "it became weak or sick" is an expression of someone ill (John 11:1; Xenophon, *Anab.* 1.1.1; 6.2.19).

5. Paul uses this term ὁμοιώματι for similarity (Rom 1:23; 5:14; 6:5; 8:3) rather than identity as claimed by Barth, *Romans*, 90.

6. Such compliance to the Law is expected from Second Temple Spirit empowerment (*Jub.* 6.17; *Charter of a Jewish Sectarian Association* [1QS; 4Q255–264a; 5Q11] 3.15–4.1; 4.5, 18–23; 1QpHab col. 11.13; *The War Scroll* [1QM, 4Q491–496] 1.1–20; 16.11; 1QH 4, 5, 18; 4Q548 frag. 1 col. 2 9–16; 11Q13 22–25; VanderKam, "Covenant," in Schiffman and VanderKam, eds., *Encyclopedia of the Dead Sea Scrolls*, 1:151–55; Blanton, "Spirit and Covenant Renewal," 137–38); this position is affirmed by the *Reformed Episcopal Articles of Religion, 1875*, art. 12, "Of the Justification of Man," in Schaff, ed., *Creeds of Christendom*, 3:818.

7. There is no need to multiply the fruit of the Spirit in this text to that of twelve fruit as is done in the Latin *Vulgate* Gal 5:23 by adding faith and modesty before, and chastity after, the fruit of self-control.

example, Spirit-fruited love (for God and one's fellow human) fulfills the Law (Rom 8:4; 13:9; Gal 5:22–23; Deut 6:4–5; Lev 19:18, 34; Matt 22:39–40; Mark 12:32–34; Luke 10:26–27).[8] The result is that the indwelling Spirit transforms the thought and life of the Christian to encourage departing from fearful, unrighteous, condemning ways in death to embrace a mindset of Christ and Spirit with an intimate relationship of prayer reflective of his adoption as a child of God (Rom 8:8, 13–15; Phil 2:5; 3:19). Foundational to this, early Judaism also identified that those who obey the Law are righteous and called sons of God, and thus heirs (usually of the Abrahamic promise, such as in Rom 4:13–14).[9] In the same manner, the Christian is seen as a new covenant person in the Spirit with a greater reality of new covenant benefits to come inherited in the eschatological kingdom. So this Christian vindication by the Spirit fosters life transformation with an ultimate kingdom inheritance role. Such spiritual life accomplishes the same life transformation that a Jewish Law-based assessment previously intended in Jewish covenant nomism. The judgment[10] removed in Romans 8:1 is thus likely a servitude to indwelling sin as a master, which fosters condemning fear and a death lifestyle (developed in Rom 7:14–25), rather than the imposition of forensic condemnation from a distant context. Mystically in the new covenant in Christ, the Christian is set free from a condemning lifestyle dominated and characterized by the flesh, redeemed to the joyous privilege of living life in the Spirit by the agency of the indwelling Holy Spirit (Rom 8:1, 6, 15).

There is a difference of opinion on whether in Romans 8:4 "requirement of the Law [which] might be fulfilled in us" is *obedience of Christ*

---

8. *T. Iss.* 5.2; *T. Dan.* 5.3; *Jub.* 36.3–8; Josephus, *Ag. Ap.* 2.206; Philo, *Spec.* 2.63; *Decal.* 20.154; 108–10; *Abr.* 208; *m. Sanh.* 10.1; Rabbi Akiba in *Sifra Lev.* 19:18; *Sifre* on Deut. 6:4; *b. Šabb.* 31a; *b. Ber.* 63a. Rabbi Akiba considered love of neighbor in Leviticus 19:18 to be also the great commandment (*Sifra Qed.* 4.200.3.7; *Sifra* on Lev. 19:18; *Gen. Rab.* 24.7; *b. Šabb.* 31a). Such love extends even to personal enemies and persecutors (Rom 12:14, 17–20; 1 Cor 4:12–13; 1 Thess 5:15; 1 Pet 3:9; Acts 7:60; *Ep. Arist.* 207, 227, 232; Philo, *Virt.* 116–18; *T. Gad.* 6.1–7; *T. Zeb.* 7.2–4; *T. Iss.* 7.6; *T. Benj.* 4.2–3; 2 *Bar.* 52.6; 2 *En.* 50.4; *b. Ketub.* 68a; *m.' Abot* 1.12; 2.11; 4.3; 5.16; Polycarp, *Ep.* 12.3; Irenaeus, *Haer.* 3.18.5; *Ps.-Clem. Hom.* 3.19; *Ep. Apost.* 18; 2 *Clem.* 13.4; Justin, *1 Apol.* 14.3; Athenagoras, *Supp.* 12.3.

9. Sir 4:10; *Ps. Sol.* 17.26–27; *Jub.* 1.24–25; Wis 16:10; *As. Mos.* 10.3.

10. This word κατάκριμα is used of penal servitude as a consequence of conviction of a crime such as non-payment of taxes (Danker, "Under Contract: A Form-Critical Study of Linguistic Adaptation in Romans," in Barth and Concroft, eds., *Festchrift to Honor F. Wilbur Gingrich*, 105; Kruse, "Kantakkrima-Strafzahlung oder Steuer?"; Deismann, *Bible Studies*, 164–65; Bruce, *Romans*, 159; Halicarnassus, *Antiq. rom.* 13.5.1 cited by Moulton and Milligan, *Vocabulary of the Greek Testament*, 327 from Rainer et al., eds., *Corpus Papyrorum Raineri*, 1.15–16).

resulting in Christian justification,[11] or the *obedience of the Christian* resulting in a lifestyle transformation fulfilling the virtues of the Law like the fruit of the Spirit,[12] or a hybrid of both.[13] The last two options could be described as a Spirit-transformation vindication or a living justification. The focus of νῦν and νυνὶ in the context is "now" within the Christian's life as opposed to initial salvation, so my preference is for lifestyle transformation, which is emphasized in the context (Rom 6:19, 21, 7:6; 17; 8:1, 18). In Paul, the term "walking" (περιπατοῦσιν) indicates ethical virtue in the Christian life or vices within an alternative lifestyle (Rom 8:4),[14] that is, not momentary commitments but long-term virtues of being a person reflective of the Spirit's qualities rather than flesh traits. In light of these Pauline virtues, the Law is fulfilled through the fruit of the Spirit, and especially through deeds of love (Rom 13:8, 10; Gal 5:13-14, 23).[15] Jewish fulfillment of the Law did not require perfection, but repentance and availing oneself of the means of recovery available within the covenant.[16] The sphere within which fulfillment is obtained is "in us" as we become broadly characterized by the Spirit (Rom 8:4-5). As such, in Romans 8:2, "The law of the Spirit of life in Christ Jesus" is the Spirit's transformative life empowerment of the person

---

11. Calvin, *Romans*, 283; Jacombe, *Sermons on the Eighth Chapter to the Epistle to the Romans*, 347-48; Hodge, *Romans*, 249; Moo, *Romans*, 481-84.

12. Augustine, *Spir. et litt.*, 26-29 and especially 46; Luther, *Lectures on Romans*, in *Luther's Works*, 25:243-44; *Lectures on Deuteronomy*, in *Luther's Works*, 9:179; Melancthon, *Loci communes von 1521*, 123; Oecolampadius, *In Hieremiam prophetam commentariorum libri tres Ioannis Oecolampadii*, 2.162a; *The Thirty-Nine Articles of the Church of England* (1571), art. 7; Augustine, Ambroisiater, and Pelagius held this Christian life view (Bray, *Romans*, 205-6); Godet, *Romans*, 302; Murray, *Romans*, 283; Cranfield, *Romans*, 1:383-84; Keck, "The Law and 'the Law of Sin and Death' (Rom 8:1-4): Reflection on the Spirit and Ethics in Paul," in Crenshaw and Sandmel, eds., *Divine Helmsman*, 52-53; Sanders, *Paul, the Law, and the Jewish People*, 93-94; Räisänen, *Paul and the Law*, 65-67; Hübner, *Law in Paul's Thought*, 146-47; Schnabel, *Law and Wisdom from Ben Sira to Paul*, 288-90; Dunn, *Romans*, 1:423-24; Wright, *Climax of the Covenant*, 212; Stuhlmacher, *Romans*, 120; Schreiner, *Law and Its Fulfillment*, 71-73; *Romans*, 404-8; Thielman, *Paul & the Law*, 242-43; Dabney, "'Justified by the Spirit,'" 50; Seifrid, *Christ, Our Righteousness*; Das, *Paul, the Law, and the Covenant*, 226; McFadden, "Fulfillment of the Law's DIKAIŌMA."

13. Melanchthon, *Romans* on 8:4a; Henry, *Matthew Henry's Commentary*, 2211; Lloyd-Jones, *Romans: An Exposition of Chapters 7:1—8:4*, 337-42.

14. Rom 6:4; 13:13; 14:15; 1 Cor 3:3; 2 Cor 4:2; Gal 5:16; Eph 2:2, 10;4:1, 17; 5:2, 8, 15; Phil 3:17-18; Col 1:10; 2:6; 3:7; 1 Thess 2:11; 4:1, 12; 2 Thess 3:6, 11; Schreiner, *Law and Its Fulfillment*, 151.

15. McFadden, "Fulfillment of the Law's DIKAIŌMA," 489-97.

16. Sanders, *Paul and Palestinian Judaism*, 137, 183; Kennard, *Biblical Covenantalism*, 2:96-130.

in Christ to be characterized by Law virtues, such as love and righteousness (Rom 7:6; 8:2, 4; Gal 5:18, 23).

The Spirit guarantees such intimate growth so as to foster thoughts and habits of: life, peace, belonging to Christ, righteousness, resurrection of the body, intimacy in prayer, and fellow inheritance with Christ (Rom 8:6, 9–11, 13–17). In this context, such life associated with belonging to Christ would include everlasting life. This is a lifestyle free from condemnation of the Mosaic Law; in Christ the inner man empowered by the Spirit is free from the peripheralized Mosaic Law related to the flesh (Rom 8:1–2). Therefore, in the way life is lived by the Spirit, the Mosaic Law of the mind does not condemn. The Mosaic Law was rendered impotent to accomplish its tasks as an external standard in light of the weakness of one's flesh (Rom 7:6; 8:3). However, Jesus' condemning of sin in his human flesh made possible the Spirit's transforming of a Christian life so that the righteousness of the Mosaic Law is fulfilled in the Christian's Spirit-produced life (Rom 8:2, 4). Instead of using the Jewish metaphor of "walk by God's Law" (Exod 16:4; Lev 18:4; 1 Kgs 6:12; Prov 20:7; Jer 44:23; Ezek 5:6–7),[17] Paul replaces it with "walk by the Spirit" (Rom 8:4; Gal 5:16, 25). Therefore, the Spirit guarantees that the Christian who appropriately has assurance of his belonging to Christ will be living a righteous life as defined by Mosaic Law virtues. The life that puts to death the deeds of the body will live (Rom 8:13; similar to Deut 30:15–20 and Dan 12:2). Such a life is the beginning of resurrected life fostered by the Spirit as guarantor of eschatological redemption (Rom 8:6, 11, 23; Eph 1:13–14). So the Spirit is the means by which the righteous may hope in the eschatological justification (Gal 5:5). Such a righteous person as a Christian produces abiding righteousness (namely, good deeds) that meets real needs (2 Cor 9:9–10). Such abiding righteousness will still have its affect when it comes to the eschatological judgment, for such a life reaps everlasting life (Gal 6:8; Rom 6:22).

Coupled with this mysticism with the Spirit is also the fact that Christ is mystically present in the believer as well (Rom 8:10; Eph 3:16–17; Col 1:27).[18] Such an internal perichoresis relationship with Christ is completely transformative. With Christ now living in the believer, the life that the believer lives reflects faith and transformation parallel to that which the Holy Spirit performs, thus provoking the believer to hope and love in Christ (Gal 2:20). Paul's and the church's purpose is to form Christ within the community of faith so as to reflect Christ's character through believers (Gal 4:19; Eph 4:15–16; Phil 2:5).

17. *T. Ash.* 6.13; 2 Macc 6:23; 1QS 3.18–4.26; *halak* 3.
18. Wright, *Paul and the Faithfulness of God*, 2:858–59.

The two διὰ clauses in Romans 8:10 should probably be taken in the same way, being in such close proximity to each other. While many take the first clause as indicating that the body is dead or enters the walking dead *because of* (διὰ) sin (Rom 6:23 causing body of death 7:24). For these clauses to be parallel the second clause would then have the sense that the Christian's human spirit is mystically alive *because of* (διὰ) the Christian's righteousness (Rom 6:19, 22). Most would find taking this second clause this way to be unusual, unless they read it through a mystical two-ways orientation (Rom 5:18). Breaking the parallel, the regeneration aliveness of one's human spirit might be *caused by* (διὰ) Christ's righteousness, where "Christ's righteousness" either in his life or in his sacrificial justification and the Spirit's effects on the Christian might be implied from Romans 8:3–4 or 5:21. Another parallel possibility of the two διὰ clauses might be that the body is dead *through the context of* (διὰ) evidential sin in the same way that the Spirit causes life to the Christian's human spirit *through the context of* (διὰ) evidential righteousness (Rom 8:10 similar to Gal 5:19–25a).

Thus, both the flesh life and the Spirit life would be evidentially recognizable and thus provide assurance for salvation by recognizing the Spirit's religious affections becoming evident within the Christian's life.[19] As such, the flesh life would be dominated by flesh thinking and broadly by flesh traits, so that hostility to God could be seen currently in their life of choices to do sin, and ultimately fear and death would ensue because they do not belong to Christ (Rom 8:5–8, 13, 15; 6:21; 14:15; Gal 5:19–21; 6:8). Anyone described in this manner over the long haul should be warned that she is not a Christian and that she is heading for damnation unless she repents.

Likewise, Spirit life would be dominated by Spirit thinking and broadly by the fruit of the Spirit because the Holy Spirit indwells the believer and thus empowers a Spirit-transformed life, which ultimately promises bodily resurrection and inheritance in the kingdom because she is among God's children (Rom 8:5–6, 9–11, 17; Gal 5:21b–23). Such bodily resurrection into immortal spirit bodies is the ultimate redemption of the believer's body because flesh and blood cannot inherit the kingdom so we must all undergo this resurrection change (Rom 8:23; 1 Cor 15:44–50–52). Until this eschatological redemption, from this Spirit empowerment, Paul exhorts those who belong to Christ to choose to live rightly by putting to death their own sinning behavior (Rom 8:9, 12–13; Gal 5:24–26).

However, these virtues concerning which the Christian is exhorted are also fruit (καρπὸς) produced automatically from the Spirit like fruit is produced from a plant. The Spirit becomes the guarantor for growth of the fruit

---

19. Edwards, *Treatise Concerning Religious Affections*.

of: love, joy, peace, patience, kindness, goodness, faithfulness, gentleness, self-control, righteousness, holiness, and truth (Gal 5:22–23; Rom 6:22; Eph 5:9; Phil 1:11). All these virtues are fruit produced by the Holy Spirit.

Such a Spirit-endowed life evidences assurance that the Christian is a child belonging to God and Christ and a coheir of God with Christ (Rom 8:9, 15, 17). Such a life of evident religious affections or fruit of the Spirit is further mystically reassured by the Spirit utilizing these transformed traits to reassure her personal human spirit that she is a child of God ("Spirit witness" Rom 8:16; also Acts 5:32 witness of Spirit given to those who obey God). The Holy Spirit utilizes the qualities of her transformed human spirit to reassure the Christian that she is in the full reality of the adoption relationship and inheritance with God and Christ. Such assurance of salvation is provided by the Spirit mystically transforming the Christian's life to show the fruit of the Spirit, evident for the individual's human spirit and likely evident as fruit of the Spirit that others can also view in and from her life as well.

Such a life quality is founded in the divine activity to adopt us as the people of God, which adoption brings intimate belonging and kingdom inheritance (Rom 8:15–17; Gal 4:5–7; Eph 1:5). With the Pauline emphasis of (1) belonging and (2) inheritance, there is more a Jewish concept of adoption that made Israel become the covenantal people in the first place; "Israel is my son, my firstborn" (LXX: Exod 4:22–23; Deut 14:1; 32:5; Isa 1:2; 30:9; 63:8; Jer 31:9; Hos 2:1 [MT: 1:10]; 11.1; Rom 9:4).[20] This hope for the adopted son Israel is that they would be blessed in the Mosaic covenant blessings unto the kingdom (Jer 3:19). But the unfortunate reality is that as a Israel was destroyed under the covenant curse of the Babylonian captivity (Jer 10:20), only to be regathered by God from the dispersion for kingdom blessing (Isa 43:6; 45:11). Philo eventually expresses that the proselyte also is adopted into the Mosaic covenant community as part of Israel,[21] showing that the adoption metaphor works on an individual level of conversion as well as that of Yahweh's corporate election of the community. Such an expression of adoption in Paul also works on the personal level because it prompts intimate prayer to "Abba, Father" (Rom 8:15; Gal 4:6).

Usually the Roman idea of adoption[22] to serve in the political networking in the senate is absent from Moses, Isaiah, Jeremiah, and Paul's adoption contexts,[23] though service is certainly a Pauline theme.

---

20. Sir 36:17; Wis 12:21; 16:21, 26; 18:13; *Jub.* 1.24; 2.20; *2 Esd.* 6.58; 4Q504 3.6–7.
21. Philo, *Sobr.* 56.
22. Scott, *Adoption as Sons of God*, 3–57.
23. Ibid., 61–267; Burke, *Adopted into God's Family*.

In fact, the hope of the *Testament of Judah* 24:3 is to see that the people Israel and the Messiah are adopted together as God's sons unto the kingdom. This sentiment of adoption merges the Mosaic covenant adoption with that of the Davidic covenant, which extends the adoption formula[24] through the Davidic covenant with its dynastic adoption[25] of the Davidic King as God's son adopted into a relationship of correction to purity and faithfulness (2 Sam 7:14), ultimately to receive everlasting eschatological kingdom benefits (2 Sam 7:16).[26] Paul replaces the Mosaic covenant adoption of Israel with the new covenant adoption of the Christian community and fuses this with the Davidic covenant adoption of the Davidic Son, Christ. The Pauline idea combining the Christian's adoption as a son resulting in the Christian's inheritor role combines these sentiments such that Christ and the Christian become coheirs in the kingdom together (Rom 8:17; Gal 4:7).[27] Such a grand stage of kingdom bodily resurrection is seen by Paul as an eschatological expression of adoption (Rom 8:23) to reflect the earlier reality of adoption into the new covenant community with the Father and identified by the Spirit (Rom 8:15–17; Gal 4:5–7; Eph 1:5).

Ultimately, such adoption ushers in an eschatological everlasting kingdom era identified in Paul as redemption (Old Greek LXX Dan. 4:34 ἀπολυτρώσεως; Eph. 4:30 ἀπολυτρώσεως; 1:14; Rom 8:15, 23 ἀπολύτρωσιν; Luke 1:68; 2:38; 21:28). This redemption is a kingdom dominated by the Holy Spirit, destroying all opposition, including indwelling sin, because the Christian's body will also be eschatologically redeemed (Rom 8:23). However, presently with creation entangled under sin's affect, all creation groans awaiting this eschatological redemption (Rom 8:18–25). However, the initiation of this redemption benefit in Christ is that of a new covenant forgiveness like at the Day of Atonement, with the Holy Spirit transforming

---

24. Adoption formula you are "my son" in 2 Sam 7:14 parallel to 2 Kgs 16:7; parallel to the Hittite treaty between Šuppiluliuma and Šattiwazza as contained in Weidner, *Politische Dokumente aus Kleinasien*, 2:22–26; Weinfeld, "The Covenant Grant in the Old Testament and in the Ancient Near East," *JAOS* 90 (1970) 191, reprinted in Greenspahn, ed., *Essential Papers on Israel and the Ancient Near East*, 69–102; "Addenda to *JAOS* 90 (1970) 469; similar language is used in the "Testament of *Hattušili* adopting *Labarna*," 1.4–5, 37, and 3.24–25, in *Die hethitisch-akkadische Bilingue des Hattušili I (Labarna II)*. Sommer and Falkenstein, 2–7, 12; Kalluveettil, *Declaration and Covenant*, 368–72.

25. God is Father to king as Son; ancient Near East examples include from: Egypt: Pharaoh as son of Re; Ugarit and Mesopotamia: Keret is son of El; and Roman: Caesar as Son of God; cf. von Martitz in *TDNT*, 8:336–40; Hengel, *Son of God*, 24; Dunn, *Christology in the Making*, 14–16; Deissmann, *Light from the Ancient East*, 346.

26. 4Q174 3.11.

27. Similar to *T. Jud.* 24.3.

the Christian's character (Eph 1:7, 14; Rom 8:23; Col 1:14; Heb 9:12, 15). The present transformation of the Christian's character by the Holy Spirit seals and operates as a pledge guaranteeing her eschatological redemption (Eph 1:14; 4:30).

In Christ, the Holy Spirit empowers fruit of the Spirit to grow into Christian consistency, fulfilling the Law as a living justification, adoption, and redemption of the Christian. Those adopted, redeemed, and justified are reassured that they will continue in an everlasting relationship with God, inheriting with Christ and having their bodies redeemed into eschatological glory (Rom 8:17–39).

21

Paul Identifies that Jesus Is Lord

THE JEWISH CONFESSION OF faith, the *Shema*, has been rewritten by Paul in the terms of 1 Corinthians 8:6: "There is one God, the Father, from whom are all things, and we *exist* for him; and one Lord, Jesus Christ, through whom are all things, and we *exist* through him." This Pauline creed, N. T. Wright contends, is the content of Paul's gospel.

> The heart of the Pauline doctrine of justification by faith: that the community of the people of God, those declared in the present to be δικαιος, are those whose faith has precisely this content ... [Justification by faith means] justification by *belief*, i.e. covenant membership demarcated by that which is believed.[1]

The content of such faith is this affirmation of God and Christ. The prominent placement and choice of titles like "Lord" for Jesus, coupled with the pronoun "our," also supports this allegiance to Christ rather than Caesar, with much the same language as a loyalty oath (Rom 5:1, 11, 21; 7:25 κυρίου ἡμῶν; 10:9–10).[2] This focus of the content of gospel, identified as one's loyalty to God and Christ, is also apparent from the content of Paul's gospel messages in Acts, which focus on God and Christ but nowhere spell out the efficaciousness of Christ's substitutionary death and regularly have listeners believing and becoming saved (Acts 13:16–48; 16:31; 17:22–32; 18:3–6;

---

1. Wright, *Climax of the Covenant*, 2; *Justification*, 46; Smith, *Justification and Eschatology*, 15.

2. Josephus, *J.W.* 7.418; Suetonius, *De Vita Caesarum* 13.2; Hofius, "ὁμολογεω ὁμολογια," in *EDNT* 2 (1991) 515–16; Bietenhard, "Lord, Master," in *DNTT*, 2:511; Cullmann, *Christology of the New Testament*, 197–99.

19:1-7; 20:21).³ So believing gospel essentially is allegiance to God and to Jesus Christ as Lord.

In Romans 1:1-4 the gospel of God is identified as "Jesus is Lord," promised beforehand by the holy prophets, born according to Davidic lineage, and boldly declared by the Spirit through his resurrection.⁴ This gospel statement becomes authoritative for Paul's disciples as well, for, speaking about the Lord, Paul says, "Remember Jesus Christ, risen from the dead, descendant of David, according to my gospel" (2 Tim 2:8).

Paul identified in Romans 10:9-10, "if you confess with your mouth Jesus as Lord, and believe in your heart that God raised him from the dead, you shall be saved; for with the heart man believes, resulting in righteousness, and with the mouth he confesses, resulting in salvation." Such confession appears here as a "specifically Christian religious usage" that "affirms Jesus as authoritative and identifies the confessor as his follower."⁵ Such a confession identifies the speaker as subservient and belonging to the Lord as her final loyalty.⁶ So each belief or confession that "Jesus is Lord" saves. As Paul, quoting Joel 2:32, maintained, "Whoever will call upon the name of the Lord will be saved" (Rom 10:13). In this context, confessing "*Jesus is Lord*" is essentially gospel.

---

3. Kennard, *Messiah Jesus*, 439-70.

4. Pokorny, *From the Gospel to the Gospels*, 9-10.

5. Jewett, *Romans*, 629-30; Hofius, "ὁμολογεω ὁμολογια," *EDNT* 2 (1991) 515-16; von Campenhausen, "Das Bekenntnis im Urchistentum," *ZNW* 63 (1972) 211; Michael in *TDNT*, 5:209; Hurtado, *One God*, 112.

6. Josephus, *J.W.* 7.418-9; Suetonius, *De Vita Caesarum* 13.2; Jewett, *Romans*, 629-30; Dunn, *Romans*, 2:607-8; Hofius, "ὁμολογεω ὁμολογια," *EDNT* 2 (1991) 515.

22

Redemption Victory Procession

PAUL DESCRIBES HIS MINISTRY of the gospel (εὐαγγέλιον) of Christ preached in Troas as an open door in the Lord (2 Cor 2:12–13). Paul's ministry in Macedonia is described as a victory prompting him to break out in triumphal thanksgiving.

In 2 Corinthians 2:14–17 Paul's praise is to God as a military victor, indicated through a triumphal procession.[1] Such triumphal processions come after the military victory is complete and the conquering general returns to his home city from which the campaign emerged. Trumpeters would announce the procession. At the head of the procession came the magistrates and the senators. Many individuals along the procession would waft incense and carry the spoils of victory. The notable captives would be led in chains or transported as part of these spoils, usually to be sold in the slave market or given to the patrons of the campaign. Then the general would ride in a chariot, being acclaimed for the greatness of his conquest. The conquering soldiers would follow, marching down the main street, showing the might of the general's troops.

Many take the Christians or Paul as slaves of conquest in 2 Corinthians 2 based on the Philemon 23 reference indicating that they are "fellow prisoners" (συναιχμάλωτός) in Christ. This is possible, but the other references of συναιχμάλωτός in Romans 16:7 and Colossians 4:10 clarify that Paul as "fellow prisoner" is actually a Roman prisoner for the cause of Christ as he writes these letters. All three references could be taken as being written from prison, removing any identification with this 2 Corinthians 2 context developing Christians as conquered slave spoils. Taking this view to

---

1. Josephus, *J.W.* 7.153–55; Dio Cassius, *Roman History* 6.23; Plutarch, *Aemilius Paulus* 32.1–36.6; Versnel, *Triumphus*; Marshall, "Meaning of Social Shame," 304.

the extreme, Scott Hafemann extends the prisoner image to requiring that Christians are slaves heading to death in the arena.[2] Even if someone would grant Christians were conquered slaves (which I have not here, but do in Eph 4:8–13), there are many instances of triumphal procession in which the conquered did not end in martyrdom in the arena but rather service to a new master.[3] The reference in Ephesians 4:8–13 develops such service as being gifted to the church.

Instead, 2 Corinthians 2:14 indicates Christians are a fragrance in this procession. In a triumphal procession this fragrance would be accomplished by either perfume or flowers sprinkled along the route.[4] Such fragrance would be a sweet smell of victory for the conquerors and a stench of defeat for the conquered. In Paul's illustration in 2 Corinthians 2:14, the Christian people are the fragrance. The splitting of a people into the metaphor of being both fragrance and stench is also utilized by 2 *Apoc. Bar.* 67:6 as those who live rightly by the Law or the impious violators.[5] Therefore, for Christians, those who know Christ become a sweet aroma of victory "from life to life" (2 Cor 2:14–15). However, for the conquered who resist such knowledge of Christ, the Christian's presence is a stench of their damning defeat, an aroma "from death to death." The focus is on being in Christ and that others in Christ recognize the hope of resurrection that all in Christ have and are encouraged by that fragrance.[6]

Such a divine gospel message is honestly presenting the truth in Christ with integrity before God (2 Cor 2:17). God is the one who has won the victory and authored the gospel. However, the message is that in Christ there is life and victory. The Spirit transformation of Christians through the new covenant showcases the evidence of this fragrant transformation (2 Cor 3).

---

2. Hafemann, *Suffering and the Spirit*, 33–39.

3. Augustus, *Res Gestae* 1.4; Appian, *Mithridatic Wars* 12.117; Plutarch, *Reg.* 76.6–7; 77.2; *Flam.* 13.3–6; Livy, *Hist. Rom.* 33.23.1–6; 34.52.11–12; Hafemann (*Suffering and the Spirit*, 108–9) acknowledges the majority of prisoners were sold into slavery; Guthrie, *2 Corinthians*, 171–73. Eph 4:8–13 does not identify as gospel though it supports God and Christ resourcing and setting the agenda for the church.

4. Horace, *Odes* 4.2.50–51; Suetonius, *Nero* 25.2; Appian, *Punica* 66.

5. Fragrance echoed as *Torah* in *Deut. Rab.* 1.6; *B. Šabb.* 88b; *b. Yoma* 72b; Bruce, *1 and 2 Corinthians*, 188. Judaism also identifies the way of wisdom (Sir 24:15) and the tree of life with attractive fragrance (*1 En.* 24–25; Furnish, *2 Corinthians*, 188).

6. Harris, *Second Corinthians*, 248.

23

Paul's Narrow Way to Everlasting Life

IN A TWO-WAYS SALVATION framework, the narrow way to everlasting life can be considered to be the gospel because it provides the good news for how a person obtains the encouraging outcome of everlasting life through God's eschatological judgment. Paul develops this two-way salvation model in Romans 2, 6, and 11.

Paul occasionally frames salvation as a narrow way to live within a two-ways approach to salvation (Rom 2:5–11).[1] For Paul, such a forensic justification is eschatological and evidential (Rom 2:5, 8). Paul positions himself within early Judaism, including future eschatological righteous judgment as "rendering to every man according to his deeds" (ἔργα, Rom 2:6, 13; 14:10–12; 1 Cor 3:8; 2 Cor 5:10; Col 3:25).[2] With Paul extending the Jewish eschatological forensic pattern, any past Christian justification is better seen within another metaphor than forensic, such as a covenantal

---

1. Also Rom 6:16–22; 11:17–21.

2. This judgment according to deeds fits the Jewish narrow way pattern: 1 Kgs 8:32; Job 34:11; Pss 28:4; 62:12; Prov 24:12; Jer 16:18; 17:10; 21:14; 32:19; Ezek 7:4; Hos 4:9; Mic 7:13; Dan 7:9–10, 18, 26; Matt 16:27; 25:41–46; Rom 2:6; 14:12; 1 Cor 3:5; 2 Cor 5:10; Eph 6:8; Col 3:25; Rev 2:23; 20:11–15; 22:12; Sir 11:26; 16:12, 14; 32.24; *Jub.* 5.11, 15; 20.2; 23.20–21; *1 En.* 9.4; 47.3 with 46.2; 60.2; 62.2–16; 63:1–12; 82.4; 90:20–36; 95.5; 100.7; *2 En.* 63.1–2; *Pss. Sol.* 2.7, 7, 16, 25, 34–35; 17.8–9; *Jos. Asen.* 28.3; 1QS 2.7–8; 9.18–21; 10.21; 11.13; 1QSa 1.2; 1QHa 12.18–25; 14.10, 23–24; 1QX 10.11, 17–18; 1QH 4.18–19; 5.5–6; 14.24; 1QM 11.3–4; 18.14; CD 1.11, 13, 16; 2.3; 3.4–5; 5.15–16; 7.9; 20.24; 1QpHab 12.2–3; 1Q22 2.8; 4QpPs 37.4–9; 4Q185 1.1–2; 2.1–2, 4; 4Q246 col. 2; 4Q260 5.1; 4Q400 1.1, 14; 4Q405 23.1.11; 4Q429 4.1.10; 4Q473 1; 4Q511 2.1.6; 11Q5 22.10; 11Q Melch. 2.13; 11QT 54.17; *L.A.B.* 3.10; 44.10; 64.7; *2 Bar.* 54.21; 72. 2, 6; 73–74.4; *4 Ezra* 5.1; 7.37, 76–77; *T. Abr. A* 11.11; 12.1–18; 13.12; 14A; *Sib. Or.* 2.183–84, 239–54, 283–338; *b. Ned.* 39b–40a; *Midr. Ps.* 118.19. Yinger, *Paul, Judaism and Judgement According to Deeds*; Kim, *God Will Judge Each One According to Works*.

sacrifice (rather than a legal fiction, which affirms and denies the same meaning simultaneously). That is, there are two ways and two forensically judged outcomes possible for human life: (1) everlasting life for those who are known as doing good, and (2) God's wrath for the unrighteous (Rom 2:7-8). Much of the church continues to reflect Paul's concern that eschatological justification is rendered to every human according to her deeds.[3] To a stubborn unrepentant person who is selfishly ambitious and does not obey the truth, the characterization of unrighteousness describes his life with the outcome of God's wrath and indignation. So the wrath of God comes presently and eschatologically upon the sons of disobedience (Rom 1:18; 2:5, 8; 9:22; Eph 5:6; Col 3:6; 1 Thess 2:16; Matt 3:7; Luke 3:7; John

---

3. This judgment according to deeds is continued in the two-ways teaching of the church: *Did.* 1.1.1-4; 4.14b; *1 Clem.* 34-35; *2 Clem.* 6.8; 8.4; Polycarp, *Phil.* 10; Ignatius, *Phil.* 5.1; *Eph.* 3.1; *Barn.* 16.7-8; 18.1-2; 19; Justin Martyr, *Dial.* 3.4; *1 Apol.* 16.8-9; *2 Apol.* 9; Irenaeus, *Haer.* 3.1.10 maintained this as the universal teaching all Christians held at the time; *Herm. Mand.* 2.7; *Herm. Sim.* 3.8.6-11; Clement of Alexandria, *Strom.* 4.6; Quis div.; Commodianus, *Instructions* 28; Origen, *Comm. Matt.* 14.10-13; *Fr. Prin.* 2.9.7-8; 3.1.12; Cyprian, *Fort.* 12-13; Dionysius of Alexandria, *Exegetical Fragments 7 Reception of Lapsed*; Methodius of Olympus, *The Banquet of the Ten Virgins* 9.3; *Oration Concerning Simeon and Anna* 8; Lactantius, *Inst.* 3.12; 6.3-7; 7.10; Eusebius, *Hist. eccl.* 3.20.6-7; 5.8.5; *Council of Sardica Lengthy Creed*: Socrates Scholasticus, *Hist. eccl.* 2.19=Athanasius, *Syn.* 26; A.D. 351 and 359 *Sirmium Creed*: Socrates Scholasticus, *Hist. eccl.* 2.30=Athanasius, *Syn.* 27; *Synod at Ariminum Creed*: Socrates Scholasticus, *Hist. eccl.* 2.37; A.D. 359 *Seleucia Creed*: Socrates Scholasticus, *Hist. eccl.* 2.40=Athanasius, *Syn.* 8; A.D. 359 *Confession at Niké* and A.D. 360 *Constantinople Creed*: Athanasius, *Syn.* 30; A.D. 359 *Ariminum Creed* and modified for the A.D. 381 Council at Constantinople: Socrates Scholasticus, *Hist. eccl.* 2.41; Cyril, *Catechetical Lectures* 15.1, 24-25, 33; Gregory of Nyssa, *On Pilgramages*, para. 1; *The Great Catechism* 40; Gregory Nazianzen, *Letter 4 to Basil*; Ambrose, *Duties of the Clergy* 1.16.59; Augustine, *Civ.* 13.8; 14.25; 19.11; 20.1-8, 12, 14, 22; 21.1; *Enchir.* 15; 31-32; 55; 107; 113; *Perf.* 42-44; *Ennarat. Ps.* 31.25; 112.5; *Tract. Ev. Jo.* 124.5; Hilary of Poitiers, *On the Trinity* 12.45; Leo the Great, *Sermons* 46.3; 49.2, 5; 63.2, 7; 67.5-6; 72.1; 95.1-9; Vincent of Lérins, *The Commonitory* 23.57-59, which he claims is the teaching everyone held at that time 23.4-6; John Cassian, *Cassian's Conferences* 1.5; 6.8; 13.13; 14.3; John Climacus, *The Ladder of Divine Ascent*, 9.1; summary on step 30; Thomas à Kempis, *Of the Imitation of Christ*, especially 1.23; 2.7; 3.44, 56; Bunyan, *Pilgrim's Progress*, especially 18, 187; Willard, *Divine Conspiracy*; Yinger, *Paul, Judaism, and Judgment According to Deeds*, 285 summary but argued through the book; Dunn, *New Perspective on Paul*, 72-73; "If Paul Could Believe both in Justification by Faith and Judgment According to Works, Why Should That Be a Problem for Us?" and "Response to Thomas Schreiner," in Gundry, ed., *Four Views on the Role of Works at the Final Judgment*, 135, 106-8. However, this view can be granted from outside the two-ways tradition, such as from the Reformed tradition: Calvin, *Institutes*, 3.15.8; 3.16.1, "we are justified not without works, and not by works, since in the participation in Christ, by which we are justified, is contained not less sanctification than justification," 16.3; 18.1; Schreiner, "Justification Apart from and by Works: At the Final Judgment Works Will *Confirm* Justification," in Gundry, ed., *Four Views on the Role of Works at the Final Judgment*, 78-79.

3:36). However, to the one who perseveres in doing "good works" (ἔργου ἀγαθοῦ) and seeks his own[4] glory, honor, and immortality, the outcome of God's judgment is his own everlasting life, glory, honor, and peace (Rom 2:7, 10), while eschatological judgment is made according to "deeds" (Rom 2:6, ἔργα, 2:7, ἔργου ἀγαθοῦ), which show the character of a person. This eschatological salvation way should not be considered an earned salvation, for the human basis is located instead in the virtues of consistent goodness and seeking noble ends, similar to that of early Judaism's gracious emphasis. God's eschatological righteous judgment welcomes all the righteous into the kingdom with a crown of righteousness while damning those who persecute them (2 Thess 1:5-6; 2 Tim 4:8). Paul elsewhere ties the hope of this eschatological justification to the present new covenant work provided through the Spirit (Rom 2:14-16; Gal 5:5).[5] Likewise, from his work comparing the *Psalms of Solomon* to the letters of Paul, Mikael Winninge reminds that Jewish materials join Paul in presenting a universality of sinfulness such that the righteous within the narrow way could be more accurately called the "sinfully righteous" as opposed to the "stubbornly disobedient 'sinners.'"[6]

Christian traditions (such as Orthodox, Roman Catholic, Anglican, Episcopalian, Wesleyan, and Anabaptist) retain the possibility of gaining the kingdom by following Christ through a Spirit-fostered faithful love relationship with God, as is expressed in the Decalogue.[7] From a Gentile perspective, these traditions diminish the Mosaic Law to essentially the Decalogue instead of the ancient Nazarene approach affirming the whole Law for Jewish Christians. Furthermore, these are the same traditions that embrace a two-ways soteriology and consider that, in this two-ways salvation, the Law matters. For example, N. T. Wright addresses this perspective from the ac-

---

4. Glory, honor, and immortality could refer to God or human, though in the immediate context with humans receiving glory, honor (Rom 2:10), and everlasting life (Rom 2:7) (and everlasting life being a virtual synonym for immortality), it is best to take these objects sought as for man who seeks and finds them.

5. Wesley's sermon "The Circumcision of the Heart, Rom 2:29"; Zahn, *Brief des Paulus an die Römer*; Mundle, "Zur Auslegung von Röm 2:13ff," *ThBl* 13 (1934) 249-56; Flückinger, "Die Werke des Gesetzes bei den Heiden (nach Röm 2.14ff)," *ThZ* 8 (1952) 17-42; Barth, *Romans*, 36-39; Souček, "Zur Exegese von Röm 2, 14ff.," in *Antwort*, 99-113; Cranfield, *Romans*, 1:155-63; König, "Gentiles or Gentile Christians?: On the Meaning of Romans 2:12-16," *JTSA* 15 (1976) 53-60; Salas, "Dios premia según las obras (Estudio exegético-teólogico de Rom. 2,6-11)," in *La idea de Dios*, 265-86; Bergmeier, *Gesetz im Römerbrief*, 31-102; Watson, *Paul, Judaism, and the Gentiles*, 118-22; Wright, "The Law in Romans 2," in Dunn, ed., *Paul and the Mosaic Law*, 131-50; Jewett, *Romans*, 212-14.

6. Winninge, *Sinners and the Righteous*, 264, 305.

7. Origen, *Homily 8.1 on Exodus*; Augustine, *Contra Faustum* 10.2; *Spirit and Letter* 17.29; Wright, "The Law in Romans 2," in Dunn, ed., *Paul and the Mosaic Law*, 143-44.

count of the rich young ruler: "The Torah was the boundary marker of the covenant people: those who kept it would share the life of the coming age."[8] Wright explains how the Law matters for a forensic eschatological justification view within a two-ways soteriology from Romans 2:12–16.

> It is vital to note that the justification and the judgment spoken of in this paragraph are inalienably *future*. This is not *present* justification; Paul will come to that in chapter 3. Nor can the two be played off against one another. They belong together: present justification, as Romans makes clear, is the true anticipation of future justification. And in Romans as elsewhere in Paul, it is present justification, not future, that is closely correlated with faith. Future justification, acquittal at the last great Assize, always takes place on the basis of the totality of the life lived.[9]

Wright goes on to explain that "'Justification' in the first century was not about how someone might establish a relationship with God. It was about God's eschatological definition, both future and present, of who was, in fact, a member of his people."[10] Similarly, E. P. Sanders describes *justification* as not so much about *getting in*, or even *staying in*,[11] as the *status* and *assurance* of how you can tell *who was in*. After establishing this two-ways soteriology, N. T. Wright continues to place the Law as mattering within it.

> First, we may consider the peculiar situation of those described here. [Romans] 2.13 and 2.14, taken together, indicate quite clearly that those described in the latter as 'doing the law' will, according to the former, be justified (remember, again that we are here dealing with *future*, not present, justification).[12]

Within this two-ways framework, the Mosaic Law informs the way of salvation so that those who manifest the virtue of doing the Law will be justified by God (Rom 2:13). While obviously not the full picture, this narrow way is not merely self-mastery, while God stores up sins not atoned until the Day of Judgment, as Stanley Stowers claims.[13] In Stowers' view, the Gentiles need the atonement Christ provides but the Jews, who have atone-

---

8. Wright, *Jesus and the Victory of God*, 301.

9. Wright, "The Law in Romans 2," in Dunn, ed., *Paul and the Mosaic Law*, 143–44; *Paul and the Faithfulness of God*, 2:935–39.

10. Wright, *What Saint Paul Really Said*, 119.

11. Sanders, *Paul and Palestinian Judaism*, 544–46.

12. Wright, "The Law in Romans 2," in Dunn, ed., *Paul and the Mosaic Law*, 146; similarly Stettler, "Paul, the Law and Judgment by Works," *EQ* 76 (2004) 195–215.

13. Stowers, *Reading of Romans*, 32, 36, 106, 129, 176, 190.

ment means, would possibly not have this need. Rather, Paul develops this narrow way as an inner transformation that would indicate whether this Gentile is kingdom bound[14] and the Law-violating Jew is damned.[15] Those who hear the Mosaic Law but do not apply it are judged as sinners under the Law (Rom 2:12–13; Gal 3:10). Furthermore, those who do not have the Mosaic Law are not judged by the Mosaic Law's standards but by the standards of their own conscience, by which God reveals and judges them in the eschatological forensic judgment (Rom 2:1–3, 12, 15–16). These Gentiles without a textual copy of the Law but with new covenant transformation[16] ("Law written in the hearts," Jer 31:33; Rom 2:15 and "circumcision of heart by the Spirit," Deut 30:6; Rom 2:29) keep the Law (Rom 2:26). Christian Stettler identifies that such behavior fulfills the Law by keeping the primary virtues of the Law, like love, mercy, and justice, without keeping all of the details of the Law (Rom 8:4; 13:8, 10; Gal 5:14, 23).[17] Such an orientation is not a natural law perspective in one's own efforts but a Spirit-transformed new covenant empowering to live Law virtues such as love of God and fellow human. Such a person who "observes the righteous requirement of the Law" fulfills the condition for the Mosaic covenant stipulations (Rom 2:26; Exod 15:26 LXX: Ἐὰν . . . φυλάξῃς πάντα τὰ δικαιώματα αὐτοῦ; Deut 4:40;

---

14. Consistent with a minority of Second Temple texts that allow for an internally transformed Gentile to be saved (Philo, QE 2.2).

15. Consistent with mainstream Second Temple Judaism (T. Jos. 18.1; Jub. 5.10; 10.17; 22.22; 2 Bar. 48.22b; CD 3.11–16, 20–21; 7.5, 9; 13.11; 20.17–20, 25–27; 4Q228 frag. 1 1.9; 4Q266, frag. 11; 4QMMT C; 1QS 3.7–12).

16. Sectarian Second Temple Judaism viewed the new covenant as being realized among their new covenant community in Israel: *Charter of a Jewish Sectarian Association* (1QS, 4Q255–264a and 5Q11) 3.7–12, 26; 4.22–23; 5.5, 21; *Damascus Document* (CD 4Q268 frag. 1=4Q266 frag. 2 Col. 1) ver. 6; 6.19; 8.21; 14.1–2; B col. 19, ver. 12–13 here the new covenant is clearly still law like Jer 31:33 Hebrew; 19:33; 20:12; 1QpHab 2.3; 11.13, "circumcision of heart's foreskin"; *4 Ezra* 9.31; Freedman and Miano, "People of the New Covenant" and Evans, "Covenant in the Qumran Literature" in Porter and de Roo, eds., *Concept of the Covenant in the Second Temple Period*, 7–26 and 55–80 respectively. Paul is extending this to Gentiles. Wesley's sermon "The Circumcision of the Heart, Rom 2:29" presents a Gentile new covenant Christian showing that she is saved because of the life transformation wrought by the Spirit of God to obey the Law (Rom 8:2, 4; Gal 5:23).

17. Stettler, "Paul, the Law, and Judgment by Works," *EQ* 76 (2004) 203–5, 208–11; Wesley, "The Circumcision of the Heart, Rom 2:29"; Gorman, *Becoming the Gospel*, 63–64 extends the narrow way through a gospel of faith(fulness), love, and hope from 1 Thess.

6:2; 7:11; 26:17; 28:45; 30:10, 16).[18] Such Law-obedient Gentiles become the foil for judging Jewish disobedience (Rom 2:13–16, 26–29).[19]

There is no discussion of a natural law informing such a person's conscience, rather, merely the conscience is that fallible personal assessment by which a person critiques others' and her own deeds. This expression of the Mosaic Law is said to be "in her nature" (φύσει; Rom 2:14) in the sense that it is lived consistently with one's *whole nature*, not through the means of a transcendental intuition as in Stoicism or natural law.[20] Whatever subjective standard one uses to judge others' lives is a standard one binds upon one's own life, usually bringing judgment. When a person without the Mosaic Law uses her conscience, she might possess notable virtues that the Mosaic Law also addresses, like doing good, loving, or seeking to live honorably. When such a person lives this way, she is instinctively doing some of the things of the Mosaic Law, not all (Rom 2:14). The conscience itself does not justify a person but the Lord's judgment does (2 Cor 4:4). So, to the extent that her conscience reflects Mosaic Law concerns, she evidences what would normally be attributed as a new covenant benefit of having the Mosaic Law written in her heart, which would identify her with the way of salvation. Paul does not here tell us how this person might have a new covenant benefit without having the Mosaic covenant, but it is unlikely that Paul is setting forth an alternative salvation than faith in Christ since he sums up all under

---

18. Other examples of this technical covenant formulation are: Pss 104:45; 118:5, 8; Prov 2:8; Ezek 11:20; 18:9; 20:13, 18, 19, 21; 43:11; Mic 8:16; 3 Kgdms 2.3; Freedman and Miano, "People of the New Covenant," in Porter and de Roo, eds., *Concept of the Covenant in the Second Temple Period*, 7–26. Philo describes a Gentile proselyte to Judaism in this manner as one who is "circumcised not in foreskin but in pleasures, desires, and other passions of the soul." (*QE* 2.2).

19. Those who also agree that this text is describing a Christian new covenant Gentile (rather than natural law) as a foil for Jewish disobedience: Zahn, *Brief des Paulus an die Römer*; Mundle, "Zur Auslegung von Röm 2:13ff," *ThBl* 13(1934) 249–56; Flückinger, "Die Werke des Gesetzes bei den Heiden (nach Röm 2.14ff)," *ThZ* 8(1952) 17–42; Barth, *Romans*, 36–39; Souček, "Zur Exegese von Röm 2, 14ff.," in *Antwort*, 99–113; Cranfield, *Romans*, 1:155–63; König, "Gentiles or Gentile Christians?: On the Meaning of Romans 2:12–16," *JTSA* 15 (1976) 53–60; Salas, "Dios premia según las obras (Estudio exegético-teólogico de Rom. 2,6–11)," in *La idea de Dios en la Biblica XXVIII semana biblica española (Madrid 23–27 Sept. 1968)*, 265–86; Bergmeier, *Gesetz im Römerbrief*, 31–102; Watson, *Paul, Judaism, and the Gentiles*, 118–22; Wright, "The Law in Romans 2," in Dunn, ed., *Paul and the Mosaic Law*, 131–50; Jewett, *Romans*, 212–14; Kennard, *Biblical Covenantalism*, 1:11–15; 3:64–70.

20. The word φύσει refers to wholistic nature of the person and consistency with this condition in other instances in the NT (Gal 2:15; 4:8; Eph 2:3; Jas 3:7), and that is also how other instances of φύσις broadly are used in Romans (1:26; 2:27; 11:21, 24). So in Rom 2:14 the term "nature" is a new covenant nature from which the Gentile operates and fulfills the Mosaic Law.

sin, including the denial that there are righteous and good people in order to bring them to Christ's redemption (Rom 3:9-12, 23-24). However, it is likely that Paul conceives of a human with this new covenant transformation of his conscience, such that he could do good, as seeking Mosaic Law virtues without the Mosaic Law text, and thereby being justified in God's eschatological judgment. In Paul, such a description would be one way to describe a Gentile person who has faith in Christ. If this is the case, then Mosaic Law virtues (such as consciously doing Mosaic Law deeds as an intrinsic motivation of one's conscience) have salvific value as a statement of gospel in aiding this person on the way of salvation.

In Romans 6, the issue is enslavement and the consequences that follow from being rescued from the realm of sin (or the realm of the Law) as an "old human," rescued into the more powerful realm and person of Christ as a "new human" (Rom 5:13; 6:1, 14; 7:1-4; Gal 2:20). This exodus from the realm of sin into new covenant transformation within Christ is what Paul means by the present experience of redemption (Rom 3:24; 1 Cor 1:30). To follow these strands, Romans 6 has two primary points, as indicated by the questions in verses 1 and 15. First, in mystically connecting with Christ's death and resurrection we are changed into new humans with a new covenant relationship in Christ and removed from the realm of sin ("old man," ὁ παλαιὸς ἡμῶν ἄνθρωπος), so we should think and live differently reflecting this change (Rom 6:1-14; Gal 2:20).[21] This mystical beginning is visibly identified as occurring at a Christian's conversion marked by the initiation rite of baptism into Christ, after the pattern of early Jewish proselyting baptism into Moses (Rom 6:3-4; Gal 3:27)[22] and John the Baptist's baptism into kingdom-oriented Judaism (Matt 3:6, 11; Mark 1:4, 8; Luke 3:3, 6; John 1:26; 3:5; Acts 19:3-5 baptism into [εἰς] John or Christ). Paul describes that the

---

21. Kennard, *Messiah Jesus*, 313-21, 342-44; Schweitzer, *Mysticism of Paul the Apostle*, 101-40. Some see a parallel metaphor with that of mythical death and resurrection from Isis (Apuleius, *Met.* 11.21), but I think Kim's proposal from Paul's conversion is a closer metaphor (Kim, *Origin of Paul's Gospel*).

22. Baptism into Moses as a Jewish metaphor is evident on the Dura Europa synagogue west wall with a beehive-shaped rock pouring water like a fountain running to the tents of Israel, as described in Goodenough, *Jewish Symbols in the Greco-Roman World*, vol. 11, plate 12; Exod 17:6; Num 20:8-11; 1 Cor 10:2; Josephus, *Ant.* 10.7; *Num. Rab.* 1.2; 19.25-26; Targum *Onkelos* on Num 21:17; Etheridge, *The Targums of Onkelos*, 142-3; *Sifre* on Num. 11:21; *b. Šabb.* 35a; Ap. Eusebius, *Praep. Ev.* 9; 29.16; Ellis, *Paul's Use of the Old Testament*, 66-67; Willis, *Idol Meet in Corinth*, 133. Convert baptism to Qumran (1QS 3.3-9; 4QTLevi ar). Gentile proselyte baptism to Judaism (Josephus, *J.W.* 2.150; *Ant.* 14.285; 18.93-4; 18.117; *T. Levi* 2.3.1-2; *Sib. Or.* 4.162-70; Epictetus, *Diatr.* 2.9.19-20; *Apoc. Moses* 29.6-13; *m. Tohar* 7.6; *b. Yebam.* 46a-48b; Midrash Sifre Num. 15.14; *t. Yoma* 4.20; *t. Pesaḥ* 7.13). Christian convert baptism (Rom 6:3-4; 1 Cor 1:13-16; John 18:28; Acts 2:38-41; 10:28).

believer is baptized into (εἰς) Christ, that is, mystically baptized into (εἰς) Christ's death (Rom 6:3–4).[23] Such a mystical awareness that we are new humans in Christ is conceived after the pattern in which Paul was rendered a new human by meeting Christ on the Damascus road (Rom 6:6; Acts 9:1–22; 22:3–21).[24] Kim develops that in the same manner that the murderous sinning Paul died when Christ met him on the Damascus road to become mystically Christ's new human in new covenant, so it is when anyone comes into faith in Christ. So the "old man" (ὁ παλαιὸς ἡμῶν ἄνθρωπος) is all we were prior to coming to Christ (Rom 6:6; Col 3:9).[25] So the death of the non-Christian self is accomplished by Christ as a person enters into Christ (Rom 6:6 and Eph 4:22 are passive verbs; Col 3:9 middle). Likewise, the "body of sin" (τὸ σῶμα τῆς ἁμαρτίας) is a holistic description of the embodied life prior to Christ because in this context "body" (σῶμα) is used holistically (Rom 6:6, 12–13). Therefore, the intended outcome of having "the body of sin done away" either means that we lose our flesh body when we resurrect in a spiritual body (Rom 6:6; 7:24–25; 8:23; 1 Cor 15:42–44) or that within a person's embodiment she would progressively be utilizing her members as instruments *for worship and allegiance*[26] to God instead of as weapons[27] of idolatrous allegiance to sin (Rom 6:12–13). This new beginning in Christ makes an individual a "new creation" in which these old allegiances have passed away and new empowerment and allegiances have begun (1 Cor 5:17; Gal 5:17; 6:15 καινὴ κτίσις). Such a *mystical entrance into Christ could also be considered to be gospel because of the transformation Christ brings*. This new beginning ushers the Christian into a continuing ministry of peace and reconciliation. A similar idea for this growth is evident in Ephesians 4:22–24 in replacing (4:24 infinitive) the removed (Eph 4:22 passive) old human clothes with the clothes of the new human as we

---

23. Paul provides no explanation for how the baptism mystically transforms the Christian, as is provided in Valentinian Christianity by the Spirit transforming the baptismal water to then transform the initiate by removing evil from her (*Exc. Theod.* 81.2; 82.2; also *Gos. Phil.* 59.19; 68.22–69.8; 74.18–21), but Paul ties the mystical transformation to that which is accomplished in Christ's death (similar to Gregory Nazianzen, *In Defense of His Flight to Pontus* 1.3–4 and *Second Oration on Easter* 24).

24. Kim, *Origin of Paul's Gospel*.

25. Though the Augustinian-Dispensationalist Christian life tradition takes this concept as a sin nature that is part of a person, no other Christian life tradition joins them in this and the context does not support their view. It is better to see this exchange of the old self as a regenerational idea like Paul losing his old self on the Damascus road.

26. The word "present" (παραστῆσαι) indicates loyalty and worship (Rom 6:13, 19; 12:1).

27. The word ὅπλα can mean helpful "instruments" or threatening "weapons" (Rom 6:13; 13:12; 2 Cor 10:4).

reflect God's qualities of righteousness, holiness, and truth. It is possible that this concept includes already an aspect of embodied worship and allegiance to God in a transformed lifestyle, while there is a not yet reality of her resurrected spirit body, with previous character traits being removed. So this death with Christ ceases the previous way of life so that the new way of life may be thought through and lived by faith in Christ (2 Cor 5:17; Gal 2:20). Being a new human means that we shouldn't let sin and death reign as master in our lives as we had done before we came to Christ (Rom 6:6, 9–20, contrast with 5:14, 17, 21).

Such a new human (in the new covenant) is created with a new mindset[28] to choose to live in righteousness (Eph 4:17–24; Rom 6:9–14; 8:5). The choices made as a new human in Christ should be appropriate: that of righteous deeds (Rom 6:13, 16, 18–19). This *mystically transformed life full of choices within the narrow way should reflect the Christian's new allegiance* and could also be considered gospel because it is *the narrow way that leads to everlasting life* (Rom 6:22). Secondly in Romans 6, we should not do acts of sin because such behavior shames us and leads to damnation (in a two-ways salvation in this context: "the wages of sin is death" Rom 6:23). That is, sin comes to maturity (τέλος) in a person earning her death (Rom 6:21). Focusing on the narrow way, *we are heading for everlasting life, so we should choose consistent righteous behavior that leads to and matures* (τέλος, Rom 6:22) *unto that goal of everlasting life* (Rom 6:15–23). This discussion is developed by alluding to slavery terminology that describes the old person entangled with impurity and lawlessness (Rom 6:19). However, to be freed from this previous enslavement is redemption from this previous slavery unto a redemption lifestyle reflective of allegiance to Christ (Rom 6:18–20).[29] Paul explains the Christian's thought and choices through the lens of everyday implications of redemption. In this narrow way, righteousness should grow and deepen through a habituated commitment developing more consistency (Rom 6:11, 16, 19, 22). The lifestyle impact is that of (Christ mystically [Rom 6:4–8] along with our choices [Rom 6:11–22]) setting a person apart more and more like Christ as we head toward everlasting life, a gift of God (Rom 6:22–23; 1 Tim 6:12–14). The fact of Christ mystically transforming us (Rom 6:4–8) serves as the basis upon which the

---

28. A similar mindset and lifestyle is presented in Jewish texts in contrast to that of Gentiles (Wis 12–15; 1QS 3–4). In this context sin is more a metaphor and an allegiance unlike the entrapping indwelling sin of Rom 7:17 and 20, so righteousness works in the same vein as a metaphor and an allegiance rather that a personification of Christ (contra Southhall, *Rediscovering Righteousness in Romans*).

29. Morris, "Redemption," in Hawthorne et al., eds., *Dictionary of Paul and His Letters*, 785.

reflective commitment (λογίζεσθε) is made to corral one's life to be dead to sin and alive to God in Christ (Rom 6:11). In this the Christian is choosing Christ's narrow way as opposed to the broad way of sin and death (Rom 6:21-23). Such a commitment ushers in the implication of not allowing sin to reign within one's own mortal body (Rom 6:12). Such faithful allegiance to Christ's narrow way leads toward everlasting life, but this is not a goal earned, since everlasting life is a gift of God (Rom 6:22-23), whereas the life lived in sin earns the outcome of death (Rom 6:21, 23).

Eventually, in God's plan and mercy, the nation of Israel will convert to Christ (Rom 11:12, 31-32). This conversion will bring in a new covenant kingdom that will provide riches[30] for the world (Rom 11:12). The kingdom transformation for Israel is as though it is life from the dead (Rom 11:15). Such a kingdom will permeate and purify the whole (Rom 11:16). This imagery sets up a warning of two ways for the church: either pride unto destruction or believing unto reconciliation (Rom 11:15-18).

The extended metaphor of the olive tree shows the place of blessing and salvation (Rom 11:16-24). While not explicit in Paul, Jewish texts develop Abraham as the chosen root.[31] Additionally, God uses the olive tree metaphor to indicate a people planted by him and at risk in rebellion for being destroyed by removing branches for burning.[32] So this text works to communicate inclusion of the elect and exclusion of the rejected by God (after the previous pattern of both imageries, Ps 92:13; Jer 11:16-17).[33]

In agricultural grafting, one normally has a hearty root appropriate for the region. Theophrastus compares the effect of wild and cultivated grafted trees in an orchard in Mykonos.

> It is also reasonable that grafted trees are richer in fine fruit, especially when a scion from a cultivated tree is grafted onto a stock of a wild tree of the same bark, since the scion receives more nourishment from the strength of the stock. This is why people recommend that one should first plant wild olives trees and graft in buds or branches later, for the grafts hold better to the stronger stock, and by attracting more nourishment the tree bears rich fruit. If, on the other hand, someone were to graft a

---

30. Paul treats πλοῦτος as wealth (2 Cor 8:2; 9:8-10; Phil 4:19) but in this context it is obviously spiritual wealth.

31. T. Jud. 24.5; Jub. 16.26; 1 En. 93.5, 8; Philo, Her. 279.

32. 1Q20 13.13-17.

33. Pss. Sol. 14.3-4; 1 En. 84.6; Paul's point is echoed by Clement of Alexandria, Strom. 4.15 and Tertullian, Adv. Jud. 12-13.

wild scion into a cultivated stock, there will be some difference, but there will be no fine fruit.[34]

Whichever root is chosen, the root supports and enlivens all that is connected to it (Job 18:16; Jer 17:8; Ezek 31:8; Hos 9:16).[35] Almost never would wild branches be grafted into this root because their fruit would not normally be useful, though these wild branches might be cut off from the root to provide a hearty root for other fruit-bearing branches to be engrafted. Cultivated branches with a proven record of bearing hearty, good-tasting fruit are grafted into this root stock so as to increase fruit production. Columella, a contemporary to Paul, describes when a rarity of a cultivated olive tree has a wild olive grafted into it for rejuvenation.

> It happens also frequently that, though the trees are thriving well, they fail to bear fruit. It is a good plan to bore them with a Gallic augur and to put tightly into the hole a green slip taken from a wild olive tree; the result is that the tree, being as it were impregnated with fruitful offspring, becomes more productive.[36]

Thus this kind of grafting replaces part of the root. Paul has either conflated these two types of grafting (grafting a wild root to invigorate the tree and cultivated branches to produce good fruit) or, more likely, simply mixed the metaphor into the same process of grafting branches. Neither the Jewish nor the Gentile branches support the root; rather they both are to bear fruit from the nourishment that the root supplies (Rom 11:17–18).

The Old Testament and early Jewish writing envision Gentile nations making pilgrimage to Jerusalem for kingdom salvation (Ps 22:27; Isa 2:2–4; 56:6–8; Micah 4:1–5; Zech 2:11; 14:16).[37] However, Paul sees the Gentile participation in salvation preceding and not replacing salvation for Israel (Rom 11:13–14, 25–27). So counter to N. T. Wright, who sees Israel is replaced supercessionally by the church,[38] ultimately both a national Israel and the church will be saved on earth. In the context, Israel does not include the church (Rom 9:6; 11:7 Israel hardened and referred as "them," Rom

---

34. Theophrastus *Caus. Plant.* 1.6.10, quoted by Esler, *Conflict and Identity in Romans*, 302; also *m. Kil'ayim* 1.7 excludes grafting of a different kind of branch to a root, except that Rabbi Judah permits this.

35. Sir 1:20; 40:15.

36. Columella, *Rust.* 5.9.16 as quoted in Jewett, *Romans*, 684; also supported by Palladius, *Instit.* 53–54.

37. Tob 13:11, 13; 14:6–7; *Pss. Sol.* 17. 30–31, 34; *T. Zeb.* 9.8; *T. Benj.* 9.2; *Mekhilta* 33.1.1.

38. Wright, *Climax of the Covenant*, 54; *Romans*, 689; "Romans 9–11 and the 'New Perspective,'" in Wilk and Wagner, eds., *Between Gospel and Election*, 37–59.

11:11, 20–23), while the church joins Israel in the place of salvific blessing (Rom 11:11–13 referred as "Gentiles" and "you," Rom 11:13, 17–22, 24).[39] Jewish hopes for Israel's restoration in the kingdom[40] and Gentile hopes for the kingdom on earth will both be realized within the same eschatological kingdom.

Such a kingdom salvation includes resurrection with immortal bodies so that Christians will always be like and with the Lord Jesus Christ (1 Cor 15:42–57; 2 Cor 5:8; 2 Thess 2:1). So even though a Christian may die, she will live for Christ everlastingly. So the narrow way of God's kindness is for those Christians who believe and fear (Rom 11:20). Thus again, the gospel of a narrow way provides access to God's merciful forgiveness (Rom 11:27).

The imagery of an olive tree works metaphorically within a two-ways salvation in which each group has the possibility to head toward eschatological salvation and there is possible risk at not gaining that outcome (Rom 11:16–24). Israel's corporate (as indicated by the plural "them") rejection of Christ has meant that they, the natural branches, were cut off from this place of blessing and salvation. Individual Gentiles (as indicated by the singular "you") were grafted into the place of blessing and salvation because of each one's faith. Individual Gentiles stand within the place of salvation and blessing only humanly, because of each one's faith. However, if a Gentile becomes arrogant in unbelief, then in joining the broad way he will also be broken off and damned. Such arrogance (uppity-mindedness) is reminiscent of the boasting and bragging earlier in Romans 2:23; 3:27; and 4:2. To realize one's vulnerability should motivate personal fear, humility, and faith, for God shows severity to those he excludes and kindness to those he includes. No one is saved by his efforts; the whole argument of Romans so far is summed up in the concluding verse: "For God has shut up all in disobedience that he might show mercy to all" (Rom 11:32).

Such two-ways views in Paul are immersed in God's mercy but they provide real warnings for the Christian to live consistently for Christ, reflective of the character that Christ mystically provides. Such is a legitimate gospel providing everlasting life and forgiveness. The alternative way threatens Christians with damnation to warn of the unfortunate life and consequences if they do not live for God.

---

39. A point also made by Das, *Solving the Romans Debate*, 237–38.
40. *1 En.* 90.34–38; *Jub.* 1.15–25; *Pss. Sol.* 17.21–46; *m. Sanh.* 10.1.

24

Christ's Atonement in Hebrews

IN HEBREWS, CHRIST'S ATONEMENT is compared to the corporate pattern of the Jewish Day of Atonement and to Moses' initial cleansing of the people and tabernacle. Corporate atonement is accomplished for the group in each pattern. However, Christ's new covenant pattern also accomplished everlasting forgiveness for all time (Heb 8:12; 10:17), new-covenantly transforms the heart and conscience from within (Heb 8:10; 10:16), and brought believers to inherit everlasting salvation (Heb 1:14; 6:12; 9:15).

The atonement in Hebrews is a definite[1] or "direct application" to the community of followers of Christ, but applied indefinitely[2] or "available but not immediately applied" on an individual basis with regard to forgiveness and definitely with regard to a cleansed conscience. Two things should be immediately apparent: (1) I think Hebrews has crafted a view of atonement between the limited atonement of Calvinism and the unlimited atonement of Arminianism,[3] Wesleyanism,[4] and Amyraldianism;[5] and (2) Hebrews'

---

1. "Definite" is a technical term indicating "direct application to" the individual for whom Jesus died and normally identified with limited atonement in the wake of the Dortian Calvinistic reaction to Arminianism.

2. "Indefinite" is a technical term indicating "available for but not immediately applied" to the individual for whom Jesus died and normally identified with a form of unlimited atonement which is advocated by Arminians, Weslyans, and Amryaldians. That is, either the human choice or God's additional grace is needed to apply Jesus' death for the individual's sins.

3. Jesus' death is a substitute for sinners in the sense that it is available for the sinners to believe and then have it applied by God to remedy their sin condition.

4. Jesus' death is a substitute for sinners in the sense that it is available for the sinners who are elevated by God's prevenient grace so that they might believe and then have it applied by God to remedy their sin condition.

5. Jesus' death is a substitute for sinners in the sense that it is available for the

concept of salvation is primarily communal, rather than the Western reformation concept of salvation as primarily individuals obtaining everlasting life. Unpacking this further, the atonement in Hebrews should be understood as definitely accomplished by Christ for the new covenant community. Hebrews applies this new covenant in two ways. The first application of Hebrews' new covenant atonement identifies that it is the community that is everlastingly forgiven. However, individuals who identify with this community are obligated to continue to believe in the supremacy of Christ to enter into the rest (or everlasting salvation) and the forgiveness that this new covenant relationship provides, thus reflecting an indefinite aspect of the atonement for the individual. This sets up a two-ways soteriological strategy of faith in Christ, in contrast to their temptation to depart from new covenant benefits. The other feature that Hebrews focuses upon with regard to the new covenant is that of an individually definite application of Christ's atonement in a kind of Edwardsian religious affection identified as a cleansed conscience.

In contrast to the traditional individual-reformation soteriology of the Reformed, Lutheran, and Arminian traditions, Hebrews paints within a communally covenantal background. We need to be careful of applying modern constructs like individualism on a text. A better strategy is to notice the constructs available in the historical-cultural context and allow them to evidence something of the range of the possible views. Then, more specifically, we should prefer those constructs that the text itself floats as models it identifies as setting up the foundation for the teaching it develops. And of course, any clear statement in the text takes priority over these inclinations of the possible and the likely.

The context of Hebrews is rather clearly that of Jewish followers of Jesus, who need to think through the covenantal frameworks that govern them. The book of Hebrews draws out discussions about the Mosaic covenant and builds its teaching on the new covenant, in part against the Mosaic covenant and in part extending it. To enter Hebrews' thought forms is to enter into an analysis of the aspects of the Mosaic covenant that Hebrews builds upon. This analysis emphasizes a corporate covenantal perspective that sets up an exclusive two-ways view of salvation.

Further, the new covenant emphasizes corporate and internal transformation for the nation of Israel. The new covenant is presented with the people and nation Israel; "'Behold days are coming' declares Yahweh, 'when I will make a new covenant with the house of Israel and with the house of

---

sinners to have the divine efficacious grace applied to them, which evidences itself in believing, and then the sinner has Christ's atonement applied by God to remedy their sin condition.

Judah.'" (Jer 31:31; also quoted in Heb 8:8). The Essenes' eschatological hope was in the new covenant.⁶ For example, the whole of the people of Israel were to be regathered by God into their land again (Isa 49:6; Jer 31:27–28).⁷ The new covenant is predicted to be a work of God, with corporate Israel internalizing the Law; "this is the covenant which I will make with the house of Israel after those days, 'I will put my Law within them, and on their heart I will write it; and I will be their God and they will be my people'" (Jer 31:33; also quoted in Heb 8:10; 10:16). The singular of תּוֹרָתִי ("my Law") in Jeremiah 31:33 promises that the people Israel would have an internal transformation of responsiveness for obeying the Law of Moses. The Jews in the wake of their regathering in the land from the Babylonian captivity saw passion for the Law as a realization of the new covenant in which God was giving them a "new heart" and a "new spirit,"⁸ though the LXX retranslates this into a plural "my laws," which internally transform them into broadening obedience to whatever God commands. This new covenant was a whole community transformation; "they shall not teach again, each man his neighbor and each man his brother, saying, 'know Yahweh,' for they shall all know Me, from the least of them to the greatest of them,' declares Yahweh" (Jer 31:34 also quoted in Heb 8:11). The forgiveness to be found in this new covenant is also understood to be a corporate one as well; "I will forgive their iniquity, and their sin I will remember no more" (Jer 31:34 also quoted in Heb 8:12; 10:17). I realize the individualism of Western approaches often assumes an individually applied forgiveness, but the corporateness of the pronouns throughout this text and the corporate contextual emphasis with the Day of Atonement better fits into a premodern corporate construct of the group as being regathered and forgiven as a corporate entity.

New covenant corporate forgiveness is developed by Hebrews as mirroring the corporate atonement of the Day of Atonement (Heb 9:7, 11). The pattern by which Hebrews extends Christ's new covenant atonement is built upon that of corporate Israel at the Day of Atonement, so it is fitting to return to the Mosaic covenant to understand how atonement worked within the Day of Atonement. Within the Mosaic covenant, Yahweh demands that Israel be kept clean and holy (Lev 11:44–45). Ultimately, sins defile Yahweh's holy name and bring covenant curse (Ezek 43:7–8). For Israel to ignore this mandate and become unclean defiles the tabernacle and puts Israel at risk

---

6. CD 6.19; 8:21; 20:12; 1QpHab. 2.3f.

7. Sir 35:11; 48:10; Bar 4:37; 5:5; 2 Macc 1:27; 2:18; *Jub.* 1:15; *Ps. Sol.* 11:2; 17:28–31, 50; 8:34; 1QM 2.2, 7; 3.13; 5.1; 11QT 8.14–16; 57.5; Philo, *Rewards* 164; Kennard, *Biblical Covenantalism*, 2:79–89, 129–30.

8. As in Jer 31:31–34 and Ezek 36:24—37:28 so too in: *Jub.* 1:22–25; 1Q3 4, 5; 1QH 4, 5, 18; 4Q Shir Shalb.

to be cut off in covenant curse (Lev 15:31; Num 19:13). This defilement of tabernacle penetrates to defile the holy place and altar as well (Lev 16:16, 18; Num 19:20). For example, high-handed unrepentant sin, such as refusing to purify oneself after touching a dead body, defiles both the tabernacle and holy place (Num 19:13, 20). Jacob Milgrom developed that this uncleanness defiles the tabernacle in three stages.[9] First, the individual's inadvertent misdemeanor or severe physical impurity defiles the courtyard altar. This altar is cleansed by daubing its horns with the blood of the sin offering (Lev 4:25, 30; 9:9). Secondly, the inadvertent misdemeanor of the high priest or the entire community pollutes the shrine. This area is cleansed by the high priest placing the blood of the sin offering on the inner altar and before the veil that divides the holy place from the holy of holies (Lev 4:5–7, 16–18; Heb 9:7). Finally, high-handed unrepentant sin not only pollutes the outer altar and penetrates into the holy place, but pierces the veil to the holy place and the holy ark, the throne of God (Lev 16:16; Num 19:20; Isa 37:16). Since the high-handed rebellious sinner is barred from bringing a sin offering (Num 15:27–31; Heb 9:7), the uncleanness wrought by his offense must wait for the cleansing of the sanctuary on the Day of Atonement. This Day of Atonement cleansing consists of two steps: the cleansing of the tent, and the cleansing of the outer altar and the people with atonement (Lev 16:16–19, 30). Thus, all the sin of the most holy place and of the people is cleansed on the Day of Atonement with the sin offering blood. In this way the nation of Israel is able to continue on for another year in Mosaic covenant relationship with Yahweh because their sin has been atoned for at the yearly Day of Atonement. Hebrews 9:7 acknowledges this process and develops that the high priest enters the holy place once a year with the blood of the atonement, "which he offers for himself and for the ignorance of the people." The phrase τῶν τοῦ λαοῦ ἀγνοημάτων, retains this corporate emphasis (of the people's ignorance or sin) from the Mosaic description of the Day of Atonement, so that the people and tabernacle are cleansed to continue in the relationship with Yahweh for another year; however, the new covenant promise of a perfected conscience does not get accomplished by the Day of Atonement (Heb 9:9).

Christ's new covenant corporate atonement is also developed by Hebrews as mirroring the corporate atonement practice that Moses applied to initiate the Mosaic covenant cleansing in the first place (Heb 9:19–21; Exod 24:5–8; also 1 Pet 1:2). All the different tabernacle implements and the people are sprinkled with blood[10] to initially cleanse them and to serve as

---

9. Milgrom, *Numbers*, 445–46; Kennard, *Biblical Covenantalism*, 1:277–303.

10. This is an opportunity for Hebrews to discuss that blood is the dominant means

in the beginning of the Mosaic covenant. The statement that Hebrews 9:20 reports Moses as saying ("This is the blood of the covenant which God commanded you") is a shortened form combining Moses' Exodus 24:8 statement ("Behold the blood of the covenant, which Yahweh has made with you in accordance with all these words") with Israel's complete submission in obedience ("All Yahweh's spoken word we will do, and we will be obedient"). Both the shortened and longer forms clearly describe the group as Israel and thus have a corporate role of binding Israel to this Mosaic covenant, and now that they are cleansed this atonement enters them as a group into the fearful experience with the glory of God (Exod 24:9–18). Hebrews conflates this initiation of Mosaic covenant with the experience of Moses cleansing the earthly tabernacle parts constructed by the Spirit-empowered craftsmen after the heavenly pattern (Exod 40:9). So this later corporate event of tabernacle initiation and cleansing is seen by Hebrews as an extension of the divine covenant binding on the corporate community.

Hebrews presents Christ as a new Melchizedekian high priest who has also entered the heavenly tabernacle to atone after these two patterns of Day of Atonement and initial covenantal cleansing (Heb 9:11–28).[11] The initial cleansing by Moses served to support the initiation of a covenant by blood, of which Christ's new covenant is initiated with his sacrifice. Christ's death in the new covenant is toward redemption so that the called may receive everlasting salvation inheritance (Heb 9:15 with 1:14). However, Christ's death deals with transgressions under the first covenant (τῶν ἐπὶ τῇ πρώτῃ διαθήκῃ παραβάσεων), not that Christ's death satisfies something of the inadequate Mosaic covenant.[12] The initiation of the new covenant

---

for cleansing in the Mosaic covenant (Heb 9:22), however Christian tradition often reads this as the only way to cleanse, and thus emphasizes further the need for Christ's death. Hebrews is however very explicit with the use of "almost" (σχεδὸν) at the start of the clause that "one may almost say, that all things are cleansed with blood." There are other Mosaic means of cleansing, including time, cleaning, removing the material, destruction of the object and a baptism in the *miqvuaoth* or ritual baths as developed by Lev 13–15. Also the scapegoat would be offered as atonement and then led into the wilderness to bear Israel's sin away from the temple and the people, without shedding its blood (Lev 16:10; *m. Yoma* 4.2a; 6.1–4; 8.9; *y. Yoma* 8.9, 45c; *b. Yoma* 65 ab; *Sifra Ahere Mot* 8.5; *Bar.* 7.7–9). Additionally, the poor could bring a sacrifice of grain without blood and be cleansed by atonement (Lev 5:11). There is even an odd instance in which Israel is atoned for by bringing gold instead of animal sacrifice (Num 31:50). However, the usual way of cleansing is through animal sacrifice and that is what this verse says.

11. Kennard, *Messiah Jesus*, 353–75.

12. The placement of the article τῶν associated with "transgressions" (παραβάσεων) identifies that the transgressions were committed under the Mosaic covenant by the surrounding phrase (ἐπὶ τῇ πρώτῃ διαθήκῃ), *not* that Christ's death was under or governed by the "first" or Mosaic covenant (Heb 9:15).

is also identified with a brief discussion of a will and testament in which Hebrews explains that Christ must die or this covenant cannot take effect (Heb 9:16–17). The Day of Atonement pattern served to develop the priestly role with tabernacle and thus set up the inadequacies of a repeated Mosaic covenant Day of Atonement. Christ's once-for-all new covenant atonement polemics both corporate Mosaic covenant patterns (Mosaic covenant initiation and Day of Atonement), because Christ brings a better sacrifice,[13] and offers it in a better place,[14] a heavenly tabernacle.

---

13. Christ's death is a better sacrifice but Christian tradition often overstates this by reinterpreting Heb 10:4, "For it is impossible for the blood of bulls and goats to take away sins," to mean no forgiveness is possible at all on account of such animal sacrifices, and thus the absolute need for Christ's death or all Jews before Christ remain unforgiven. This common view ignores the clear statement of the biblical text that in the divine provision of the animal sacrifices atonement and forgiveness is in fact declared to be realized (Lev 1:4; 4:20, 26, 31, 35; 5:6, 10, 13, 16, 18 . . . ; Kennard, *Biblical Covenantalism*, 1:289–313; Milgrom, *Leviticus 1–16*, 253–54; Gane, *Cult and Character*, xx, 47–49, 299; Gammie, *Holiness in Israel*, 39; Kiuchi, *Purification Offering*, 41, 59, 72–74). So that if animal sacrifices provide a legitimate means for God to forgive sin in a Mosaic covenant framework, Heb 10:4 "take away sins" needs to be interpreted in light of its place in the argument of the Hebrews context. The point being made about the new covenant sacrifice is that Christ' sacrifice occurs once and that settles the matter for all time (Heb 9:28; 10:12). In contrast to this complete atonement even for future sins, the Mosaic covenant sacrifices continue to need to be done on a yearly basis (alluding to the Day of Atonement again) and thus never finally "take away sins." That is, the forgiveness for past sins wonderfully accomplished by God through the Mosaic covenant sacrifices do not settle the future issue regarding sins as Christ's sacrifice does. So Christ provides a greater sacrifice than the Mosaic means even if they do in fact provide past forgiveness. Kennard, *Biblical Covenantalism*, 3:162–72.

14. Often the better place of heaven is developed through a Platonic framework but this is foreign to the text. In Platonism the heavenly forms are the only reality, with the earthly objects being merely a shadow of this reality imposed upon our senses through our souls' recollection of preincarnate life among those heavenly forms. In Platonism if the truth is present in the heavenly then it is present in the earthly as well, because the earthly is a mere shadow of the heavenly. Here in Heb 9:23–25 both the heavenly tabernacle and the earthly copies of the heavenly tabernacle are real as evidenced by the Hebraic pattern of *Merkabah* mysticism. That is, both the heavenly and earthly temples are real and different things may be occurring in these different realities. For example, the heavenly temple is normally thought to be where God's presence dwells (Isa 6:4), but the amazing thing is that with the cleansed tabernacle God also dwells on earth, with the ark of the covenant serving as his throne (Exod 40:34–38). However, the uncleanness of the earthly temple dislodges the divine presence from the earthly temple, while he remains in the heavenly temple (Ezek 1:4–28; 11:22–25). The different conditions of the pure heavenly temple and the occasionally unclean earthly temple show that they are both real in this multidimensional Hebraic framework rather than the idealism of the earthly shadows that Platonism portrays. Kennard, *Epistemology and Logic in the New Testament*, 220–21.

Hebrews applies the new covenant in two ways: perfected conscience and everlasting forgiveness. These two issues are where the text quotes aspects of the Jeremiah 31 quote again (Heb 8:10, 12; and 10:16–17) and thus shows the selection and emphasis of the new covenant in Hebrews.

The Day of Atonement (Heb 9:7–9) and the initiation of the Mosaic covenant (Heb 9:18–22) are developed as the framework through which Christ's new covenant atonement is to be viewed (Heb 9:11–14, 23–28). Both these Mosaic covenant frameworks bring corporate atonement and belonging. Thus, the individual is a beneficiary of this corporate Mosaic covenant atonement by continuing in the covenant way with faithfulness and loyalty. This Mosaic covenant pattern would mean that Christ's atonement after this pattern would be an indefinite atonement for individuals and yet definite atonement for the community of the new covenant. This definiteness for the new covenant community is apparent in such statements as Christ "obtained everlasting redemption" and died "once to bear the sins of the many" (Heb 9:12, 26, 28; 10:10, 12). That is, Christ's death has accomplished the atonement for the group. So it is now time to turn to the issue of how this atonement is applied and to whom. Throughout these allusions of Christ's atonement, after the Mosaic pattern the corporateness of atonement is implied, and occasionally stated as in "the many" (Heb 9:28). From this corporate pattern (inherited out of their Mosaic covenant heritage and development in the context) and perhaps the indefiniteness of "the many," there is indefiniteness with regard to individuals in this new covenant forgiveness. In such a covenantal structure one would expect a two-ways strategy to launch, and that is what occurs in especially the warning sections of the book.[15] Therefore, the readers should heed Jesus' miraculously attested great salvation and obediently press on into the rest by continuing to trust God (Heb 2:3–4; 3:8, 11–13, 15, 19; 4:2–4, 11; 11:1—12:13). This is also said in the negative: "do not harden your heart," as when Israel provoked God in the wilderness, for such rebellion and disbelief brings judgment, as when Israelites died on the wilderness journey (Heb 3:8, 13, 15–19; 4:5–7; 6:6; 10:26–31). Faithfulness in the narrow new exodus way is a disposition of continuing faith for those whom God has called to inherit everlasting salvation, which he will generously give (Heb 1:14; 6:12; 9:15). Jesus and Abraham are provided as positive examples of continuing faithfully to inherit (Heb 1:4; 11:8) and Esau provides a warning pattern of an unrepentant rebel to avoid, for he could not inherit even though he wished inheritance (Heb 12:17). The issue is not obtaining the gospel message in the first place, but rather maintaining a loyal relationship to Jesus as the

---

15. Kennard "Warnings in the Book of Hebrews."

Christ and his new covenant instead of returning to Judaism with its Mosaic covenant (Heb 7:1—10:31). So the Jewish framework of atonement brings a Jewish perspective on life that requires continuing belief in Christ, which is an exclusive soteriological strategy. For those who continue in this faith, forgiveness is their benefit along with kingdom rest. For those who do not continue, they identify themselves to be unbelievers and rebels, much like Israel did and died in the wilderness (Heb 3:16–19), which means that the issue is not a conversion point or a moment of faith; it is continuing faith. Remember that Hebrews' construction frames faith in the future for benefits that have not been realized yet for those who are believers (Heb 11:1–39). This emphasis of future looking faith further supports a two-ways strategy unto salvation. Thus, the Jewish followers of Jesus are called to continue in future looking faith, for that is the way that they as individuals each realize the corporate new covenant benefit of everlasting forgiveness.

The new covenant is superior over the Mosaic covenant as the heavenly pattern, but the Mosaic is a close earthly copy of the heavenly tabernacle shown to Moses on the mountain (Heb 8:5; 9:23). The priestly and sacrificial functioning of the Mosaic tabernacle train the Jews in basic concepts that the new covenant completes in the one sacrifice of Jesus Christ. Jesus' one sacrifice as a once-for-all sacrifice is emphasized in Hebrews (Heb 7:27; 9:12, 14, 25, 28; 10:10, 12, 14, 18), so why when the heavenly things are cleansed for new covenant effectiveness does Hebrews say that they are cleansed with "sacrifices" (plural: θυσίαις) instead of Jesus' one sacrifice (Heb 9:23)?

Might these plural sacrifices hint at the burnt offerings and sin offerings that the Levitical priests use to cleanse Ezekiel's altar (Ezek 43:18–27)? With Hebrews' emphasis, the plural cleansing sacrifice should be argued to be the singular sacrifice of Jesus, here rendered plural "sacrifices" (θυσίαις) out of attraction to the plural "with these" (τούτοις),[16] or as Gutherie's theological appeal that Christ's single sacrifice sufficiently replaces all of the Levitical sacrifices (Heb 9:23).

> The plural is used in the sense that the one sacrifice stands as the complete fulfillment of all the different sacrifices in the old order. It may be said that the sacrifice of Christ is so many sided that it required a whole range of sacrifices to serve as adequate copies.[17]

Hebrews develops Christ's one sacrifice as the one in the context that was done in the heavenly temple.

---

16. Lane, *Hebrews*, 2:247.
17. Guthrie, *Hebrews*, 196.

Amid the final exhortations of Hebrews, a devotional homily reminds the reader to follow her Christian leader's faith in grace, thereby worshipping God and doing good in the new covenant (Heb 13:7–16). The rationale reminds the reader that we live in grace, so the faith of Christian leadership should be emulated (Heb 13:7–9). Such a gracious life contrasts with that of those diminishing grace with strange teaching that sees real benefit in food. Perhaps this food issue refers to a Jewish liturgical meal with peace offering because of the Jewish context in which the Jewish worshippers eat major portions of the sacrifice and the priest officiating obtains the right thigh of the sacrifice for his food (Heb 13:9–10; Lev 7:15–17, 32–33).[18] Such eating was festive as an expression of thanks to God, often with the blessing that the food strengthens the heart (Ps 104:14–15).[19] The use of the plural "foods" (βρώμασιν) in Hebrews 13:9 may also indicate the issue of kosher, which was a significant Jewish issue at that time,[20] and because the LXX only uses the plural βρῶμα to refer to kosher food in contrast to that which is impure (Lev 11:34)[21] and that the other instance of the plural word in Hebrews is broader than a sacrificial sense (Heb 9:10). However, in either view the food was merely physical food passing through one's body, so such food is polemiced without lasting benefit to the one who partakes of it (Heb 13:9), a theme Philo acknowledged as he saw the value in the heart transformation being far more important than food.[22] The polemic continues in that new covenant Christians have an altar, presumably Christ's original heavenly altar, which is aligned with the new covenant so those Levitical priests of the Mosaic covenant do not have a right to eat from it (Heb 9:23–24; 13:10 in contrast to Lev 7:32–33).

18. *M. Pesaḥ.* 10.6; *Jub.* 22.3–9; 32.7; 49.6.

19. *M. Ber.* 6.1, 3.

20. Dan 1:1–21; Esth 3:28; 4:16; Tob 1:9–12; 4:12–13; Jdt 10:5; 12:1–2, 9–19; 13:8; 2 Macc 7 especially 7:9 and 8:2; 3 Macc 3:4–7; 7.11; 4 Macc 1:8, 10; *Jos. Asen.*; *Letter of Aristeas* 139–42; Josephus, *Ant.* 14.185–267; *Vita* 14 includes Jewish priests imprisoned in Rome in A.D. 61 abstaining from meat on kosher grounds; *T. Isaac* 4.5; Macrobius, *Sat.* 2.4.11; Riggenbach, "Die Starken und Schwachen in der römischen Gemeinde," *ThStK* 66 (1893) 655–68; Strathmann, *Geschichte der frühchristlichen Askese bis zur Entstehung des Mönchtums im religionsgeschichtlichen Zusammenhange*, 1:1–13; Rauer, *Die "Schwachen" in Korinth und Rom nach den Paulusbriefen*, 138–69; Behm, "ἐσθίω," in *TDNT* 2:694; Dunn, *Romans*, 2:799–802; Elliott, "Asceticism among the 'Weak' and 'Strong' in Romans 14–15," in Vaage and Wimbush, ed., *Asceticism and the New Testament*, 231–51 but especially 239–45; Winter, "Roman Law and Society in Romans 12–15," in Oakes, ed., *Rome in the Bible and the Early Church*, 90–91; Pucci Ben Zeev, *Jewish Rights in the Roman World*, 381–408; Hellerman, "Purity and Nationalism in Second Temple Literature: 1–2 *Maccabees* and *Jubilees*," *JETS* 46 (2003) 401–21.

21. Lane, *Hebrews*, 2:534.

22. Philo, *Spec.* 2.193–94, 198–99.

The Day of Atonement sacrifice from which the high priest took blood into the holy place had its remains burned outside the camp (Heb 13:11; 9:7–8; Lev 16:27).[23] By connecting Jesus' sacrifice with the blood sacrifice at the Day of Atonement, Hebrews identifies Jesus' sacrifice as a vicarious substitution. Since Jesus was excluded and killed outside the Jewish camp, the Jewish Christians could relate to his exclusion. By similarity, Jesus suffered outside the gate in his death so as to sanctify the people (Heb 13:12). Upon this basis the author exhorts, "let us go outside the camp, bearing his reproach," presumably calling his readership to remove themselves from mainstream Judaism by identifying with Jesus as their Messiah and atonement, with its hope of an everlasting kingdom to come (Heb 13:13–14). Ignatius extends these phrases in his *Letter to Magnesians* to argue for abstinence from kosher and Jewish sacrifices.

> Gather together-all of you-to the one temple of God, as it were, to one altar, to one Jesus Christ . . . Do not be led away through strange teachings and outmoded fables, which are not useful. If we still go on observing Judaism, we acknowledge that we never received grace.[24]

However, the metaphor of "going outside the camp" (ἔξω τῆς παρεμβολῆς) may function on a level of positively identifying with Christ in "bearing his reproach," rather than necessarily leaving Jewish practices, since this metaphor also is used positively in LXX Exodus 33:7–8 three times for where the tabernacle was set up and where Moses met Yahweh in this tabernacle.[25]

With our messianic kingdom hope, the Christian's life should be characterized by worship, doing good, and sharing with others, "for with such sacrifices God is pleased" (Heb 13:15–16). In aligning with Christ we should continually offer up a sacrifice of praise to God, especially giving thanks to Christ's name. Joining these sacrifices are those that meet practical needs like doing good and sharing with others. All these forms of worship and doing good are sacrifices that please God.

Hebrews' perspective realizes many factors of the Davidic and new covenants so that its readers see that the Mosaic covenant has been superseded, prompting them to not place their trust in it. Jesus is already the Davidic King over his house of believers in Christ (Heb 1:5—2:8; 3:6). The new covenant makes believers already partakers of rest if we continue in faith

---

23. Rabbinics saw that the Day of Atonement forgave all sin between the worshipper and God (*m. Yoma* 8.9; *y. Yoma* 8.9, 45c; *b. Yoma* 65 ab; *Sifra Ahere Mot* 8.5).

24. Ignatius, *Magn.* 7.2—8.2.

25. Lane, *Hebrews*, 2:542–44.

(Heb 4:3). The new covenant establishes a lasting relationship with Yahweh in forgiveness (Heb 8:12; 10:17). The new covenant matures the conscience by internalizing God's laws (Heb 10:14–16).

Jeremiah 31:33 (singular in the Hebrew text תּוֹרָתִי, "my Law") left the whole Mosaic Law as a binding internalized code within the new covenant for the Jewish person heading into the kingdom. However, in the LXX (which is Jer 38:33 plural νόμους, "laws") the dispersion Jewish community saw God's generic commands as internally binding without identifying them as the Mosaic covenant. Hebrews indicates the Mosaic covenant is obsolete for the Jewish Christian but is less clear as to what are the continuing internalized laws of God. However, Jeremiah and Ezekiel (in Hebrew and LXX) left the hope of Levitical priests offering Mosaic sacrifices within a temple. These sacrifices include burnt offerings and purification-sin offerings, so that forgiveness and atonement (כִּפֶּר/*kpr*) for sins will be obtained from God by these means (Jer 33:18; Ezek 43:18–27; 44:11, 15, 29; 45:15, 17, 18–20, 21–25; 46:2, 4, 12, 13–15).

Hebrews identifies that with Jesus' sufficient sacrifice to obtain forgiveness "there is no longer any offering for sin" (Heb 10:18).

How are these tensions between the Levitical sacrifices in Ezekiel (and Jeremiah) and Christ's sacrifice in Hebrews to be worked out? Most attempts to resolve these issues ignore or leave out various features that show they are inadequate solutions. One way to resolve this is to merge all the factors together with clear indicators as to when and whom they refer. When this is done we find Hebrews has clear teaching on Jesus' sacrifice as sufficient to obtain forgiveness so that the Jewish Christian does not need to offer another sacrifice for sin. The new covenant is in place, perfecting the conscience of the Jewish Christian so that he does not have the external Mosaic covenant as binding upon him. Laws of the Mosaic covenant may float freely from the Mosaic covenant into the new covenant and into the conscience and life of the Jewish Christian. Any transfer of laws, like faithfulness and obedience to enter into rest, excel beyond a suzerainty treaty framework as they penetrate into the conscience and life of the Jewish Christian under the covenant grant of the new covenant. Within this new covenant there is the necessary identification with Jesus as the Messiah for the kingdom. Ultimately, when national Israel is benefited by the new covenant they will find themselves as a national group forgiven and transformed in their hearts to do the Mosaic Law within the new covenant grant framework. In this kingdom state the Levitical priests may offer sin and guilt offerings for forgiveness and atonement purposes (because God did not make a mistake when he established the Mosaic covenant framework). When such obedience and sacrifice is done regarding the Mosaic covenant, there are redundant affirmations from both Mosaic and new covenants that Israel is blessed and forgiven. The individual responsiveness under this new covenant transformation supersedes any need for multigenerational judgment, so individual responsibility and judgment is what is affirmed in the new covenant. In this new covenant, the relationships of a Jewish Christian and kingdom Israelite with Yahweh are forever in forgiveness.

The other new covenant application is the perfected conscience. The warning charge to the readers rings out: "don't harden your hearts" (Heb 3:8, 11, 15; 5:5). In light of this call and Israel's failure to obey this call, the Law is seen to be impotent. The inability of the Law to perfect a person's conscience is the basis for the Mosaic covenant being set aside or annulled (Heb 7:18–19). Since this perfection is not through the Mosaic covenant and the Levitical priesthood, the Law is changed from the Mosaic covenant to the new covenant. Likewise, the Mosaic covenant's cleansing of the flesh left it impotent to cleanse the conscience (Heb 9:13–14). Part of the problem is that the Mosaic covenant repeatedly reminds the sinner with the need to sacrifice, so the consciousness of sins remains before the individual. However, Christ perfects those who are sanctified or set apart in the new covenant (Heb 10:14). This sanctification alludes to those sanctified by Christ's atonement (Heb 10:10). Again, this sanctification should be seen through the contextual lens of the Mosaic covenant, which is the condition for sanctification to set apart Israel (in the flesh) as holy (Heb 9:13; Exod 19:14). Thus, for the Mosaic covenant the cleansing of the people identifies them as appropriately in the covenantal community (Exod 19:14; Lev 12–16). However, in the new covenant an internal cleansing of the heart is realized, which Hebrews identifies as the cleansing of the conscience (Heb 8:10; 9:14; 10:2, 16). This is also stated as perfecting conscience (Heb 10:1–2) in contrast to the lack of perfecting conscience from the Mosaic covenant (Heb 9:9). This cleansing or perfecting of conscience is done to the follower of Jesus as part of Jesus' new covenant atonement cleansing. So this perfection is a definite work of Christ for those individuals within the new covenant. It serves to balance the human responsibility side of continuing to be faithful with this divine work noticeable in the mind of each believer. It is then like an Edwardsian religious affection and thus provides reassurance to the cleansed in conscience that they are among the community of everlastingly forgiven. Perhaps this cleansed conscience is part of the way that we believers already enter rest (responsively believing instead of hardened in heart), even though the dominant expression of rest is still future and would be identified with Christ's kingdom (Heb 1:8–13; 3:14; 4:1–11). Additionally, this cleansed conscience also provides the basis of a new covenant command to draw near to God and his cleansed community with a future-looking faith (hope) because God is himself faithful (Heb 10:22–25). The fact that the cleansed conscience becomes a basis for an appeal to continue in the faith may softly hint at this cleansed conscience as Hebrews' analog to the new birth (in John and Peter) or that of becoming a new man (in Paul). That is, it looks like the cleansed conscience is Hebrews' regeneration metaphor. As such, it fits rather well as an Edwardsian religious affection, evidencing where authentic salvation is being realized and thus provides assurance for this salvation.

In summary, in Hebrews, Christ's new covenant atonement is vicariously definite for the community of Jesus' followers in a two-ways strategy that provides: (1) everlasting forgiveness as an indefinite blessing to those in the community who continue in the faith, and (2) new covenant cleansed conscience as a definite blessing corroborating their faith. With the concepts framed by the Day of Atonement and Moses' initial cleansing of the tabernacle, Hebrews' priestly covenantal vicarious sacrifice framework resists being reworked into a legal penal atonement. Each individual's cleansed conscience and continuing in faith to the kingdom provides reassuring evidence of the believer's kingdom salvation.

25

Petrine Redemption unto the Narrow Way to the Kingdom

PETRINE REDEMPTION IS CHRIST'S work setting people free from their previous lifestyles. Peter does not use Paul's exhaustive redemption concept, which includes features such as justification, forgiveness, and the ultimate resurrection departure from the sinful body (Rom 3:24; 8:23; Eph 1:7, 14), nor Luke's eschatological kingdom concept of redemption (Luke 1:68–69; 2:38; 24:21; also in Old Greek LXX Dan 4:34). Rather, Peter's concept of redemption emphasizes a change "from your futile way of life" (1 Pet 1:18).

The concept of redemption is the exchanging of ownership, often by paying a price either in a market or on a battlefield. Initially the concept of redemption is grounded in the exodus with Yahweh's rescue and release of Israel to inherit the land and serve the living God (Deut 7:8; 9:6; Pss 74:2; 77:15). Emerging from the exodus, the first born were to be redeemed by the Levites, vicariously replacing them in living service and a payment to be made to Aaron (Num 3:11–51). By extension, any Israelite entangled in debt and selling himself into slavery was to be redeemed by those family members around him, since such slavery was inappropriate for those whom Yahweh had redeemed (Lev 25:25–27; 47–49). Peter expressed this thought with two words. First, ἐλυτρώθητε means "to set free, redeem or rescue" and often includes paying a ransom (1 Pet 1:18; LXX Ps 118[119]:134; Isa 44:22–24; Hos 13:14).[1] The second word, ἀγοράσαντα, emphasizes the market imagery of purchasing goods or people (2 Pet 2:1; 1 Cor 6:20; 7:23).[2] In such an exchange the goods or people are set free from the seller, usually to be

---

1. BAG, 484; 1 Macc 4:11; *Pss. Sol.* 8.30; 9.1.
2. BAG, 12; 1 Macc 13:49; Josephus, *J.W.* 2.127.

possessed and obligated to the purchaser. Both Greek words for redemption are used to describe the purchasing of slaves resulting in either enslavement to a new owner or being set free.[3] Furthermore, these words express the idea of ransom, wherein a conqueror may free prisoners by defeating their master in battle.[4] In such an example, the one redeemed exchanges allegiance to the previous dominating power for allegiance to the one bringing about the redemption. However, the redemption of people does not require the one redeemed to have a new owner; the person may simply be set free.

The purchase price of the redemption Peter talks about was the death of Christ. Jesus died as a substitution on behalf of others.[5] Peter develops this theme by first designating what the price of redemption was not and then identifying what it was (1 Pet 1:18–19). For example, the price was not perishable (φθαρτοῖς), that which is subject to corruption or destruction.[6] Additionally, silver and gold are mentioned as dross compared to the extreme value of the actual price paid. In contrast, the actual price paid is the precious blood of Christ. The imagery of the blood refers to Christ's death in a Jewish sacrificial lamb pattern (1 Pet 1:2, 19, 21; Acts 1:19; 5:28), not a Bengelian effusion (draining Christ dry in order to obtain his blood as the imperishable material substance of value).[7] Thus, Christ's death is characterized by a simile: Christ's shed blood was like that of the sacrificial lamb: unblemished and spotless, indicating the required purity of the sacrifice in a priestly covenantal context.

There is no description of a price being paid to another, either to God or to Satan, for Peter describes redemption in the Old Testament pattern of Yahweh delivering Israel from bondage and captivity (Exod 6:6; Isa 52:3; 2 Pet 2:1). Additionally, by this time among the Jews the concept of ransom had become identified with vicarious sufferings and martyrdom of the righteous without giving anyone a payment because the martyrs' lives were just spent on the battlefield.[8] The situation would be analogous to that whereby

---

3. Both words used this way in Deissmann, *Light from the Ancient East*, 328, 333.

4. Büchsel, "λύτρον," in *TDNT*, 4:344; Moulton and Milligan, *Vocabulary of the Greek Testament*, 4:383.

5. Büchsel, "λύτρον," in *TDNT*, 4:343.

6. Harder, "φθαρω," in *TDNT*, 9:103–4.

7. Contra Bengel, *Gnomon of the New Testament*, 4.474; human martyr blood as redemption during battle (4 Macc 17:22) and the priest's prayer for that redemptive victory outcome (4 Macc 6:29); cf. Hughes, "The Blood of Jesus and His Heavenly Priesthood in Hebrews," *BSac* 131 (1973) 99–109; Jewett, *Romans*, 286.

8. Human martyr blood as redemption during battle (4 Macc 17:22) and the priest's prayer for that redemptive victory outcome (4 Macc 6:29).

slain soldiers of a conquering army accomplish the freeing of slaves through the shedding of the soldiers' blood in a decisive battle that wins a war.

Peter additionally ties this sacrificial death with the Jewish sacrifice concept in Isaiah 52–53 (1 Pet 1:2; 2:22–25; Isa 52:15; 53:5–6, 9). Therefore, Jesus is the pure sacrifice who died to accomplish human redemption. However, this completed redemption emphasizes a life transformation "that we might die to sin and live to righteousness" (1 Pet 2:24). Such is the life healing that Jesus' atonement provides, which transforms the believer from her "straying like sheep" condition to that of following Jesus in mimetic atonement and suffering if necessary (1 Pet 2:24–25, 20–21). Furthermore, in his sanctified purity and just character, Jesus died for unjust people so that he might bring us to God through the resurrection he initiated and we participate within (1 Pet 3:18, 4:6).

Likewise, redemption includes purification from their former sins. Utilizing καθαρισμοῦ clarifies that a "purification" or "sin offering" cleanses and provides atonement as recovering from leprosy or the flow of blood (2 Pet 1:9; Mark 1:44; Luke 2:22; 5:14; LXX: Exod 29:36; 30:10; Neh 12:45). In such Jewish sacrifices as purification or sin offering there is no development of a penal aspect.

The accomplishment of Petrine redemption is that of freeing people from their previous futile sinning and straying ways of life (1 Pet 1:18; 2:24–25). A prior lifestyle was characterized by ματαίας, which means "idle, empty, fruitless, useless, powerless, lacking truth."[9] This futile lifestyle was inherited from the forefathers as the worthless commitments of a pagan.[10] For example, this prior lifestyle was composed of ignorant lusts (1 Pet 1:14), diverse evil actions (1 Pet 2:1), and Gentile dissipation (1 Pet 4:3–4). No doubt there were Jews among those with such lifestyles since in 1 Peter so many Jewish imageries are used. These Jews, however, either had a milder former lifestyle or else ran in the same Gentile excesses. In either case their lives before redemption through Christ had been futile (1 Pet 1:18). Now Christ has freed from (ἐκ) such futility. They no longer need to be involved in their previous lifestyles. As such, Petrine redemption is an act that focuses on requiring the redeemed to live differently. For example, the repeated commands throughout 1 Peter remind believers of their obligation. The act of Christ redeeming them must be followed by their own action. However, Petrine redemption does not extend through the believer's life with any continual monergistic enablement. The continued soteriological enablement described by Peter is identified with other soteriological motifs, such as the

---

9. BAG, 496.
10. Bauernfeind, "ματαίας," in *TDNT*, 4:521–24.

continued presence of the Spirit upon the believer (1 Pet 4:14). Petrine redemption, then, is a definite act wherein Christ initially frees a person from his former futile way of life and thus renders him under obligation to obey synergistically in his new changed lifestyle.

Petrine redemption is not equated with Petrine salvation. In Peter, "salvation" is a present process (1 Pet 3:21; 4:18; σῴζω) that is not complete until one enters into the kingdom in the end times (Acts 2:21, future indicative σωθήσεται; 1 Pet 1:5, 9; 2 Pet 3:15). In contrast, Petrine redemption is a past fact, fully accomplished by Christ when the life is transformed (1 Pet 1:18; 2 Pet 2:1). Peter never describes salvation as a past fact. Things can be presently soteriological, however, if they normally lead to the future salvation. Additionally, Petrine salvation focuses on freedom from judgment and obtaining the kingdom within a gracious strictured two-ways framework in contrast to apostasy (1 Pet 1:3–9; 2 Pet 1:2–11; 2:1–22). Petrine redemption focuses on the past transformation of a futile lifestyle to vital righteous living. In Peter, one can be soteriologically redeemed without having been saved. Furthermore, while Peter includes redemption within the total process of salvation, he indicates by the extent of redemption that the redemption of an individual does not guarantee that she will be ultimately saved. Calvin floats this view of the apostatizing of previously non-saved knowers of the truth.[11]

The redemption is not that of bringing Israel out of Egypt, because 2 Peter is written to a mixed group of Christians, some of whom have come from Gentile backgrounds. Most notably, in 2 Peter 2:1 "the people," who should be understood as Israel,[12] were distinguished from the recipients of Peter's letter. That is, Israel had false prophets; the present recipients of Peter's letter will be harassed when false teachers rise from among them.

The context of 2 Peter develops soteriological concerns.[13] For example, the recipients of the letter have the same kind of faith as Peter (2 Pet 1:1). Additionally, the recipients have been granted everything pertaining to life and godliness through the true knowledge of Christ (2 Pet 1:3). These magnificent promises provide the group, each individually, with everlasting life by obtaining immortality of the divine nature (2 Pet 1:4 reflecting the change between plural verb and individual nouns and adjectives).[14] "Divine"

---

11. Calvin, *Catholic Epistles*, in *Calvin's Commentary*, 22:393; Bauckham, *Jude–2 Peter*, 240–41, 274–81.

12. Strathmann, "λαός," in *TDNT*, 4:50–57.

13. Parallel to 2 Peter, Jude develops a similar common salvation (Jude 3), judgment (Jude 5–16) and exhortations to guarantee salvation (Jude 17–23) and the security from Christ the Savior (Jude 24–25).

14. Echoed by *2 Clem.* 5.5.

(θείας) as an adjectival description of "divine" power facilitates the promises and "divine" nature as the outcome of those promises (2 Pet 1:3-4). "Nature" (φύσεως) describes the whole condition of a person. When these words are combined in Jewish contexts of "corruption" (φθορᾶς), they often have the sense of indicating incorruptibility or immortality of the resurrection body after death (2 Pet 1:4).[15] Such a condition is not realized until the individual escapes corruption of mortality and lusts to participate in the resurrection nature (2 Pet 1:4 aorist of ἀποφυγόντες; 2 Pet 2:19-20). To turn this passage into the teaching for deification, in which humans participate in the very life and being of God mystically, one would have to read the Jewish resurrection in a very Platonic idea, but that would actually diminish Jewish bodily resurrection to make humans into gods,[16] which is foreign to the Jewish metaphors throughout the book. Such a mystical participation within the persons of God is better claimed from perichoresis passages in Paul and John (John 4:23-24; 14:16-20, 23; 15:45; 17:21; Rom 8:9; 1 Cor 3:16; 2 Cor 5:17; Phil 2:13; Col 1:27; 3:3). However, being in the divine persons and the divine persons in Christians is not developed in 2 Peter.

Upon this foundation of promises unto resurrection, Peter develops a narrow way of virtues unto the everlasting kingdom (2 Pet 1:5-11). Beginning with the faith granted, Christians are to apply moral excellence, knowledge, self-control, perseverance, godliness, brotherly kindness, and love in their lives as they pursue the kingdom (2 Pet 1:1, 5-6, 11). By living into these virtues in an increasing manner, the Christian reassures herself that her election and entrance unto the kingdom is ensured (2 Pet 1:8, 10-11). These virtues growing in the believer's life become the synergistic evidence for them knowing that they have been elected by God and that they will be in the kingdom. Following this, Peter guarantees that kingdom salvation shall be fulfilled by appealing to earlier stages of the prophecy that have already occurred, such as Peter's observation of Jesus' transfiguration (1 Pet 1:16-19).

Those who do not pursue such kingdom virtues shall be severely judged and miss salvation (2 Pet 1:9; 2:2-9). Some have escaped such defilement through this knowledge of Christ only to be re-entangled, which results in being worse off than at first (2 Pet 2:20-22). That is, these scoffers

---

15. 4 Macc 18:3; Wis 2:23.

16. *Pseudo-Phocylides* 103-4 fuses Jewish resurrection, transforming humans into Hellenistic divine deities similar to Josephus, *Ag. Ap.* 1.232 and Plutarch, *Def. orc.* 10; *Mor.* 415C; whereas Philo, *QE* 2.29 develops a Platonic idea with humans undergoing angelification without becoming Yahweh; *Abr.* 144; *Conf.* 154; Origen, *Comm. Jo.* 13.25; thus Bauckham, *Jude-2 Peter*, 180-82 and Bigg, *Epistles of St. Peter and St. Jude*, 255-56 argue against deification here.

shall be condemned while the beloved shall be saved (2 Pet 3:3–15). The temporal deliverances of Noah and Lot in the midst of temporal judgments are subsumed under the greater soteriological concerns (2 Pet 2:5, 7, 9). These deliverances are not developed to make the great judgment day seem less. Rather, they reinforce the fact that since God has judged previously he will certainly do so again in this greater future judgment when he also saves those who are his.

The buying (ἀγοράσαντα) is best seen as soteriological "redemption." Even though ἀγοράσαντα does not translate OT words for soteriological redemption, the word always means soteriological redemption in the NT when it refers to people as the object of the purchase (1 Cor 6:20; 7:23; Rev 5:9; 14:3–4). Furthermore, the context clearly develops soteriological issues. Within this development there is a major emphasis on lifestyle, which is quite appropriate to Petrine redemption. For example, those who have knowledge of Christ are to abundantly appropriate in their lives: faith, moral excellence, knowledge, self-control, perseverance, godliness, brotherly kindness, and love (2 Pet 1:2–7). This meaningful way of life assures the believer that she shall bear fruit and enter into the everlasting kingdom (2 Pet 1:8–11). This meaningful way is the reverse of the preredemptive futile sinful way of life (1 Pet 1:18; 2 Pet 1:9). So ἀγοράσαντα here is best seen as soteriological redemption. The lack of a mentioned price in this context is no reason to overthrow this soteriological meaning since half of the NT soteriological meanings of this word omit any mention of a price (2 Pet 2:1; Rev 14:3–4).

The master (δεσπότην) who is denied by the false teachers is Jesus Christ (2 Pet 2:1). First, since the redemption accomplished by the master is soteriological (2 Pet 2:1) and Peter describes only Christ as the one who soteriologically redeems people (1 Pet 1:18–19), then Christ is the master of whom Peter speaks in 2 Peter 2:1. Second, Christ is the master because the context emphasizes soteriological concerns. However, Peter elsewhere uses δεσπότην of the sovereign Creator (Acts 4:24) but the sovereign book is an unlikely reference in 2 Peter 2:1 since the Creator is only a minor element in 2 Peter, subservient to the greater concern of eschatological salvation and judgment (2 Pet 3:4–7). Additionally, Peter elsewhere uses δεσπόταις of earthly slave masters (1 Pet 2:18). However, there is no indication of earthly masters and their slaves in 2 Peter. In fact, the false teachers are free with the human freedom to pursue a multitude of different actions inappropriate for slaves, most notably their own licentious living. Third, 2 Peter is broadly parallel to Jude, and Jude 4 uses δεσπότην to refer to Christ within a context of common salvation in which the false teachers are denying the only Master and Lord, Jesus Christ.

It is inappropriate to appeal to a hypothetical redemption in 2 Peter 2:1 patterned after Luke 14:15-24. For example, A. Chang maintains such a hypothetical purchase.[17] But Chang nullifies his position by arguing that the statements of purchase are outright lies. He argues for false statements of actual purchase rather than true statements of hypothetical purchase. Such an argument better supports the view of charity, calling someone something that they call themselves even though it is false. However, I. H. Marshall does develop the hypothetical nature of the purchase in Luke. In that case "the purchase may well have been arranged on the condition of later inspection and approval," where the reference to necessity (ἀνάγκην in Luke 14:18) "implies the legal obligation of the purchaser to complete the sale."[18] However, this Lukan example is in the middle of an actual transaction and does not develop the effect of a rejection of a completed purchase such as 2 Peter 2:1 develops. The meaning of Petrine redemption as actual or hypothetical is then not determined by an appeal to Luke but by the context of 2 Peter.

A contextual appeal to 2 Peter surfaces three groups who have actually experienced the change of life normally resulting from Petrine redemption. The first is that body of believers who are growing in the qualities of salvation (2 Pet 1:4-6). For example, this group escaped lusts through moral excellence and godliness. Second, the theoretical possibility of a second group is admitted by Peter in the context: those who have begun with these changed qualities and then left them, having forgotten their purification from their former sins (2 Pet 1:9-11). Peter condemns these apostates as doubly blind, unfruitful, and in danger of missing the kingdom. Peter then develops this theoretical group as two actual groups: the false teachers, and those who barely escape lusts only to be enticed back into their former lifestyles (2 Pet 2:18-22; Simon of Acts 8:13, 20).[19] These two groups experience the lifestyle change that the knowledge of Christ produces. For example, those who barely escape from the ones who live in error still actually escape for a time (2 Pet 2:18). The

---

17. Chang, "Second Peter 2:1 and the Extent of the Atonement," *BSac* 142 (1985) 55-56.

18. Marshall, *Luke*, 589.

19. Two groups are indicated because the accusative of 2 Pet 2:18 cannot be identified with the subject, the false teachers who entice them; contra Jerome, *Jov.* 2 n. 3; Augustine, *Fid. Op.* c. 45; *Vg*. Simon Magnus is an example of such a false teacher who had believed, been baptized, and aligned with believers (Acts 8:13) but upon seeing the power of the bestowal of the Holy Spirit is warned by Peter about Simon's precarious situation of impending damnation (σὺν σοὶ εἴη εἰς ἀπώλειαν, Acts 8:20 similar to Theodotion LXX Dan 2:5; 3:96 and Old Greek LXX Dan 2:18; 6:23) due to his root of bitterness and bondage to iniquity (Acts 8:20, 23). Justin Martyr, *1 Apol.* 26.3; 56.2 later identifies that he did not repent and he died trying to perform a miracle that would lead others astray and was therefore damned. Bock, *Acts*, 333-36.

repetition of ἀποφυγόντες in 2 Peter 2:18 and 20 identifies the possibility of some people barely escaping only to be overcome again. The context of verse 20 is primarily to do with the false teachers, who are the third group. This is demonstrated contextually since the false teachers are those who entice the vulnerable escapees by fleshly desires, promising freedom while they themselves are slaves overcome[20] by judgment[21] (2 Pet 2:18-19). Furthermore, the use of γάρ in 2:19-20 connects this immediately preceding material with what follows, so that false teachers remain the primary subject.[22] The false teachers are indicated as the subject through the repetition of "overcome," emphasizing the judgment that "overcomes" the false teachers (2 Pet 2:20 ἡττῶνται; 2:19 ἥττηται). Since verse 20 primarily has to do with the false teachers, they also had actually escaped the defilements of the world by the knowledge of Christ. They have experienced the change of life normally resulting from Petrine redemption (1 Pet 1:18; 2 Pet 2:20).

The false teachers have been redeemed soteriologically under Peter's concept of redemption. (1) They have been redeemed soteriologically because Christ has bought them in a soteriological manner (2 Pet 2:1). (2) The soteriological redemption was not hypothetically applied but actually accomplished, since the false teachers experienced the results of Petrine redemption: a changed life (2 Pet 2:20). Thus, where the results of the work have been present one should consider the work of redemption as having been accomplished. (3) Redemption results were accomplished by the knowledge of Christ, which further identifies the redemption as having been soteriologically accomplished. For example, the divinely-given true knowledge of Christ is within the precious and magnificent salvation promises (2 Pet 1:3-4). This soteriological knowledge is a commitment to truth that leads to salvation and the kingdom (2 Pet 1:8-11; 3:18). So the one who diligently continues in soteriological knowledge shall arrive at kingdom salvation. It is then best to see the false teachers as actually having begun by Petrine soteriological redemption, which resulted in their transformed lives through Christ's death.

20. As in a battle, those overcome are slaves of their enemy; Bauckham, *Jude-2 Peter*, 277.

21. The use of φθορᾶς refers to the divine judgment (2 Pet 2:12) and its mortality (2 Pet 1:4). The word is not used by Peter for moral corruption (Harder, "φθορω," in *TDNT*, 9:104; and Köster, "φύσις," in *TDNT*, 9:275).

22. Perhaps in the focus on the false teachers the enticed ones barely escape (ἀποφεύγοντας; 2 Pet 2:18) and are warned of a similar fate by the repetition of ἀποφυγόντες in 2:20. However, the conceptual relationship between v. 18, "enticed by fleshly desires" and v. 20, "the defilements of the world" is not significant because there is no verbal connection (as with the false teachers in 2:10). Since the context emphasizes the false teachers as the subject, any conceptual appeal should maintain this emphasis.

The false teachers have in turn exchanged their knowledge and moral living for an ignorant life of rampant sin and certain condemnation. Having come to know (ἐπεγνωκέναι) the way of righteousness and experience (ἐπιγνοῦσιν) it, they have then rejected it (2 Pet 2:21), which in turn has plunged them into an ignorant life (2 Pet 2:12 ἀγνοοῦσιν). Such ignorance is akin to the unbeliever's condition of practicing sinful lust and persecuting Christ (Acts 3:17; 1 Pet 1:14; 2:15). These false teachers are worse off than if they had remained unredeemed ignorant unbelievers (2 Pet 2:21). (1) They know the commandment that they must live righteously. In being overcome by the entanglements of the world, they know judgment will follow their disobedience. (2) Their true bent demonstrates clearly that they are fools (2 Pet 2:22). Proverbial statements such as a dog returning to its vomit and a washed sow returning to the mire recall the contextual use in Proverbs 26:11 signifying a fool returning to his folly. These false teachers cannot say they never knew better. They have committed high-handed sin, knowingly rejecting both Christ and the way they must live. Such an unrighteous life will be kept by the Lord under impending punishment for the day of judgment (2 Pet 2:9).

Such a concept renders Petrine redemption superabundant rather than impotent. First, the elect are redeemed, accomplishing for them a new covenant transformation of life that leads toward their guaranteed salvation (1 Pet 1:1–5, 18). In Peter's terminology, salvation is identified with the resurrection and the kingdom (1 Pet 1:5, 9–10). Things can be considered presently soteriological, however, if they normally lead toward that salvation even if they do not fully accomplish it (1 Pet 3:21; 4:18; 2 Pet 3:15). Redemption as a soteriological work of Christ is effective in its transformation of the lives of the elect on their journey toward salvation. Second, redemption is no less effective where it accomplishes its full work of life transformation among some, like the false teachers who are not recipients of other soteriological works, which are needed if they would be saved. One should not fault a work of Christ that does more than is soteriologically necessary. A work of Christ may go beyond the limits of the elect to benefit others for a time. This redemption is not universalism, however, because it is actually applied to all who are transformed. Petrine redemption should then be conceived of as a limited redemption that nevertheless extends beyond the limits of the elect. It also includes all who experience the transformation of life by means of Christ's death, even for a time.

26

Christ's Propitiation in 1 John

1 JOHN 1:5—2:2 IS viewed differently in three Christian traditional ways. The Keswick, Augustinian-Dispensationalist, and Holiness traditions develop a carnal and a higher spiritual life, thus rendering the passage irrelevant to gospel.[1] The Lutheran and Wesleyan approaches recognize that the Christian is both sinner and saint simultaneously, and thus public acknowledgment that they are in this tension as both sinner and saint is relevant to the gospel.[2] The Reformed approach tends to recognize this text as gospel about initial salvation to initiate salvific forgiveness and fellowship.[3] Therefore, the public confession is one of testifying about their sin condition in order to become initially saved. When it comes to 1 John 2:2, the Reformed and Lutheran traditions tend toward limited atonement while the Wesleyan, Keswick, Holiness, and Augustinian-Dispensationalist traditions tend toward unlimited atonement enlivened by either faith or election applied. John Calvin holds a unique approach between these options by framing Christ's Johannine propitiation within Christ's present advocacy ministry,

---

1. Mitchell, *Fellowship*, 27–46; Hodges, "Fellowship and Confession in 1 John 1:5–10."

2. Wilder and Hoon, "First, Second, and Third Epistles of John," 234; Barclay, *Letters of John and Jude*, 33; Marshall, *Epistles of John*, 112; Black, "First, Second, and Third Letters of John," 386; Smalley, *1, 2, and 3 John*, 30 "daily forgiveness."

3. Calvin views confession of sins as more characteristic of the saved (*Catholic Epistles*, 22:168). The usual Reformed approach is to view the confession as occurring in a baptismal context (Matt 3:6; Mark 1:5; *Did.* 4.14; 8.2; Westcott, *Epistles of St. John*, 23; Law, *Tests of Life*, 130–31; Dodd, *Johannine Epistles*, 9; Brown, *Epistles of John*, 208; Yarbrough, *1–3 John*, 63).

thus identifying a present salvation option.[4] Kennard follows Calvin's approach in this gospel text.

Like most of John's larger writings, 1 John is anchored by an introduction of the historical Jesus (1 John 1:1-4). The Word of Life was in the beginning, heard, seen, handled, and proclaimed as everlasting life from the Father to us. This proclamation of Christ is the gospel because it results in everlasting life received by its responsive audience (1 John 1:2).

Jewish texts promised life as a continued life in Deuteronomic *Torah* blessings (Deut 30:6, 15-16, 19),[5] until early Judaism deepened this blessing into everlasting life[6] and personal resurrection where the dead will awake from their sleep among the dust to either everlasting life or everlasting contempt (Dan 12:2-3).[7] Such everlasting life cannot be merely realized eschatology, for it continues without end as an expression of the kingdom (Dan 12:2-3; John 3:15-17; 1 John 5:11-13).[8] This sort of eschatological resurrection hope becomes common in Pharisaic, rabbinic, and sectarian early Judaism.[9] Additionally, a minority Pharisaic view that Jesus embraces

---

4. Calvin, *Catholic Epistles*, 22:168.

5. Bar 3:9; 4:1-2; *Pss. Sol.* 14.1-2; *L.A.B.* 23.10; *2 Bar.* 38.2; *m. 'Abot* 2.7; *b. 'Abot* 6.7, bar.; *'Abot R. Nat.* 34A; 35B; *Sipre Deut.* 306.22.1; 336.1.1; *b. Ḥag.* 3b; *Roš Haš.* 18a; *p. Ber.* 2.2, section 9; *Ex. Rab.* 41.1; *Lev. Rab.* 29.5; *Num. Rab.* 5.8; 10.1; 16.24; *Deut. Rab.* 7.1, 3, 9; *Tg. Eccl.* 6.12.

6. 1QS 4.6-8; CD 3.20; 4Q181 3-4; *1 En.* 37.4; 40.4; 58.3; 4 Macc 15:3; *Ps. Sol.* 3.12; *Sib. Or.* 3.49 frag. 3.

7. 1QS 4.6-8; CD 3.20; 4Q181 3-4; *1 En.* 37.4; 40.4; 58.3; 4 Macc 15:3; *Ps. Sol.* 3.12; *Sib. Or.* 3.49 frag. 3; Baldwin, *Daniel*, 204-6; Wright, *Resurrection of the Son of God*, 108-10.

8. 1QS 4.6-8; CD 3.20-21; 1QH 3.10-22; 6.34; 11.12; 1QM 12.1-4.; 2 Macc 7:9-14, 22-23.

9. 1QH 3.10-22; 6.34; 11.12; 1QM 12.1-4; *1 En.* 58.3; 62.14-16; 91.10; 92.2; 108.11-14; *2 Bar.*[Syriac] 30.1-5; 2 Macc 7:9-14, 22-23; 14:43-46; 4 Macc 7:19; 16:25; 4 Ezra 7.32; *Sib. Or.* 4.180; *T. of Ben.* 10.6-8; *T. Levi* 18; *T. Jud.* 24; *T. of Hos.* 6:2 interprets this text to be resurrection, whereas the text speaks of the reviving of Israel on the third day; *Tg. Jon.* on Isa 27:12f describes salvation as being accomplished on the third day; *b. Sanh.* 90b, where Gamaliel claims that God would give the resurrected patriarchs land, not merely their descendants and Johanan Num 18:28 the portion of YHWH given to Aaron is taken that he will be alive again; likewise Num 15:31 is claimed that the remaining guilt of the offender will be accountable in the world to come; 91b-92a; *B. Ta'an.* 2a; *B. Ket.* 111; *m. Sanh.* 10.1, 3; *T. Mos.* 10.8-10; *Gen. Rab.* 14.5; 28.3; *Lev. Rab.* 14.9; *Messianic Apocalypse* adds resurrection to a modification of Ps 146:5-9 as a messianic expectation to be done to others; *T. Jud.* 25.4 claims this messianic resurrection would begin with Abraham, Isaac, and Jacob; *T. Benj.* claims that after these are raised the whole of Israel will be raised; *Ps. of Sol.* 3.11-12; 4Q521 frag. 2, cols. 2.1-13; frags. 7 and 5, cols. 2.1-7; 1QH 14.29-35; 19.10-14; *Targum Songs* 8.5; the benediction in the *Amidah*, the *Shemoneh Esre*. However, Wis 3:1; 8:19-20; 9:15 and Josephus' description of the Pharisees (*Ant.* 17.152-154; 18.1.3-5; *J.W.* 2.151-153; 2.8.14; *Ap.* 2.217-18)

anticipates resurrection life for the faithful believer resurrecting upon death, thus affirming the monotheistic God as the God of living Abraham, Isaac, and Jacob (Exod 3:6; Luke 16:19-30; 20:39).[10]

John's perspective brings resurrection into this life even before death but continuing beyond this bodily experience (John 3:16; 11:26). In Johannine writing, this everlasting life is a mystical reality that is already true of the one who believes (John 3:16-18). Calvin identified that the genitive "Word *of Life*" indicates that Jesus is the "life-giving" agent.[11] Thus, Jesus as agent himself embodies the everlasting life gospel message.[12]

This everlasting life proclamation of Jesus as the historical Word of Life results in fellowship with Christians, the Father, and the Son (1 John 1:3 κοινωνία). That is, John's concept of fellowship is not a higher level of spirituality within the Christian life; fellowship is the Christian life with the emphasis on relationship. Fellowship is akin to saving covenantal relationship. Such a relationship continues with God, Christ, and Christians. Reception of the proclaimed gospel brings "fellowship with us" (John and perhaps apostles or other Christians). Yet this fellowship with one another also connects the gospel receiver in a fellowship with the Father and with his Son, Jesus Christ (1 John 1:3, 7). John is overjoyed as his readers realize that receiving the gospel brings them into a vibrant fellowship with God, Christ, and other Christians.

This gospel message heard from Christ and announced identifies God as light, such that all darkness is excluded (1 John 1:5; 4:8, 16, 24 Spirit; 2:8 Christ).[13] This approach continues the sectarian Jewish way of mystical light at Qumran and the Gospel of John, in opposition to the broad way of dark-

---

follow more a Platonic immortality of the soul view, but even here the soul eventually is given a body to match (Wis 9:15; Josephus, *J.W.* 2.163). Also the biblical authors (Matt 22:23-33; Mark 12:18-27; Acts 23:6-7) and the *Eighteen Benedictions* present the Pharisees as believing the bodily resurrection of the dead; cf. Gillman, *Death of Death*, 101-42; Wright, *Resurrection of the Son of God*, 129-206 for the post-biblical Jewish view. The early church from patristic through medieval eras embraced bodily resurrection instead of Platonic immortality of the soul with regard to personal eschatology (Bynum, *Resurrection of the Body in Western Christianity*; Wright, *Resurrection of the Son of God*, 480-552).

10. Jesus view (cf. Luke 16:19-31) is consistent with Jewish tradition (*Abr.* 50-55; 4 Macc 7:18-19; 13:17; 16:25; Philo, *Sacr. CA* 1.5; *T. Abr.* 20.8-14; *Qoh. Rab.* 9.5.1; *b. Sanh* 90b; *Ex. Rab.* 1.8; *Deut. Rab.* 3.15; *LAB* 4.11; *T. Isaac* 2.1-5; *T. Benj.* 10.6; *Apoc. Sed.* 14.3; *3 En.* 44.7). The sages could also read "living God" as "God of the living" (*Pesiq. R.* 1.2).

11. Calvin, *Catholic Epistles*, 22:159.

12. Calvin, *Catholic Epistles*, 22:161, 165, 168.

13. Ps 119:130; Isa 5:20: Mic 7:8; 1QS 1.5, 9-10; 5.19-21; 1QH 4.5-6; 18.29; 1QM 13.15; Philo, *Deus* 29.

ness (John 1:4-9; 3:19-21; 5:35; 6:17, 19; 8:12; 9:5; 11:9-10; 12:35-6, 46).[14] Such dualism is grounded upon the Old Testament hope that Yahweh is the archetypical light: "The LORD is my light and my salvation, whom shall I fear?" (Ps 27:1). This revelational light metaphor is balanced by 1QS and the Gospel of John insisting on the invisibility of God present among Jewish monotheism (John 1:18; 6:46).[15]

Interpreters propose a range of people who are in darkness, who depart from Christianity as the foil to the true light Christians (1 John 1:6, 8, 10; 2:19; 5:16).[16] One view considers that the foil is Gnostic, similar to Cerinthus.[17] However, there is no evidence that such Gnosticism was present before the mid-second century, emerging with Valentinus and Basilides in Alexandria, usually after most commentators consider when John wrote this epistle. This means that a pre-Gnostic heresy is a conjecture without sufficient first-century evidence.[18] A second foil often combined with Gnosticism is a Docetic apostasy considering that Jesus merely appeared as a specter instead of being fully human.[19] While Docetism did occur early, the epistle only raises the physical reality of Jesus mildly as to support the truthfulness of John being an eyewitness to Jesus' life (1 John 1:1-3; 4:2; 2 John 7). Furthermore, the fact of Jesus' death argues against Jesus as a Docetic specter (1 John 1:7; 5:6). An alternative foil is sought among those who consider prophecy providing special spiritual knowledge.[20] However, any spiritual knowledge that denies Jesus Christ has come in the flesh is not Christian (1 John 4:1-3). A fourth option for a foil is that of Jewish

14. 1QS 3.17-4.1; 1QM 13.5-6, 14-15; Philo, *Opif.* 33; *Did.* 1-6; Barn. 18-20.

15. 1QS 11.20; 2 *En.* 48.5; '*Abot R. Nat.* 2, 39 A; *Sipra VDDen. Pq.* 2.2.3.2-3; *Tg. Ps.-J* on Gen 16:13; *Tg. Neof.* on Exod 33:23; *Tg. Onq.* on Exod 33:20, 23; Kennard, "Analysis of Theological Similarities between the *Charter of a Jewish Sectarian Association* (1QS, 4Q255-264a, 5Q11) and 'The Gospel of John,'" in *Epistemology and Logic in the New Testament*, 181-99.

16. Street, *They Went Out from Us*, 7-100 provides a nice analysis; Jobes, *1, 2, and 3 John*, 125 summarizes his options.

17. Gnosticism is attacked by Irenaeus, *Haer.* 1.26.1; 3.3.4; 3.11.1; 3.16; Tertullian, *Carn. Chr.* and *Marc.*; Epiphanius made significant later polemical use of 1 John against Gnostic sects in *Panarion*; Windisch and Preisker, *Katholischen Briefe*, 127-28; Bultmann, *Johannine Epistles*, 8, 11, 38-39; Law, *Tests of Life*, 26-38; Dodd, *Johannine Epistles*, xvii, xix-xxi.

18. Appreciating the contributions of Yamauchi, *Pre-Christian Gnosticism* and *Jewish Gnosticism?* indicate that Gnosticism is not sufficiently early to inform 1 John.

19. Docetism may be evident in *Gosp. Peter* 10 and is attacked by Polycarp, *Phil.* 7.1; Ignatius, *Trall.* 10; *Smyrn.* 2; Tertullian, *Carn.* 14; Law, *Tests of Life*, 26-38; Dodd, *Johannine Epistles*, xvii, xix-xxi.

20. Maybe after a pattern in 1 Cor 12-14; Büchsel, *Johannesbriefe*, 4-5; Brown, *Epistles of John*, 49-50.

Christians departing from the Christian community to return to synagogue (1 John 2:7–11, 19).[21] A fifth option is carnality in contrast to a higher spiritual life presented by Keswick, Augustinian-Dispensationalist, and Holiness traditions.[22] However, this approach and maybe the others are insensitive to the gospel and everlasting life proclaimed in the preceding context (1 John 1:1–3). A sixth option refuses to mirror-read a specific foil and places the emphasis on what John actually says in the epistle.[23] This last approach will be followed here.

This Johannine gospel approach sets up tests of life[24] that extend for the rest of the epistle. What we know is that 1 John 1:5–10 develops alternating conditional[25] statements of inclusion and exclusion, so that if someone claims to have a relationship with Christ (as in 1 John 1:6) there is enough to test whether in fact the claimant has this everlasting life. These tests are apparent in instances of exclusion (such as 1 John 1:6, 8, 10). For example, if one claims to have a relationship with Christ but his life identifies him as within a lifestyle of darkness (not receiving Christ's revelation, nor reflecting Christ's life in his life), then he lies and does not practice the truth (1 John 1:6).[26] Furthermore, if anyone claims that he in a condition of no sin or as though he has not sinned, he deceives himself and the truth is not in him (1 John 1:8, 10). God's word declares that we do sin, so such a liar attempts to make God a liar and in the end identifies that God's word is not in him (1 John 1:10).

In contrast, if we walk in the light as God himself is in the light, our lives demonstrate the righteous quality as to identify that we have relationship with God and one another (1 John 1:7). Such a privilege of covenantal relationship also provides the cleansing associated with sanctification within

---

21. Maybe after the pattern of Heb 6:4–8; 10:25–36; Wurm, *Irrlehrer im Ersten Johannesbrief*; Street, *They Went Out from Us*, 2, 90–100.

22. Mitchell, *Fellowship*, 27–46; Hodges, "Fellowship and Confession in 1 John 1:5–10."

23. Griffith, "Non-Polemical Reading of 1 John," 28.

24. Law, *Tests of Life* is an excellent biblical theology that develops this theme throughout the whole of 1 John. One of the major purposes of the writing of 1 John is that the readers might know that they have everlasting life (1 John 5:13).

25. The series of third-class conditional statements are uncertain but still likely and thus live conditions.

26. Such a condition is akin to the Jews who did not abide in Christ's word but sought to kill Christ (John 8:31, 37). They were of their father the devil, who as a liar has no truth in him (John 8:44). They sought to convict Christ of sin while justifying that in such a move they were not sinners (John 8:46). Christ teaches the truth, so that if anyone does not keep Christ's word they do not practice the truth (John 8:45–46, 51–52). If they claim to know God in such a condition they are liars (John 8:55).

the community (Notice plurals: 1 John 1:7 καθαρίζει ἡμᾶς, 1:9 καθαρίσῃ ἡμᾶς within Leviticus framework: Lev 12:8; 14:18–21, 31, 53; 15:15, 30; 16:30; Acts 10:15; 11:9; Heb 9:14, 22–23; Eph 5:26; Tit 2:14). Or, if we characteristically publicly acknowledge our sins,[27] God demonstrates himself to be characteristically faithful and righteous to forgive us and cleanse us of our sins (1 John 1:9). In fact, unlike the reluctant pagan deities who need to be cajoled into forgiveness, God initiated propitiation by sending his Son as an expression of his love (1 John 4:10). Faithfulness and righteousness are demonstrated as present characteristics of God in his forgiving condition.[28] These things are written so that John's audience could be characterized presently by not sinning, but if they do sin now there is encouragement of propitiation from Christ the Comforter (1 John 2:1).

As in the Gospel of John, an idiolect study of 1 John also emphasizes the present-ness[29] of salvation, in that Jesus Christ presently provides salvific forgiveness through the ongoing advocacy role (1 John 1:7, 9; 2:1–2). Jesus' historical death provides the metaphor of the blood of Jesus, which makes cleansing possible. However, such salvific forgiveness (in contrast to those who don't have fellowship and everlasting life) is developed in the present[30] and discussed as present realizations (of cleansing, forgiveness, and propitiation) for the one who presently identifies with God and Christ and publicly acknowledges that he sins. That is, Jesus *presently cleanses us* from all sin (1 John 1:7 present tense: καθαρίζει). Likewise, God *is* characteristically faithful and righteous (1 John 1:9 present tense: ἐστιν) in the cleansing and forgiveness process that takes care of all unrighteousness. This is a present realization of Christ's atonement death being applied to those who acknowledge that they are sinners.

27. The word ὁμολογῶμεν means "confess" as in public declaration, never as a form of prayer (John 1:20; 9:22; 12:42; 1 John 1:9; 2:23; 4:2–3, 15). Usually the public declaration is a characteristic of acknowledging Christ as Lord. Calvin, *Catholic Epistles*, 22:168 takes this instance as characteristic as well. In this instance, the present tense takes on a public characteristic of acknowledging I am a sinner in contrast to the liars who deny their sin.

28. From the characteristic use of the present tense and the near context present activity.

29. This point is not built from taking the present tense as absolute time but on an idiolect study of the Johannine context of 1 John that identifies the propitiation with Jesus' continuing advocacy role. Additional support comes from: Wallace, *Greek Grammar*, 523 n. 26 "customary present," also 621 argues for this conclusion from the broad use of soteriological verbs using the present tense in the NT. Also, Campbell, *Verbal Aspect*, 50–53 argues for present tense emphasizing proximity of salvation.

30. This point is not built from taking the present tense as absolute time but on an idiolect study of the context of 1 John that identifies the present reception of salvific benefits from Jesus' continuing advocacy.

God reveals himself as light in *Shekinah* and fire.[31] Extending this revelation of divine light, Jesus in John has both seen the Father and reveals him to the Christian community. The fact that Yahweh epitomizes this light identifies him from Old Testament and early Jewish sources as the Orderer among chaos in a manner where he continues to penetrate the threatening chaos with light: to create (John 1:3–5),[32] to enable visibility in the creation,[33] to enlighten humans to become children of the light (John 1:9–12),[34] to provide good moral guidance unto everlasting life (John 8:12; 12:46; 1 John 1:6–7),[35] also to protect (the point of the synonymous parallelism of Ps 27:1), and ultimately to bring about kingdom salvation of his making.[36] Within this kingdom, ultimately Yahweh's messianic servant is a light to the nations by which he establishes a covenant relationship with them (Isa 42:6; 49:6; John 8:12; 9:5).[37]

Believers in Jesus become a community of light having their habitation as of light (1 John 1:5; 2:8–10).[38] Such a habitation of light is further developed as indicated by "walking" in the path of light (John 3:20; 12:35–36; 1 John 1:7).[39] This habitation goes deeper than reception of communication and a transformed lifestyle; the life in the light deepens into an everlasting

---

31. Exod 13:22; 40:34–48; Pss 27:1; 104:1–2; Rev 21:23; 1QH 7.24–25; 4 *Bar.* 9.3; *L.A.E.* 28.2; *T. Zeb.* 9.8 (paraphrasing Mal 4:2); *PGM* 4.1219–1222; perhaps 4Q451 frg. 24, line 7; *Sib. Or.* 3.285; *b. Menaḥ.* 88b; *Gen. Rab.* 3.4 (citing Ps 104:2); 59.5 (citing Isa 60:19; *Ex. Rab.* 50.1 (citing Ps 104:2); *Num. Rab.* 15.2; *Pesiq. Rab.* 8.5 (citing Pss 27:1; 119:105); 21.5 (citing Isa 60:19); *Shekinah* glory (Wis 17; 18:1–3; *b. Menaḥ.* 86b; *Ex Rab.* 14.3; *Sipre Num.* 41.1.1; *b. Ber.* 60b).

32. Some Second Temple sources see light as a primeval light before creation (2 *En.* 24.4; *Ex. Rab.* 50.1) while others identify early in the creation light is used by God to limit chaos (Gen 1:3–5; *Gen. Rab.* 42.3; *b. Ḥag.* 12a).

33. 3 *En.* 5.3; *b. Ḥag.* 12a; *p. Ber.* 8.6 section 5; *Gen Rab.* 42.3; *Lev. Rab.* 11.7; *Num. Rab.* 13.5; *Ruth Rab.* Proem 7; *Pesiq. Rab.* 23.6.

34. Sir 31:17; 1QS 1.9–10; 2.16; 3.13; 3.17–4.1; 4Q392 frg. 1.

35. 1QS 3.3; also 1Q27 1.5–6; 4Q183 2.4–8; 1Q185 1–2 2.6–8; *T. Job* 43.6/4; *Sib. Or.* frg. 1.26–27; 1 *En.* 108.12–14.

36. Job 30:26; Ps 35:8–10; Isa 9:2–7; 45:7; 60:1–11; Matt 13:43; Rev 18:1; 21:23; 22:5; 1 *En.* 1.8; 5.7; 108.11–14; 1QM541 9 1.4–5; *Sib. Or.* 2.316; *'Abot R. Nat.* 37. 95 B; *b. Ḥag.* 12b; *Pesaḥ.* 50a; *Taʿan.* 15a; *Pesiq. Rab Kah.* 21.3–5; *Pesiq. Rab Kah.* Sup. 5.1; *Ex. Rab.* 14.3; 18.11; *Lev. Rab.* 6.6; *Song Rab.* 1.3, section 3; *Eccl. Rab.* 11.7.1; *Pesiq. Rab.*36.1; 42.4. This includes the restoration of light after this present era of sin affect (*b. Ḥag.* 12a; *Gen. Rab.* 11.2; 42.3; *Ex. Rab.* 18.11; *Lev. Rab.* 11.7; *Num. Rab.* 13.5; *Pesiq. Rab.* 23.6 42.4).

37. 1 *En.* 48.4 (alluding to Isa 42:6; 49:6); 1QSb 4.27; *Pesiq. Rab Kah.* Sup. 6.5; *Gen. Rab.* 1.6; 85.1; *Pesiq. Rab.* 36.1–2; 37.2; *Tg.*1 *Chr.* 8.33.

38. Similar to 1QS 3.19.

39. Similar to 1QS 3:20.

fellowship with God, Christ, the Holy Spirit, and one's comrades in the light (John 14:6–7, 17; 1 John 1:3–7).[40]

That is, Jesus Christ as Advocate is the solution if any of John's readers should sin. As advocate (παράκλητον),[41] Christ provides a role of championing the believer before God, a real priestly present consolation and encouragement to deal with present salvific needs of sin.

Christ is himself the propitiation in this advocacy role. That is, the reflexive pronoun αὐτὸς identifies that it is Christ *himself*[42] and not a personified metonymy: Jesus standing for a historically past deed done by him, that is, the propitiation is in his contextually developed advocacy role. For example, the priestly role of the Levitical priest in the functioning Jewish temple and the high priest at the Day of Atonement would facilitate this propitiation advocacy role for as long as the temple stood to function on behalf of the Jewish sinner (LXX: Exod 25:17–22; 31:7; 35:12; 38:5–8; Lev 16:2, 13–15; Num 7:89; Ezek 43:14–20). An additional historical pattern for this is evident in 4 Maccabees 6:28–29, where Eleazar the priest fused the role of priestly intercession into the martyrs' (including his own) mimetic atonement for the sins of the people, thus the priestly intercession continued to apply the atonement to the believer. However, Christ provides a vicarious atonement in Johannine writings. Instead of the Maccabean instance of advocate and death for atonement, *Jesus' death provides the means*, decisively in a vicarious manner (1 John 1:7 "blood of Jesus"), *by which Jesus' present advocacy role as priest propitiates presently for the sins of his people* (1 John 2:2).[43] *The present tense of the propitiation* further identifies Christ himself in the *present advocacy role as being an ongoing provision to deal with divine appeasement concerning sin* (1 John 2:1–2; 4:10 ἱλασμός).[44] This is an unusual present framing of the issues that Paul and Hebrews develop decisively as offering a sacrifice and climactically Jesus offering himself in his death. However, the present salvation emphasis in Johannine theology

40. Similar to 1QS 2.25.

41. The word παράκλητον is used repeatedly by John. The Holy Spirit and Christ are similar comforters who provide this kind of encouragement (John 14:26; 15:26; 16:7, 13–14; 1 John 2:1).

42. Blass et al., *Greek Grammar*, p. 148, sec. 283 identify that the reflexive pronoun is "used almost exclusively as the direct complement of the verb referring to the subject." Wallace, *Greek Grammar*, 350.

43. Similar to 4 Macc 6:28–29 but instead Jesus' prayer advocacy applies Jesus' own vicarious atonement death rather than martyrs' mimetic atonement deaths.

44. This point is not built from taking the present tense as absolute time but on the context of 1 John that identifies the propitiation with Jesus' continuing advocacy and present tense emphasizing proximity of the context (Campbell, *Verbal Aspect*, 50–53). This is a conclusion from contextual emphasis, not a myopic grammatical one.

and the advocacy context within which Jesus is referred to as propitiation in person shift the action to an ongoing ministry of Christ on our behalf. This should not surprise us because elsewhere (in John's Gospel and Epistles) John presents salvation in the present tense as well. Likewise, the priest's intercession and sacrifice roles can fuse.[45] Here they do as Jesus continues to function as Priest. Such a propitiation salvifically deals with sin in the present and brings cleansing and forgiveness for all one's sin (1 John 1:7, 9; 2:1–2; 4:10).

At this point, I follow John Calvin in crafting an option between the limited atonement of Dortian Calvinism and the unlimited atonement of Arminius or Amyrald. Calvin identifies that in 1 John the present intercession of Christ is the framework within which the Father is propitious.

> Christ so intercedes by the sacrifice of his death, that the Father is propitious to us... The intercession of Christ is a continual application of his death for our salvation. That God then does not impute to us our sins, this comes to us, because he has regard to Christ as intercessor... the simple truth ought to be retained, that the fruit of his death is ever new and perpetual, that by his intercession he renders God propitious to us.[46]

Christ as propitiation is available not merely for those who are already identified with him and his everlasting life, but also for those of the whole world (1 John 2:2). So there is an unlimited availability of Christ as a present salvific priestly propitiation for people's sins. However, only those who are identified as in relationship with Christ as come in the flesh are beneficiaries of his everlasting life (1 John 1:2–3; 2:2–23; 4:10–16), limiting the extent of propitiation as realized to those who actually benefit from it. Furthermore, John has moved the atonement from the past historical event of Jesus' death to the present active advocacy role of Christ available for all but only efficacious for those who actually benefit by identification with him. Thus, John identifies Christ's salvation as divinely intended to be available for all but only efficacious for those presently believing. 1 John 2:1–2 develops Jesus' present advocacy role by which John and Calvin urge us to broaden our categories regarding the extent of atonement. Christ's propitiation is available for all through his advocacy role but this propitiation is only applied to actual beneficiaries who have faith in Christ.

---

45. 4 Macc 6:28–29; and in Hebrews we have seen the new covenant cleansing of conscience to be partly due to Jesus' sacrifice and partly due to Jesus' priestly intercession.

46. Calvin, *Catholic Epistles*, 22:170–72.

The Gospel of John records that John the Baptist identified Jesus as the "Lamb of God, who takes away the sin of the world" (John 1:29, 36). This is likely an allusion of the Isaianic sin or guilt offering applied to ethnic groups even beyond Israel (Isa 52:15 "sprinkle many nations"; 53:10–11 "justify the many"). The book of Revelation indicates that this Lamb was slain in accomplishing his mission of salvation and is worthy to be worshipped in this accomplishment (Rev 5:6–13; 7:9–14; 13:8; 15:3). However, Jesus' vicarious atonement redeems us from our sins through his priestly sacrifice on our behalf (Rev 1:5 λύσαντι ἡμᾶς ἐκ τῶν ἁμαρτιῶν ἡμῶν).[47] This reference may identify a redemption effect that goes beyond a Jewish sacrifice to impact life based on the preposition ἐκ separating us *from* our sins. 1 John might supply the rationale by which Christ separates the believer *from* his sins. In 1 John there is a concern that the Christian not sin habitually but practice righteousness (1 John 2:1; 3:4–9). However, if the Christian sins then there is reassurance toward atonement. John describes the effect of Jesus' death as providing cleansing for those who identify with Jesus (1 John 1:7), though this cleansing continues through the consistent character of God and the compassionate comfort role of Christ presently in the believer's life as we acknowledge our sin condition and need (1 John 1:9; 2:1–2, 12). These references make the allusion more generally to Jesus being a purification offering for the world, with forgiveness and the recovery from sin especially emphasized.

In 1 John, the prayer and advocacy by Jesus penetrates to a deep level of salvation experience. Jesus is described as παράκλητον, which in this instance could fit the Greek legal "defender" advocate role. However, the metaphors here are mixed with priestly imagery that presents a different picture. Elsewhere in John and the OT, παράκλητον stands primarily for the roles of helping, comforting, and prophecy (LXX: Gen 24:67; Job 2:11; Isa 10:32; 21:2; 22:4; 35; 38:16; 40:1–2, 11; John 14:16–18, 26; 15:26–27; 16:7–14; Acts 2:33; 1 John 2:1; 4:6; 5:6),[48] so it is better to see Jesus as "Comforter" in a broadly priestly ministry of comfort rather than in a forensic defender role here.

The propitiation (1 John 2:1; ἱλασμός) accomplished by Christ identifies with what is accomplished on behalf of Israel at the "mercy seat" on the Day of Atonement (LXX: Exod 25:17–22; 31:7; 35:12; 38:5–8; Lev 16:2, 13–15; Num 7:89; Ezek 43:14–20). Framing Christ's corporate atonement accomplishment through the lens of the Day of Atonement is a profoundly

---

47. Similar to Exod 24:8; Lev 16:14–19; Beale, *Revelation*, 191; Loenertz, *Apocalypse of St. John*, 43.

48. *Jub.* 25:14; 2 Macc 6:12; *T. of Jud.* 20.1, 5; 1QS 2.3; 3.13–26; 4.21; 4Q381 frag. 69, line 4; Johnston, *Spirit-Paraclete in the Gospel of John*.

priestly image, especially developed in Hebrews 9:1—10:18. Propitiation in 1 John is not a legal fiction but a priestly restoration of covenantal relationship. Hebrews, John, Paul, and the early church viewed Christ's death through this covenantal sacrificial model rather than a legal one, so such metaphors are not to be seen as inventions of the New Perspective on Paul (Heb 9:7-28; John 1:29, 36; 1 John 2:1; Rom 3:25).[49] Remember that in a Levitical sacrifice the animal sacrificed is not declared to receive a covenant curse but the scapegoat is to be released into the wilderness to bear Israel's sin away (Lev 16:21-22).[50] However, even though there is no mention of a

---

49. John 1:29; Heb 9:1—10:18; *Barn.* 7-8 Jesus' death parallel to Day of Atonement and red heifer cleansing; Justin Martyr, *Dial.* 13.1-9, 40.1-4, 72.1, 111.2-3 develop Jesus' death as parallel to paschal lamb, Day of Atonement, and Isa 53 sacrificial lamb (Markschies, "Jesus Christ as a Man before God: Two Interpretive Models for Isaiah 53 in the Patristic Literature and Their Development" and Baley, "'Our Suffering and Crucified Messiah' [*Dial.* 111.2]: Justin Martyr's Allusions to Isaiah 53 in His Dialogue with Trypho with Special Reference to the New Edition of M. Marcovich," in Janowski and Stuhlmacher, eds., *Suffering Servant*, 332-33 and 378-79; Cyprian, *Test.* 15 Jesus' death is parallel to Jewish sacrifice, Isa 53, and Passover lamb; *Letter* 63.14.4 in Filium, ed., *Corpus Scriptorum Ecclesiasticorum Latinorum*, 3c:410-11; Origen, *Comm. Jo.* 6.32-38 and Augustine, *Trin.* 4.14 or 19 and *On Forgiveness of Sins and Baptism* 54-55 identify Jesus' death parallel to Jewish daily sacrifices; Theodoret of Cyrrhus, *Interpretation of the Letter to the Romans*, in Migne, ed., *Patrologia graeca*, 82; Chrysostom, *Hom. Rom.* 7 in Schaff, ed., *Nicene and Post-Nicene Fathers*, 11:378; both mentioned in Oden, *Justification Reader*, 62; Origen, *Romans* 2:110 cited in Oden, *Justification Reader*, 65; Cyril, *Catechetical Lectures* 13.3 develops Jesus' death parallel to Day of Atonement; Eusebius, *Theoph.* 3.59, *Comm. Isa.* 2.42 on Isa 53:5-6 and 11-12, and *Dem. ev.* 3.2.61-2 develop Jesus' death as a Jewish sacrifice and sin offering (Markschies, "Jesus Christ as a Man before God: Two Interpretive Models for Isaiah 53 in the Patristic Literature and Their Development," in Janowski and Stuhlmacher, eds., *Suffering Servant*, 305, 308, 312-33); Gregory Nazianzen, *In Defense of His Flight to Pontus* 1.3-4 develops Jesus' atonement parallel to Passover; Ambrose, *Fid.* 3.11.67 parallel to Melchizedek sacrifice; Leo the Great, *Sermons* 55.3; 56.1; 59.5, 7; 68.3 parallel to daily Jewish sacrifice and Passover; Presbyterian Church of England, *Articles of the Faith*, 1890, art. 13, "Justification by Faith," in Schaff, ed., *Creeds of Christendom*, 3:918; also the abundance of early church iconography presenting Jesus as a sacrificial lamb show the profusion of Jesus' death conceived through the lens of Jewish sacrifice, for example: a third-century Roman catacomb lamb image for Christ, Jesus as lamb with cruciform halo in the apex of the dome in a 6th-century church of Ravenna, the 6th-century basilica of Saints Cosmos and Damian in Rome shows the Lamb of God on a rock surrounded by the twelve apostles as lambs indicating mimetic atonement, a 7th-century Roman altar portraying the Lamb of God on the altar with the cross, the 82nd canon of the A.D. 692 Council of Trullo affirmed Jesus was incarnate in human flesh by banning the very common practice of representing Jesus' death as a lamb, "we decree that henceforth Christ our God must be represented in his human form but not in the form of the ancient lamb"; *Nicene and Post-Nicene Fathers*, 14:401; Sanday and Headlam, *Romans*, 122-24; Kennard, *Biblical Covenantalism*, 1:289-313; 3:43-110, 162-74.

50. No mention of the death of the scapegoat occurs until *m. Yoma* 6.4 and *Bar.* 7.7, 9 describe pushing the scapegoat off a cliff after Israel no longer can do the Day of

sacrifice receiving a covenant curse, the sacrifices are part of the means to avert covenant curse in order to recover believers in covenant.

However, in 1 John propitiation is described as referring to Jesus himself by the choice of the personal pronoun (αὐτὸς), rather than to a deed Jesus accomplishes.[51] That is, propitiation contextually is tied to Christ's ministry of advocacy[52] (which is a present priestly function) and provides everlasting life (1 John 2:2; 4:10). While Hebrews and Pauline propitiation focus on the death of Jesus as sacrifice, in 1 John propitiation is extended into his continued advocacy role,[53] from the basis of having died for our sins (1 John 1:7; 2:1–2). So this Johannine advocacy theme extends Hebrews' role of priestly intercession (Heb 7:25) soteriologically into a present atonement recovery from the status and the practice of sin to that of intimate forgiven everlasting life fellowship with God and fellow believers (1 John 2:1–2). That is, Hebrews frames our life on the narrow way as heading toward the

---

Atonement in Jerusalem because they were banned by Rome and the temple was rebuilt to worship Jupiter. Perhaps some see propitiation as penal by analogy from *Oedipus Rex* 1290–93 but John conceives of atonement through Jewish imagery, "the lamb of God who takes away the sin of the world" (John 1:29, 36).

51. Grammatically, the personal pronoun (αὐτὸς) *focuses the attention on the person of Jesus* (Porter, *Idioms of the Greek New Testament*, 129, para. 2.1.1; Robertson, *Grammar of the Greek New Testament*, 676), even though grammarians argue on whether such use would make it emphatic (some argue for emphasis: Blass et al., *Greek Grammar*, 145, para. 277; Winer, *Treatise on the Grammar of New Testament Greek*, 190; others usually see emphasis but not true in all examples: Robertson, *Grammar of the Greek New Testament*, 676; Moulton, *Grammar of New Testament Greek*, 85). Allowing the personal pronoun to focus on the person honors John's present emphasis more than turning it into a personalized metonymy of cause for the effect of atonement in the past (which is the emphasis in Paul and Hebrews focus on the deed).

52. Propitiation is tied to Jesus' advocacy rather than Jesus' death in the 1 John 2:1–2 statement: παράκλητον ἔχομεν πρὸς τὸν πατέρα Ἰησοῦν Χριστὸν δίκαιον· 2 καὶ αὐτὸς ἱλασμός ἐστιν περὶ τῶν ἁμαρτιῶν ἡμῶν. Campbell, *Verbal Aspect*, 50–53 argues for present tense to emphasize proximity, thus ἐστιν in 1 John 2:2 is focused on the near-context priestly advocacy role rather than the more removed death of Christ (1 John 1:7). Such a priestly action occurs as the high priest performs atonement in early Judaism, where an appropriate sacrifice is provided for the guilty and unclean people at the "mercy seat" on the Day of Atonement (ἱλαστήριον); Kraus, *Tod Jesu als Heiligtumsweihe*, 21–32 lists six instances in pagan sacrifice (the most telling is Josephus, *Ant.* 16.182 in which a votive offering placates the wrath of God) and thirty-nine in Jewish sacrificial atonement texts (twenty-one times in *Torah*: LXX Exod 25:17–22; 31:7; 35:12; 38:5–8; Lev 16:2, 13–15; Num 7:89; 5 in Ezek 43:14–20; one in Amos, six times in Philo and one in the Rahlfs ed. of 4 Macc 17:22, twice in Symmachus, one in *T. Sol.*); Heb 9–10; Markus Tiwald, "Christ as Hilasterion (Rom 3:25), Pauline Theology on the Day of Atonement in the Mirror of Early Jewish Thought," in *The Day of Atonement*, 189–209 argues for this Jewish atonement meaning while the temple still functioned not being abrogated by Rom 3:25.

53. Similar to priestly redemption through prayer in 4 Macc 6:29.

kingdom,[54] while John places the salvation motifs as primarily in the present tense: believers remain within everlasting life as a present possession and presently receive propitiation from Christ's advocacy while we live in the tension of reflecting God's light and unfortunately sinning as well.[55] Christ the Advocate recovers Christians from their sin.

---

54. Kennard, "Warnings in the Book of Hebrews."

55. This point is not built from taking the present tense as absolute time but on the context of 1 John that identifies the propitiation with Jesus' continuing advocacy.

27

The Overcomer in Revelation

THE BOOK OF REVELATION begins with a vision of Christ wherein He, as the *alpha* and *omega* Son of Man, commissions John to write letters to seven churches in Asia to call them all to overcome the hardships surrounding them and thereby promise them resurrection kingdom benefits (Rev 1:8–9, 11, 19; Dan 7:13).[1] John was taken up to the heavens on the Lord's Day[2] to be presented with a vision of the divine Christ. John saw a transcendent glowing solar[3] white-[4] and bronze-colored Christ surrounded by seven lampstands,[5] which are the seven churches to which John was to write (Rev 1:13–15, 20). In Christ's right hand he held seven stars, which are the recipient messengers to the seven churches (Rev 1:16, 20).[6] From out of Christ's

---

1. The Son of Man phrase refers to Christ as the divine cloud rider who comes up to the Ancient of Days (Dan 7:13; Rev 1:13; 14:14; Matt 24:30; 26:64; Mark 13:26; 14:62; Luke 21:27; *Did.* 16.8; *Apoc. Pet.* 1; Justin, *1 Apol.* 51.9; *Dial.* 14.8; 31.1; 120.4; *4 Ezra* 13.3; *b. Ḥag.* 14a).

2. Sunday when Christians gathered (1 Cor 16:2; Acts 20:7; Justin, *1 Apol.* 67; Ignatius, *Magn.* 9.1; *Did.* 14.1).

3. Glowing like the sun (Matt 17:2 transfiguration; Rev 10:1; *2 En.* J and A mss 1.5; 19.2; *4 Ezra* 7.97, 125; *Apoc. Zeph.* 6.11; *1 En.* 14.21; 106.2). There is no need to appeal to a Hellenistic Apollo to make sense of this picture but this picture might polemic Apollo as the divine patron of Patmos Island and of Miletus (*1 Pat* 33; Koester, *Revelation*, 241). Eyes glowing like flames is a common divine vision trait (Rev 1:14, 19:12; Apollodorus, *Library* 2.4.9; Suetonius, *Aug.* 79.2).

4. Divine in white hair (Rev 1:14; Dan 7:9; *1 En.* 46.1; 71.10) and white clothing (Rev 19:14; *1 En.* 14.18–21) is common.

5. "Menorahs" indicating the heavenly throne room (Aune, *Revelation*, 65, 88–90; Philo, *QE* 2.73, 81, 95).

6. The seven stars could have been visually presented as the seven planets of which Hellenists were aware or a constellation of either the Great Bear or the Pleiades (Aune,

glowing face a long double-edged spear sword[7] extended in front of his mouth, perhaps as a metaphor for Christ's speech, to show John that Christ's commands carry consequences if the churches do not respond to these letters (Rev 1:16; 2:12; 19:15, 21).

The vision following the letters returns to the heavenly throne room, with God and Christ being worshipped (Rev 4–5). Here the image of Christ changes from the Christophany on the throne before the letters to one standing near the Father's throne identified as "Lion of Judah, Root of David, and a Lamb alive after being slain (Rev 5:5–8, 12–13). No doubt the Lamb imagery draws from the Gospel of John's "lamb that takes away the sin of the world" (John 1:29, 36), but the book of Revelation does not develop this significance for the good news. What is developed as gospel in the book of Revelation is the exhortation to overcome the challenges in following Christ. John frames salvation through a two-ways strategy, even though Jesus' Jewish vicarious atonement is part of the background.

Each of the seven letters begins with restating part of this vision to indicate that it is not just John who writes but the comments to the respective churches also come from Christ himself (Rev 2:1, 8, 12, 18; 3:1, 7, 14). Christ's omniscience permeates the letters with knowledge[8] of the contextual condition of the churches, followed by appropriate authoritative commands for those churches to remedy their respective situations. The Christians are treated corporately, and not individually, as a group making up a church that has a problem or can repent or is corporately encouraged in their faithfulness. Each letter closes with a call for overcoming (νικῶν) and a command that every church should heed what Christ says to each church.

Christ's call to overcome focuses the narrow way unto the kingdom. The letters refer to the *overcomer* or *victor* through a present active participle, "he who overcomes" (νικῶν). However, the idea of a *Christian overcomer* (Rev 2:7, 11, 17, 26; 3:5, 12, 21; 12:11; 15:2) is grounded on the pattern of Christ as *victor* in the book (Rev 3:21; 5:5; 17:14; 21:7). Beale identifies that those who overcome receive the benefit of God's salvific presence.[9] Stewart develops the gospel in the book of Revelation as *faithful overcoming through Christ's return and judgment*.

Revelation, 97–98, 111–12). Perhaps the seven stars imagery polemic Domitian's reign, which minted a Roman coin in A.D. 88–96 that showed Domitian surrounded by seven stars.

7. 1QM 5.11–14.

8. Especially evident in the perfect-tense use of οἶδα (Rev 2:2, 9, 13, 19; 3:1, 8, 15).

9. Beale, *Revelation*, 235.

Throughout the Apocalypse, John presents salvation as a future event that would not decisively culminate until Christ's return in order to motivate his hearers to overcome in the present through complete faithfulness to Jesus unto death. Those who responded positively to his call to repentance, worship, witness, perseverance, and obedience would be saved with God's people in the final day of salvation and judgment, while those who did not respond appropriately would be judged with God's enemies.[10]

The Christian overcomer is promised resurrection life and coregency with Christ in the kingdom. The clearest promise to this outcome is the one Christ makes in Revelation 3:21: "He who overcomes, I will grant to him to sit down with me on my throne, as I also overcame and sat down with my Father on his throne." Obviously, overcoming may entail one's self-sacrifice in martyrdom death and resurrection, since Christ died and was raised to ascend to coregency with the Father and live forever (Rev 1:18; 2:8; 3:5, 21; 5:5–10; 12:11; 13:8; 17:8; 20:12, 15; 21:27).[11] Since Christ is the Living One, those affiliated with him also will share in life (Rev 1:18; 2:8; 3:21). Such overcoming grants the privilege of eating of the tree of life, in paradise,[12] and thus living forever (Rev 2:7; Gen 3:22–24)[13] and receiving the crown of life[14] (Rev 2:10; 3:11; James 1:12). Having the keys to Hades, Christ re-

10. Stewart, *Soteriology as Motivation in the Apocalypse of John*, 5–6.

11. Martyrdom is still seen as a live prospect if the readers identify as a Christian in a Roman court (Rev 2:10, 13; 12:11; 20:4; Pliny, *Ep.* 10.96.3–4; Justinian, *Dig.* 1.16.6, 11; 48.19.8.1; Tacitus, *Ann.* 15.44; *Mart. Pol.* 12.3; Ignatius, *Rom.* 4.1) but in such a death one can be an "overcoming victor" (4 Macc 9:30; Seneca, *Ep. Mor.* 67.10–11) because one's names will be retained in the book of life (Rev 3:5; Exod 32:32–33; Pss 9:5; 69:28; 87:6; Isa 4:3; Ezek 13:9; Dan 7:10; 12:1–2; Luke 10:20; Phil 4:3; Heb 12:23; *Jub.* 30.22; 1QM 12.2–5; *Jos. Asen.* 15.4); du Rand, "Soteriology in the Apocalypse of John," in Van der Watt, ed., *Salvation in the New Testament*, 474; Minear, *I Saw a New Earth*, 59–61; Shin, "More than Conquerors").

12. Paradise was the kingdom on earth where the resurrected dead live eating from the tree of life (Rev 2:7; 22:2; Gen 2:9; 3:22–24; Ezek 47:12; *1 En.* 24.3–4; 25.4–6; 32.3; 60.8; 70.3; 77.3; *2 En.* 8.3–7; *3 En.* 23.18; Philo, *QE Gen* 4.51; *Adam and Eve* 25.1–3; 40.1–2; *4 Ezra* 2.12; 7.36; 8.52; *T. Abr.* [rec. B] 10.2; *T. Levi* 18.10–11; *Ps. Sol.* 14.2–3, 10; *Apol. Sedr.* 9.1; 12.1; 16.6; *Apoc. Mos.* 28.2–4; Theophilus, *Ad Autolycum* 2.24; *Odes Sol.* 20.7).

13. 1QH 6.17–18; *T. Levi* 18.11; *Apoc. Elijah* 5; *Odes Sol.* 11.19; *Gilgamesh Epic* 9.266–95.

14. Crown (στέφανον) is broadly a metaphor for *victory* (in athletics: 1 Cor 9:25; 1 Pet 5:4; 1QS 4.7; 2 *Bar.* 15.8; military: Jdt 15:13; Josephus, *Ant.* 14.299; Pliny the Elder, *Nat.* 16.3.7–8; 16.5.14; 22.4.6–8; Vellius Paterculus, *Rom. Hist.* 1.12.4; 2.81.3; Aulus Gelius, *Noct. Att.* 5.6.1–27; *ISmyr.* 609–10), *martyrdom* (4 Macc 17:15; *Mart. Pol.* 17.1; 19.2; *Mart. Asc. Isa.* 9.18), and *co-regency* (Ps 8:5 LXX; Wis 5:16; or public service *ISmyr.* 515.7–8; 578.34–24; 579.23–24; *IPerg.* 459; *IThyat.* 903; *IEph.* 27.89; *ISard.* 27;

leases Christians from death's entrapment so that they might join him in the privilege of everlasting life (Rev 1:18). These metaphors identify the believer with everlasting life, guaranteeing that the overcomer will not be hurt by the second death (Rev 2:11; 20:6, 14–15; 21:8). In fact, Christ promised a more personal clothing of the overcomer with white,[15] a guarantee that her name will not be erased from the book of life, and a personal confessing of her name before the Father and his angels (Rev 3:5, 18). Kingdom access is pictorially described by the overcomer having an open door to the kingdom by the key of David along with the keys of death and Hades (Rev 3:7; 1:18),[16] and being made into a pillar[17] named for God in God's temple in the New Jerusalem, which comes down from heaven (Rev 3:12). The figures expand to include the overcomer as partaking of hidden manna[18] and given an affirming white stone or vindication[19] (Rev 2:17). The overcomer's benefits include coregency, which fulfills the Psalm 2:8 "authority over the nations" to rule and judge them with Christ (Rev 2:26–27).

This *overcoming* is modified by synonyms "be faithful" and "hold fast" until Christ comes, to which are also promised the crown of life and that crown would not be removed (Rev 2:10, 25; 3:11). Christ provides the model to emulate in endurance (Rev 1:9). Such faithfulness would entail persevering in suffering (Rev 2:2–3, 9–10, 19; 3:10) and cultivating a vital

---

IPhil. 1894; Koester, *Revelation*, 277–78).

15. White signifies purity, holiness, and honor (Rev 3:18; 7:9–14; Josephus, *Ant.* 11.327, 331; 1 *En.* 14.20; Koester, *Revelation*, 314, 347). Though Rev 7:14 provides a later explanation for how the robes were made white by washing them in the blood of the lamb, and thus vicarious atonement, but maybe also mimetic atonement since they come out of the tribulation as well.

16. This keeper of the keys elevates above Hellenistic Aeacus, keeper of the key to Hades (Apollodorus, 3.12.6; *CIG* 3.933), or Jewish angel Michael, keeper of the key to the kingdom (3 *Apoc. Bar.* 11.2).

17. "Pillar" (στῦλον) can identify leaders (Gal 2:9; 1 *Clem.* 5.2; Euridides, *Iph. Taur.* 57; Pindar, *Olymp.* 2.81–82; Lycophron, *Alex.* 281) but here it is better understood as a kingdom temple architecture blessing similar to Jachin and Boaz pillars in the Solomonic temple or Baucis and Philemon becoming pillars of the temple to Zeus in Lycaonian (1 Kgs 7:15–21; 2 Chr 3:15; Josephus, *Ant.* 8.77–78; *Jos. As.* 17.6; Ovid, *Metam.* 8.626–725; Hernas, *Vis.* 3.8.2).

18. Manna as an eschatological expectation in early Judaism's kingdom food (Exod 16:32–34 with 2 Macc 2:4–7; 2 Bar. 29:8; *Sib. Or.* 7.149; *b. Ḥag.* 12b; *Midr. Rab. Eccl.* 1.9) and in that setting banned from idolaters (*Sib. Or.* 3.24–49). The eating of the hidden manna is a benefit from heaven that brought life in contrast to eating what has been sacrificed to idols (Rev 2:14–17; Exod 16:3–4).

19. A white stone was a positive vote to affirm an individual and can merge with the pillar affirmation (Ovid, *Metam.* 15.41–42; Aeschylus, *Eum.* 737–56; Plutarch, *Alc.* 2.22; *Mor.* 186F; white square column archeological example in Pergamum engraved with honored names; Koester, *Revelation*, 290).

intimate growing committed love relationship with Christ (Rev 2:4-5, 19; 3:1). Overcomers show their love for Christ in practical deeds by refusing idolatry, immorality, and capitalistic gain perverting Christianity (Rev 2:14-15, 20, 22; 3:17-18), and in practical deeds that refresh and benefit others (Rev 2:5, 19; 3:15-16). The virtues called to here are the narrow way unto the kingdom. The vices lead astray to damnation if one does not repent from this broad way.

There are consequences of exclusion unto damnation if they do not overcome in faithfulness. Jesus warns that if the Ephesus church does not regain its first love of God and Christ, then Jesus will remove the church's lampstand out of its place, presumably displacing the church from the presence of Christ (Rev 2:5). The church in Smyrna is warned that the second death awaits those who do not overcome (Rev 2:11; 20:6, 14; 21:8). Any who align with the apostasies of idolatry and immorality associated with Balaam or the Nicolaitans or Jezebel or Satan will have Christ war against them with his sword of judgment (Rev 2:6, 14-16, 22-24; 3:9). The church of Sardis is warned about being dead because their deeds do not show signs of life (Rev 3:3). The church at Laodicea is warned that its wealthy lackadaisical attitude is not refreshing[20] to others and thus is provoking Christ to spew them out as rejected (Rev 3:15-17).

This narrow way is not earned, though one can tell by life choices which way one is traveling because there are deeper issues at work here. For example, Christ's kingdom is guaranteed to come in a context that will judge Satan (Rev 12:10; 19-20). In this context, the overcomers are victorious over Satan because of the vicarious atonement that is provided through the blood or death of Christ the Lamb and they remained faithful if necessary unto martyrdom (Rev 12:11; 5:6).

Fitting early Judaism's pattern at the eschatological judgment before the great white throne, all humans will be judged by what is written in the book of life and the books recording their deeds (Rev 20:11-15; 17:8).[21] All humans

---

20. The refreshing import is carried metaphorically by the sources of water in their context: the Travertine hot springs about a mile outside Laodicea toward Hierapolis is refreshing to bathe in (Strabo, *Geogr.* 13.4.14), or a cup of cold spring water at the Laodicean fountain house, which was refreshing to drink (fourth century inscription, Hedychrous, *ILaod.* 13; Corsten, *Inschriften*, 49; *Sib. Or.* 3.471-72), but at that time much of Laodicea piped its water supply from the Travertine spring into town, resulting in non-refreshing lukewarm mineral water prone to make one gag and spit unless one camouflaged its taste (Koester, *Revelation*, 337).

21. In early Judaism, God possesses and refers to a book of deeds (*T. Abr.* 12.12; *Apoc. Zeph.* 7.1-11; *1 En.* 81.1-4; 89.61-64; 90.17, 20; 97.6; 104.5-7; 108.7; *2 En.* 19.3-5 rec. J and A; 52.15; 53.2 rec. J and A; *3 En.* 30.2; 44.8-9; *Jub.* 5.12-13; 23.30-32; 30.20-23; 32.21-22; 36.10; *Apoc. Zeph.* 3.8-9; *Asc. Isa.* 9.21-23; *T. Abr.* 12.7-18; *m. 'Abot* 2.1;

will be judged according to their deeds by God and his co-regent Christ (Rev 20:12-13; Ps 62:12; Matt 16:27; 25:34-46; Rom 2:6; 1 Pet 1:17).[22] Much of the church continues to reflect John's concern that eschatological justification is rendered to every human according to her deeds.[23] Those who were included

---

b. Ta'an. 11a; *b. Ned.* 22a; *Lev. Rab.* 26 on 21:1; *Gen. Rab.* 81 on 35:1) and a book of the righteous as the book of life (Exod 32:32-33; Ps 69:28; Luke 10:20; 1QM 12.1-5; *Jub.* 30.21-23; 36.10; 1 *En.* 43.3; 108.3; *Apoc. Zeph.* 3.6-9; *T. Jac.* 7.27-28; *Jos. Asen.* 15.4; Herm. *Vis.* 1.3.2; *Mand.* 8.6; *Sim.* 2.9; *Odes Sol.* 9.11-12; *Jos. As.* 15.4; *b. Roš Haš* 16b, 32b). The books are opened at eschatological judgment and provide a basis upon which divine judgment is decided (Dan 7:10; *1 En.* 47.3; *4 Ezra* 6.20; *2 Bar.* 24.1).

22. This judgment according to deeds fits the Jewish narrow way pattern: 1 Kgs 8:32; Job 34:11; Pss 28:4; 62:12; Prov 24:12; Jer 16:18; 17:10; 21:14; 32:19; Ezek 7:4; Hos 4:9; Mic 7:13; Dan 7:9-10, 18, 26; Matt 16:27; 25:41-46; Rom 2:6; 14:12; 1 Cor 3:5; 2 Cor 5:10; Eph 6:8; Col 3:25; Rev 2:23; 20:11-15; 22:12; Sir 11:26; 16:12, 14; 32:24; *Jub.* 5.11, 15; 20.2; 23.20-21; *1 En.* 9.4; 47.3 with 46.2; 60.2; 62.2-16; 63:1-12; 82.4; 90:20-36; 95.5; 100.7; *2 En.* 63.1-2; *Pss. Sol.* 2.7, 7, 16, 25, 34-35; 17.8-9; *Jos. Asen.* 28.3; 1QS 2.7-8; 9.18-21; 10.21; 11.13; 1QSa 1.2; 1QHa 12.18-25; 14.10, 23-24; 1QX 10.11, 17-18; 1QH 4.18-19; 5.5-6; 14.24; 1QM 11.3-4; 18.14; CD 1.11, 13, 16; 2.3; 3.4-5; 5.15-16; 7.9; 20.24; 1QpHab 12.2-3; 1Q22 2.8; 4QpPs 37.4-9; 4Q185 1.1-2; 2.1-2, 4; 4Q246 col. 2; 4Q260 5.1; 4Q400 1.1, 14; 4Q405 23.1.11; 4Q429 4.1.10; 4Q473 1; 4Q511 2.1.6; 11Q5 22.10; 11Q Melch. 2.13; 11QT 54.17; *L.A.B.* 3.10; 44.10; 64.7; *2 Bar.* 54.21; 72. 2, 6; 73-74.4; *4 Ezra* 5.1; 7.33, 37, 76-77; *T. Abr.* A 11.11; 12.1-18; 13.12; 14A; *Sib. Or.* 2.183-84, 2.214-20, 230-54, 283-338; *b. Ned.* 39b-40a; *Midr. Ps.* 118.19; *Targ. Eccl.* 9.7-8. Yinger, *Paul, Judaism and Judgement According to Deeds*; Kim, *God Will Judge Each One According to Works*.

23. This judgment according to deeds is continued in the two-ways teaching of the church: *Did.* 1.1.1-4; 4.14b; *1 Clem.* 34-35; *2 Clem.* 6.8; 8.4; Polycarp, *Phil.* 10; Ignatius, *Phil.* 5.1; *Eph.* 3.1; *Barn.* 16.7-8; 18.1-2; 19; Justin Martyr, *Dial.* 3.4; *1 Apol.* 16.8-9; *2 Apol.* 9; Irenaeus, *Haer.* 3.1.10 maintained this as the universal teaching all Christians held at the time; Herm. *Mand.* 2.7; Herm. *Sim.* 3.8.6-11; Clement of Alexandria, *The Strom.* 4.6; *Quis div.*; Commodianus, *Instructions* 28; Origen, *Comm. Matt.* 14.10-13; *Fr. Prin.* 2.9.7-8; 3.1.12; Cyprian, *Fort.* 12-13; Dionysius of Alexandria, *Exegetical Fragments* 7 *Reception of Lapsed*; Methodius of Olympus, *The Banquet of the Ten Virgins* 9.3; *Oration Concerning Simeon and Anna* 8; Lactantius, *Inst.* 3.12; 6.3-7; 7.10; Eusebius, *Hist. eccl.* 3.20.6-7; 5.8.5; *Council of Sardica Lengthy Creed*: Socrates Scholasticus, *Hist. eccl.* 2.19=Athanasius, *Syn.* 26; 351 and A.D. 359 *Sirmium Creed*: Socrates Scholasticus, *Hist. eccl.* 2.30=Athanasius, *Syn.* 27; *Synod at Ariminum Creed*: Socrates Scholasticus, *Hist. eccl.* 2.37; A.D. 359 *Seleucia Creed*: Socrates Scholasticus, *Hist. eccl.* 2.40=Athanasius, *Syn.* 8; A.D. 359 *Confession at Niké* and A.D. 360 *Constantinople Creed*: Athanasius, *Syn.* 30; A.D. 359 *Ariminum Creed* and modified for the A.D. 381 Council at Constantinople: Socrates Scholasticus, *Hist. eccl.* 2.41; Cyril, *Catechetical Lectures* 15.1, 24-25, 33; Gregory Nyssa, *On Pilgrimages*, para. 1; *The Great Catechism* 40; Gregory Nazianzen, *Letter 4 to Basil*; Ambrose, *Duties of the Clergy* 1.16.59; Augustine, *Civ.* 13.8; 14.25; 19.11; 20.1-8, 12, 14, 22; 21.1; *Enchir.* 15; 31-32; 55; 107; 113; *Perf.* 42-44; *Ennarat. Ps.* 31.25; 112.5; *Tract. Ev. Jo.* 124.5; Hilary of Poitiers, *On the Trinity* 12.45; Leo the Great, *Sermons* 46.3; 49.2, 5; 63.2, 7; 67.5-6; 72.1; 95.1-9; Vincent of Lérins, *The Commonitory* 23.57-59 which he claims is the teaching everyone held at that time 23.4-6; John Cassian, *Cassian's Conferences* 1.5; 6.8; 13.13; 14.3; John Climacus, *The Ladder of Divine Ascent*, 9.1; summary on step 30; Thomas a Kempis, *Of the Imitation*

in the book of life were included in the kingdom, whereas those not found in the book of life were thrown into the lake of fire (Rev 20:15).[24]

The gospel in Revelation can be described as: *Jesus Christ is (1) the vicarious Jewish sacrifice (2) who should be worshipped and obeyed to show through one's good deeds that you have followed in his narrow way to overcome, and (3) one's life is assessed eschatologically at Christ's second coming by the Father and the Son through the books of life and deeds.*

---

of Christ, esp. 1.23; 2.7; 3.44, 56; Bunyan, *Pilgrim's Progress*, 18, 187; Willard, *Divine Conspiracy*; Yinger. *Paul, Judaism, and Judgment According to Deeds*, 285 summary but argued through the book; Dunn, *New Perspective on Paul*, 72–73; "If Paul Could Believe both in Justification by Faith and Judgment According to Works, Why Should That be a Problem for us?" and "Response to Thomas Schreiner," in Gundry, ed., *Four Views on the Role of Works at the Final Judgment*, 135, 106–8. However, this view can be granted from outside the two-ways tradition, such as from the Reformed tradition: John Calvin, *Institutes*, 3.15.8; 3.16.1, "we are justified not without works, and not by works, since in the participation in Christ, by which we are justified, is contained not less sanctification than justification," 16.3; 18.1; Schreiner, "Justification Apart from and by Works: At the Final Judgment Works will *Confirm* Justification," in Gundry, ed., *Four Views on the Role of Works at the Final Judgment*, 8–9.

24. Those of second death are placed in the lake of fire (Rev 20:14; 21:8; perhaps Isa 66:24; 1 En. 90:24–27; 4 Ezra 7.36, 38; 2 Bar. 44.15; Tg. Onq. Deut 33:6; Tg. Isa. 65:5–6, 13–15; Tg. Jer. 51:40, 57; Pirque R. El. 34; CD 2.5; 1QS 2.7–8).

28

Putting it all Together

THIS BOOK EXPLORED ANY biblical statement that either (1) identifies itself as gospel, or (2) promises forgiveness, or (3) promises everlasting life, or (4) promises the kingdom, or (5) promises resurrection with Christ. There were several strategies present in the biblical text that have funded historical views of gospel within Christendom including: *a messianic expression of Jewish sacrificial atonement and redemption, believing Jesus' died for our sins and was raised, believing Jesus' teachings and the narrative story of Jesus living those teachings, the affirmation that Jesus is Lord, following Jesus in the narrow way unto the kingdom, allow the Holy Spirit to transform believers into new covenant people expressing the fruit of the Spirit, loving God and others as one loves oneself, forgiving others and showing mercy as Jesus would, and believing Jesus is the object of our faith.* Some of these models also mix into hybrids. Based on this variety one can see how a tradition could latch onto their traditional model in theological hermeneutics and turn a blind eye to the other options or perhaps selectively value a biblical author such as Protestants higher valuing of Paul's epistles and penal atonement, or Orthodoxy's valuing of John's mysticism, or Roman Catholic valuing of synoptics, James and Peter as they develop character change following Jesus in his narrow way. The approach that insists that the only salvation way is the one of "my tradition" often has damned the other approaches and ignores a number of biblical passages. Such an approach may have some biblical grounding but it also neglects much biblical grounding of legitimate gospel statements.

If the reader agrees with the author that these are all legitimate biblical gospel statements then an exclusive salvation in Christ on the basis of this variety of gospel statements ensues that affirms in different ways the salvation message that Jesus Christ provides. That is, every biblical salvation strategy has Jesus Christ within it so that salvation is not provided outside of Christ. However, there are several ways that gospel can be said and still be effective in both promising and delivering Christ's abundant salvation. Hopefully, the reader will choose to express the gospel in one or more of these ways that is sensitive to the context into which they are trying to communicate. Also, hopefully when we listen to other's expression of the gospel statement we listen with tolerance by not requiring every tradition to describe the gospel in our preferred manner.

Several historical ways of communicating the gospel do not have biblical textual support. Those traditions that do not have biblical support for a view should jettison that view as an interesting historical oddity, rather than repeating a view that the biblical text does not warrant. For example, the approaches that develop a ticket Christianity promising a forensic generosity with little or no life change except past faith and an experience prepare a major section of the church for Jesus Christ to say to them, "Depart from Me, I never knew you!" The concept of forensic throne room decision is repeatedly eschatological in the New Testament on the basis of good works showing that one's whole life matters. Furthermore, with vicarious atonement framed within Jewish covenantal sacrifice as the early church developed, there is no clear text that requires a penal element for this past substitutionary atonement. Additionally, the Anselmic Satisfaction view is not warranted mostly for logical reasons (as the appendix develops).

The author's wish and prayer is that all readers might recognize that the gospel is multifaceted with abundant means of conceptualizing salvation, and that the reader would appropriate all the available biblical means for receiving their abundant salvation. So hopefully, this volume will draw the readers to unity around Jesus Christ and God's gracious salvation. Additionally, hopefully this volume will draw the reader to rethink and appropriate biblical gospel patterns as a new reformation for fullness of salvation in Christ and his kingdom on earth.

Appendix

A Critique of Anselm's *Cur Deus Homo* (*Why the God-Man?*)
Argument from Atonement

ANSELM WRITES CUR DEUS Homo (*Why the God Man?*) within a context of late medieval interpretation of the LXX, feudal obligation, and chivalry in order to defend through reason the Chalcedonian formula of Christ's hypostatic union (Jesus Christ is fully God and fully human within a unified person). Within this context, Anselm weaves an argument intended to be logically necessary and inescapable even to Jews and pagans.[1] Part 1 of his book attempts to answer the questions Anselm considers such a mixed audience might have, while part 2 provides a positive argument for his satisfaction model. However, most consider that there are lapses of logic but within Anselm's context the argument might be plausible. A literary

---

1. Anselm, *Cur Deus Homo* 1.1; Leftlow, "Anselm on the Necessity of the Incarnation," *Rel. Stud.* 31 (1995) 167–85; the "must" reflects Anselm's attempt to provide a *logical necessary argument* to describe what is *fitting for God's honor* without binding God to human logical necessity reflecting Athanasius, *De Incarnatione* 6; Root, "Necessity and Unfittingness in Anselm's *Cur Deus Homo*," *SJT* 40 (1987) 213; Noble, "The Necessity of Anselm: The Argument of the *Cur Deus Homo*," *Wesleyan Theological Journal* 50.1 (2015) 57. Asiedu demonstrates that Anselm's claim that the "infidels" (in the "Preface") include Jews and Muslims as a literary construct contemporaneous with the First Crusade and while Jews were massacred nearby at Rouen in the spring of 1096 and while William Rufus compelled Jewish converts to deny Christ to return to Judaism ("Anselm and the Unbeliever: Pagans, Jews, and Christians in the *Cur Deus Homo*," *TS* 62 [2001] 530–48; Guibert of Nogent, *De vita sua* 2.5 translated by Archamlault, *A Monk's Confession*, 111; Crispin, *Disputatio ludei et Christiani*; Southern, "St Anselm and Gilbert Crispin, Abbot of Westminster," *Mediaeval and Renaissance Studies* 3 [1954] 78–115).

opponent, Boso, is constructed to highlight aspects of the argument and to be a yes-man to compel the reader to grant the logic of the argument. Anselm's argument is as follows:

1. God must act for his greatest honor and such immutable honor cannot be diminished (1.14, 15).[2]
2. God made man for happiness and everlasting life (1.10, 21).
3. Such human happiness and everlasting life cannot be obtained without freedom from sin (1.10).
4. All humans and communities of humans sin by not giving God his due honor (1.11).
5. Such sin obligates humans to the devil as their feudal lord (1.7, 22).
6. Therefore, to obtain human happiness, remission of sin is necessary by rehonoring God (1.10, 11, 24).
7. In a chivalry context, rehonoring God requires an infinite amount to be sufficient compensation or punishment (1.12, 13).
8. God's honor will not permit the same treatment being given for individuals who are guilty and forgiven individuals; either debt must be repaid or, in a chivalry context, guilt must be righteously punished to rehonor God (1.14).
9. In chivalry, God can be rehonored with regard to sin by judging the sinner to damnation (that is, a limited being dishonoring an infinite Being requires an infinite payment of everlasting damnation to rehonor God (1.15).
10. Repayment can't come from a human for his own dishonoring of God because he already owes everything to God (1.15).
11. Therefore, repayment must come from another with appropriate resources of at least equal value (1.14, 20).
12. To maintain God's honor for his creation design, the number and level of angels that fell must be made up by an equal number and level of procreated beings associated with rehonoring God (1.16, 18; 2.22; LXX Deut 32:8).
13. Angel numbers cannot be made up by God creating more of that kind of angel because any increase of angelic creation would entail God's design had been flawed (1.17).

---

2. References in parentheses are from sections of Anselm's *Cur Deus Homo*.

14. Therefore, the replacement beings for the angels that fell must be redeemed humans since they are the only procreated beings (thus able to expand beyond the original two, Adam and Eve) that can be elevated to sufficient angelic levels (1.17).

15. Therefore, divine atonement enables humans to replace fallen angels to complete kingdom happiness and despoil the devil (1.22, 23).

16. For redeemed humans to obtain happiness, they must be transformed to choose good in a restored condition as if they had never sinned (2.1, 3).

17. Therefore, in redemption sin must be removed from these human lives by God (2.4).

18. Atonement must be done by a human, so rehonoring God is from humanity (2.6).

19. Atonement must be accomplished by someone of sufficient value for all the creation, therefore a divine one other than God the Father must rehonor God (2.6).

20. For 18 and 19 to be accomplished, Divine and human natures must be fully instantiated in a hypostatic union with no alteration, comingling, or changing of these natures (2.7).

21. Christ's humanity can't be directly created by God or he would not be of the human family as needed to satisfy rehonoring God from them (2.8).

22. A virgin is purer (2.8).[3]

23. Christ's humanity is from a virgin woman (2.8).

24. Christ should come from woman alone as women originally came from man alone (2.8).

25. Only one of the Trinity should be incarnated, so there is only one Son (2.9).

26. Christ's humanity must have the ability to sin so that Christ's impeccability and the devil's defeat is by a choice that rehonors God (2.10).

3. An undeveloped element in *Cur Deus Homo* is a likely Augustinian inclination for traducianism of the soul and seminalism in which each human participated in the sin of Adam and has that transferred to them through the sensual sex act. So to be free of the Adamic effect of sin is to be without a human father and the concupiscence of the sex act. So in this line of reasoning conception by a virgin is purer. In *Cur Deus Homo* the argument is that it is fitting that Jesus be born of a virgin, whereas in *De Conceptu* 13, 23, and 26 Anselm argues that Jesus must have been born of a virgin. Hopkins, *Companion to the Study of St. Anselm*, 202–12.

27. Humans are not essentially sinners, nor mortal, so that Christ willingly dies, and thereby he can resurrect as immortal (2.11, 17).

28. The Son set a pattern of generously giving to God beyond God's demand (2.18).[4]

29. Christ lived the designed human life, preserving God's original honor (2.19).

30. Therefore, in all respects God's honor is preserved and restored.

Within the original context of medieval interpretation, feudal obligation, and chivalry, the argument could compel a generous reader to the conclusions. Boso images such a generous reader and is compelled by Anselm's argument. However, several of the premises are framed more from worldview assumptions than from logical necessity. For example, Aquinas raises several questions from a similar context to Anselm's, showing that the argument had vulnerabilities in its own day even for those who worked within a two-ways soteriology and embraced a Chalcedonian Christology. These contemporary critiques will be included in the subsequent discussion.

There are really three arguments in Anselm's: (1) God's original design must be maintained in the resolution to preserve God's honor; (2) within a narrow-way eschatological judgment model, God's original design wisdom must show the narrow way is possible to be lived by Jesus living it, and redeeming humans so they can live the narrow way unto kingdom;[5] and (3) to redeem the elect of humanity there must be an appropriate sacrifice (thus human) and an infinite sacrifice (thus divine) to rehonor God from human dishonoring rebellion.

The eschatological kingdom returning to the original Eden design is a prominent patristic tradition. For example, Origen advocated that, "The goodness of God through Christ will restore his entire creation to one end."[6] This view continue with an elaborate identification of levels of salvation to replace the ranks of fallen angels from their stars or planets by redeemed humans. The view continued to be advocated by Augustine, Thomas Aquinas,

---

4. Christ's voluntary death satisfies our debt (following Athanasius, *De Incarnatione* 9.1–2) and worthy God utilizes such offering (following ibid., 6.4–10).

5. Often the living quality is ignored by evangelicals but John Wesley retains this factor as Christians are to fulfill the Law of God (*Principles of a Methodist*, 3; *Works*, 9:51; Noble, "The Necessity of Anselm: The Argument of the *Cur Deus Homo*," *Wesleyan Theological Journal* 50.1 [2015] 53).

6. Origen, *On First Principles* 1.6.1.

Dante Alighiriei, and John Milton.⁷ Aquinas concluded with Anselm that for restoration of humanity to happen divine incarnation must occur.⁸

The move to return to the original design number was driven by the LXX reading of Deuteronomy 32:8, "according to the number of the angels" (κατὰ ἀριθμὸν ἀγγέλων θεοῦ).⁹ Such was the authoritative biblical text among early Judaism dispersion and Eastern fathers of the church. However, Protestants tend to see the Hebrew as more authoritative, and Catholics especially during the medieval era would see the Latin Vulgate as more authoritative. These texts read, "according to the number of Israel," which makes better sense in the context of exodus to promised land (מִסְפַּר בְּנֵי יִשְׂרָאֵל; *juxta numerum filiorum Israël*). Such a reading would cut the center out of Anselm's argument for returning to the original design parameters and it was the more authoritative reading in his context. This likely shows that Anselm is proof-texting from a less authoritative reading to support a dominant traditional understanding of eschatology. Such a conclusion is evident, since Anselm discusses both readings and concludes for a fusion in the text, showing human and angel could function on the level of "angel," but by the end of the section he concludes that it is fallen angels that then must be replaced by redeemed humans.¹⁰

Contemporary American evangelicals tend not to read Anselm's argument through this lens. Unless an evangelical maintains a literary salvation history approach to the Bible, one is likely to consider the eschatological kingdom to be an improvement over the original garden condition, thus replacing the first argument. In this new framework the original design requirement is superseded by however one's tradition conceives of the eschatological kingdom. Such an evangelical move shifts the framework out of preserving God's honor because a better re-creation into kingdom will certainly bring more glory to God. This is an efficient move because few contemporary evangelicals see the need to preserve each rank of angel on a planet or star with the design number. As such, a contemporary evangelical perspective cuts the middle out of Anselm's argument.

Premise 16 transforms a human into a glorified condition such that the "old man" is made into a "glorified new man." An Orthodox tradition could view this move as deification toward resurrection transformation and

---

7. Augustine, *Trin.* 3.4; Aquinas, *Summa Theologica* 1.102.2 claim, "I answer that," and "reply to obj. 1;" Dante Alighieri, *Divine Comedy: Paradise*, canto 2–22, 30–31; Milton, *Paradise Lost*, 3.679–91.

8. Aquinas, *Summa Theologica* 3.1.1.

9. Anselm, *Cur Deus Homo* 1.18.

10. Ibid.

thereby find in Anselm traction for their soteriological models.[11] However, Anselm does not use this terminology.

Immanuel Kant had problems viewing Anselm's, the Orthodox, and Pauline terminology retaining a continuity of person, since the natures are so different.[12] However, I think Kant had arbitrarily severed these natures within humanity instead of viewing human nature through the Pauline lens of realms of sin and Christ, or the feudal realms of Satan and Christ.

Albert Schweitzer developed that being in these realms transforms the nature through a distinctive mystical relation that each realm brings. From this perspective, Romans 6:4-14 is a prolonged discussion of mystically dying and rising with Christ. The believer now lives mystically in a post-resurrection manner already in kingdom but also continues to live in the soulish body as well. However, Christians have begun toward kingdom in the second Adam, Christ. Schweitzer developed Christ funding this mysticism:

> But it is by His coming in the flesh and His dying and rising again that He first becomes man, from whom a new humanity can go forth. Since the humanity destined to Messianic glory, which takes its rise from Him, follows as the second humanity after the humanity which proceeds from Adam, Paul speaks of Him as the second Adam.[13]

This mystical participation (through Christian baptism in Christ's dying and rising) grafts the believer into the corporeity of Christ such that "he loses his creatively individual existence and his natural personality. Henceforth, the Christian is only a form of manifestation of the personality of Jesus Christ, which dominates that corporeity."[14] Schweitzer envisioned that this Pauline mysticism is a real and physical union.

> What is in view in the Pauline mysticism is an actual physical union between Christ and the Elect is proved by the fact that "being in Christ" corresponds to and, as a state of existence, takes the place of the physical "being in the flesh."[15]

---

11. Hart, "A Gift Exceeding Every Debt: An Eastern Orthodox Appreciation of Anselm's *Cur Deus Homo*," *ProEccl* 7.3 (1998) 334-36.

12. Kant, *Religion within the Limits of Reason Alone*, 54, 67, 73, 97; also discussed by Hare, "Atonement, Justification, and Sanctification," in Quinn and Taliaferro, eds., *Companion to Philosophy of Religion*, 550-51.

13. Schweitzer, *Mysticism of Paul*, 167, see also 166, 219.

14. Ibid., 115-16.

15. Ibid., 127.

Most of NT scholarship expresses that the physicality of Schweitzer's mysticism is overplayed and probably replaces it with the ministry of the Holy Spirit.[16] Such an approach might resolve the bitheistic option of Father and Son into a more wholesome Trinitarian one with the role of the Spirit, however, Anselm does not go that way. Furthermore, if we recognize that the term "body" (σῶμα) also greatly emphasizes relationship and not merely physicality, I think we would be closer to the emphasis of Paul's concept of "the body of Christ." Perhaps also Schweitzer was a bit extreme on the loss of personality within the believer's union with Christ (a weaker sense of Kant's concern), but there is some sort of fusion going on to describe the believer as a *new human*.

Wilhelm Bousset proposed a communal model of mysticism that facilitates believers gathered in worship to be mystically absorbed into Christ and thereby become partakers of his death and resurrection.[17] Bousset saw that the death and resurrection that are attributed to Christ represent the historicism and fusion of two Hellenistic myths, the dying and rising of the god and the descent and ascent of the Primal Human. Applying these traditions, Bousset writes:

> One will not be able to avoid the impression that here is given the spiritual atmosphere within which the Pauline dying-with Christ and rising-with-Christ is located . . . The parallel again becomes quite close when we set the Pauline "in Adam die, in Christ be made alive" over against the falling and rising with the divine hero in Hellenistic piety . . . The pious person experiences in mystical fellowship the same thing which the divine hero previously and fundamentally has experienced in exemplary power. The experience of the believers is only the consequence, victoriously being worked out, of the one given beginning.[18]

Elsewhere, Marv Pate and I have critiqued Bousset's view as: (1) recovering a helpful communal focus, (2) not appreciating the depth of Christian suffering, (3) too dependent upon a late somewhat dissimilar Hellenistic model, and (4) not appreciating the possible earlier Jewish apocalyptic contribution to these issues.[19]

---

16. Dunn, *Theology of Paul*, 393.

17. Bousset, *Kyrios Christos*.

18. Ibid., 193–94.

19. Pate and Kennard, *Deliverance Now and Not Yet*, 132–33, 157–62; in this context we also discuss Deissmann's mystical model of suffering because of its applicability for mystical participation in the messianic woes.

The current trend among scholarly exegesis identifies this Pauline mysticism with Jewish *merkabah* (divine throne/chariot) mysticism,[20] the ecstatic ascent to heaven by the righteous as participating in the age to come, which has already dawned in heaven but not yet descended to earth (Ezek 1:15–26; Rom 6:3–14; Eph 1:1—2:7).[21] The worshipper encounters the glory of God by being raised into his presence (Ezek 1:15–26; Eph 1:3, 6, 12, 14, 18, 20–22).[22] Both the Pauline and Second Temple sources appreciate that this form of mysticism occurs within the community of believers rather than for an individual mystic. Such a view employs the notion of corporate personality, where a representative figure does a deed and others align themselves in the benefits made available by mystically being identified within the representative, especially in Adam, Abraham, Moses, or Christ (Matt 3:9; Luke 3:8; John 9:28; Rom 4:1–16; 5:14–21; Gal 3:6–18).[23] The very same community of believers lives on in bodily form within the world. In this way, the community of believers and the individuals within it are both in the present age and the age to come simultaneously in different ways. In community identification, position, obligation, and blessing we are already in the age to come, whereas in our soulish bodies and the choices we sometimes make, it is apparent that we are not yet glorified as fully righteous but retain a lingering effect of Adam.

This is the analog in Paul for what John and Peter refer to as "born again." However, it has been argued convincingly by S. Kim that this old human/new human transformation reflects the radical break in allegiance (from Paul's Jewish hatred for Christians to loyalty to Christ) that Saul experienced on his Damascus road encounter with the risen Christ.[24] That is, the non-Christian old human with all his relationships bathed in sin is no more, for it has been crucified with Christ as pictured in the burial in baptism. Now the rising from the baptismal water pictures a real mystical change of life with Christ. That is, the new life of the new human with all his relationships (which now also involve Christ) has changed the new Christian

---

20. Pioneering studies in this area include: Davies, *Paul and Rabbinic Judaism*, 198, 210ff.; Lincoln's whole work addressed this topic, *Paradise Now and Not Yet*; as did James Tabor's study on 2 Cor 12:1–10, *Things Unutterable*; Segal, "Paul and Ecstasy," in Richards, ed., *Society of Biblical Literature 1986 Seminar Papers*, 550–80; *Paul the Convert*; Pate and Kennard, *Deliverance Now and Not Yet*, 78–92, 130–36, 211, 215, 225, 229–32, 240–41; Dean-Otting, *Heavenly Journeys*; Scholem, *Jewish Gnosticism, Merkabah Mysticism, and Talmudic Tradition*.

21. 1 *En.* 14; 37–71; 4Q 400–405; 11Q 17; 2 *En.* 15–16; 3 *En.*; *Ascent of Isaiah* 9; *The Books of Adam and Eve* 37; *Apoc. Ab.* 29; Hekalot [places] Rabbati.

22. This is particularly apparent in *1 En.* 9.4; 25.3; 60.2; 71.7.

23. Wedderburn, *Baptism and Resurrection*, 186.

24. Kim, *Origin of Paul's Gospel*.

sufficiently so that he might walk in newness of life (Rom 6:4–8; 2 Cor 5:17). In fact, Paul describes this new life as "Christ lives in me" (Gal 2:20). It is a life still lived in the flesh but it is lived by faith in the Son of God, whose motives of love for me now are to motivate me from within for love for others as well. Christ mystically infuses such an abundant gift of righteousness so that it reigns in the life of the one in Christ (Rom 5:17). Righteousness is then to reign in the new human. So Christ's resurrection (as in the enlivening of Abraham's deadened body in Rom 4:17) charts a course through[25] our righteousness by faith (Rom 4:25). Because becoming a Christian is such a radical metaphysical and relational change, we should be aware of this and choose to present the members of our soulish body to righteous service loyal to God (Rom 6:12–13; Eph 4:21–24; Col 3:1–4, 9–10). Our present mystical resurrected life now in the soulish body is a mystical uniting with the resurrected Lord through newness of the Holy Spirit (Rom 7:4–6). This change is at least a metaphysical change in a person's spirit dimension. Where one's spirit had been dead, it becomes enlivened within him, fostered by the Holy Spirit (Rom 8:6, 10). This aliveness of spirit is accomplished because of[26] the vitality of righteousness that the Holy Spirit fosters in the Christian's life (Rom 8:4–6, 10). This aliveness of one's spirit is an expression of the new covenant work of the Holy Spirit bringing the age to come into our lives as the promise of resurrection of our bodies (Rom 8:11; Eph. 1:13–14). In this, the Spirit is the guarantor of growth. Such growth is apparent when the Christian has his mind set upon the things of the Spirit such that his visible life shows that it is lived according to the Spirit (Rom 8:4–5). In this, our choice to side with the Spirit for righteousness identifies us for resurrection, sonship and coinheritance with Christ (Rom 8:12–17). N. T. Wright frames this resurrection imagery as the inbreaking of the age to come into a person who still lives in the present age.

> The context for the discussion has already been established: the overlap of the 'two ages' (1 Cor 2:6–8). The 'soulish' person, it seems, is one whose life is determined by the 'present age', animated merely by the ordinary 'soul' (*psyche*) that everyone has. The Spirit is the gift of the creator god, coming from the future where the divine plan for the complete new age is already secure (having been made secure, as we shall learn, through

---

25. This phrase reflects ἠγέρθη διὰ τὴν δικαίωσιν ἡμῶν with the parallel that Christ was delivered up through (διὰ) the context of our transgressions. Both transgressions and righteousness in this verse are identified as "our" human sin and righteousness.

26. This phrase reflects πνεῦμα ζωὴ διὰ δικαιοσύνην with the parallel that the body is dead because of (διὰ) sin. Both the sin and righteousness are descriptions of the person, bringing about the consequent condition, whether death or one's spirit life.

the resurrection of Jesus the Messiah); and the Spirit is breaking into 'the present age' which still rumbles on, unaware that the future has decisively invaded it. The 'spiritual' person is the one in whose heart and mind the living god has worked by the Spirit so that he or she understands the strange new truths of the strange new age, and can see into the mystery, the wisdom, which Paul longs to impart. The contrast is sharpened in verse 16: Isaiah 40:13 declares that nobody in the present age could guess what YHWH had in mind, but Paul responds that those whose minds are illuminated by the gospel know 'the mind of the Messiah'. This, by implication, refers to the divine plans, laid up in the Messiah, already unveiled in the gospel but still to be implemented.[27]

The beginning of this mystical regeneration is approximated in philosophical discussion by Sören Kierkegaard's Lutheran mystical repentance as droned by Judge William in *Either/Or*: "What is required is the suffering of the 'new human' on behalf of the 'old human' in what the judge calls 'repentance.' I repent myself out of the whole of existence . . . Repentance specifically expresses that evil essentially belongs to me and at the same time expresses that it does not essentially belong to me."[28]

Returning to Anselm, Boso asks, "Why couldn't God save man in some other way?" (1.10).[29] For example, Boso asks, "Why can't God simply forgive humans?" (1.6). Jesus forgave the paralytic, without an exchange, based on the faith of his friends (Matt 9:2). Contemporary Peter Abelard also considered that God retains his honor in simply forgiving sinners motivated by his essential intrinsic love rather than by any extrinsic necessary argument, and that Jesus demonstrated this generous forgiveness to believers even without atonement (Matt 9:2; Luke 8:2).[30] Additionally, in an Arabic honor context, a lord could be appealed to for mercy of forgiveness and it would be an increase of high honor to be praised for one to forgive beyond what is done by others.[31] This is evidenced by multiple instances of caliphs

---

27. Wright, *Resurrection of the Son of God*, 282.

28. Kierkegaard, *Either/Or*, 2:224 also summarized by Hare in "Atonement, Justification, and Sanctification," in Quinn and Taliaferro, eds., *A Companion to Philosophy of Religion*, 552–23 and further recapitulated by Heidegger, *Being and Time*, 325–48.

29. Aquinas, *Summa Theologica* 3.1.2 agrees with Boso against Anselm here. At this point, Judaism (Sir 28.2–5; b. Šabb. 151b; T. Zeb. 5.3; 8.1–2; T. Jos. 18.2; m. Yoma 8.9; t. B. Qam. 9.29; b. Meg. 28a; Polyc. 6.2) and Islam (*Quran* especially Surah az-Zumar 53 but also present in *Quran* 12.92; 24.22; 7.199; 42.43) advocated generous forgiveness so that God would generously forgive those who forgive.

30. Abelard, *Romans*, 3:26, p. 163 and "Question," 115, pp. 165–66.

31. Leaman, *The Qur'an: An Encyclopedia*, 213–16; Amanullah, "Just Retribution

forgiving either a repentant military enemy or a traitor as a response to the sinners prostrating themselves before the caliph. Boso asks essentially, "Why couldn't God do the same" and be praised for his generosity? Furthermore, in Anselm's own tradition Athanasius argued that if God could not save by his fiat then he is not the omnipotent deity.[32] However, Anselm engaged neither Athanasius' implication of omnipotence nor an oriental context of honor. Anselm approached the question simply with regard to the Western chivalry forgiveness of a heinous sin. Anselm's focus was to rehabilitate all of humanity so that we would be transformed and prepared for judgment and kingdom. So, Anselm's argument approaches the concept of forgiveness from the eschatological orientation, rather than the praise of God's generous character. Aquinas joined Anselm in considering that sin stains the soul and brings feudal bondage to the devil.[33] Such an effect of sin makes humans deserving of punishment.[34] However, Aquinas considered that a mere human could satisfy God for the whole human race if God permitted, and recounts a story in the fathers in which saints satisfy some of the dishonor of God for fellow humans.[35] Countering Anselm's inference, Aquinas joined Boso and an oriental perspective, concluding that it would not be unjust for God to free humans from sin without any satisfaction being made.[36] Boso's questions are good ones to consider since much of evangelicalism and much of a biblical approach follow a different trajectory.

Anselm recognized that in a chivalry context the level of the dishonored required a similar level of honor to rehonor God (1.14, 15, 20). Because God is an infinite being, human sin dishonors God infinitely requiring an infinite rehonoring, and thus the divinity of the Son is required in having a role in rehonoring Father God. This serves as the rationale for why the atonement must include divinity within the incarnation. Aquinas had a similar sentiment for the infinity of rehonoring,[37] so the corroboration of these two satisfaction theologians is reassuring that in their chivalry context the inference of human dishonoring of God requires an incarnated divine one to rehonor God.

(Qisas) Versus Forgiveness ('Afw')," in *Islam*, 871–83.

32. Athanasius, *De Incarnatione* 6.

33. Aquinas, *Summa Theologica* 1–2.86.1 and 3.48.4.

34. Ibid., 1–2.87.1.2.

35. Ibid., 3.1.2; suppl.13.2

36. Ibid., 3.46.2.3; 3.47.3.1; Quinn, "Aquinas on Atonement," in Feenstra and Plantinga, eds., *Trinity, Incarnation, and Atonement*, 158.

37. Aquinas, *Summa Theologica* 3.1.2.2.

Much of evangelicalism does not approach salvation through an eschatological lens with a narrow way to ensure entry through the divine judgment. Many traditions (such as Lutheran, Keswick, Augustinian-Dispensational, Holiness, Pentecostal and others) focus on the initial salvation being able to be obtained as a ticket on the basis of Jesus Christ's atonement for our sins. This "ticket Christianity" removes the felt need to have Jesus demonstrate that the narrow way can be lived and the need for God to transform living humans so that we too might follow Christ through eschatological judgment. "Ticket Christianity" removes the second trajectory through Anselm's argument. What is left in salvation is an external forensic legal penal substitute justification by Christ that saves believers unto kingdom.

For Anselm's argument to be resurrected for this form of "ticket Christianity," it would work out as follows:

31. To justify humans, God requires a just payment.

32. Jesus Christ as human provides an appropriate kind of payment for human atonement and Jesus Christ as God provides the unlimited righteousness of the payment to overwhelm human sin.

33. Therefore, Christian salvation is obtained by the God-man Jesus Christ.

This is a significantly simpler argument than Anselm's, yet an argument that evangelicalism tends to find more compelling than Anselm's. Usually the argument is funded by a court scene where a fine is to be paid. The judge pronounces the criminal guilty, requiring the payment of the appropriate fine. However, since the judge is also the criminal's father, the judge steps down from the bench and pays the criminal's fine. Perhaps this is reminiscent of the ubiquitous parental aid in moving a minor beyond a traffic ticket.

However, this argument needs to deepen with the recognition that the wages of such a sinning condition is death of the sinner (Rom 5:12; 6:23; 7:6, 9–11; 1 Cor 15:22). At the center of this argument is a view of an exact precise scale of justice keeping track of every sin and an exchange theory that provides for another who can pay for that death penalty. No law court should change the status of a sinner to that of declared righteous, producing a "legal fiction," for only an unrighteous judge violating the Law of God would pervert justice in that manner (Deut 25:1–2). No judge would have the right to legally substitute another forensic representative to take the sinner's place, for even if others died in such a capital punishment within a forensic model, the guilty sinner would still be under a death sentence

(Deut 25:2; 27:19).³⁸ Furthermore, Yahweh brought a covenant lawsuit upon Israel casting them out of the land unto Babylonian captivity partially for those who deserved capital punishment not being brought to justice (Isa 1:15; Jer 7:8–9). Only if the guilty could not be found could the nearest community to a murder offer a young heifer sacrifice to remove themselves beyond blood guiltiness and obtain covenantal communal forgiveness in their innocence (Deut 21:1–9). However, in Paul's framework the criminals are every human (Rom 3:23) and we are all culpable to capital punishment (Rom 5:12; 6:23; 7:6, 9–11; 1 Cor 15:22). Unlike a payment of a fine assessed in a forensic context, a death sentence is not a legal sentence another can pay to release the culpable sinner from the demands of the Law regarding his active deeds of sin.

Perhaps divine penal justification is like a literary motif, such as when Sydney Carton dies as a replacement to free the good Doctor Manette at the end of *A Tale of Two Cities*.³⁹ However, God does not permit executing an innocent human through human law courts to redeem the guilty (Deut 25:1), nor do the Hebrew, Greek, Roman, or American legal systems. If an innocent human is executed (as occurred in *A Tale of Two Cities*), such an act does not remove the guilt or the penal obligation of capital punishment for the guilty. If the criminal can be found out and brought to justice through our contemporary penal system, it should be accomplished even if an innocent human has already suffered capital punishment as judgment for the crime. This rehabilitated argument only inclines intuitions as a broad literary metaphor might. However, if the legal precision does not work out, shouldn't we resist such a metaphorical appeal that entices us to violate such a legal standard of righteousness?

Another substitute model is sometimes built off the Union Enrollment Act of 1863, which identifies a drafted person, "or he may pay ... three

---

38. Sometimes a significant fine could be paid by the guilty person to replace capital punishment if the victim's family requested it but such fine would still be paid by the criminal (Exod 21:29–30; 4Q251 frag. 8 5; Beckman, *Hittite Diplomatic Texts*, p. 109 #18 B "Treaty Between Hattusili 3 of Hatti and Ulmi-Teshhup of Tarhuntassa" 1 obv. 7'–14'; p. 119 #18 C "Treaty Between Tudhaliya 4 of Hatti and Kurunta of Tarhuntassa" 20 ii 95–iii 20; p. 145 #23A "Letter from a King of Hatti to an Anatolian Ruler" 4 obv. 31–35; Roth, *Law Collections from Mesopotamia and Asia Minor*, 82; *Laws of Hammurabi* 5). Under Roman law a criminal under death sentence might make an appeal to the whole populous to have banishment substituted for capital punishment in *provocation ad populum*, but if granted the criminal would suffer banishment from the community. No evidence of any ancient Near Eastern law provides for an innocent person dying in place of a criminal of a capital crime to legally expunge the criminal's guilt. Furthermore, no person could stand in the place for another person (Kant, *Religion within the Limits of Reason Alone*, 66).

39. Dickens, *Tale of Two Cities*, 324, 328, 333.

hundred dollars . . . for the procuration of such substitute . . . and thereupon such person so furnishing the substitute, or paying the money, shall be discharged from further liability under the draft."[40] Anselm does not consider a substitute living in the narrow way (like Christ, 2.19) to be an adequate replacement, for the Christian must also live the narrow way unto kingdom (1.17, 22–2.4). If the substitute Union soldier got killed in the war, the person paying the money would still have discharged his draft duty. This, however, is not a legal replacement for a capital sentence; it is merely a legal replacement that happens to die. This model does not sufficiently fund a penal substitution model.

Furthermore, in stepping from the chivalry context to that of the penal law court there no longer remains an infinite amount of rehonoring to be accomplished, so one would not need an infinite payment (of divine incarnation) to be made for the sin of the world; merely an enormously huge payment for sin could accomplish the judicial judgment. In such a setting as this, perhaps an enormously valuable elect angel, say Michael or Gabriel, or a group of elect angels equal to the task of tipping the penal scales, could suffice to be sacrificed so as to redeem the elect humans. However, in this case the argument would not work at all, since a God-man would not be required for such a finite (though huge) payment, and if a God-man was sacrificed then overpayment would occur. Would not there be some injustice in overpayment?

At the core of this evangelical argument is a central premise of Anselm's argument for substitution: Only man *ought* to and only God can, therefore, the God-man *ought* to come (2.18). However, Anselm uses the same Latin verb, *debere* ("ought"), for both premises but with different meaning.[41] That is, the first instance has the meaning that humans must redress God's honor or be damned. The second instance is only that an omnipotent God who pays willingly has sufficient resources to affect the situation meaningfully. Jasper Hopkins calls this argument equivocal at this point. The same flaw stands against the evangelical rehabilitation as well. Humans must pay for the penal consequences of their sins but there is no logical necessity for either an innocent human or for divinity to do such measures. In the evangelical argument God is not in a logically necessary bind of providing atonement to retain his honor, for God could simply damn all sinners and be righteous through forensic penal judgment. So, in a legal framework, God's atonement is volitional and shows his generosity. If generosity is the motive,

---

40. *A Century of Lawmaking for a New Nation: US Congressional Documents and Debates, 1774–1875*, 733, statute 731, 37th Congress, 3rd session, ch. 75, sec. 13.

41. Hopkins, *Companion to the Study of St. Anselm*, 195–97.

we return to Boso's previous argument and muse, "Why could God not just forgive without a substitutionary atonement?" If a substitutionary atonement was chosen by God, why did he utilize a God-man's human death when biblical atonement has been accomplished for God by Israel: (1) paying gold to the tabernacle (Num 31:50), (2) the poor giving grain offerings (Lev 5:11), and (3) the usual pattern of animal sacrifice (Lev 1–7, 16)? The first two atonement options satisfied God without blood or a death occurring. The third option has the standard pattern of animal sacrifice. This is why it is important to remember the emphasized word "almost" (σχεδὸν) at the beginning of Hebrew 9:22, "Almost all things are cleansed with blood." Obviously, in a few instances something other than sacrificial death is used for atonement. Why can't God opt for a non-blood atonement for human sin, since he has done it before on multiple occasions (Lev 5:11 repeated grain offerings by the poor; Num 31:50 coin payment)?

Neither of these Anselmic arguments enters into the biblical framework and worldview. Could an Anselmic argument be cogent and compelling if we enter such a biblical worldview? It is my contention that the closest argument within the biblical worldview is the prophetic expectation being fulfilled by Christ. However, this biblical framework is far less than an argument from necessity, and with regard to atonement probably does not require Christ's divinity to fulfill Isaiah 53.

Select Bibliography

Abelard, Peter. *Commentary on the Epistle to the Romans*. Translated by Steven Cartwright. Washington, DC: Catholic University of America, 2011.
———. *A Dialogue of a Philosopher with a Jew and a Christian*. Translated by Pierre Payer. Toronto: Pontifical Institute of Mediaeval Studies, 1979.
Abrahams, Israel. *Studies in Pharisaism and the Gospels*. Cambridge: Cambridge University Press, 1924.
Anderson, A. A. *The Book of Psalms*. 2 vols. Grand Rapids: Eerdmans, 1972.
Anderson, Bernard. *Out of the Depths: The Psalms Speak for Us Today*. Philadelphia: Westminster, 1983.
Anderson, Gary. *Charity: The Place of the Poor in the Biblical Tradition*. New Haven, CT: Yale University, 2013.
Anselm. *Cur Deus Homo*. In *Basic Writings*, translated by S. N. Deane. La Salle, IL: Open Court, 1962.
Aquinas, Thomas. *Summa Theologica*. Great Books of the Western World 19, 20. Chicago: Encyclopedia Britannica, 1952.
Aulén, Gustav. *Christus Victor: An Historical Study of the Three Main Types of the Idea of Atonement*. Translated by A. G. Herbert. New York: Macmillan, 1969.
Aune, David. *Jesus, Gospel Tradition and Paul in the Context of Jewish and Greco-Roman Antiquity: Collected Essays II*. WUNT 303. Tübingen: Mohr, 2013.
Balch, D. L. "The Areoagus Speech: An Appeal to the Stoic Historian Posidonus against Later Stoics and the Epicureans." In *Greeks, Romans, and Christians*, edited by D. L. Balch, Everett Ferguson, and Wayne Meeks, 52–79. Minneapolis: Fortress, 1990.
Baldwin, Joyce. *Daniel: An Introduction and Commentary*. Tyndale Old Testament Commentary Series. Downers Grove, IL: InterVarsity, 1978.
Balz, H., and G. Schneider, eds. *Exegetical Dictionary of the New Testament*. Grand Rapids: Eerdmans,1990.
Barclay, William. *The Gospel of Matthew*. Philadelphia: Westminster, 1975.
———. *The Letters of John and Jude*. Philadelphia: The Westminster, 1976.
Barr, James. *The Semantics of Biblical Language*. London: Oxford University, 1961.

Barrett, Charles Kingsley. *A Commentary on the Epistle to the Romans*. London: Black, 1957.

———. "Paul's Speech on the Areopagus." In *New Testament Christianity for Africa and the World: Essays in Honor of Harry Sawyer*, edited by M. E. Glasswell and E. W. Fashole-Luke, 69–77. London: SPCK, 1974.

Barth, E. M., and R. E. Concroft, eds. *Festchrift to Honor F. Wilbur Gingrich: Lexicographer, Scholar, Teacher, and Committed Christian Layman*. Leiden: Brill, 1972.

Barth, Karl. *A Shorter Commentary on Romans*. Richmond: John Knox, 1959.

Bates, Matthew. *Salvation by Allegiance Alone: Rethinking Faith, Works, and the Gospel of Jesus the King*. Grand Rapids: Baker, 2017.

Bauckham, Richard. *Jesus and the Eyewitnesses: The Gospels as Eyewitness Testimony*. Grand Rapids: Eerdmans, 2006.

———. *Jude–2 Peter*. WBC 50. Waco: Word, 1983.

———. "The Rich Man and Lazarus: The Parable and Parallels." In *The Fate of the Dead: Studies on the Jewish and Christian Apocalypses*, 97–118. Novum Testamentum Supplement 93. Leiden: Brill, 1998.

———. "The Scrupulous Priest and the Good Samaritan: A Communal Exegesis Approach." *NTS* 44(1998) 475–89.

Bauer, Walter, ed. *Orthodoxy and Heresy in Earliest Christianity*. Minneapolis: Fortress, 1971.

Bautch, Richard. *Developments in Genre between Post-Exilic Penitential Prayers and the Psalms of Communal Lament*. Atlanta: Society of Biblical Literature, 2003.

Beale, G. K. *The Book of Revelation*. New International Greek Testament Commentary. Grand Rapids: Eerdmans, 1999.

Beckman, Gary. *Hittite Diplomatic Texts*. Atlanta: Society of Biblical Literature, 1999.

Behrens, Achin. "Gen. 15.6 und das Vorverständnis des Paulus." *ZAW* 109 (1997) 327–41.

Beiringer, Reimund, and Didier Pollefeyt, eds. *Paul and Judaism: Crosscurrents in Pauline Exegesis and the Study of Jewish-Christian Relations*. London: T. & T. Clark, 2012.

Bellinger, William, ed. *Jesus and the Suffering Servant: Isaiah 53 and Christian Origins*. London: SPCK, 1959.

Bettenson, Henry, and Chris Maunder., eds. *Documents of the Christian Church*. 3rd ed. Oxford: Oxford University Press, 1999.

Betz, Otto. "Jesus' Gospel of the Kingdom." In *The Gospel and the Gospels*, edited by Peter Stuhnmacher, 53–74. Grand Rapids: Eerdmans, 1991.

Bietenhard, Hans. "Natürliche Goetteserkenntnis der Heiden?: Eine Erwägung zu Röm 1." *ThZ* 12(1956) 275–88.

Bigg, Charles. *A Critical and Exegetical Commentary on the Epistles of St. Peter and St. Jude*. Edinburgh: T. & T. Clark, 1978.

Bird, Michael. *The Gospel of the Lord: How the Early Church Wrote the Story of Jesus*. Grand Rapids: Eerdmans, 2014.

Bird, Michael, and Preston Sprinkle. *The Faith of Jesus Christ: Exegetical, Biblical, and Theological Studies*. Milton Keyes: Paternoster, 2009.

Black, C. Clifton. "The First, Second, and Third Letters of John." In *The New Interpreter's Bible*, vol. 12. Nashville: Abingdon, 1998.

Black, David Alan. *New Testament Textual Criticism: A Concise Guide.* Grand Rapids: Baker, 1994.

Blanton, Thomas. "Spirit and Covenant Renewal: A Theologoumenon of Paul's Opponents in 2 Corinthians." *JBL* 129 (2010) 129–51.

Blass, A., Debrunner, and R. Funk. *A Greek Grammar of the New Testament and Other Early Christian Literature.* Chicago: University of Chicago Press, 1961.

Block, Daniel. *The Gospel According to Moses: Theological and Ethical Reflections on the Book of Deuteronomy.* Eugene, OR: Cascade, 2012.

Blomberg, Craig. *Interpreting the Parables.* Downers Grove, IL: InterVarsity, 1990.

Bock, Darrell. *Blasphemy and Exaltation in Judaism: The Charge Against Jesus in Mark 14:53–65.* Grand Rapids: Baker, 2000.

———. *Luke 9:51—24:53.* Grand Rapids: Baker, 1996.

———. *Proclamation from Prophecy and Pattern: Lucan Old Testament Christology.* JSNTSS 12. Sheffield: JSOT, 1987.

Bokzer, B. Z. *Judaism and the Christian Predicament.* New York: Knopf, 1967.

Bousset, Wilhelm. *Kyrios Christos: A History of Belief in Christ from the Beginnings of Christianity to Irenaeus.* Translated by John E. Steely. Nashville: Abingdon, 1970.

Braaten, Carl, and Robert Jenson, eds. *Union with Christ: The New Finnish Interpretation of Luther.* Grand Rapids: Eerdmans, 1998.

Bray, Gerald. *Romans.* Downers Grove, IL: InterVarsity, 1998.

Brichto, Herbert Chanan. "On Slaughter and Sacrifice, Blood and Atonement." *HUCA* 47(1976) 19–55.

Brown, Raymond. *The Epistles of John.* Garden City, NY: Doubleday, 1985.

———. *The Gospel According to John.* 2 vols. Anchor Bible 29, 29A. Garden City, NY: Doubleday, 1982.

Bruce, F. F. *Commentary on the Book of Acts.* Grand Rapids: Eerdmans, 1979.

———. *The Epistle of Paul to the Romans.* Grand Rapids: Eerdmans, 1985.

———. *1 and 2 Corinthians.* Grand Rapids: Eerdmans, 1971.

———. *New Testament History.* Garden City, NY: Doubleday, 1972.

———. "The Speeches in Acts—Thirty Years After." In *Reconciliation and Hope: New Testament Essays on Atonement and Eschatology Presented to L. L. Morris on His 60th Birthday*, edited by Robert Banks, 53–68. Exeter: Paternoster, 1974.

———. *The Speeches in the Book of Acts the Apostles.* London: Tyndale, 1942.

———. *The Time Is Fulfilled: Five Aspects of the Fulfilment of the Old Testament in the New.* Grand Rapids: Eerdmans, 1978.

Brueggemann, Walter, and William Bellinger. *Psalms.* New Cambridge Bible Commentary. New York: Cambridge University, 2014.

Bucer, Martin. *Metaphrasis et enarratio in epist. d. Pauli apostolic ad Romanos.* 1536, 1562. Latin text retrieved online from *The Digital Library of Classic Protestant Texts.* Alexandria, VA: Alexander Street, 2007. https://alexanderstreet.com/products/digital-library-classic-protestant-texts.

Büchsel, Friedrich. *Die Johannesbriefe.* Leipzig: Deichert, 1933.

Bultmann, Rudolf. *The Johannine Epistles.* Philadelphia: Fortress, 1973.

———. *The Second Letter to the Corinthians.* Minneapolis: Augsburg, 1985.

———. *Theology of the New Testament.* Waco: Baylor, 2007.

Buttrick, David. *Speaking Parables: A Homiletic Guide.* Louisville: Westminster John Knox, 2000.

Bynum, Caroline Walker. *The Resurrection of the Body in Western Christianity, 200–1336.* New York: Columbia University, 1995.

Cadbury, Henry. "The Speeches in Acts." In *The Beginnings of Christianity: Part One, The Acts of the Apostles,* edited by J. Foakes Jackson and Kirsopp Lake, 402–26. Grand Rapids: Baker, 1979.

Calvin, John. *Calvin's Commentary.* 45 vols. Grand Rapids: Baker, 1979.

———. *Institutes of the Christian Religion.* Translated by John Allen. Philadelphia: Presbyterian Board of Christian Education, 1936.

Campbell, Constantine. *Verbal Aspect, the Indicative Mood, and Narrative: Soundings in the Greek of the New Testament.* New York: Peter Lang, 2007.

Campbell, Douglas A. *The Rhetoric of Righteousness in Romans 3:21–26.* Sheffield: JSOT Press, 1992.

Campbell, Ted. *The Gospel in Christian Traditions.* New York: Oxford, 2009.

Carter, Warren. *Households and Discipleship: A Study of Matthew 19–20.* Sheffield: JSOT Press, 1994.

Cary, Phillip. "Anxious about Assurance." *Christianity Today,* March 2013, 53–55.

Chalmers, Aaron. "The Influence of Cognitive Biases on Biblical Interpretation." *BBR* 26.4 (2016) 467–80.

Collins, R. F. "Matthew's ΕΝΤΟΛΑΙ: Towards an Understanding of the Commandments in the First Gospel" In *The Four Gospels: Festschrift Frans Neirynck,* edited by F. van Seobroeck, C. M. Tuckett, G. van Belle, and J. Verheyden, 2:1325–48. Leuven: University Press, 1992.

Conzelmann, Hans. *Acts of the Apostles.* Hermenia. Philadelphia: Fortress, 1972.

———. *Die Mitte der Zeit: Studien zur Theologie des Lukas.* Tübingen: Mohr, 1954.

———. *The Theology of St. Luke.* Translated by Geoffrey Buswell. Philadelphia: Fortress, 1961.

Cope, O. Lamar. "'The Good Is One': Mt 19:16–22 and Prov 3:35—4:4." In *Matthew: A Scribe Trained for the Kingdom of Heaven,* 111–20. Washington, DC: Catholic Biblical Association of America, 1976.

Catechism of the Catholic Church. Vatican: Libreria Editrice Vaticana, 1997.

Cothenet, Eduard, et al. "Imitation du Christ." *Dictionnaire de Spiritualité* 7 (1971) 1536–1601.

Cox, Harvey. *The Secular City.* New York: Macmillan, 1965.

Cranfield, C. E. B. *A Critical and Exegetical Commentary on the Epistle to the Romans.* 2 vols. Edinburgh: T. & T. Clark, 1979.

Creed, J. M. *The Gospel According to St. Luke.* London: Macmillian, 1930.

Crenshaw, James L., and Samuel Sandmel, eds. *The Divine Helmsman: Studies on God's Control of Human Events: Presented to Lou H. Silberman.* New York: KTAV, 1980.

Crossan, John Dominic. *The Power of Parable: How Fiction by Jesus Became Fiction about Jesus.* San Francisco: HarperOne, 2012.

Crouzel, Henri. "L'imitation et la 'suite' de Dieu et du Christ dans les premiers siècles chrétiens, ansi que leurs sources gréco-romaines et hébraiques." *JAC* 21(1978) 7–41.

Cullmann, Oscar. *The Christology of the New Testament.* Philadelphia: Westminster, 1959.

Dabney, D. Lyle. "'Justified by the Spirit': Soteriological Reflections on the Resurrection." *International Journal of Systematic Theology* 3.1 (March 2001) 46–68.

Daly, Robert J. "The Soteriological Significant of the Sacrifice of Isaac." *CBQ* 39 (January 1977) 45–75.
Das, A. Andrew. *Paul and the Jews*. Peabody, MA: Hendrickson, 2003.
———. *Paul, the Law, and the Covenant*. Peabody, MA: Hendrickson, 2001.
Daube, D. "Public Pronouncement and Private Explanation in the Gospels." *ET* 57 (1945–46) 175–77.
Davies, W. D., and Dale Allison. *The Gospel According to Saint Matthew*. 3 vols. Edinburgh: T. & T. Clark, 1988.
De Boer, Willis Peter. *The Imitation of Paul: An Exegetical Study*. Kampen: Kok, 1962.
deClaissé-Walford, Nancy, Rolf Jacobson, and Beth Tanner. *The Book of Psalms*. Grand Rapids: Eerdmans, 2014.
Deissmann, Adolf. *Bible Studies: Contributions, Chiefly from Papyri and Inscriptions, to the History of the Language, the Literature, and the Religion of Hellenistic Judaism and Primitive Christianity*. Translated by Alexander Grieve. Eugene, OR: Wipf and Stock, 2004.
———. *Light from the Ancient East: The New Testament Illustrated by Recently Discovered Texts of the Graeco-Roman World*. Translated by Lionel Strachan. New York: George Daron, 1927.
———. *Paulus: Eine Kultur- und religionsgeschichtliche Skizze*. Tübingen: Mohr, 1925.
———. *St. Paul: A Study in Social and Religious History*. Translated by William E. Wilson. London: Hodder and Stoughton, 1926.
Dibelius, Martin. "Paul on Areopagus" In *Studies in the Acts of the Apostles*, edited by H. Greeven, 26–77. New York: Scribner, 1956.
———. "The Speeches in Acts and Ancient Historiography." In *Studies in the Acts of the Apostles*, edited by H. Greeven, 138–85. New York: Scribner, 1956.
Dickson, John. "Gospel as News: εὐαγγελ from Aristophanes to the Apostle Paul." *NTS* 51(2005) 212–30.
Dihle, Albrecht. "The Gospels and Greek Biography." In *The Gospel and the Gospels*, edited by Peter Stuhlmacher, 361–86. Grand Rapids: Eerdmans, 1991.
Dobbeler, Axel von. *Glaube als Teilhabe: Historische und semantische Grundlagen der paulinischen Theologie und Ekklesiologie des Glaubens*. WUNT 2. Tübingen: Mohr, 1987.
Dodd, C. H. "HILASKESTHAI, Its Cognates, Derivatives, and Synonyms in the Septuagint." *JTS* 32 (1931) 352–60.
———. *The Apostolic Preaching and Its Developments*. London: Hodder and Stoughton, 1936.
———. *The Epistle to the Romans*. London: Hodder and Stroughton, 1932.
———. "The Framework of the Gospel Narrative." *ExpTim* 43 (1931–32) 396–400.
———. *The Johannine Epistles*. London: Hodder and Stoughton, 1946.
———. *The Parables of the Kingdom*. New York: Scribner, 1961.
Donaldson, Terence. *Paul and the Gentiles: Remapping the Apostle's World*. Minneapolis: Fortress, 1997.
Dunn, James. *Jesus, Paul, and the Law: Studies in Mark and Galatians*. Louisville: Westminster/John Knox, 1990.
———. *Jews and Christians: The Parting of the Ways, A.D. 70 to 135*. Grand Rapids: Eerdmans, 1992.
———, ed. *Paul and the Mosaic Law*. Grand Rapids: Eerdmans, 1996.
———. *Romans*. 2 vols. Anchor Bible 38, 38A. Dallas: Word, 1988.

———. *The Christ and the Spirit: Collected Essays of James D. G. Dunn*. Vol. 1, *Christology*. Grand Rapids: Eerdmans, 1998.

———. "The Gospel and the Gospels." *EQ* 85(2013) 291–308.

———. *The New Perspective on Paul*. Grand Rapids: Eerdmans, 2008.

———. *The Theology of Paul the Apostle*. Grand Rapids: Eerdmans, 1998.

———. "When Did the Understanding of Jesus' Death as an Atoning Sacrifice First Emerge?" In *Israel's God and Rebecca's Children: Christology and Community in Early Judaism and Christianity*, edited by David Capes, April DeConick, Helen Bond, and Troy Miller, 169–81. Waco: Baylor, 2007.

Dunn, James, and Alan Suggate. *The Justice of God: A Fresh Look at the Old Doctrine of Justification by Faith*. Grand Rapids: Eerdmans, 1993.

Edwards, Jonathan. *A Treatise Concerning Religious Affections*. London, 1796.

Egelkraut, H. L. *Jesus' Mission to Jerusalem: A Redaction Critical Study of the Travel Narrative in the Gospel of Luke, Lk 9:51—19:48*. Bern: Lang, 1976.

Eichrodt, Walter. *Theology of the Old Testament*. 2 vols. Philadelphia: Westminster, 1961, 1967.

Elliott, Mark Adam. *The Survivors of Israel: A Reconsideration of the Theology of Pre-Christian Judaism*. Grand Rapids: Eerdmans, 2000.

Elliger, Karl. *Leviticus*. Tübingen: Mohr, 1966.

Ellis, E. E. *The Gospel of Luke*. Grand Rapids: Eerdmans, 1974.

Eubank, Nathan. *Wages of Cross-Bearing and Debt of Sin: The Economy of Heaven in Matthew's Gospel*. Berlin: De Gruyter, 2013.

Evans, A. Craig. *Jesus and the Remains of His Day: Studies in Jesus and the Evidence of Material Culture*. Peabody, MA: Hendrickson, 2015.

Evans, C. F. *Saint Luke*. Trinity Press International New Testament Commentaries. Philadelphia: Trinity, 1990.

Farmer, William. "The Patriarch Phinehas: A Note on 'It Was Reckoned to Him as Righteousness.'" *AThR* 34.1 (January 1952) 26–30.

Feder, Yitzhaq. "On *Kuppuru*, *Kippēr* and Etymological Sins that Cannot Be Wiped Away." *VT* 60 (2010) 535–45.

Feuillet, A. "Mort du Christ et mort du Chrétien." *RBib* 66 (1959) 481–513.

Ficino, Marsilio. *Platonic Theology*. Translated by Michael J. B. Allen. 6 vols. Cambridge, MA: Harvard University, 2004.

Fiensy, David, and James Strange, eds. *Galilee in the Late Second Temple and Mishnaic Periods*. Vol. 1, *Life, Culture, and Society*. Minneapolis: Fortress, 2014.

Filium, C. Geroldi, ed. *Corpus Scriptorum Ecclesiasticorum Latinorum*. Vienna: Vindobonae, 1972.

Finkel, Asher. *The Pharisees and the Teacher of Nazareth: A Study of their Background, Their Halachic and Midrashic Teachings, the Similarities and Differences*. Leiden: Brill, 1964.

Fiore, Benjamin. *The Function of Personal Example in the Socratic and Pastoral Epistles*. Analecta biblica 105. Rome: Biblical Institute, 1986.

Fitzmyer, Joseph. *Romans*. Anchor Bible 33. New York: Doubleday, 1993.

———. *The Gospel According to Luke*. 2 vols. Anchor Bible 28. Garden City, NY: Doubleday, 1985.

Flint, Peter, ed. *The Bible at Qumran: Text, Shape, and Interpretation*. Grand Rapids: Eerdmans, 2001.

Ford, Richard. *The Parables of Jesus: Recovering the Act of Listening.* Minneapolis: Fortress, 1997.
Fornara, Charles William. *The Nature of History in Ancient Greece and Rome.* Eidos Studies in Classical Kinds. Berkeley: University of California Press, 1983.
Fortna, Robert. "Exegesis and Proclamation." *Journal of Theology for Southern Africa* 72 (1990) 66–72.
Freed, Edwin. "Did John Write His Gospel Partly to Win Samaritan Converts?" *NovT* 12 (1970) 241–56.
Freyne, Seán. *The Jesus Movement and Its Expansion: Meaning and Mission.* Grand Rapids: Eerdmans, 2014.
Friedlander, Gerald. *The Jewish Sources of the Sermon on the Mount.* New York: KTAV, 1991.
Friedrich, Gerhard. "ἁαρτία οὐκ ἐλλογεῖται, Röm. 5,13." *ThLZ* 77 (1952) 525–27.
Fryer, Nico S. L. "The Meaning and Translation of *Hilastērion* in Romans 3:25." *EvQ* 59 (1987) 105–11.
Furnish, Paul. *2 Corinthians.* Garden City, NY: Doubleday, 1984.
Gammie, John. *Holiness in Israel.* Minneapolis: Fortress, 1989.
Gane, Roy. *Cult and Character: Purification Offerings, Day of Atonement, and Theodicy.* Winona Lake, IN: Eisenbrauns, 2005.
Garland, D. E. *2 Corinthians.* Nashville: Broadman, 1999.
Garret, James Leo. *Systematic Theology: Biblical, Historical, and Evangelical.* Grand Rapids: Eerdmans, 1990.
Gärtner, B. *The Areopagus Speech and Natural Revelation.* Translated by Carolyn Hannay King. Lund: C. W. K. Gleerup, 1955.
Gathercole, Simon. *Defending Substitution: An Essay on Atonement in Paul.* Grand Rapids: Baker, 2015.
———. *Where Is Boasting?: Early Jewish Soteriology and Paul's Response in Romans 1–5.* Grand Rapids: Eerdmans, 2002.
Gese, Hartmut. "Die Sühne." In *Zur biblischen Theologie Alttestamentliche Vorträge*, 85–106. Munich: Kaiser, 1977.
———. "The Atonement." In *Essays on Biblical Theology*, 93–116. Minneapolis: Augsburg, 1981.
Gillman, Neil. *The Death of Death: Resurrection and Immortality in Jewish Thought.* Woodstock, VT: Jewish Lights, 2000.
Godet, Frederic Louis. *Commentary on Romans.* Grand Rapids: Kregel, 1977.
Gorman, Michael. *Becoming the Gospel: Paul, Participation, and Mission.* Grand Rapids: Eerdmans, 2015.
Graver, Margaret. *Stoicism and Emotion.* Chicago: University of Chicago Press, 2007.
Gregory, Bradley. "Abraham as the Jewish Ideal: Exegetical Traditions in Sirach 44:19–21." *CBQ* 70 (2008) 66–81.
Greear, J. D. "Should We Stop Asking Jesus into Our Hearts?" *Christianity Today*, July 13, 2012.
———. *Stop Asking Jesus into Your Heart: How to Know for Sure You Are Saved.* Nashville: B & H, 2013.
Green, Joel. *The Theology of the Gospel of Luke.* Cambridge: Cambridge University Press, 1995.
Griffith, Terry. "A Non-Polemical Reading of 1 John: Sin, Christology, and the Limits of Johannine Christianity." *TynBul* 49 (1998) 253–76.

Grindheim, Sigrud. "Ignorance Is Bliss: Attitudinal Aspects of the Judgment according to Works in Matthew 25:31–46." *NovT* 50 (2008) 313–31.

Gubler, Marie-Louise. *Die Frühesten Deutungen des Todes Jesu: Eine motifgeschichtliche Darstellung aufrung der neuen exegetischen Forschung.* Freiburg Schweiz: Universtatsverlag, 1977.

Guilbert, P. "The Message of Salvation in the Acts of the Apostles: Composition and Structure." *Lumen-Vitoria* 12 (1957) 406–17.

Gundry, Robert. *Matthew: A Commentary on His Literary and Theological Art.* Grand Rapids: Eerdmans, 1982.

Guthrie, Donald. *The Letter to the Hebrews.* Leicester: InterVarsity, 1983.

———. *New Testament Theology.* Downers Grove, IL: InterVarsity, 1981.

Guthrie, George. *2 Corinthians.* Grand Rapids: Baker, 2015.

Gutiérrez, Gustavo. *A Theology of Liberation: History, Politics, and Salvation.* Translated and edited by Sister Caridad Inda and John Eagleson. Maryknoll, NY: Orbis, 1973.

Gutierrez, Pedro. *La Paternité spirituelle selon S. Paul.* Paris: Gabalda, 1968.

Hafemann, Scott. *Suffering and the Spirit: An Exegetical Study of II Cor. 2:14—3:3 within the Context of the Corinthian Correspondence.* Tübingen: Mohr, 1986.

Hägerland, Tobias. *Jesus and the Forgiveness of Sins: An Aspect of His Prophetic Mission.* Cambridge: Cambridge University Press, 2012.

Hagner, Donald. *Matthew.* 2 vols. Word Biblical Commentary 33A, 33B. Dallas: Word, 1995.

Hahn, Scott. *Kinship by Covenant: A Canonical Approach to the Fulfillment of God's Saving Promises.* New Haven, CT: Yale University, 2009.

Hallo, William, ed. *The Context of Scripture.* Vol. 1: *Canonical Compositions from the Biblical World.* Leiden: Brill, 1997.

Hantzler, H. B. *Moody in Chicago.* New York: Revell, 1894.

Harnack, Adolf von. "Gospel: History of the Conception in the Earliest Church." In *The Constitution and Law of the Church in the First Two Centuries*, edited by Adolf von Harnack, Frank Pogson, and H. D. A. Major. London: William & Norgate, 1910.

———. *What Is Christianity?* Translated by Thomas Bailey Saunders. London: Harper, 1957.

Harrington, Wilfrid. *Luke—Gracious Theologian: The Jesus of Luke.* Blackrock: Columba, 1977.

Harris, Murray. *The Second Epistle to the Corinthians.* Grand Rapids: Eerdmans, 2005.

Hays, Richard B. *Echoes of Scripture in the Gospels.* Waco: Baylor University Press, 2016.

———. *The Faith of Jesus Christ: An Investigation of the Narrative Substructure of Galatians 3:1—4:11.* Chico, CA: Scholars, 1983.

Hemer, Colin J. *The Book of Acts in the Setting of Hellenistic History.* Winona Lake, IN: Eisenbrauns, 1990.

———. "The Speeches in Acts II: The Areopagus Address." *TynB* 40(1989) 239–59.

Hengel, Martin. *Four Gospels and the One Gospel of Jesus Christ.* Harrisburg, PA: Trinity, 2000.

Hennecke, Edward, and Wilhelm Schneemelcher, eds. *The New Testament Apocrypha.* 2 vols. Philadelphia: Westminster, 1965.

Henninger, Joseph. *Sanctus Augustinus et doctrina de duplici iustitia.* Mödling: Typus Domus Missionum ad Sanctum Gabrielem, 1935.

Hermann, Johannes. *Die Idee der Sühne im Alten Testament: eine Utersuchung über Gebrauch und Bedeutung des Wortes kipper.* Leipzig: Hinrichs, 1905.

Herzog, William. *Parables as Subversive Speech: Jesus as Pedagogue of the Oppressed*. Louisville: Westminster/John Knox, 1994.
Hiecke, Thomas, and Tobias Nichlas. *The Day of Atonement: Its Interpretations in Early Jewish and Christian Traditions*. Leiden: Brill, 2012.
Hildesheimer, Azriel, ed. *Halakbot G'dolot*. Berlin: Mekize Nirdamim, 1888.
Hoag, Gary. *Wealth in Ancient Ephesus and the First Letter to Timothy: Fresh Insights from Ephesiaca by Xenophon of Ephesus*. Winona Lake, IN: Eisenbrauns, 2015.
Hodge, Charles. *Commentary on the Epistle to the Romans*. Grand Rapids: Eerdmans, 1950.
Hodges, Zane. "Fellowship and Confession in 1 John 1:5–10." *BibSac* 129 (1972) 48–60.
Hofius, Otfried. "Sühne und Versöhnung: Zum paulinischen Verständis des Kreuzestodes Jesu." In *Paulustudien*. Tübingen: Mohr, 1989.
Holtzmann, H. J. *Die Apostelgeschte*. Hand-Commentar zum Neuen Testament ½. Tübingen: Mohr (Paul Siebeck), 1901.
Hooker, Morna. *From Adam to Christ: Essays on Paul*. Cambridge: Cambridge University Press, 1990.
———. *Jesus and the Servant: The Influence of the Servant Concept of Deutero-Isaiah in the New Testament*. Edited by William Bellinger and William Farmer. London: SPCK, 1959.
———. "πίστις Ἰησοῦ." *NTS* 35 (1989) 321–42.
———. *The Gospel According to Saint Mark*. Peabody, MA: Hendrickson, 1991.
Hopkins, Jasper. *A Companion to the Study of St. Anselm*. Minneapolis: University of Minnesota Press, 1972.
Horbury, William. "'Gospel' in Herodian Judea." In *The Written Gospel*, edited by M. Bockmuehl and D. A. Hagner, 7–30. Cambridge: Cambridge University Press, 2005.
Horsley, G. H. R. "Speeches and Dialogue in Acts." *NTS* 32 (1986) 609–14.
Hübner, Hans. *The Law in Paul's Thought*. Edinburg: T. & T. Clark, 1984.
Irons, Charles. *The Righteousness of God: A Lexical Examination of the Covenant-Faithfulness Interpretation*. Tübingen: Mohr, 2015.
Isaac, Jules. *Jesus and Israel*. New York: Holt, Rinehart and Winston, 1971.
Jacombe, Thomas. *Sermons on the Eighth Chapter to the Epistle to the Romans (Verses 1–4)*. Edinburgh: Banner of Truth Trust, 1996.
Jahnow, Hedwig. "Das Abdecken des Daches [Mc 2,4/Lc 5,19]." *ZNW* 24 (1925) 155–58.
Janowski, Bernd. *Sühne als Heilsgeschehen: Studien zur Sühnetheologie der Priesterschrift und zur Wurzel KPR im Alten Testament*. Neukirchen-Vluyn: Neukirchener, 1982.
Janowski, Bernd, and Peter Stuhlmacher, eds. *The Suffering Servant: Isaiah 53 in Jewish and Christian Sources*. Grand Rapids: Eerdmans, 2004.
Jeremias, Joachim. *Neotestamentliche Theologie*. Gütersloh: Gütersloher, 1971.
Jervell, Jacob. *The Theology of the Acts of the Apostles*. Cambridge: Cambridge University Press, 1996.
Jewett, Robert. *Romans*. Minneapolis: Fortress, 2007.
Jobes, Karen. *1, 2, and 3 John*. Zondervan Exegetical Commentary on the New Testament 19. Grand Rapids: Zondervan, 2013.
Johnston, George. *The Spirit-Paraclete in the Gospel of John*. Cambridge: Cambridge University Press, 1970.

Jones, D. L. "The Christology of the Missionary Speeches in the Acts of the Apostles." PhD diss., Duke University, 1966.

Kant, Immanuel. *Religion within the Limits of Reason Alone*. Translated by Theodore M. Greene and Hoyt H. Hudson. New York: Harper Torchbooks, 1960.

Karis, Robert. *Luke: Artist and Theologian: Luke's Passion Account as Literature*. New York: Paulist, 1985.

Käsemann, Ernst. *Commentary on Romans*. Grand Rapids: Eerdmans, 1980.

Kee, Howard Clark. *Good News to the Ends of the Earth: The Theology of Acts*. London: SCM, 1990.

Keener, Craig. *A Commentary on the Gospel of Matthew*. Grand Rapids: Eerdmans, 1999.

———. *Miracles: The Credibility of the New Testament Accounts*. Grand Rapids: Baker, 2011.

———. *The Gospel of John*. 2 vols. Peabody, MA: Hendrickson, 2003.

Kennard, Douglas W. "A Biblical and Philosophical Critique of Anselm's Argument for the Chalcedonian Formula for Christ's Hypostatic Union as Presented in *Cur Deus Homo*." Paper presented at the Evangelical Philosophical Society annual meeting, March 2010.

———. *A Critical Realist's Theological Method: Returning the Bible and Biblical Theology to Be the Framer for Theology and Science*. Eugene, OR: Wipf and Stock, 2013.

———. "An Analysis of Theological Similarities between the *Charter of a Jewish Sectarian Association* (1QS, 4Q255–264a, 5Q11) and 'The Gospel of John.'" Paper presented at the SBL annual meeting, March 2011.

———. *Biblical Covenantalism: Engagement with Judaism, Law, Atonement, the New Perspective, and Kingdom Hope*. Vol. 1: *Biblical Covenantalism in Torah: Judaism, Covenant Nomism, and Atonement*. Eugene: Wipf and Stock, 2015.

———. *Biblical Covenantalism: In Prophets, Psalms, Early Judaism, Gospels, and Acts*. Vol. 2: *Judaism, Covenant Nomism, and Kingdom Hope*. Eugene, OR: Wipf and Stock, 2015.

———. *Biblical Covenantalism: Engaging the New Perspective and New Covenant Atonement*. Vol. 3: *Biblical Covenantalism in New Testament Epistles*. Eugene, OR: Wipf and Stock, 2015.

———. *Epistemology and Logic in the New Testament: Early Jewish Context and Biblical Theology Mechanisms That Fit within Some Contemporary Ways of Knowing*. Eugene, OR: Wipf and Stock, 2016.

———. "Jeremiah and Hebrews: Mosaic, Davidic, and New." Paper presented at the Evangelical Theological Society annual meeting, March 1994.

———. "The Law in James." Paper presented at the Evangelical Theological Society Mid-West regional meeting, March 1993.

———. *Messiah Jesus: Christology in His Day and Ours*. New York: Peter Lang, 2008.

———. "Paul and the Law." Paper presented at the Evangelical Theological Society Mid-West regional meeting, March 1996.

———. *The Relationship between Epistemology, Hermeneutics, Biblical Theology and Contextualization*. Lewiston, NY: Edwin Mellen, 1999.

———. "The Way to Kingdom Salvation: Synoptics and the Law." Paper presented at the Evangelical Theological Society Mid-West regional meeting, March 1992.

———. "Warnings in the Book of Hebrews: The Two-Ways Tradition." Paper presented at the Evangelical Theological Society annual meeting, March 1998.

Kennedy, George. *New Testament Interpretation through Rhetorical Criticism.* Chapel Hill: University of North Carolina Press, 1984.
Kilgallen, J. J. "Acts 13,38–39: Culmination of Paul's Speech in Psidia." *Bib* 69 (1988) 480–506.
Kim, Kyong-Shik. *God Will Judge Each One According to Works: Judgment According to Works and Psalm 62 in Early Judaism and the New Testament.* Berlin: De Gruyter, 2011.
Kissinger, Warren. *The Parables of Jesus: A History of Interpretation and Bibliography.* Metuchen, NJ: Scarecrow, 1979.
Kiuchi, N. *Purification Offering in the Priestly Literature: Its Meaning and Function.* Sheffield: Sheffield Academic, 1987.
Klijn, A. F. J. "Stephen's Speech—Acts 7,2–53." *NTS* 4 (1957–58) 25–31.
———. "The Study of Jewish Christianity." *NTS* 20 (1973–74) 419–31.
Klijn, A. F. J., and G. J. Reinink. *Patristic Evidence for Jewish-Christian Sects.* Leiden: Brill, 1973.
Köstenberger, Andreas. *John.* Baker Exegetical Commentary on the New Testament. Grand Rapids: Baker, 2004.
Kraus, Hans-Joachim. *Psalms 1–59.* Vol. 1 of 2. Translated by Hilton C. Oswald. Minneapolis: Augsburg, 1989.
Kraus, Wolfgang. *Der Tod Jesu als Heiligtumsweihe: Eine Untersuchung zum Umfeld der Sühnevorstellung in Römer 3.25–26a.* Neukirchen-Vluyn: Neukirchen, 1991.
Kruse, Colin. *Paul's Letter to the Romans.* Grand Rapids: Eerdmans, 2012.
Kruse, Thomas. "Kantakkrima-Strafzahlung oder Steuer?" *Zeitschrift für Papyrologie und Epigraphik* 124 (1999) 166–90.
Kühl, Ernst. *Der Brief des Paulus an die Römer.* Leipzig: Hinrichs, 1929.
Kuhn, Karl. *The Kingdom According to Luke and Acts: A Social, Literary, and Theological Introduction.* Grand Rapids: Baker, 2015.
Kurtz, Johann Heinrich. *Sacrificial Worship of the Old Testament.* Edinburgh: T. & T. Clark, 1863.
Kurz, William. "Narrative Models for Imitation in Luke-Acts." In *Greeks, Romans, and Christians*, edited by D. L. Balch, Everett Ferguson, and Wayne Meeks, 171–89. Minneapolis: Fortress, 1990.
Kuula, Kari. *The Law, the Covenant and God's Plan.* Vol. 1: *Paul's Polemical Treatment of the Law in Galatians.* Göttingen: Vandenhoeck & Ruprecht, 2003.
———. *The Law, the Covenant and God's Plan.* Vol. 2: *Paul's Treatment of the Law and Israel in Romans Galatians.* Göttingen: Vandenhoeck & Ruprecht, 2006.
La Place, Josué de. *De Imputatione Primi Peccati Adami.* Franequerae: Johannis Gyzelaar, 1702.
Lambrecht, Jan. "Why Is Boasting Excluded?: A Note on Rom. 3,27 and 4,2." *EThL* 61 (1985) 366–67.
Lampe, G. W. H. "The Lucan Portrait of Christ." *NTS* 2 (1955, 1956) 160–75.
Lapide, Phihas. *The Sermon on the Mount.* Maryknoll, NY: Orbis, 1986.
Law, George. "The Law of the New Covenant in Matthew." *American Theological Inquiry* (online) 5.2 (July 15, 2012) 27–29.
Law, Robert. *The Tests of Life: A Study of the First Epistle of St. John.* Grand Rapids: Baker, 1914.
Levine, Amy-Jill. *The Short Stories by Jesus: The Enigmatic Parables of a Controversial Rabbi.* New York: Harper One, 2014.

———. *The Social and Ethical Dimensions of Matthean Salvation History*. Studies in the Bible and Early Christianity 14. Lewiston, NY: Edwin Mellen, 1988.

Levine, Baruch. *In the Presence of the Lord: A Study of Cult and Some Cultic Terms in Ancient Israel*. Leiden: Brill, 1974.

Lightfoot, John. *A Commentary on the New Testament from the Talmud and Hebraica*. Grand Rapids: Baker, 1979.

Loader, William. *Jesus' Attitude towards the Law: A Study of the Gospels*. Grand Rapids: Eerdmans, 1997.

Locke, John. *Concerning Human Understanding*. Great Books of the Western World 35. Chicago: Encyclopaedia Britannica, 1952.

———. "A Discourse of Miracles." In *The Works of John Locke*, 9:256–65. London: C. & J. Rivington, 1824.

———. "The Reasonableness of Christianity." In *The Works of John Locke*, vol. 6. London: C. & J. Rivington, 1824.

Loehr, Hermut. "Jesus and the Ten Words." In *Handbook for the Study of the Historical Jesus*, edited by Tom Holmén and Stanley Porter, 4:3135–54. Leiden: Brill, 2011.

Loenertz, R. J. *The Apocalypse of St. John*. London: Sheed and Ward, 1947.

Lohse, Eduard. *Märtyrer und Gottesknecht: Untersuchungen zur urchristlichen Verkündigung vom sühntod Jesu Christi*. Forschungen zur Religion und Literatur des Alten und Neuen Testaments 49. Göttingen: Vandenhoeck & Ruprecht, 1963.

Long, Thomas. *Matthew*. Louisville: Westminster John Knox, 1997.

Longenecker, Richard N. *The Christology of Early Jewish Christianity*. London: SCM, 1970.

———. *The Epistle to the Romans: A Commentary on the Greek Text*. Grand Rapids: Eerdmans, 2016.

Lossky, Vladimir. *In the Image and Likeness of God*. Edited by John H. Erickson and Thomas E. Bird. Crestwood, NY: St. Vladimir's Seminary Press, 1974.

Luther, Martin. *Luther's Works*. General editor Helmut Lehmann. Philadelphia: Fortress, 1955–86.

Maldonatus, John. *A Commentary on the Holy Gospels: Saint Matthew's Gospel Chapters XX to the End*. London: John Hodges, 1888.

Marcus, Joel. *Mark*. 2 vols. Garden City, NY: Doubleday, 2000.

Marshall, I. Howard. *Luke: Historian and Theologian*. Grand Rapids: Zondervan, 1970.

———. *The Acts of the Apostles*. Grand Rapids: Eerdmans, 1980.

———. *The Epistles of John*. Grand Rapids: Eerdmans, 1978.

Marshall, L. H. *The Challenge of New Testament Ethics*. New York: Macmillan, 1947.

Marshall, P. "The Meaning of Social Shame: ΘPIAMBEYEIN in 2 Cor. 2:14." *NovT* 25 (1983) 302–17.

Martin, Ralph. *2 Corinthians*. Nashville: T. Nelson, 1986.

Martyn, Louis. *Theological Issues in the Letters of Paul*. Edinburgh: T. & T. Clark, 1997.

Mason, Steve. *Josephus, Judea, and Christian Origins: Methods and Categories*. Peabody, MA: Hendrickson, 2009.

Mayordomo, Moisés. *Argumentiert Paulus logisch?: Eine Analyse vor dem Hintergrund antiker Logik*. Tübingen: Mohr Siebeck, 2005.

McArthur, Harvey, and Robert Johnston, eds. *They Also Taught in Parables: Rabbinic Parables from the First Centuries of the Christian Era*. Grand Rapids: Zondervan, 1990.

McFadden, Kevin W. "The Fulfillment of the Law's *DIKAIŌMA*: Another Look at Romans 8:1–4." *JETS* 52 (2009) 483–97.
McGrath, Alister. *Iustitia Dei: A History of the Christian Doctrine of Justification.* Cambridge: Cambridge University Press, 1998.
McKnight, Scot. *The King Jesus Gospel: The Original Good News Revisited.* Grand Rapids: Zondervan, 2011.
Meier, John. *A Marginal Jew: Rethinking the Historical Jesus.* Vol. 2: *Mentor, Message, and Miracles.* New York: Doubleday, 1994.
Melanchthon, Philip. *Commentary on Romans.* In *Melanchthons Werke* 15, edited by Robert Stupperich. Gütersloh: Mohn, 1965.
———. *Loci communes von 1521.* In *Melancthons Werke* 2.1, edited by Hans Engelland. Gütersloh: Bertelsmann, 1952.
———. *Loci communes.* In *Corpus Reformatorum*, edited by Karl Gottlieb Bretschneider. Berlin: C. A. Schwetschke, 1834.
Menard, Jacques E. "*Pais Theou* as a Messianic Title in the Book of Acts." *CBQ* 19 (1957) 83–92.
Metzger, Bruce. *A Textual Commentary on the Greek New Testament.* 2nd ed. Stuttgart: United Bible Societies, 2002.
Meyers, Eric. *Galilee Through the Centuries: Confluence of Cultures.* Winona Lake, IN: Eisenbrauns, 1999.
Michel, Otto. *Der Brief an die Römer.* Göttingen: Vandenhoeck & Ruprecht, 1978.
Migne, J.-P., ed. *Patrologia graeca.* 162 vols. Paris, 1857–1886.
———, ed. *Patrologia latina.* 217 vols. Paris, 1844–64.
Milgrom, Jacob. *Leviticus 1–16.* Anchor Bible 3. New York: Doubleday, 1991.
———. *Numbers [=Be-midbar]: The Traditional Hebrew Text with the New JPS Translation.* JPS Torah Commentary. Philadelphia: Jewish Publication Society, 1990.
Mitchell, John. *Fellowship: A Devotional Study of the Epistles of John.* Portland: Multnomah, 1974.
Montague, G. T. "Paul and Athens." *TBT* 49 (1970) 14–23.
Moo, Douglas. *The Epistle to the Romans.* New International Commentary on the New Testament. Grand Rapids: Eerdmans, 1996.
Morris, Leon. *John.* Grand Rapids: Eerdmans, 1971.
Moser, Paul, ed. *Jesus and Philosophy: New Essays.* Cambridge: Cambridge University Press, 2009.
Moulton, J. H. *A Grammar of New Testament Greek.* Vol. 1: *Prolegomena.* Grand Rapids: Eerdmans, 1985.
Murray, Gregory. "The Rich Young Man." *Downside Review* 103 (1985) 144–46.
Murray, John. *Collected Writings of John Murray.* 4 vols. Edinburgh: Banner of Truth Trust, 1977.
———. *The Epistle to the Romans.* Grand Rapids: Eerdmans, 1959.
Neusner, J. *Sifre to Numbers: An American Translation and Explanation.* 2 vols. Brown Judaic Studies 118, 119. Atlanta: Scholars, 1986.
Neyrey, Jerome H. "Acts 17, Epicureans, and Theodicy: A Study in Stereotypes." In *Greeks, Romans, and Christians*, edited by D. L. Balch, Everett Ferguson, and Wayne Meeks, 118–34. Minneapolis: Fortress, 1990.
Nickelsburg, George. *Resurrection, Immortality, and Eternal Life in Intertestamental Judaism.* Cambridge, MA: Harvard University, 1972.

Nicoll, W. R., ed. *The Expositor's Greek New Testament*. Grand Rapids: Eerdmans, 1970.
Noland, John. *Luke*. 2 vols. Word Biblical Commentary 35A, 35B. Nashville: T. Nelson, 1993.
Nygren, A. *Commentary on Romans*. Philadelphia: Fortress, 1949.
Oakman, Douglas. "The Buying Power of Two Denarri." *Forum* 3(1987) 33–38.
Oden, Thomas. *The Justification Reader*. Grand Rapids: Eerdmans, 2002.
Oecolampadius, Johannes. *In Hieremiam prophetam commentariorum libri tres Ioannis Oecolampadii*. Argentinae: in officinae Matthiae Apiarii, 1533.
Oeming, Manfred. "Ist Gen. 15.6 ein Beleg für die Anrechnung des Glaubens zur Gerechtigkeit?" *ZAW* 95 (1983) 185–96.
Oswalt, John. *The Book of Isaiah: Chapters 40–66*. Grand Rapids: Eerdmans, 1998.
O'Toole, Robert. *The Unity of Luke's Theology: An Analysis of Luke-Acts*. Wilmington, DE: M. Glazier, 1984.
Overman, Andrew. *Matthew's Gospel and Formative Judaism: The Social World of the Matthean Community*. Minneapolis: Fortress, 1990.
Packer, J. I. "What Did the Cross Achieve?: The Logic of Penal Substitution." *TynBul* 25 (1974) 3–45.
Padilla, Osvaldo. *The Acts of the Apostles: Interpretation, History, and Theology*. Downers Grove, IL: InterVarsity, 2016.
Park, Eugene Eung-Chun. "Covenant Nomism and the Gospel of Matthew." *CBQ* 77.4 (2015) 668–85.
Parker, T. H. L. *Commentaries on the Epistle to the Romans, 1532–1542*. Edinburgh: T. & T. Clark, 1986.
Pate, C. Marvin, and Douglas W. Kennard. *Deliverance Now and Not Yet: The New Testament and the Great Tribulation*. New York: Peter Lang, 2003.
Plantinga, Alvin. *Knowledge and Christian Belief*. Grand Rapids: Eerdmans, 2015.
———. *Warrant and Proper Function*. New York: Oxford University Press, 1993.
Plummer, A. *A Critical and Exegetical Commentary on the Gospel According to St. Luke*. ICC. Edinburg: T. & T. Clark, 1896.
Pokorny, Petr. *From the Gospel to the Gospels: History, Theology and Impact of the Biblical Term "Euangelion"*. Berlin: De Gruyter, 2013.
Porter, Stanley. *Idioms of the Greek New Testament*. Sheffield: Sheffield Academic, 1992.
———. "Thucydides 1.22.1 and Speeches in Acts: Is There a Thucydidean View?" *NovT* 2(1990) 121–42.
Porter, Stanley, and Jacqueline C. R. de Roo, eds. *The Concept of the Covenant in the Second Temple Period*. Supplements to the Journal for the Study of Judaism 71. Atlanta: Society of Biblical Literature, 2003.
Rad, Gerhard von. *Old Testament Theology*. Translated by D. M. G. Stalke. 2 vols. New York: Harper & Row, 1962, 65.
———. *The Problem of the Hexateuch and Other Essays*. Translated by E. W. Trueman Dicken. Edinburgh: McGraw Hill, 1966.
Rainer, Archduke, Carl Wessely, and Ludwig Mitteis, eds. *Corpus papyrorum Raineri*. Vienna: Holinek, 1895.
Räisänen, Heikki. *Paul and the Law*. WUNT 29. Tübingen: Mohr (Siebeck), 1983.
Rashdall, Hastings. "The Abelardian Doctrine of the Atonement." In *Doctrine and Development: University Sermons*, 128–45. London: Methuen, 1898.

Reed, Jonathan. "Reappraising the Galilean Economy: The Limits of Models, Archeology, and Analogy." Paper presented at the Westar Jesus Seminar spring meeting, March 2008.
Reiche, Bo. "The New Testament Concept of Reward." In *Aux sources de la tradition chréttiene: Mélanges offerts à M. Maurice Goguel*, edited by P. H. Menoud and Oscar Cullman, 195–206. Paris: Delachaux and Niestlé, 1950.
Rhee, Helen. *Loving the Poor, Saving the Rich: Wealth, Poverty, and Early Christian Formation*. Grand Rapids: Baker, 2012.
Ricoeur, Paul. *Oneself as Another*. Translated by Kathleen Blamey. Chicago: University of Chicago Press, 1992.
Ridderbos, H. N. *The Speeches of Peter in the Acts of the Apostles*. London: Tyndale, 1962.
Riesenfeld, Ernst H. *Jesus Transfiguré: L'arrière-plan du récit évangélique de la Transfiguration de Notre-Seigneur*. Copenhagen: Munksgaard, 1947.
Robertson, A. T. *A Grammar of the Greek New Testament in Light of Historical Research*. Nashville: Broadman, 1934.
———. *Word Pictures in the New Testament*. 6 vols. Nashville: Broadman, 1930–.
Robinson, W. C. "'The Way of the Lord': A Study of History and Eschatology in the Gospel of Luke." PhD diss., University of Basel, 1960.
Rosenberg, Roy A. "Jesus, Isaac and the Suffering Servant." *JBL* 84 (1965) 381–88.
Ross, J. T. "The Concept of σωτηρία in the New Testament." PhD diss., University of Chicago, 1947.
Roth, Martha. *Law Collections from Mesopotamia and Asia Minor*. Atlanta: Society of Biblical Literature, 1997.
Rottzoll, Dirk. "Gen. 15.6—Ein Beleg für den Glauben als Werkgerechtigkeit." *ZAW* 106 (1994) 21–27.
Ruether, Rosemary Radford. *Introducing Redemption in Christian Feminism*. Sheffield: Sheffield Academic, 1998.
Saldarini, Anthony. *Matthew's Christian-Jewish Community*. Chicago: University of Chicago Press, 1994.
Sanday, William, and Arthur Headlam, *A Critical and Exegetical Commentary on the Epistle to the Romans*. 5th ed. Edinburgh: T. & T. Clark, 1902.
Sanders, E. P. *Jesus and Judaism; Paul, the Law, and the Jewish People*. Philadelphia: Fortress, 1985.
———. *Jewish Law from Jesus to the Mishnah*. London: SCM, 1990.
———. *Judaism: Practice and Belief 63 BCE–66 CE*. London: SCM, 1992.
———. *Paul and Palestinian Judaism*. Philadelphia: Fortress, 1977.
———. *Paul, the Law, and the Jewish People*. Minneapolis: Fortress, 1983.
Sanders, Jack. *The Jews in Luke-Acts*. Philadelphia: Fortress, 1987.
Saussure, Ferdinand de. *Cours de linguistique générale*. Paris: Payot, 1969.
Schaff, Philip, ed. *The Nicene and Post-Nicene Fathers of the Christian Church*. Grand Rapids: Eerdmans, 1952–56.
———. *Creeds of Christendom*. New York: Harper, 1877.
Schenker, Adrian. "*Koper* et expiation." *Bib* 63 (1982) 32–46.
Schiffman, Lawrence. *Reclaiming the Dead Sea Scrolls: Their True Meaning for Judaism and Christianity*. Anchor Bible Reference Library. New York: Doubleday, 1995.
Schiffman, Lawrence, and James VanderKam, eds. *Encyclopedia of the Dead Sea Scrolls*. New York: Oxford University, 2000.

Schlatter, Adolf. *Romans: The Righteousness of God*. Peabody, MA: Hendrickson, 1995.
Schlier, Hinrich. *Der Römerbrief*. Freiburg: Herder, 1977.
Schnabel, Eckhard. *Law and Wisdom from Ben Sira to Paul: A Tradition Historical Enquiry into the Relation of Law, Wisdom, and Ethics*. Tübingen: Mohr, 1985.
Schniewind, Julius. *Euangelion: Ursprung und erste Gestalt des Begriffs Evangelium, Untersuchung*. Gütersloh: Bertelsmann, 1927.
Schoeps, Hans-Joachim. *Jewish Christianity: Factional Disputes in the Early Church*. Translated by Douglas R. A. Hare. Philadelphia: Fortress, 1969.
———. *Paul: The Theology of the Apostle in the Light of Jewish Religious History*. Translated by Harold Knight. Philadelphia: Westminster, 1961.
———. *Theologie und Geschichte des Judenchristentums*. Tubingen: Mohr, 1949.
Schreiner, Thomas. *Romans*. Grand Rapids: Baker, 1998.
———. *The Law and Its Fulfillment: A Pauline Theology of Law*. Grand Rapids: Baker, 1993.
Schreiner, Thomas, and Ardel Caneday. *The Race Set before Us: A Biblical Theology of Perseverance & Assurance*. Downer's Grove, IL: InterVarsity, 2001.
Schroeder, H. J., trans. *The Canons and Decrees of the Council of Trent*. St. Louis: Herder, 1941.
Schubert, P. "The Final Cycle of Speeches in the Book of Acts." *JBL* 87(1968) 1–16.
———. "The Place of the Areopagus Speech in the Composition of Acts." In *Transitions in Biblical Scholarship*, edited by J. Coert Rylaarsdam, 235–61. Chicago: University of Chicago Press, 1968.
Schweitzer, Albert. *The Kingdom of God and Primitive Christianity*. Translated by L. A. Garrard New York: Seabury, 1968.
———. *The Mystery of the Kingdom of God: The Secret of Jesus' Messiahship and Passion*. Translated by Walter Lowrie. New York: Macmillan, 1950.
———. *The Mysticism of Paul the Apostle*. Translated by William Montgomery London: A. & C. Black, 1931.
Schweizer, E. "Concerning the Speeches in Acts." In *Studies in Luke–Acts*, edited by L. E. Keck and J. L. Martyn, 208–16. London: SPCK, 1968.
Scott, E. F. *The Ethical Teaching of Jesus*. New York: Macmillan, 1924.
Scott, Ian. *Implicit Epistemology in the Letters of Paul: Story, Experience and the Spirit*. Tübingen: Mohr Siebeck, 2006.
———. *Paul's Way of Knowing: Story, Experience, and the Spirit*. Grand Rapids: Baker, 2009.
Scott, James. *Adoption as Sons of God: An Exegetical Investigation into the Background of Hyiothesia in the Pauline Corpus*. WUNT 2.48. Tübingen: Mohr, 1992.
Seeley, David. *The Noble Death: Greco-Roman Martyrology and Paul's Concept of Salvation*. Sheffield: JSOT, 1990.
Seifrid, Mark. *Christ, Our Righteousness: Paul's Theology of Justification*. Downers Grove, IL: InterVarsity, 2000.
———. *Justification by Faith: The Origen and Development of a Central Pauline Theme*. New York: Brill, 1992.
Shields, B. E. "The Areopagus Sermon and Romans 1.18ff: A Study in Creation Theology." *ResQ* 20 (1977) 23–40.
Shin, Eun-Chul. "More than Conquerors: The Conqueror (NIKÁΩ) Motif in the Book of Revelation." PhD diss., Pretoria University, 2006.

Sievers, Joseph. "'Where Two or Three...': The Rabbinic Concept of Shekhinah and Matthew 18:20." In *The Jewish Roots of Christian Liturgy*, edited by Eugene Fisher, 47–61. New York: Paulist, 1990.
Sikes, J. G. *Peter Abailard*. New York: Russell & Russell, 1965.
Sjöberg, E. *Der Menschensohn im ältiopischen Henochbuch*. Lund: Gleerup, 1946.
Sklar, Jay. *Sin, Impurity, Sacrifice, Atonement: The Priestly Conceptions*. Sheffield: Sheffield Phoenix, 2005.
Smalley, Stephen. *1, 2, and 3 John*. Word Biblical Commentary 51. Nashville: T. Nelson, 2007.
Snodgrass, Klyne. *Stories with Intent: A Comprehensive Guide to the Parables of Jesus*. Grand Rapids: Eerdmans, 2008.
Soards, M. *The Speeches in Acts: Their Content, Context, and Concerns*. Louisville: Westminster/John Knox, 1994.
Stamm, Johann Jakob. *Erlösen und Vergeben im alten Testament: Eine begriffsgeschichtliche Untersuchung*. Bern: A. Francke, 1940.
Stanley, Alan, and Robert Wilkin, eds. *Four Views on the Role of Works at the Final Judgment*. Grand Rapids: Zondervan, 2013.
Stanley, David. "The Conception of Salvation in Primitive Christian Preaching." *CBQ* 18 (1956) 231–54.
Stanton, Graham. *Jesus and Gospel*. Cambridge: Cambridge University Press, 2004.
Stegman, Thomas. "Paul's Use of Dikaio-Terminology: Moving beyond N. T. Wright's Forensic Interpretation." *TS* 72(2011) 496–524.
Stewart, Alexander. *Soteriology as Motivation in the Apocalypse of John*. Piscataway, NJ: Gorgias, 2015.
Stewart, Robert, ed. *The Message of Jesus: John Dominic Crossan and Ben Witherington III in Dialog*. Minneapolis: Fortress, 2013.
Strack, Hermann, and Paul Billerbeck. *Kommentar zum Neuen Testament aus Talmud und Midrash*. Munich: Beck, 1956.
Strecker, Georg. *Das Judenchristentum in den Pseudoklementinen*. Texte und Untersuchungen zur Geschichte der altchristlichen Literatur 70. Berlin: Akademie, 1981.
Street, Daniel. *They Went Out from Us: The Identity of the Opponents in First John*. Berlin: De Gruyter, 2011.
Stuhlmacher, Peter. *Das paulinische Evangelium*. Göttingen: Vandenhoeck & Ruprecht, 1968.
———, ed. *The Gospel and the Gospels*. Grand Rapids: Eerdmans, 1991.
———. *Paul's Letter to the Romans*. Translated by Scott J. Hafemann. Louisville: Westminster/John Knox, 1994.
Sylvia, Mary. *Pauline and Johannine Mysticism*. London: Darton, Longman and Todd, 1964.
Talbert, Charles. *Matthew*. Grand Rapids: Baker, 2010.
Talbert, G. W. "Biographies of Philosophers and Rulers as Instruments of Religious Propaganda in Mediterranean Antiquity." *ANRW* 2.16.2 (1978) 1619–51.
Taylor, J. E. "The Phenomenon of Early Jewish Christianity: Reality or Scholarly Invention?" *VC* 44 (1990) 313–34.
Theissen, G., and A. Merz. *The Historical Jesus: A Comprehensive Guide*. Translated by John Bowden. Minneapolis: Fortress, 1998.

Thielman, Frank. *Paul & the Law: A Contextual Approach*. Downers Grove, IL: InterVarsity, 1994.
Thiselton, Anthony. *The First Epistle to the Corinthians*. Grand Rapids: Eerdmans, 2000.
Tolkien, J. R. R. *The Two Towers*. The Lord of the Rings. Boston: Houghton Mifflin, 1965.
Torrance, T. F. "Justification: Its Radical Nature and Place in Reformed Doctrine and Life." *Scottish Journal of Theology* 13(1960) 223–46.
Trompf, G. W. *The Idea of Historical Recurrence in Western Thought: From Antiquity to the Reformation*. Berkeley: University of California Press, 1979.
Thornton, T. C. G. "Propitiation or Expiation?" *ExpTim* 80(1968–9) 53–55.
Twelftree, Graham. *Jesus: The Miracle Worker*. Downers Grove, IL: InterVarsity, 1999.
Van der Watt, Jan, ed. *Salvation in the New Testament: Perspectives on Soteriology*. Supplements to Novum Testamentum 121. Leiden: Brill, 2005.
VanDrunen, David. "Israel's Recapitulation of Adam's Probation Under the Law of Moses." *WJT* 73(2011) 303–24.
Vanhoozer, Kevin, and Daniel Treier. *Theology and the Mirror of Scripture: A Mere Evangelical Account*. Downers Grove, IL: InterVarsity, 2015.
Van Seters, John. *Abraham in History and Tradition*. New Haven, CT: Yale University, 1975.
Van Voorst, Robert E. *The Ascents of James: History and Theology of a Jewish-Christian Community*. SBLDS 112. Atlanta: Scholars, 1989.
Velasco, Jesus Maria, and Leopold Sabourin. "Jewish Christianity of the First Centuries." *BTB* 6 (1976) 5–26.
Versnel, H. S. *Triumphus: An Inquiry into the Origin, Development and Meaning of the Roman Triumph*. Leiden: Brill, 1970.
Vidu, Adonis. *Atonement, Law, and Justice: The Cross in Historical Contexts*. Grand Rapids: Baker, 2014.
Vermès, Géza. *Scripture and Tradition in Judaism: Haggadic Studies*. Studia Post-Biblica 4. Leiden: Brill, 1961.
Wainwright, A. W. "The Confession 'Jesus Is God' in the New Testament." *Scottish Journal of Theology* 10.3 (1957) 274–99.
Wallace, Dan. *Greek Grammar: Beyond the Basics*. Grand Rapids: Zondervan, 1996.
Waltke, Bruce. *The Book of Proverbs*. 2 vols. Grand Rapids: Eerdmans, 2004.
Ward, R. B. "The Works of Abraham: James 2:14–16." *HTR* 59 (1968) 283–90.
Weingart, Richard. *The Logic of Divine Love: A Critical Analysis of the Soteriology of Peter Abailard*. Oxford: Clarendon, 1970.
Westcott, B. F. *The Epistles of St. John*. London: Macmillan, 1909.
Wilder, Amos, and Paul Hoon. "The First, Second, and Third Epistles of John." In *The Interpreters Bible*, vol. 12. New York: Abingdon, 1957.
Willard, Dallas. *The Divine Conspiracy: Rediscovering Our Hidden Life in God*. San Francisco: HarperSanFrancisco, 1998.
Williams, Prescott. "The Poems about Incomparable Yahweh's Servant in Isaiah 40–55." *SwJT* 11 (1968) 73–87.
Windisch, Hans, and Herbert Preisker. *Die katholischen Briefe*. Tübingen: Mohr, 1951.
Winer, G. B. *A Treatise on the Grammar of New Testament Greek*. Translated by W. F. Moulton. Edinburgh: T. & T. Clark, 1882.
Witherington, Ben, III. *The Acts of the Apostles: A Socio-Rhetorical Commentary*. Grand Rapids: Eerdmans, 1998.

Wittgenstein, Ludwig. *Philosophical Investigations*. Translated by G. E. M. Anscombe. New York: Macmillan, 1953.

Wood, J. Edwin. "Isaac Typology in the New Testament." *NTS* 14 (July 1968) 583–89.

Wright, N. T. "4QMMT and Paul: Justification, 'Works' and Eschatology." In *History and Exegesis: New Testament Essays in Honor of Dr. E. Earle Ellis for his 80th Birthday*, edited by Sang-Won Son, 104–32. London: T. & T. Clark, 2006.

———. *The Climax of the Covenant: Christ and the Law in Pauline Theology*. Minneapolis: Fortress, 1992.

———. *Jesus and the Victory of God*. Christian Origins and the Question of God 2. Minneapolis: Fortress, 1996.

———. *Paul and the Faithfulness of God*. 2 vols. Christian Origins and the Question of God 4. Minneapolis: Fortress, 2013.

———. *Pauline Perspectives: Essays on Paul, 1978–2013*. Minneapolis: Fortress, 2013.

———. *The Resurrection of the Son of God*. Christian Origins and the Question of God 3. Minneapolis: Fortress, 2003.

———. *What Saint Paul Really Said: Was Paul of Tarsus the Real Founder of Christianity?* Grand Rapids: Eerdmans, 1997.

Wurm, Alois. *Die Irrlehrer im Ersten Johannesbrief*. Freiburg im Breisgau: Herder, 1903.

Yamauchi, Eduard. *Jewish Gnosticism?: The Prologue of John, Mandaean Parallels, and the Trimorphic Protennoia*. Leiden: Brill, 1981.

———. *Pre-Christian Gnosticism: A Survey of the Evidences*. Grand Rapids: Eerdmans, 1973.

Yarbrough, Robert. *1–3 John*. Baker Exegetical Commentary on the New Testament. Grand Rapids: Baker, 2008.

Yinger. Kent. *Paul, Judaism, and Judgment According to Deeds*. Cambridge: Cambridge University Press, 1999.

Yitzhaq of Berdichev. *Imre Tzaddiqim*. Edited by Tz'vi Hasid. Zhitomir: n.p., 1899.

Yoder, John Howard. *The Politics of Jesus: Vicit Agnus Noster*. Grand Rapids: Eerdmans, 1994.

Zehnle, R. F. *Peter's Pentecost Discourse: Tradition and Lukan Reinterpretation in Peter's Speeches of Acts 2 and 3*. Nashville: Abingdon, 1971.

Zerwick, M., and M. Grosvenor. *A Grammatical Analysis of the Greek New Testament*. Translated and revised by Mary Grosvenor 2 vols. Rome: Pontifical Biblical Institute, 1974.

Author Index

Abelard, 7, 9, 13, 256
Abrahams, 79
Absalom, 62
Acha, 50
Aeschylus, 143, 240
A Kempis, 11, 191, 242
Akiba, 6, 56, 179
Alighieri, 103, 251
Allison, 33–5, 41, 48–50, 52–3, 59, 61–2, 66, 74–5, 88, 101
Altereatio, 10
Amanullah, 256
Ambroisiater, 12, 180
Ambrose, 9, 191, 242
Amyrald, 232
Anderson, 82, 169
Anselm, 14–7, 243, 245–61
Apollodorus, 240
Appian, 76, 189
Apuleius, 196
Aquinas, 7–8, 14, 89, 250–1, 256–7
Aratus, 141–2
Aristeas, 56, 210
Arius, 4
Arminius, 232
Athanasius, 11, 13–4, 191, 242, 250, 257
Athenagorus, 57, 81, 179
Augustine, 3, 5, 7–13, 16, 47, 55–6, 79, 82, 85–7, 89–91, 152, 175, 180, 221, 234, 242, 250–1

Augustus, 189, 192
Aulén, 10
Aulus G, 76, 239,
Aune, 2, 73, 76, 237
Aurelius, 2–3, 140
Averbeck, 154
Azulai, 49

Bailey, 8–9, 24, 152
Balch, 119, 142
Baldwin, 107, 225
Baley, 234
Barber, 12
Barclay, 85, 224
Barr, 154
Barrett, 119
Barth, 178, 192, 195
Basel, 105
Bates, 2
Bauckham, 30, 57, 99, 218–9, 222
Bauenfeind, 217
Bauer, 6, 79
Bautch, 151
Beale, 233, 238
Beckman, 148–9, 171–2, 259
Behm, 210
Behrens, 150, 158
Bellinger, 22, 151
Bengel, 216
Ben Zeev, 210
Bergemeier, 192, 195

Bernard, 158
Bettenson, 3–4, 13,
Betz, 2, 22, 24
Bielfeldt, 176
Bietenhard, 129, 142, 186
Bigg, 219
Billerbeck, 21–2
Bird, 2, 80, 165
Black, 8, 106, 224
Blanton, 177–8
Blass, 231, 235
Block, 2
Blomberg, 90
Bock, 88, 99, 169, 221
Bokzer, 49
Bousset, 176, 253
Bray, 12, 180
Bretschneider, 17
Brichto, 154
Brown, 111, 114, 224, 227
Bruce, 111, 133, 135–6, 179, 189
Brueggemann, 151
Bucer, 17
Büchsel, 216, 227
Bultmann, 3, 157, 227
Bunyan, 11–2, 191
Burke, 183
Buttrick, 88
Bynum, 108, 226

Cadbury, 119–20
Caesarius, 4
Calvin, 11, 17, 89, 180, 191, 218, 224–5, 229, 232, 243
Campbell, 4, 106, 153, 229, 231, 235
Carter, 88
Cary, 19
Cassian, 2, 191
Cassiodorus, 13
Cato, 27
Celsus, 3
Chalmers, 20, 85
Chang, 221
Chiyah, 57, 81, 91
Chrysippus, 140
Chrysostom, 2, 9, 30, 82, 86, 105, 142, 152, 234
Cicero, 17, 140, 142

Cleanthes, 142
Clement A, 2, 11, 14, 41, 73, 76, 84, 86, 142, 191, 199, 242
Clement R, 2, 11, 13, 73, 76, 81, 83, 191, 218, 240, 242
Cleon, 140
Climacus, 11, 191
Collins, 79
Columella, 200
Commodianus, 11, 86, 191
Conzelmann, 117–8, 120, 124
Cope, 79
Corsten, 241
Cothenet, 31
Cox, 13, 35
Cranfield, 12, 162, 180, 192, 195
Creed, 88
Crenshaw, 12
Crispin, 247
Crossan, 99
Crouzel, 31, 121
Cullmann, 21, 129, 186
Cyprian, 2–3, 9, 11, 83, 191, 241
Cyril, 9–11, 153, 191, 234

Dabney, 13, 180
Daly, 21–2
Danker, 179
Das, 13, 173, 180, 201
Davies, 33–5, 41, 48, 50, 52–3, 59, 61–2, 66, 74, 76, 88, 101
De Boer, 31, 121
De Claissé-Walford 151
Deissmann, 130, 165, 184, 216, 253
Delhaye, 7
Demonax, 27
Demosthenes, 140
De Roo, 147, 162
Dibelius, 117, 120, 140
Dickens, 259
Dickson, 2
Dihle, 30
Dio Cassius, 188
Diogenes, 27
Dionysius A, 11, 31, 105, 191, 242
Dobbeler, 175
Dodd, 90, 119, 153, 160, 224, 227
Donaldson, 166

AUTHOR INDEX

Dulles, 7
Dunn, 2, 6, 11–2, 36, 45–6, 55, 158, 174, 176, 180, 187, 191, 210, 243, 253
DuRand, 239

Edwards, 13, 182, 214
Egelkraut, 57
Eichrodt, 169
Elinger, 153
Elliott, 46, 49, 210
Ellis, 196
Epictetus, 39, 104, 134, 141, 196
Epicurus, 140
Epiderxis, 10
Epiphanius, 4, 47, 227
Esler, 200
Eubank, 88
Euripides, 110, 141, 240
Eusebius, 3–5, 7, 9, 11, 30, 47, 56, 72, 80, 143, 153, 191, 196, 234
Evans, 69, 157, 194

Fadden, 180
Farmer, 150
Feder, 154
Felix, 3
Feuillet, 176
Ficino, 13
Finkel, 72
Finney, 18
Fiore, 120
Fisher, 53
Fitzmyer, 21–2, 58, 97–8, 142
Flückinger, 195
Ford, 92
Fornara, 31, 121
Fortna, 93
Freed, 111
Freedman, 194
Freyne, 78
Friedrich, 172
Fryer, 8, 152
Furnish, 189

Gamaliel, 66, 107
Gammie, 155, 207
Gane, 154–5, 207

Garland, 157
Garret, 175
Gärtner, 119, 140
Gathercole, 1, 160–1, 163
George, 8
Gese, 154
Gillman, 108
Goodenough, 196
Gorman, 194
Graver, 140
Greear, 19
Green, 120
Gregory Great, 128, 160
Grosvenor, 157
Gubler, 21–2
Guilbert, 118, 247
Gundry, 64, 170
Guthrie, 157, 189, 209
Gutiérrez, 10, 31

Hackett, 7
Hagner, 84
Hägerland, 151
Hafemann, 189
Hahn, 157
Halicarnassus, 174, 179
Hantzler, 18
Harder, 216, 222
Hare, 252, 256
Harnack, 2, 13, 32, 35, 168
Harrington, 120
Harris, 157, 189
Hart, 252
Hays, 74, 165
Headlam, 9, 153
Hedychrous, 241
Hellerman, 210
Hemer, 119, 140, 143
Hengel, 5, 8, 24, 152
Hennecke, 6, 56
Henninger, 12
Henry, 180
Hermann, 154
Hermes, 98
Herodotus, 140
Herzog, 88, 92
Hesiod, 39, 83
Hicks, 140

Hilary, 10–1, 191, 242
Hildesheimer, 49
Hillel, 52, 72
Hoag, 84
Hodge, 180
Hodges, 224, 228
Hofius, 8, 151, 155, 186–7
Holtzmann, 132
Homer, 2
Honnah, 50–1
Hooker, 14, 165
Hopkins, 16, 249, 260
Horace, 45, 189
Horbury, 2
Hoshaia, 50–1
Horsley, 119
Howard, 47
Hübner, 12, 162, 180
Hugh SV, 13
Hughes, 216
Hume, 8

Ignatius, 2–3, 11, 13, 30, 42, 175, 191, 211, 227, 239
Irenaeus, 2–3, 5, 7, 10, 13–4, 30, 47, 57, 79, 81, 89, 136, 179
Irons, 17
Isaac, 53
Ishmael, 58

Jahnow, 68
Janowski, 8–9, 24, 153
Jeremias, 21, 102
Jerome, 5, 30, 47, 65, 75
Jervell, 120
Jewett, 142, 159, 161–3, 165, 174, 187, 192, 195, 200, 216
Johanan Z, 59, 107, 225
Johnston, 95, 233
Jones, 118
Josephus, 2, 6, 38–9, 41–2, 45–6, 48–9, 55–6, 58, 75–76, 78–80, 83, 93, 98–9, 108, 111–3, 122, 134, 145, 147, 157–8, 163–4, 186–8, 210, 215, 225–6, 239
Judah, 200
Justin M, 2–3, 7, 9, 11, 30, 56–7, 64, 79, 81, 152, 179, 191, 221, 234, 237

Justinian, 17, 239

Kalluveettil, 184
Kant, 8, 18, 149, 252, 259
Käsemann, 167
Karis, 120
Keck, 12, 180
Kee, 120
Keener, 75, 110, 112, 114
Kennard, 2, 4–6, 9, 20–1, 26–7, 31–2, 43–4, 47, 49–50, 55–6, 59, 74, 79, 83, 112–3, 117, 118, 121, 127–8, 130, 132–3, 136, 140, 144, 147–8, 155, 157, 176, 180, 187, 195–6, 204–8, 225, 227, 236, 253–4
Kennedy, 119
Kierkegaard, 256
Kilgallen, 119, 143, 145
Kim, 11, 102, 196–7, 242, 254
Kissinger, 87, 89–90, 93
Kiuchi, 207
Klijn, 6, 56, 79, 119
Koester, 240–1
König, 192, 195
Kostenberger, 113
Köster, 222
Kraus, 151–2, 235
Kruse, 8, 152, 179
Kühl, 167
Kurtz, 153
Kurz, 31, 120
Kuula, 176

Lachs, 53
Lactantius, 11, 191
Laertius, 42, 140–1
Lambrecht, 162
Lampe, 175
Lane, 209
Lapide, 53
Law, 224, 227–8
Leaman, 256
Leftlow, 14, 247
Leo the Great, 11, 13–4, 35, 84
Levine, 47, 92–4, 154
Lightfoot, 51
Lincoln, 254
Loader, 49

AUTHOR INDEX

Loenertz, 233
Lohse, 21
Long, 89
Longenecker, 149
Lossky, 13
Lucian, 3, 38, 142
Lucretius, 142
Luther, 8, 10, 12, 17-8, 117, 180
Lycophron, 240

Macrobius, 210
Maldonatus, 90
Manoder, 13
Marcellus, 4
Markschies, 9, 152-3, 234
Marshall, IH, 5, 169, 221, 224
Marshall, L, 13
Marshall, P, 188
Martin, 158
Martyn, 10
Matthew A, 14
Maunder, 3-4
Mayordomo, 142
McArthur, 95
McFadden, 13, 180
McGrath, 12, 14, 17
McKnight, 5, 118-9
Meier, 73, 76, 127
Meir, 62
Melanchthon, 12, 17-8, 180
Menard, 21
Merz, 73, 76
Methodius, 191
Metzger, 105-6, 112
Meyers, 78
Miano, 194
Michael, 187
Michel, 167
Milgrom, 154, 205, 207
Milligan, 148, 179, 216
Milton, 251
Mitchell, 224, 228
Montague, 119, 140
Moo, 180
Moody, 18
Morris, 115, 198
Moser, 143
Moulton, 148, 179, 216, 235

Mundle, 192, 195
Murray, 12, 79, 172, 174

Nazianzen, 9-11, 30, 191, 197, 242
Nehemiah, 62
Neyrey, 119, 140
Nickelsburg, 27
Noble, 247, 250
Noland, 98-9
Nonnus, 105
Nygren, 160
Nyssa, 11, 13, 242

Oakman, 89, 92
Oden, 9, 152-3, 234
Oecolampadius 12, 180
Oeming, 150
Origen, 2-3, 5-6, 9, 11, 30, 78, 86, 105,
    149, 152, 192, 219, 234, 242, 250
Oswalt, 26
O'Toole, 120
Overman, 47, 92
Ovid, 137, 240

Packer, 17
Palladius, 200
Pannenberg, 7
Papias, 5
Park, 47, 56, 79
Parker, 17
Pate, 21, 26-7, 31, 74, 121, 127-8,
    132-3, 136, 144, 157, 253-4
Pausanias, 141
Pelagius, 12, 180
Philo, 10, 31, 33, 38-40, 45, 48, 56,
    78-81, 83-4, 87, 98, 147, 152,
    157-9, 163-6, 172, 179, 183, 194-5,
    199, 204, 210, 219, 226-7, 235, 239
Philostratus, 98, 141
Phineas, 62
Pindar, 240
Placeus, 175-6
Plato, 7, 39, 83, 140-1, 219
Pliny Elder, 239
Pliny Younger, 3, 42, 60, 88, 112
Plummer, 58
Plutarch, 2, 27, 31, 75, 140, 142, 188-9,
    219, 240

AUTHOR INDEX

Pokorny, 2, 187
Polybius, 39, 83
Polycarp, 11, 39, 56, 73, 76, 81, 83, 179, 191, 227, 242
Porphry, 3
Porter, 119, 235
Preiske, 227

Quinn, 257
Quintilian, 31

Rahlfs, 235
Rainer, 179
Räisänen, 12, 180
Rashdal, 13
Rauer, 210
Reed, 92
Reiche, 11, 102
Reinink, 6, 56, 79
Rhee, 83
Riesenfeld, 158
Riggenbach, 210
Robertson, 157, 235
Robinson, 126
Root, 247
Rosenberg, 21–22
Ross, 124
Roth, 149, 259
Rottzoll, 158
Ruether, 10
Rufinus, 3
Rufus, 4, 247

Sabourin, 56, 79
Salas, 192, 195
Saldarini, 6, 47, 56, 79
Sanday, 9, 153, 234
Sanders, 6, 12, 46, 48–9, 55, 79, 127, 175–6, 180, 193
Sandmel, 12
Sapp, 22
Saussure, 154
Schaff, 9, 152–3, 178, 234
Schiffman, 23
Schlatter, 167
Schmidt, 8, 88
Schnabel, 12, 180
Schneemelcher 56

Schoeps, 6, 21–2, 56, 79
Scholem, 254
Schreiner, 11, 13, 174, 180, 191, 243
Schrenk, 174
Schubert, 140, 143
Schweitzer, 35, 175–6, 196, 252
Schweizer, 117
Scott, 35, 142, 183
Scotus, 13
Seebass, 155
Seeley, 27
Segal, 254
Seifrid, 13, 148
Seneca, 27, 239
Sextus, 72
Shields, 119, 140
Shin, 239
Shinall, 92, 94
Sievers, 74
Simeon E, 91
Sjöberg, 27
Sklar, 154
Smalley, 224
Snodgrass, 90
Soads, 119–20
Socrates, 11, 27, 191
Solon, 39, 83
Souçek, 192, 195
Southhall, 198
Sprinkle, 165
Stahlmacher, 180
Stamm, 153
Stanley, 118
Stanton, 2, 143
Stegman, 165
Stettler, 193–4
Stewart, 238–9
Stowers, 193
Strabo, 60, 142, 241
Strack, 21–22
Strathmann, 210, 218
Strecker, 6, 56, 79
Street, 227–8
Stuhlmacher, 2, 5, 8–9, 13, 24, 32, 117, 168
Stupperich, 17
Suetonius, 129, 186, 189
Suggate, 45

Sylvia, 176

Tacitus, 27, 31, 83, 88, 93, 239
Talbert, 31, 88, 121
Taylor, 6, 56, 79
Tertullian, 3, 5, 7, 10, 30, 56, 72, 103, 143, 157, 199, 227
Thackery, 122
Theissen, 73, 76
Theodoret, 5, 9, 30, 35, 105, 152, 234
Theophilus, 239
Theophrastus, 60, 199
Thielman, 13, 181
Thucydides, 140, 174
Tiwald, 152, 235
Tolkien, 175
Torrance, 176
Trajan, 3
Treier, 2
Troeltsch, 7
Trompf, 31, 121

Van Dam, 25
VanderKam, 177–8
Van Drunen, 172
Van Gemeren, 25
Vanhoozer, 2
Van Seters, 147
VanVoorst, 6, 56, 79
Varro, 60
Velasco, 79
Vellius, 239
Vermès, 21–2
Versnel, 188
Vidu, 17
Vincent L, 11, 191, 242
Vital, 49
Von Campenhausen 187
Von Dobbeler, 176
Von Martitz, 184
Von Rad, 147, 169

Wainwright, 2
Wall, 159
Wallace, 70, 106, 229, 231
Waltke, 82
Ward, 159
Watson, 192, 195
Wedderburn, 254
Weidner, 184
Weinfeld, 184
Weingart, 7, 9
Wesley, 18, 192, 250
Westcott, 224
Wikenhauser, 176
Wilder, 224
Willard, 11, 243
Williams, 24
Willis, 196
Windisch, 227
Winer, 235
Winninge, 192
Winter, 210
Witherington, 134
Wood, 21–2
Wright, 5–6, 12, 22–3, 55, 79–80, 108, 117, 123, 145, 167, 169–70, 180–1, 186, 192–3, 195, 200, 225, 255
Wurm, 227

Xenophon, 140, 178

Yarbrough, 224
Yinger, 11, 102, 190, 242–3
Yitzhaq B, 48–9
Yoder, 35

Zahn, 192, 195
Zehn, 119
Zehnle, 119
Zerwick, 157

Scripture Index

Genesis

3	239
5	175
15	147–8, 150, 159
17	160
18	164
20	40
22	22
24	233
26	110, 160, 162
32	154

Exodus

3	108, 226
4	183
6	216
12–19	10, 156, 213, 230
20	80, 171, 172
21	24, 154
23	80
24	205–6, 233
25	8, 152, 231, 233, 235
29	155–6
30	42, 154
31	8, 152, 231, 233, 235
32	239
33	211
34	171, 172
35	8, 152, 231, 233, 235
38	8, 152, 231, 233, 235
40	28, 206–7, 230

Leveticus

1	207, 261
2	42, 261
3	261
4	149, 205, 207, 210, 261
5	26, 149, 153, 207, 261
6	155, 261
7	150, 155, 261
9	205
10	26, 153, 155
11	66, 204, 210
12	213, 229
13	205, 213
14	154, 205, 213, 229
15	205–6, 213, 229
16	8, 10, 26, 149, 153–5, 205–6, 211, 213, 229, 231, 233–5, 261
17	26, 154
18	157
19	6, 56, 80–1, 89, 179
20:19	26
21	68, 112
22	51
25	154
26	25
27	149

Numbers

3	215
4	155
7	8, 152, 231, 233, 235
9:13	26
11	25
14:34	26
15	194, 205
19	205
20	156
21	106
22	25
25	150
27	156
31	154, 261
35	25, 154

Deuteronomy

4	194
5	80, 171–2
6	51, 54, 56, 179, 195
7	195, 215
9	215
14	183
15	149
18	111
21	133, 149, 154, 157, 259
23	172
24	72, 89, 158
25	148, 158, 258–9
26	195
27	148
28–30	25, 35, 52, 194–5, 225
32	14, 183, 251

Joshua

7	171

Judges

9	175

1 Samuel

1	151
2	95
17	72
23	83
24	80
31:9	2

2 Samuel

1:20	2
4:10	2
5	68, 112
7	129, 169, 184
18:19–31	2
19	80, 148, 150

1 Kings

1:42	2
3	80
8	101, 175, 190, 242

2 Kings

8	72

1 Chronicles

10:9	2
22	40

2 Chronicles

2	156
36	171

Ezra

6	42

Esther

3	210

Job

2	233
4	71
5	71, 95
6	42
8:5–6	34
12	95
15	95
18	200
19	40
29:2–3	34

30	72
31	80
34	101, 190, 242
38:15	34

Psalms

2	133, 240
4:6	34
7	80
8	173
9	239
11	40
15	147
16	155, 169–70
17	40
18:28	34
21	155
22	200
24:3–4	39–40, 147
27	34, 230, 230
28	101, 190, 242
32	149–151
34:14	40
37	39, 95
39	150–1
42:2	38
48:3	34
51	149
56:13	34
62	101, 190, 242
63:1	38
67:11	2
69	239
72	39, 83
73	155
74	215
77	215
87	239
92	199
95:2	2
97	164
104	34, 195, 210, 230
105	148, 150
107	39, 95
110	130, 173
116	215
118	195
119	226
126:2–6	37
132	39, 169
139	111
143:6	38
146	95
147	95
150	51, 155

Proverbs

2	195
6:34–35	154
9:8	71
10:10	40
11	71, 82
13	110
14	39, 83
18	110
20:25	156
22:8	71
23:9	71
24	80, 101, 190, 242
25:21–22	80

Isaiah

	8
1	25, 149, 183, 259
2	34, 200
4	239
5	63, 226
6	28, 61
10	25, 36, 233
11	155
14	25
21	233
22	233
25	39–40
26	36, 40
27	25, 150
30	25, 40, 42, 183
32	39
33	233
35	10, 46
37	205
40	2, 24, 40, 151, 233, 256
42	21, 24, 34, 43, 144, 230
43	21–22, 183
44	215

Isaiah (cont.)

45	183
49	10, 21, 24, 34, 39–40, 43, 144, 230
50	40
51	26
52:2–7	2, 10, 40
52:13–53	9, 21–29, 113, 132, 136, 148, 151, 154, 169–70, 216, 233, 261
55	39
56	200
57	40, 155
58	95
60	2, 34, 37–8
61	2, 10, 35, 38, 40, 46, 95–6, 123, 125, 149
63	183
64	40
65	39
66	25, 37, 243

Jeremiah

2	110
3	183
5	51
6	158
7	149, 259
8	158
12	158
14	158
16	101, 158, 190
17	95, 101, 110, 190, 200
21	101, 190
23	158
24	40
28	158
29:7	80
31	37, 40, 49, 52, 177, 183, 194, 204
32	101, 190
33	158, 212
41	149

Lamentations

3	158

Ezekiel

1	28, 207, 254
7	101, 190
11	28, 195, 207
13	239
18	147, 195
20	195
21	25
22:13	25
31	200
34	177
36	44, 177
37	44
43	8, 42, 152, 195, 204, 209, 212, 231, 233, 235
44	212
45	212
46	212
47	42, 110
49	155

Daniel

1	210
2	221
3	34, 221
6	221
7	155, 190, 237, 239, 242
12	43, 107, 225, 239

Hosea

2	183
4	101–2, 190
9	200
10:12	34
11	183
13	215

Joel

2	2, 134, 177, 187

Amos

2	156
8:1	38

Jonah

4	56, 80

Micah

4	200
6:8	39
7	190, 226
8	195

Nahum

1:15	2

Habakkuk

3:3–4	34

Zephaniah

2	42

Zechariah

2	200
9:9	38
12:10–11	24
13:7	25
14	110, 200

Matthew

1	86
2:18	37
3	40, 77, 191, 196, 254
4	5, 30, 32, 40, 54, 77–78, 87
5	5–6, 32–54, 60, 62, 71, 74, 78, 81, 83–4
6	34, 39, 72–4, 76–78, 83–4, 86
7	32–34, 48, 50, 60, 70–2, 78, 83, 91, 166
8	27, 34, 78, 87
9	10, 30, 32, 39, 68, 70, 78, 83–4, 87, 115, 128, 256
10	41, 58, 78, 86
11	32, 50, 53, 60, 78
12	10, 50, 61, 70, 78, 81, 83, 110, 169–70
13	34, 41, 59–67, 77–8
15	39, 71, 83
16	40–1, 65, 78, 86, 91, 102, 111, 169–70, 190, 242
17	39–40, 83, 91, 169–70
18	34, 39, 53, 60, 74–8, 83, 86, 91, 166
19	5, 55, 77–94, 107
20	39, 77–94, 170
21	62–3
22	5–6, 34, 50, 56–7, 77–8, 81, 89, 173, 179
23	40–1, 48, 54, 78, 83
24	5, 30, 40, 50, 65, 74, 78, 101, 107
25	12, 34, 52, 84, 101–3, 107, 166, 190, 242
26	10, 30, 40, 50, 78, 89, 135, 170
27	40, 50, 170

Mark

1	30, 68, 196
2	68, 84, 87
3	10, 61, 70
4	41, 43, 59–67
5	10, 39, 83, 115
6	111
8	30, 41, 170
9	40, 42, 170
10	5, 39, 41, 55, 77–94, 107
11	39, 73, 83
12	6, 56, 62–3, 77, 12, 179
13	5, 30, 40, 65, 107
14	30, 40, 135, 170, 221
15	170
16	5, 30, 37

Luke

1	36, 39, 42, 83–4, 88, 95, 106, 123–5, 184, 215
2	42, 123, 125, 184, 215
3	123, 125, 190, 196, 254
4	32, 35–6, 72, 95, 123, 125–6
5	37, 67–9, 84, 87, 126
6	32–43, 54, 56, 71, 81, 88, 95–6, 124, 126

Luke (cont.)

7	32, 36–7, 46, 62, 70, 115–6, 123–4, 126–7
8	10, 37, 43, 59–67, 116, 123–4, 126–8, 256
9	32, 41, 58, 107, 111, 123–4, 126, 128–9, 170
10	5–6, 42, 55–8, 62, 77, 80–1, 83, 106, 126, 179
11	10, 34, 43, 70, 72, 74, 126, 129
12	84, 95, 126, 128
13	34, 91, 122, 126
14	36, 42, 106, 126, 128
15	42, 62, 70
16	5, 32, 36–7, 50–1, 84, 96, 97–9, 226
17	39, 83, 124, 170
18	5, 36, 39, 55, 70, 73, 77–94, 106, 124, 161–2, 170
19	36, 84, 87, 126, 129
20	32, 40, 63, 123, 126, 226
21	36, 41, 65, 95, 97, 107, 124, 128, 184
22	27, 126
23	56, 74, 81, 124, 127
24	42, 107, 122, 124, 129, 170, 215

John

	8
1:4–18	19, 34, 104–5, 111, 113
1:26, 29, 36	9, 148, 152, 196, 227, 230, 234–5, 238
2	170
3	104–9, 111, 116, 191–2, 225–7, 230
4	58, 110–1, 219
5	12, 112–3, 227
6	111, 113–4, 227
7	104, 107, 109
8	106–7, 111, 227, 230
9	69, 230, 254
10:9	5
11	5, 108, 115–6, 227
12	107, 227, 229
13	107
14	5, 111, 219, 231, 233
15	219, 233
16	107, 111, 233
17	107, 219
19	109

Acts

1	124, 135, 144, 216
2	84, 106, 118, 122, 129–36, 169
3	109, 122, 129–36, 223
4	117, 122, 129–36, 220
5	84, 106, 122–4, 135, 183, 216
7	56, 81, 107, 124–5
8	27, 118, 122, 135–6
9	118, 122, 145–6, 197
10	118, 124–36, 229
11	118, 122–3, 135, 146, 229
13	106, 118, 123–4, 137–46, 169, 186
14	123–4, 137–46
15	122–3, 160
16	118, 123–4, 137–46, 186
17	123, 137–46, 186
18	118, 123, 137–46, 186
19	118, 122–3, 137–46, 187, 196
20	118, 122, 137–46, 155, 187
22	118, 145–6, 197
24	118, 122
26	122–3, 145
27	124
28	143

Paul

	8

Romans

1	42, 141, 155–6, 164, 168, 187, 191, 195
2	102, 156, 190–2, 201, 242
3	9, 149, 152–3, 155, 158–62, 164–7, 196, 201, 215, 259
4	147–51, 155, 158–60, 162, 164–7, 179, 201, 254–5

SCRIPTURE INDEX

5	41, 148–9, 155–6, 158, 165–6, 171–6, 186, 196, 198, 254–5, 258–9
6	148–9, 156, 175–6, 183, 190, 196–9, 254–5, 258–9
7	148, 175, 178–82, 186, 196, 198, 255, 258–9
8	7, 28, 165, 177–85, 194, 215, 219, 255
9	148, 156, 183, 191
10:9–10	3, 186–7
11	150, 168, 190, 195, 199–201
12	56, 81
13	177
14	102, 190
15	27, 155, 168
16	168, 188

1 Corinthians

1	42, 155, 162
2	255
3	102, 156, 190, 219, 242
4	56, 81
5	149, 197
6	155–6, 178, 220
7	155, 160, 220
8	186
9	166, 168
12:3	3
13	40
15	3, 148–9, 168–70, 173, 182, 201, 258–9
16	155

2 Corinthians

1	155–6
2	11, 188–9
3	176
4	156, 195
5	12, 102, 156–8, 173, 190, 198, 201, 219, 242, 255
6	156, 173, 178
7	156
10	168
11	106, 168

Galatians

1	168
2	165, 168, 174, 181, 195, 198, 255
3	147–8, 150–1, 156, 164–5, 194, 254
4	181, 183–4, 195
5	160, 165, 168, 177–8, 180–3, 197
6	160, 181

Ephesians

1	149, 155, 173, 183–5, 215, 254
2	156, 195, 197
3	19, 155, 174, 181
4	11, 181, 184–5, 189, 198, 255
5	155–6, 183, 191, 229
6	102, 166, 190, 242

Philippians

1	12, 155, 178, 183
2	179, 181, 219
3	81, 179, 242
4	41, 168

Colossians

1	149, 155, 181, 185, 219
2	160
3	28, 102, 156, 190–1, 197, 219, 255
4	188

1 Thessalonians

1	156, 158, 166, 168
2	156, 168, 191
3	156
4	156
5	56, 81

2 Thessalonians

1	155, 192
2	155, 168, 201

1 Timothy

1	165
2	156
6	198

2 Timothy

1	39, 168
2	187
3	165
4	192

Titus

2	229
3	178

Philemon

13	168
18	172
23	188

Hebrews

	8
1	173, 202, 208
2	155, 208
3–4	10, 208–9, 212
6	202, 208
8	202, 204, 208–9, 212
9:1–10:18	8–10, 25, 152, 155–6, 185, 202, 204–12, 229, 261
11	208–9
12	12, 40
13	156, 210–1

James

1	41, 239
2	36, 148
3	195
4	106
5	40

1 Peter

1	25, 41, 155, 205, 215–20, 222–3, 242
2:18–25	27, 132, 157, 217, 223
3	41, 56, 81, 173, 217–8, 223
4	41, 217–8, 223
5	106

2 Peter

1	13, 135, 217, 219–22
2	216, 218–23
3	220, 222–3

1 John

1	34, 224–33, 235
2	109, 224, 226–35
3	40, 233
4	56, 226, 229, 231–3, 235
5	107, 225, 228, 233

Jude

	39, 218

Revelation 1

	40, 240
2	102, 190, 238–42
3	19, 238–41
4	238
5	175, 220, 238–9
12	238–9
14	65, 220
15	238
17	175, 238–9, 241
19	175, 237–8
20	102, 190, 239–43
21	230, 238–41, 243
22	40, 102, 190, 242

Subject Index

Allegiance, 2–3
Authority, 117–46

Beatitudes, 32–43

Christ in heart, 19
Christ Victor, 10–1, 188–9
Confess Lord, 2–3
Covenant Nomism 45–6
Creed affirmed 3–5
   Apostles, 3–4
   Chalcedon, 4
   Constantinople 4
   Gallican, 3
   Nicene, 3–5

Day of Atonement 8–10, 204–14, 231, 233–5
Descent to Hell 4
Deification, 13–4, 219

Eschatological Atonement 21–2
Eschatological Justification 11–3, 65–7, 74–6, 85–92, 95–103, 241–3
Eschatological Reversal 38–9, 77–100

Forgiveness, 68–76, 155, 215
Forensic atonement 17–9, 147–85, 258–61

Good news, 2

Gospel narrative 5, 30–1

Imputation, 171–6

Jesus as gospel 5, 30–31, 117–46
Jesus teaching, 5, 30–116
Jewish atonement 8–10, 21–9, 147–67, 202–14, 216–7, 231–2
Justification, 8, 11–3, 65–7, 74–6, 85–92, 95–103, 147–85, 234, 241–3

Kingship, 2, 117–46, 186–7

Law, , 5–8, 44–58, 79–85, 166, 177
Love God, 5–6, 55–58
Love humans, 5–6, 55–58, 85, 179
Loyalty, 3

Merkabah mysticism 27–8, 175–85, 207, 210, 213–4, 254–5
Mimetic Atonement 11–3, 27, 30–103, 190–223, 231, 237–43
Moral Example 13

Natural law, 7–8
New Covenant, 44–54
New exodus, 10

Orange synod, 7

Penal atonement 9, 17–9, 25–6, 29, 148–9, 156–8, 258–61
Perichoresis, 219
Persecution, 41–2
Perseverance, 41–2, 220
Poverty, 36–9, 77–100
Propitiation, 8, 152–5, 224–36

Redemption, 10–1, 188–9, 215–23
Reformation Paul 148–9
Regeneration experience 18–9

Sanctification, 155–6
Satisfaction, 14–7, 247–61

Spirit, , 8, 12–3

Theological hermeneutic 20
Ticket Christianity 18–9, 245, 258–61
Triumphal procession 10–1, 188–9
Two-ways, 10–3, 30–103, 190–23, 237–43

Vicarious Atonement 8–10, 21–9, 147–67, 202–14
Virtue, , 7, 11–3, 30–43, 77–94, 178–80, 219–20

Wealth, , 77–100

www.ingramcontent.com/pod-product-compliance
Lightning Source LLC
Chambersburg PA
CBHW071234230426
43668CB00011B/1434